SAMPSON TECHNICAL INSTITUTE

NORTH CAROLINA
STATE BOARD OF EDUCATION
DEPT. OF COMMUNITY COLLEGES
LIBRARIES

Library
Sampson Technical Institute

The Far Western Frontier

The Far Western Frontier

Advisory Editor
RAY A. BILLINGTON
Senior Research Associate
at the Henry E. Huntington Library
and Art Gallery

JOURNAL

OF THE

TEXIAN EXPEDITION AGAINST MIER

BY

GEN. THOMAS J. GREEN

ARNO PRESS
A NEW YORK TIMES COMPANY
New York • 1973

Reprint Edition 1973 by Arno Press Inc.

Reprinted from a copy in The State
Historical Society of Wisconsin Library

The Far Western Frontier
ISBN for complete set: 0-405-04955-2
See last pages of this volume for titles.

Manufactured in the United States of America

Library of Congress Cataloging in Publication Data

Green, Thomas Jefferson, 1801-1863.
   Journal of the Texian expedition against Mier.

   (The Far Western frontier)
   Reprint of the 1845 ed.
   1. Texas--History--Republic, 1836-1846.
2. Mier Expedition, 1842. I. Title. II. Series.
F390.G79 1973   976.4'04'0924 [B]   72-9447
ISBN 0-405-04975-7

JOURNAL

OF THE

TEXIAN EXPEDITION AGAINST MIER;

SUBSEQUENT IMPRISONMENT OF THE AUTHOR;

HIS SUFFERINGS,

AND FINAL

ESCAPE FROM THE CASTLE OF PEROTE.

WITH

REFLECTIONS UPON THE PRESENT POLITICAL AND
PROBABLE FUTURE RELATIONS

OF

Texas, Mexico, and the United States.

BY

GEN. THOMAS J. GREEN.

ILLUSTRATED BY DRAWINGS TAKEN FROM LIFE BY CHARLES M'LAUGHLIN,
A FELLOW-PRISONER.

NEW-YORK:
HARPER & BROTHERS, PUBLISHERS,
82 CLIFF STREET.
1845.

Entered, according to Act of Congress, in the year 1845, by
HARPER & BROTHERS,
In the Clerk's Office of the Southern District of New-York.

THIS VOLUME

IS RESPECTFULLY INSCRIBED TO THE FATHER OF THE
TEXAS REVOLUTION;
TO THE ONE WHO FIRST OF ALL STRUCK FOR THE LIBERTY
OF HIS ADOPTED COUNTRY;
TO ONE, THE LAST OF ALL WHO WOULD COMPROMIT HER
WELFARE OR HONOUR;
TO ONE AS EXALTED FOR HIS PUBLIC VIRTUES AS ESTIMABLE
FOR HIS PRIVATE WORTH,

THE HONOURABLE BRANCH T. ARCHER;

BY ONE WHO HAS KNOWN HIM LONG AND INTIMATELY IN
PRIVATE LIFE, AND WHO, IN THE SAME CAUSE, HAS
MET HIM IN THE SENATE AND THE CAMP,

HIS SINCERE FRIEND,

THOMAS J. GREEN.

PREFACE.

The Texas Revolution is one of the most remarkable political events ever recorded. A population of twenty thousand throwing off the despotic yoke of eight millions of people who claimed to be the mother state, and nine years successfully contending against such odds, with a steadily increasing ability so to do, makes the wonder of the achievement. Wonderful as it is, it is far from being bloodless. Napoleon, in twenty years' warring with nearly the whole civilized world, did not lose half as many men in proportion to the population of France as has Texas.

At the repeated request of many friends both in Texas* and the United States, the author offers to the public the following pages, in which he has endeavoured to give a faithful account of the most important incident of this sanguinary struggle, about which much has been said by the governments and people belligerent, as well as by friendly neutral powers. In doing so, as *authorship* is not his desire, he will make no apology for the manner; though, should he interest the reader with a plain tale, told in a plain way—of Texian daring, of battles won and lost, of dungeons and old castles, of imprisonment and hair-breadth escapes, of unparalleled sufferings and cruel murders—he will have fully accomplished the purpose of an impartial record while in a tyrant's chains. If the author has failed in giving the *whole* truth, it is in this, that a too studied regard for brevity has involved obscurity. The writer's position, also, in the expedition against Mier, and subsequently as a prisoner of war in Mexico, placed him in

* See Appendix No. VII.

another difficulty—that of rendering it necessary to speak of himself. If his conduct throughout has been praiseworthy or otherwise, it would be unnatural to acknowledge the one, and immodest to avow the other.

If the author has been unjust to Mexico, it is in failing to detail more at length her vices; and for fear that a too charitable community would ascribe to him personal vindictiveness, and then more charitably balance that account with his ill treatment and sufferings, he has forborne in many particulars to say what, perhaps, he should have said.

He will assert, that what he has said of the *general* degradation of that nation, of the wretched want and misery of the million, is far short of the whole truth, as a very late writer upon that country will bear witness; and what he has *particularized* no one will question.

This journal, imperfect as it may be, has been ready for the press since the writer's escape from the Castle of Perote, but has been kept back for fear of prejudicing the condition of his countrymen who were detained, until recently, prisoners of war in Mexico.

The designs accompanying the work were executed on the spot by Charles M'Laughlin, one of the Mier prisoners, who participated in all the dangers and sufferings of this eventful expedition, and to whose genius great credit is due for their faithfulness to the life.

CONTENTS.

INTRODUCTORY CHAPTER . . Page 17

CHAPTER II.

President Houston's Conduct in the Campaign.—His Newspaper War with President Santa Anna.—His Treatment of the United States Volunteers 22

CHAPTER III.

General Vascus plunders San Antonio.—The Texians to the Rescue.—General Burleson elected their Commander.—President Houston's Orders to General Somerville.—His vacillating Conduct in the Campaign.—His Call of the Congress and Veto of the War-bill . . 25

CHAPTER IV.

General Woll takes San Antonio.—His Loss.—White Flag.—Capitulation of the Citizens.—Abduction of the Court.—His Protection of the Santa Fé Prisoners.—Battle and Defeat by Colonel Caldwell at Salado.—Battle of the Musquet.—Death of Captain Dawson.—Butchery of Texians after Surrender.—Law of Retaliation.—General Woll retreats from San Antonio.—Murder of Dr. Smithers and Companions.—Death of their Wounded.—Cause of the Texians not charging him at the Rio Hondo.—Traitor Seguin.—General Burleson comes up with Re-enforcements 29

CHAPTER V.

President Houston issues another War Proclamation.—Texians again in the Field.—General Somerville arrives in Camp and Disbands the Troops.—Volunteers Organized.—Burleson's Arrival at Camp.—Houston's Refusal to issue him Orders.—Volunteers press forward to San Antonio.—Somerville's Arrival.—Montgomery Troops Return.—Operations in Camp around Bexar 37

CHAPTER VI.

General Somerville marches upon Laredo.—Gets into a Bog.—Taking of Laredo.—Neglect to Ration the Troops.—Camp moved in the Direction

B

towards Home.—Council of War.—First Texian Flag planted west of the Rio Grande.—General Somerville starts Home.—Camp without Water.—Much Discontent.—Another War Council.—Speech from the General.—200 Troops return Home, and the General marches with those remaining against the Enemy.—Cross the Rio Grande near Guerrero.—Get Sight of the Enemy.—Recross the Rio Grande for Home, and separate from the Main Body . . . . Page 52

CHAPTER VII.

Colonel Fisher elected Commander.—The Writer appointed Commander of the Flotilla.—Descent of the Rio Grande.—Capture of Carancawa Indians with a British Flag.—Occupation of Mier.—Requisition for Provision.—Arrest of the Alcalde.—Enemy's Appearance.—Council of War.—Order of Battle 70

CHAPTER VIII.

BATTLE OF MIER 82

CHAPTER IX.

White Flag.—Dr. Sinnickson's Statement.—Cavalry sent after our Camp-guard.—Camp-guard Escapes.—Major Bonnel's Death.—Return of Cavalry.—Preparation to march for Matamoras.—Dr. Sinnickson left in Charge of our Wounded.—Their Treatment and Escape.—March for Matamoras.—Suffering of our Men.—Triumphal Entry into Comargo.—Camp in a Cow-pen.—The Bull Comedy.—Camp in a Sheep-pen.—A new Comedy.—Triumphal Entry into Rhinosa.—Ridiculous Show.—Arrival at Guadaloupe.—Congratulations to Ampudia.—Visit of Tom and Esau.—Triumphal Entry into Matamoras.—Texas Negroes in Matamoras.—Our Incarceration in Prison, and Note to General Ampudia 112

CHAPTER X.

Preparations for March to Mexico.—Our Friends J. P. Schatzell, Marks, and Strother.—Protest against ironing our Men.—March for Monterey under charge of Colonel Savriego.—Held as Hostages for the good Conduct of our Men.—Interview with them in Prison.—Arrival at Caidereta.—Bad Treatment.—Letter to Ampudia.—Arrival at Monterey.—Character of Colonel Savriego.—Quartered at Colonel Bermudez's.—His Character and Family.—Interview with Governor Ortega   126

CHAPTER XI.

March for Saltillo.—Our Treatment.—Meet Captain Fitzgerald, Van Ness, and others in Prison.—Their Condition.—Arrival of Colonel Barragan with our Prisoners.—We march for San Luis Potosi.—Arrival at Salado.—Our Men arrive at Aqua Nuevo.—Captain Dimmit.—His Death.—Barragan arrives with our Men at Salado.—Concerted Attack upon the Guards.—The Charge and Victory at Salado.—Order to shoot us.—Narrow Escape.—Arrival at Cidral.—Narrow Escape from the Populace.—Narrow Escape from our new Guards.—Arrival at Mataguala.—Treatment there.—Report of the Battle of Salado
Page 140

CHAPTER XII.

Our Men take up the March for Home.—Departure from Plan of Retreat by turning into the Mountains.—Unexampled Suffering.—Killing their Horses for Food.—Many Die, and others Surrender.—Marched back to Saltillo.—March to Salado.—Decimation, and dying Words.—Our Wounded, and those who remained with them.—March from Mataguala.—Arrival at Count Zivyes.—Kind Treatment.—Arrival at San Luis Potosi.—Treatment there.—Correspondence with the Governor.—Notes to Captains Romano and Reyes.—The Valley of San Luis, Mode of drawing Water, &c. 158

CHAPTER XIII.

MARCH TO THE CAPITAL UNDER COLONEL TERRIS.

Hacienda de Plata.—Bad Treatment.—Xaral, Marquis of.—Horses taken from us.—Made to walk over the Mountain.—Our Remonstrances with the Colonel.—Billy Reese and the Catholic Crosses.—Bugler, his Wife, and Sister.—Suffer for Water.—Punishment of a Soldier.—Dolores.—Hidalgo.—Calleja.—San Miguel el Grande.—Hacienda of the Jesuits.—Burned Hacienda.—Lodged in a Stable.—The Comet.—Superstition concerning it.—Mexicans meet Danger with a Prayer.—Cruel Treatment.—Mexican Officers.—Lasso.—Lice.—Fleas: Advantage of.—Locked up.—Protest.—Quartered in a Corral.—Villanous Conduct of the Colonel.—Valley of Mexico.—Arrival at Tacubaya.—Description of.—General Jackson's Birthday.—Friends visit us.—Mr. Cursin.—Captain West.—Mr. Packenham: Interview with . . 187

CONTENTS.

CHAPTER XIV.

MARCH FROM TACUBAYA TO THE CASTLE OF PEROTE.

Marched on Foot.—General Valencia, Wife, and Daughters.—Our Reflections.—Hire Asses.—Pulque-drinking Officer.—Pass the Volcanoes.—Germans.—National Character of the Germans and other Foreigners.—Puebla.—Bad Treatment.—Lieutenant Velarde.—New Officer.—The Execution of General Mexier.—Acahita.—The Death of Mexier.—Texian Talent for Drawing.—The Honest Mexican.—Arrival at Perote.—Meeting our Countrymen Prisoners . . . . Page 223

CHAPTER XV.

IMPRISONMENT IN THE CASTLE OF PEROTE.

Three Days' Grace before Ironed.—The Castle.—Its Strength.—President Houston.—Orazabo.—Cofre de Perote.—Castle.—Its Situation.—Climate.—Description.—Bexar Prisoners.—Mexican Culprits.—Theft.—Rape.—Murder.—The Prisoner who killed a Priest for kissing his Wife.—Prisons of the Mier Men.—Their Treatment.—Ironed.—Mode of breaking off the Chains.—Tricking the Officers.—Santa Anna and the Blacksmith.—" Can't come it, Judge!"—Rations.—Ass's Milk.—Our Mess.—Cooking.—Best Way to make Coffee.—Ordered to Work.—Remonstrance to Minister of War.—To the Governor.—To the United States Minister.—Release of Judges Jones, Hutchinson, and Maverick.—Treason of Robinson: our Denunciation of.—Anniversary of the 21st of April.—Sentiments, Songs, Tecolote, and Old Guts . 236

CHAPTER XVI.

IMPRISONMENT IN THE CASTLE OF PEROTE.—Continued.

Our fat friend.—Commissariat.—Statement of Rations.—Jake upon Cowology.—Snake-bitten old Cow.—Guts in Caricature.—Old Limpy: his Character.—Lousing.—Simeon Glenn.—Louse-racing.—What is an Old Soldier?—How to select the Racers.—An Argument in favour of Phrenology.—General Austin in the Accordada.—The Old Sailing-master's Pipe.—Longing for Brandy.—Sutler, Wife, and Daughter.—Shifts to get Brandy.—Surprise of Senorito.—The Sergeant's handsome Wife.—Dan: his " Soldier's Tear."—A United States Midshipman.—How he avoided Work.—A Favourite.—" Long, long Ago."—His Heresy lost him Favour.—His intellectual Improvement.—Mr. Black, United States Consul.—Billy Reese.—Shooting of Captain Ewin Cameron.—Reminiscence of Captain Cameron.—George B. Crittenden.—O. Phelps.—Letter to President Tyler.—Letters from United States.—Letter to Mr. Calhoun.—Preparation for Emigration to Texas 262

CHAPTER XVII.

ESCAPE FROM THE CASTLE OF PEROTE.

Preparation to Escape.—Procuring a Map of the Road.—Deceiving the Officer with Shaving Tools.—Work upon Breach in the Wall.—Letter to our Prisoners in Mexico.—Santa Anna's Birthday.—President Houston's Orders to Colonel Snively prevents our Liberation.—Commodore Moore off Campeachy.—Prosecution of the Breach in the Wall.—Laying in Provisions to Travel.—Last Visit to " Guts."—Quarterlero.—Voos, his Rheumatism, and Grunts.—All decline the Escape but Sixteen.—Left Papers with Colquhoun.—Note to Santa Anna.—Take Leave of our Friends.—Turnkeys.—Mode of Counting.—Locking up.—Deceiving the Sentinels: mode of.—Monte Bank.—Bull-dance.—Commence going Out.— Toowig.— Ike Allen: his Fall.— Character.—Beeve's Bladder.— Aguardiente.—Governor.— " Guts" and the Dialogue.—Stone hung in the Hole. — The Herculean John Young. — Passing the Sentinels.—Their Hailing.—Our Response   Page 296

CHAPTER XVIII.

RESIDENCE IN THE MOUNTAINS, AND ENTRY INTO JALAPA.

Two hundred Yards east of the Castle.—Separation.—Parting Speeches.—Pass the Powder-house.—Meet with Reese and Toowig.—Divide Rations with.—Take to the Mountains.—Residence and Sufferings in.—Return to the Valley.—Charge of Cavalry and Escape.—Separation from Toowig.—Narrow Escape from a Precipice.—Make Coffee.—Approach to Jalapa.—Our Distress from Sore Feet and Thorns.—Entry and Peregrination in the City.—Our Location in the Suburbs.—Re-entry, mode of.—Don: his Wife, and warm Supper.—Meet Toowig.—Residence in City.—Kind Treatment.—Robbers employed, and we delivered over to them in a dark Hollow   326

CHAPTER XIX.

FIVE NIGHTS' JOURNEY TO VERA CRUZ UNDER CONDUCT OF ROBBERS.

Head Robber.—Coming to the Horses.—Signal.—Silence.—Winding around Precipices.—Narrow Paths.—Sure-footed Animals.—Puente Nacional.—Rio Antigua.—Lying in Swamp.—Hot Breakfast.—Lodged in vacant House.—Gray-bearded old Man.—Meeting Robbers.—Enter Antigua.—Cavalry Officer and the Gray-bearded old Man.—Narrow Escape from the Officers and Guards.—Crossing the Ferry, and deceiving the Officer.—The Gray-bearded old Man's Exultation.—

Taking the Road to Mango de Clavo.—Secreted for the Night.—Head Robber goes into Vera Cruz.—Our Location next Day.—Vessels at Sea.—Sand Storm.—Head Robber arrives with Don E.—Start for the City.—Storm and Separation.—Arrival near the City Gates.—Suspicions of the Head Robber.—Bad Night.—Don E. finds us next Day.—Our Entry into the City.—Parting with Robbers.—Valedictory of the Gray-bearded old Man.—Our Hiding-place.—United States Friends.—Dick Barclay.—Recapture of our Comrades.—A Look into the Castle after the Dénouement.—Surprise, Wonder, and Astonishment.—The Governor, Guts, and the Children . . . . . Page 343

CHAPTER XX.
EMBARCATION AT VERA CRUZ FOR HOME.

Preparation for Embarcation.—Captain Loyd and Steamer Petrita.—Pass Officers on the Mole.—Sup on board a U. S. Vessel.—Hailed by War Steamers.—Board the Petrita.—Meet my Companions and Dr. Sinnickson.—Mexican Officers come on board.—My Berth under the Boilers : its Temperature.—Dialogue with Steward.—Passage and Arrival in New-Orleans.—Once more in the Land of Liberty.—" Tom and Jerry," " Hail Storm," and " Sherry Cobbler."—St. Charles Hotel and a Soft Bed.—Sail for the " Lone Star."—Land at Velasco.—Reese and Dan.—Our Remaining Countrymen in Mexico. — Their Destitution, Sufferings, and Deaths.—The Cause, and Treasonable Armistice with Mexico 364

SUPPLEMENTAL CHAPTER.

Reflections upon the Present Political and probable Future Relations of Texas, Mexico, and the United States. — Annexation.—Abolition.—Southern Boundary 382

APPENDICES I. TO IX. 437–487

LIST OF ENGRAVINGS.

		Page
1	Mier Expedition descending the Rio Grande	71
2	Battle of Mier	82
3	Texian Charge upon the Guards, and Victory of Salado	155
4	Texians killing their Horses in the Mountains for Sustenance	161
5	Texians drawing the black Beans at Solado	170
6	Shooting of the decimated Texians at Solado	173
7	Ground-plan of the Castle of Perote	239
8	Shooting of Captain Ewin Cameron	285
9	Guts and Ike Allen at the Calaboose	324
10	Escape from the Castle of Perote	325
11	Separation after Escape	328
12	Narrow Escape from the Cavalry Officer at Antigua	350
13	Texians working upon the Road in front of the Archbishop's Palace at Tacubaya	370

JOURNAL.

INTRODUCTORY CHAPTER.

THE election of General Sam. Houston, in 1836, as first constitutional president, over Stephen F. Austin, the father of his country, did not show less confidence in the virtues and capability of that deceased patriot. In casting their votes between these distinguished individuals, a majority of the electors of Texas voted for the former, believing that, from his military reputation, he would pursue an active belligerant policy, which, at a short period, would extort an honourable peace from our enemy. They feared in General Austin a more temporizing and pacific course, which they believed less calculated to procure the peace they so much desired. Whether these were just grounds of apprehension as to the policy of that wise and good man, must to some extent remain a secret; but in frequent conversations with the author subsequent to the election, he evinced a desire to give Mexico a reasonable opportunity of settling the dispute without farther recourse to arms, and, in the event of failure, to use the most energetic means to coerce it.

Not so with General Houston. He was elected

as the war candidate; for the nation believed that a war policy would procure us a speedy peace. In this they were disappointed; for General Houston's first official act was a visit to the captive president of Mexico, then confined at Orozimbo. This artful tyrant had the address to make him believe that, if he, Santa Anna, could see Houston's old friend, President Andrew Jackson, at Washington City, they would complete the treaty which he so solemnly promised the Texians. President Houston then, in violation of the expressed will of the Congress, at that time in session, smuggled him out of the country.

When Santa Anna was once out of Texas, he laughed at his promise to Houston as neither legally nor morally binding upon him; and, though he made those promises with all the sanctity of deep contrition, and heartfelt interest for our young nation, yet the whole civilized world justified him in their breach, and wondered at the credulity of our Executive in believing that such a promise was in any way binding.

In full view, which this farce brought upon us as a nation, President Houston persisted in his "peace policy," and his next step was the disbandment of the best-appointed army Texas ever had in the field, and a total neglect of the law of Congress ordering him to build two steamers, one sloop of war, and two schooners. Thus ended President Houston's first administration, with offence enough to vex the enemy, and not energy enough to make him respect us; and it closed with a universal national conviction that a different policy was necessary. That national conviction called to the administration of the government General Mirabeau B. Lamar, a gentleman whose gallant bearing at San Jacinto, and general chivalry of character, was a sure guaranty that in him it would be fully carried out.

President Lamar did more towards carrying it out. He built the navy, and maintained the mastery of the Gulf; he beat back the Indians and extended the frontier; but, unfortunately for the nation, his administration closed without that bold and energetic strike upon our Mexican enemy which would at that time have given us peace. This war policy was advocated by the Hon. Branch T. Archer, then Secretary of War and Navy, and sustained by Vice-president Burnet, the Hon. James Webb, attorney-general, Major-general Felix Husten, and other distinguished individuals. Thus closed the sixth year of this *quasi* war, which had involved the nation in heavy debt, depreciated to a fearful extent the value of individual property, and by the ravenous operations of the courts, sheriffs, and constables, had brought misery and distress into the bosom of many a good family. An infatuation seemed to possess the land injurious as it was lasting. Most men seemed to think, when not in the immediate sight of the Mexicans, that the war was at an end. The dockets of the courts were crowded with foreign claimants in the absence of all treaty authority upon the subject, and vast amounts of property changed hands from those who had won and were still willing to fight for the country, to those who never drew a blade or contributed a dollar in the war. By thus acting, as though the war did not really exist, the chief government of the country was the government of the courts; not one of protection, but, under the peculiar circumstances of the times, of destruction to the many; because the establishment of this branch of the government, which presupposed a close of the revolution and a final accomplishment of our liberty, was premature. The people of Texas were still in the midst of revolution; a revolution which prevented men of capital from other countries making investments in ours.

There is nothing more true, that in their distress, political communities, like individuals, will frequently ascribe their calamities to wrong causes; and President Lamar's administration closed with much complaint of him as the cause of the then individual and national suffering. If this complaint had any foundation in justice, it was his neglect to procure for Texas a mild peace by the prosecution of a bold war.* Every sensible man must now believe that a

---

* Upon the authority of some of President Lamar's confidential friends, it is due to him to state, that the cause of his not prosecuting offensive measures against Mexico was the expectation of his procuring "a five million loan" in Europe, which he intended to expend by waging

bold war would have procured such a peace; that peace would have brought us emigration, and that emigration would have brought us money. In the proneness of the public mind to visit all the wrongs upon the President, men did not look to that universal commercial and pecuniary distress which had swept through all Christendom: they could not believe that a distress even greater than theirs existed in other countries. The people of Texas a third time went to the polls, and in their then individual and political sufferings they forgot the errors and wrongs of President Houston's former administration, and elected him over David G. Burnet, one alike eminent for his learning and patriotism; too honest to indulge in the trickery of the demagogue, and too proud to pander to the vitiated appetites of the corrupt.

President Houston, unlike his predecessor Lamar, who, in all his public documents, defended the honour and dignity of his country, commenced his second term by exposing to his enemies and the world his weakness, by unnecessarily magnifying that weakness, by his repudiating doctrines of public faith, by his laying violent hands upon the public archives, by his secret orders to commence civil war upon a portion of the citizens of Texas, who opposed his violent and unlawful measures to remove the seat of government, and by his advocacy

an offensive war against that country. It is certain that he was frequently flattered with the expectation of procuring said loan.

of the traitor Seguin, who at that time was leading upon the heart of our country a portion of the Mexican army; and here commences the history of the campaign which we propose faithfully to record.

CHAPTER II.

President Houston's Conduct in the Campaign.—His Newspaper War with President Santa Anna.—His Treatment of the United States Volunteers.

PRESIDENT HOUSTON'S second administration, after the foregoing catalogue as its precursor, commenced with his old siren song of peace, peace by begging, peace by negotiation. To some he would say, with a mock gravity of face and tone which would better suit a father confessor, "*In thirty days you shall have peace;*" that he was "fixing the thing." This mockery was of short duration. In rapid succession followed Santa Anna's letter of ridicule of "Mr. Samuel Houston" and the "rebel adventurers;" then General Arista's proclamation to the people of Texas; then General Vascus's capture and plunder of San Antonio. How were these insults and outrages answered by President Houston? Was it in the manly language of the cannon? To the shame of our country, we are bound to answer No! How then? In the columns of a village newspaper our president belched forth his gall and thunder upon the head of the tyrant of Mexico, whom he, Houston, "has so greatly served while in Texas."* In this newspaper war was our President victor to the extent of several columns over and above the length of his competitor, and after luxuriating under the gilded domes of the Montezumas, he insults a nation with whom we were at peace by "*unfurling the single star upon the Isthmus of Darien.*"

In this tournament of the goose-quill between the Presidents of Mexico and Texas, the partisan friends of the latter had but little time to chuckle over his victory. Santa Anna was not disposed to await the execution of his empty threat. He sends General Vascus into San Antonio, plunders that place of immense booty, and carries off our peaceable citizens. Was this outrage answered by the national ordnance which the people had placed in the hands of their President-general-in-chief? No! It was answered in the numerous war-speeches with which he lulled and cajoled the citizens of Houston and Galveston. These cities, ever devoted in their duty to their country, felt that enthusiastic patriotism which pervaded all portions of Texas. They called upon their President to avenge their country's wrongs. He says, in a public speech, "You shall have war, and war to the knife. I say it— Sam Houston says it—and no man can ever say

* See Santa Anna's letter to General Hamilton, and Houston's answer.

these lips ever uttered falsehood." In the speech alluded to, on the 21st of April, at the Tremont House in Galveston, he says, " Before July you shall have war." He authorizes the enlistment of several hundred gallant young men in the United States, and, upon their arrival on our shores, he sends them to summer it upon the Nueces, unprovided with food or the necessary equipments of an army, exposed to the sudden attack of a superior force, and the pestilence of a climate to which they were unused. These brave men were for months exposed to disease and death, placed in a situation where they could not be succoured, nor any means taken to re-enforce them.

After the President had succeeded in lulling the popular war-fever, which abated with the retirement of General Vascus from the country, he folds his arms and quietly predicts that "there must be another Fannin massacre before the people would come to their senses." If this did not take place it was no fault of the President, and in his prediction he over-estimated the bravery of the enemy, though that enemy was by him furnished with every inducement to execute his fell prediction. For the credit of our country, the following admissions we record with deep feelings of regret and mortification. These patriotic men, after suffering all that human nature was capable, returned to their homes, beggared, unpitied, and with the denunciations of our President. Their good sense will teach them that, though President Houston is the organ of the executive government of Texas, yet he is not the representative of the moral sentiment of the community; and that, while every good man in Texas sympathized in their wrongs, they will never cease to feel grateful for their heroic services.

CHAPTER III.

General Vascus plunders San Antonio.—The Texians to the Rescue.—General Burleson elected their Commander.—President Houston's Orders to General Somerville.—His vacillating Conduct in the Campaign.—His Call of the Congress and Veto of the War-bill.

THE plunder of San Antonio by General Vascus, on the 6th of March, 1842, met a response in the bosom of every patriot Texian: not in the windy gasconade of their President chief, but in that patriotic impulse which, before the 1st day of April, had carried 5000 Texians to the rescue, a large portion of whom stopped upon the Colorado. A large number had already assembled under their veteran leader, General Edward Burleson, always the first in the field and foremost in the fight. The enemy fled before them to the Rio Grande, one hundred and fifty miles distant. The Texians were anxious to pursue, having by the law of the land elected General Burleson their leader. President Houston, knowing that, if he attempted to exercise

D

the appointing power over them it would break up the expedition, sent General Somerville to take command. This dissatisfied nearly the whole camp, and General Somerville promised to retire and leave General Burleson in command. This he did, and, having returned one day's journey homeward, learning that some letters had gone on to him from President Houston, he returned to San Antonio, when General Burleson, determined not to be the means of thwarting the legal orders of the government, retired, and left the command to Somerville; most of the citizen soldiers also retired, and left General Somerville in the quiet enjoyment of the hospitalities of Bexar.

The citizens of the western counties determined to go home and prepare themselves better for a campaign the following June, calling upon their old and favourite leader Burleson to head them, which he promised with the approbation of the President, and despatched the author hereof to the President for permission so to do, which they promised should not cost the government one dollar. The President withheld his permission; and this campaign terminated with the President ordering Captain Hays to raise a ranging company for the protection of the Western frontier. Captain Hays, with but his small means, had so little success in so doing, that General Woll, in September following, absolutely entered and took possession of San Antonio without his knowledge. During this time, while all was excitement in favour of the war, President Houston joined in the cry with as much seeming patriotism as the foremost. His *Brutum Fulmen* to Santa Anna, his war proclamation, his address to the people of Texas, dated Houston, April 14th, 1842, published in the Telegraph of the 20th of June, his numerous and less destructive thunderbolts by way of grog-shop harangues, followed each other in such rapid succession, that many believed him serious in his professions. His partisans said that "he had his *own* plan of conducting the campaign; let him alone, and he would do it right;" that "if the *old chief* himself could head the army in person, then every defect in its organization would be remedied, and Mexico demolished!"

Under this state of things the President convoked the Congress at the city of Houston, to obtain, as it was alleged, more ample means to prosecute the war. The Congress convened, bringing with them the general feelings of their constituents, that "the war must be ended by manly and energetic measures." His adherents were for uniting in his person, in violation of the constitution and genius of our government, the sword and the purse. The opposition, although they had no confidence in him as a military leader, and believed that such grant of power was wholly in contravention of every principle of the government, voted him this extraordinary authority. They believed that the great public necessity of peace was paramount to all other considerations;

that a campaign upon the enemy's country would produce such peace, and that, no matter under whom it might be commenced, there was enough bravery and military intelligence among our people to prosecute it to certain victory. President Houston greatly overreached himself. He doubtless believed that the Congress would not give what his friends asked, and thereby he could defend himself from the non-prosecution of the war by saying that the Congress had tied his hands. After the Congress granted all and more than was asked, he comes out with his famous *veto* upon the war-bill, carps loudly upon the anti-republicanism of placing too much power in the hands of one individual; and, to the lasting disgrace of the office he occupied, published to our enemies and the world, in the aforesaid veto, THIRTY-SIX times, that the country had "*no means*" of prosecuting the war. We will hereafter show with how little truth this pleasing intelligence was communicated to the enemy. He at the same time despatched General M. Hunt as inspector-general to organize the militia, and muster into the service several thousand troops, thus pretending that *he* had a "plan."

CHAPTER IV.

General Woll takes San Antonio.—His Loss.—White Flag.—Capitulation of the Citizens.—Abduction of the Court.—His Protection of the Santa Fé Prisoners.—Battle and Defeat by Colonel Caldwell at Salado.—Battle of the Musquet.—Death of Captain Dawson.—Butchery of Texians after Surrender.—Law of Retaliation.—General Woll retreats from San Antonio.—Murder of Dr. Smithers and Companions. —Death of their Wounded.—Cause of the Texians not charging him at the Rio Hondo.—Traitor Seguin.—General Burleson comes up with Re-enforcements.

PRESIDENT SANTA ANNA, in contempt of all President Houston's vain boasts, again ordered the invasion of Texas, and General Woll took possession of San Antonio on the 11th September, after a determined resistance on the part of the Anglo-American portion of the population, numbering fifty-three men. The Mexican army under Woll entered the town about daylight, and was received by a warm fire from the Texians, which killed twelve and wounded twenty-nine of the enemy, and with them General Woll's favourite horse.

Although the Mexicans numbered twelve hundred, and well knew the strength of the Texians, they did not venture upon a farther attack, but had recourse to their old deception. They took one of the small boys of the town, and sent him in with a white flag, sounding a parley at the same time. The Texians sent over Dr. Booker, Mr. Van Ness, and Captain Ogden, to meet General Woll and hear his terms. They surrendered upon the following terms, that "they should be treated with all the honour and consideration of prisoners of war, and that all the Santa Fé prisoners with them should be so likewise treated." Thus General Woll captured judge, jury, clerks, lawyers, and citizens, while in the peaceable pursuit of their daily avocations. The loss of the Texians was not one killed or wounded, and the only damage done by the Mexicans was killing a chicken rooster near the position of our men.

General Woll pledged his word and honour as an officer, a gentleman, and a Frenchman, for the faithful observance of these promises, and it affords me pleasure to record the fact that he exerted himself in carrying them out. His conduct in the case of Captain Fitzgerald, Van Ness, and Hancock, Santa Fé prisoners, when they were left at San Fernandez, by order of the government, to be shot, was highly praiseworthy. He wrote to the government, if the order was persisted in, that it must also accept his resignation in the army, and thus these men were saved.

But to return to General Woll at San Antonio. He delayed his stay in that city until the 16th, by which time Colonel Matthew Caldwell (Old Paint) had assembled two hundred and ten men in the Salado bottom, about six miles east of the city, in a well-selected position. Colonel Caldwell then despatched Captain Hays, with his mounted company, to the city, to draw out the

BATTLE AT SALADO.

enemy. He approached near to the Alamo, when the enemy's cavalry, several hundred, advanced upon him. As directed, he fell back upon Caldwell's position, where the Texians lay in eager expectation to receive the enemy. They were not long kept in suspense. General Woll, with the vanity peculiar to his adopted country, said "he would go in person and drive the Texian wolves from the bushes." He accordingly marched with nearly his whole force, including a large number of the resident Mexicans of Bexar, and attacked Caldwell's position. He used every persuasion to make his men charge the Texians, but to no purpose. The Texian rifle, when directed by steady nerves, as in this case, was awfully destructive. In the attack upon the Texians, the Mexicans had sixty killed and many more wounded, while of the Texians there were only one killed and nine wounded: the one killed being a man by the name of Jet, living near San Antonio, and who was remarkable for his cool daring both in Indian and Mexican fighting.

General Woll, sorely disappointed in driving the "*Texian wolves from the bush,*" was about retreating, when he was informed that a company of Texians were advancing upon his rear, some two miles distant. This company proved to be the gallant and lamented Captain Dawson and his company of fifty-three men, mostly from Fayette county, who had determined upon succouring Caldwell; and it proved a favourable opportunity for General Woll to withdraw from Caldwell without the appearance of flight; consequently, he retreated to some distance, and despatched a large portion of his force to attack Dawson.

Dawson selected his position in a musquet thicket favourable for his rifle-shooting, and where he could have whipped a much superior force of Mexicans with small arms; but, to his surprise, after the first fire from his party, at which several Mexicans fell, their whole force withdrew to a distance beyond the reach of the rifle, and opened upon the Texians with a fieldpiece. The Texians were entirely exposed to the fire from the enemy's cannon, being in a smooth prairie, only partially protected by small musquet timbers, not sufficiently large to shield them from the cannon-shot. Thus situated, with already a loss of some eight or ten of their number, with many of their horses either killed, wounded, or otherwise broken loose from their charge, they found no means left of retreating; a surrender was therefore determined upon. Here followed a scene as disgraceful to the enemy as it was revolting to civilized man. After the Texians had surrendered up their arms, an indiscriminate slaughter took place; and, before any stop was put to it by the Mexican officers, thirty-six of our fifty-three men fell a sacrifice to their inhuman cruelty; fifteen more were taken prisoners, while two only made their escape. Of the fifteen taken prisoners, several were inhumanly butchered with swords and lances; from which wounds, however, they recovered, after long and severe suffering. Not only the officers in immediate command, but especially General Woll, and the whole Mexican nation, are responsible for this outrageous and savage butchery, after the surrender of our arms, and while the flag of peace still waved; but a day of retribution will assuredly overtake them, terrible though just.

The law of retaliation in war—the most salutary of all laws in preventing the excesses of an enemy—as yet, has never been resorted to by the Texians; that law which should have been inflicted upon Santa Anna, and each and every one of his men at San Jacinto, for his recent murder of Colonel Fannin and his four hundred, was permitted to sleep; and the cunning tyrant flattered his captor into a vain consequence, which made him forgetful of his duty to his country and these murdered heroes. Had Washington commanded at San Jacinto, with all his human kindness and Christian charity, the captive despot would have found a rope, and his men no quarter. Thus would he have balanced that bloody account, and thus would he have kept it balanced. What has the reverse of this policy benefited us? It has been, for the last seven years, an unlimited license for our enemy to plunder and murder!

To return to our narrative. After the massacre of Dawson and his men, General Woll made a triumphal entry into San Antonio with his fifteen prisoners and some two hundred of his own wounded, and prepared for a hasty retreat towards the Rio Grande. This retreat he greatly hastened, upon hearing that Colonels Mayfield, Moore, M'Cullough, and others, were coming up with re-enforcements to Caldwell.

Some days previous to this time, he had ordered Colonel John M. Seguin, with several hundred cavalry, to proceed as far as the Guadaloupe River, and report to him the condition of things there. It is believed that Seguin never went farther than the Cibelo Mineral Springs, where he knew that Dr. Smithers and two others were staying for their health. These three sick men he barbarously murdered, and thereby made himself master of Dr. Smithers's fine American horse, which his family drove in a buggy to the Rio Grande. Seguin, however, upon his return, reported to General Woll that all the Texian settlers had fled from the Guadaloupe. When General Woll found the Texian re-enforcement coming up, and that Seguin had deceived him, he laid violent hands upon every means of transportation in his reach. Among other things, he seized a large number of carts, into which he crowded his and our wounded in piles, many of whom died for want of medical assistance; and we are informed by Captain Fitzgerald and Mr. Van Ness that only two of their wounded recovered; their wounds not having been attended to for eight days, they were become past recovery.

With all General Woll's hurry in his flight homeward, at the Rio Hondo he found Caldwell upon his heels. His retreat became a flight and a panic; and had the Texians charged him, as all now agree, and as all then seemed to be anxious to do, his whole force would have fallen an easy prey. Much has been said against Caldwell and others for not so doing, and the blame has been charged upon several; but the writer has not been able to satisfy his mind that any particular individual was to blame. It seems to be one of those mischances in war, more the result of accident or the want of promptness than the absence of bravery. It was, however, a national misfortune that he was permitted to escape to the west side of the Rio Grande, after murdering forty-one, and carrying off sixty-seven of our best citizens.

General Woll had persons in his employment well calculated for spies and pilots, and adepts in robbery and murder. Among the principal of these was Antonio Periz and John M. Seguin, both of whom had been constantly in the employment of our government; and when they witnessed the determined efforts of President Houston to destroy the seat of government and break up our western settlements, their cupidity prevailed over all their love for Texas, and they determined to have a share in the general plunder, a result which is the universa consequence of a broken-up frontier. Besides, from the melancholy account which President Houston had just then promulgated to the world of the condition of Texas, they had the weakness to believe that she must again become an integral portion of Mexico. This they believed was a most favourable opportunity to reinstate themselves in the favour of their mother-country. In 1836 they had been traitors to that country—the country of their language, laws, religion, and birth—and now, Mexican-like, they sought to reinstate themselves by an act of compound treason upon us. What possible justification in the eyes of honourable men could Seguin have for this? He had enjoyed the confidence and favour of three administrations; he had uniformly been in high civil and military commissions; and yet, for this double act of perfidy, his friend, President Houston, pronounces him as pure a patriot as any in the land. I have the evidence of Captain Fitzgerald, and Messrs. Van Ness and Hancock, the three Santa Fé prisoners who were detained at San Fernando until January, that Don Erasmo Seguin, his father, then at San Antonia, was in daily correspondence with the enemy while our army was marching upon the Rio Grande.

The Texians, under Caldwell, returned from the Rio Hondo greatly exasperated at not being allowed to engage General Woll. In a few miles they met their old favourite leader, General Burleson, coming up with re-enforcements, and they believed that, with him as a commander, they would have engaged and captured their enemy; but now it was too late. General Burleson may not be considered a tactician in the strict sense of the term, but he never failed to observe one rule in winning battles more important than all the minutiæ of the drill: that rule is, to fight; and his uniform success in many a hard-fought battle proves that in this art he is abundantly proficient.

CHAPTER V.

President Houston issues another War Proclamation.—Texians again in the Field.—General Somerville arrives in Camp and Disbands the Troops.—Volunteers Organized.—Burleson's Arrival at Camp.—Houston's Refusal to issue him Orders.—Volunteers press forward to San Antonio.—Somerville's Arrival.—Montgomery Troops Return.—Operations in Camp around Bexar.

THIS second invasion of our country in the same year, and the atrocities with which it was accompanied, were well calculated to arouse anew the war feeling which President Houston's procrastinating ingenuity had in a great measure allayed. The people of Texas then viewed with dismay and indignation the wanton neglect of the navy, his refusal to prosecute war after Congress and the nation had decreed it, and his disbandment and abuse of the several hundred brave volunteers from the United States. General Woll entered Bexar on the 11th September, and, as before stated, captured judge, jury, bar, and citizens, under their own roofs, and while in discharge of their peaceable avocations. This news reached the president at

Houston on the 16th of the same month, on which day he issued another flaming war-proclamation.* Here the President meets this universal public indignation which his ruinous and deceptious policy had visited upon him, by again joining in the war-cry. The aforesaid proclamation was printed, and distributed extensively throughout the country. It called "upon the first class of drafted men from many counties to rendezvous at Bexar, to pursue the enemy into Mexico, chastise him for his insolence and wrongs," and concluded by saying, "It is hoped you will call to your lead a man of valour, wisdom, and experience." Though the laws of the country gave the citizens this latter privilege when in the field, President Houston had the spring before denied it, and yet usurped the appointing power over them. That usurpation of their lawful rights, and his endeavour to force upon them a man not of their choice, had broken up the army in the spring. Now that the war-storm raged so fiercely, he yielded this point; and all, more than all, called for in his proclamation, at the shortest possible notice were in their saddles, and moving rapidly to the seat of action. The writer was among the first two or three hundred from the middle section of the country who arrived at Columbus, upon the Colo-

---

* Volunteer corps were raised with great despatch in different portions of the country, and from the one organized in the city of Houston, which elected General Mosley Baker to its command, he (the President) required a pledge that "*they would cross the Rio Grande*" before he agreed that they should have any ammunition from the public stores.

rado, where, for the first time, they met the news of General Woll's evacuation of Bexar. Here we met many returning, some, doubtless, glad of such an opportunity to do so, while the majority deeply lamented it. What was to be done? was the question. Was this system of outrage and murder to be forever practised upon us with impunity, and a hundred miles' flight to the Rio Grande to screen our enemy from punishment? These questions were deliberately considered by every patriot present. They had in their hands the President's proclamation authorizing and commanding them to pursue the enemy into Mexico, and also to elect their own commander. One and all expressed a desire for Burleson to lead them, and said, if he would do so, they would follow the enemy home.

In this state of uncertainty and doubt, I informed them that I would go express to General Burleson's house, some sixty miles, and have him there in three days. I started for General Burleson's, and, in the mean time, General Somerville arrived at Columbus, and hearing that Burleson was expected to meet the troops at that place, he hastily disbanded them, without orders from the government, and started back to his custom-house at Matagorda Bay. The question must occur to every reflecting mind, Was this patriotic in General Somerville, after he found that he was not the choice of the troops, to disband them, and destroy all prospect of their serving their country under another leader? This was the second time General S. had dispersed the army in the same way. In March previously he pertinaciously insisted upon the command at Bexar over men who had no confidence in him, thereby driving a large and respectable army from the field. But at Columbus he was not so successful; and though he added the sanction of his authority as brigadier-general of the militia to their going home, and did *himself* go, there was a patriotism of sterner stuff which he could not control.

The gallant Captains Wm. Ryan and F. M. Gibson, of Fort Bend county, and others, called for volunteers, and when General Burleson arrived the third day, as I promised, they were ready for the onward march. General B. informed them that he would proceed to the upper Colorado counties and Washington, raise what men he could, and join them upon the San Antonio River in two weeks; adding that, if it should then be their desire for him to lead them, he would not shrink from the responsibility. He proceeded to Washington for orders from the President, not doubting that his proclamation of the 16th of the month previous, authorizing the troops to elect their own commander, would be denied. The President knew full well that, if Burleson received orders, the men would follow him and the enemy would be punished. This he never intended to perform, but merely told General B. that General Somerville had *his orders*. Burleson, always obedient to the lawful authorities of his country, returned home, and left the future conduct of the campaign to the President and General Somerville. During this time, from the last of September to the first of November, volunteers pressed forward to the San Antonio River, all eager to follow the enemy, and punish him in his own country. In the mean time, the President had sent to General Somerville, at Matagorda Bay, to proceed to Bexar and take command, at which place he arrived about five weeks after he had disbanded the troops at Columbus. Here General S. found about twelve hundred men scattered around the town, at from one to ten miles, in some six or eight different encampments; and, instead of concentrating his camp, or organizing and drilling his men, he sits down in the town for two weeks, receiving the hospitalities of those very individuals who just before had been foremost in entertaining General Woll. Much talk had been excited against these individuals in the Texian camp for their open and kind reception of the Mexican general; and now that they had a favourable opportunity of taking shelter under the protection of the Texian general by feasting and fandangoing him, no pains in this respect were spared to win that favour; and from the two weeks' carnival he held in the town, we are bound to believe that they won it. This brought about the 17th of November, and with it a most cutting north wind, which was as uncomfortable to those men without blankets, lying still in an open prairie, as General

F

S.'s luxurious indulgences in the city were to those who had blankets. During this cold weather, it was told in camp that the general would have been out "that day," but had stopped that night to attend another fandango. What was murmur and dissatisfaction before against the general's operations, now became loud and bitter denunciations. Many believed that nothing would be effected under him, while others were more highly indignant at not being provided with those absolute, indispensable munitions of war, which could have been easily obtained from the hostile citizens of Bexar. Some wanted more powder and lead, which were known to be in the town, and which had been tendered General Woll, but from the Texians an exorbitant price in silver was demanded. This was equivalent to a refusal, and those persons who held these articles well knew it. As friends of the enemy, they did not intend that the Texians should have them if in their power to prevent it. Under this state of things, nearly the whole of the Montgomery regiment returned home under feelings of indignation and disgust. Colonel Bennett and about seventy of the regiment remained. By some, blame has been attached to the Montgomery troops for returning at this time; but they returned under the known sanction of President Houston; and the writer, knowing all the circumstances of the case, can more readily excuse them; for, said they, it was easy to foresee that no good to the country would be effected under General Somerville.

After the return of these Montgomery troops, and when general dissatisfaction prevailed in camp, through the urgent request of the quartermaster-general, Colonel Wm. G. Cook, he was permitted to press into service a few sacks of salt and some lead, while Captain Bogart, of Washington county, and the writer became individually responsible for iron to shoe the barefooted horses. Did General Somerville doubt his authority to take for the use of the army absolute necessaries? If so, why was that district of country declared to be under military law? Did our enemy do less? No! they not only took absolute necessaries for the camp, but everything else which their thieving propensities instigated them to take. Was it just to Texas that these people should do less for her than for the enemy? Or was it due to Texas that General Somerville should give to these people a protection which would enable them to keep Bexar as a military granary and magazine for the enemy? Or was it due to Texas that we required of them less than they were willing to furnish the Mexicans? The bad administration of the commissariat department was a fruitful source of complaint in the Texian camp. They had not been furnished with proper rations of beef or bread-stuff. Was it because they were not to be had? No! a large number of disaffected Mexicans, who had fled with General Woll to the Rio Grande, had left the most of their cattle behind them, and the most bountiful corn crop that had been raised on the San Antonio for the last ten years. And though the troops were at this time using from fifteen to twenty beeves per day, a requisition was made upon the different *ranches* for fifty beeves to take them to the Rio Grande; a number barely sufficient for the army while these fifty were collecting. To the energy and promptness of Colonel Bennett, of the Montgomery regiment, the army was principally indebted for the beef it obtained. He detailed men from his regiment, and had three or four hundred beeves drove up, which were yet barely sufficient to last the army during its slothful march to Lovedo.

That the Texian troops complained was most natural and just. They well knew that their Mexican enemies had in their neighbourhood three or four thousand cattle. They also knew that from thirty to fifty thousand bushels of corn had been left by them, and not exceeding two thousand bushels had been used by our troops. They also knew that a grist-mill, capable of grinding 60 bushels of corn per day, which had freely supplied the Mexican army, was close by them. They also knew that salt, powder, lead, and other necessaries were in the town. Knowing these things, they complained, and rightly complained.

But did these good causes of complaint drive them home? No! most of these men left their homes in September under a solemn conviction that duty to their country and themselves required that they should pursue the enemy in his retreat, and "punish his aggressions." They rejoiced as they believed that President Houston had finally adopted that belief. They had now been from their homes from September up to the 18th of November, which found them some twenty miles west of San Antonio, upon the Precidio crossing of the Medina. They were yet 760 strong, and within five days' march of General Woll's retreating army, which had halted near Precidio to give them battle. The men were anxious for the fight, and, had General Somerville moved promptly upon Woll, we are assured by Captains Fitzgerald and Van Ness that the whole Mexican army would have been captured without a second fire; that most of the Mexican officers and men came to them, when they heard that Somerville was advancing upon Precidio, to know how they should surrender, and what to say to the Texians to save their lives.

During the six or eight days, while the remainder of the Texian army lay at this place, they were greatly cheered with the hope of speedily meeting General Woll. These days, in the absence of General Somerville, who was still in Bexar, were well improved. Many of the men left their homes during the warm days of September, with pantaloons too thin for the sharp weather of November; and now, in the absence of a uniform military clothing establishment, they in the shortest time transferred the covering of many an unwary buck to their own legs. I never saw deer so plenty; many hundreds were killed, and the whole camp for several days had more the appearance of a tremendous tanyard than an army which expected in a few days to meet the national enemy upon his own soil. Indeed, the scene here presented was no bad illustration of the facility with which Texians can accommodate themselves to unforeseen emergencies; and he who could not creep upon the most keen-sighted buck, and "ease him of his jacket," was not fit for a soldier; and many who could not or would not do it, returned home, as they said, "to get some warm clothing."

Our experience is, that those who "go home for warm clothing," a "better horse," or "better gun," almost invariably stay there; and, in my opinion, there they should stay, for I never knew a man truly anxious to meet the enemy turn back under any pretence whatever. On the contrary, I have known men to go out without either horse or gun, and never knew them to fail in being armed before the pinching time. One lad in particular I recollect to have overtaken on foot and unarmed, pressing forward to the army; and, upon my inquiring after his horse and arms, he said, with the utmost simplicity, "I have neither, sir, but expect the old general will let me fight upon my own hook with stones until one of our boys is killed, and then I can get his." I asked him if he was good at throwing stones. "I am pretty good when I get close enough, sir," was his modest answer. I need hardly add that *he* proved himself a soldier.

On the contrary, those whom I have observed with the most bloody mottoes painted upon their caps were the last to prove them true; and I do not recollect of seeing one with a "Liberty or death" motto who did not take the liberty of returning home a little too soon. One of these Republicans wore upon his hat, in large capitals, " Patriæ infelici fidelis," and he was "faithful enough to his unhappy country" to eat his full share of beef until he got sight of the enemy, but then returned home in disgust without fighting him.

This week upon the Medina was a week of anxious expectation. The "artillery was coming up," General Woll was within five days' march, the rivers low, and no impediment between us; and we believed that the last of the timid had gone home. Victory already, in the imaginations of many, had perched upon our standard; fat beef and venison hams were in the greatest profusion, and the leather breeches-making went on cheerily. Indeed, such was the contempt in which General Woll's division was held, that it looked more like a preparation for a tournament in which every man was required to be clad in deer-hides.

At the first meeting of citizen soldiers in camp, the reader must not expect to find that things are done as in a regular army. In a regular army, drilled per book, there is a mathematical monotony in all that you see, hear, or do. There the "morning reveillé" rouses you from your slumbers with that "same old beat," and there the orderly sergeants call the rolls with the "same old call." Not so in the commencement of a Texas campaign. Here the orderly sergeants are no small characters; and, at the same time that they make their men do their duty, they are ready to fight for their respective companies, will always squabble for good rations, and will see that their particular companies do no more than their due proportion of general camp-duty. Here the "crack of day" is the signal for true genius. Here the orderly sergeants are all equally busy as those in a regular army, and arrive at the same end, if not in such quick time, yet in good time. Here we have been greatly interested in the "roll-calls." Here we have seen a good-tempered farmer, in the first exercise of this important office, badly puzzled at the tardiness of his men. In his first administration, we have heard him, in his slow, easy, good-natured tone, saying, "Do, men, for God's sake, turn out here! What, in the name of Charity, is the matter with you all?" when he was promptly answered in the same long tone by some young saucebox, "Why, Uncle Bill, what makes you in such a hurry this morning?" Then one of Uncle Bill's neighbours, who at home was in the habit, thus early in the morning, of feeding his stock, and who now is as punctual in his duty to his country, took sides with Uncle Bill, and bestirred himself among his sleeping neighbours, gently shaking each by the shoulder, and saying, in the kindest manner, " Come, come, men, do get up ! don't you hear Uncle Bill ?" Now a young chap, who perhaps had not been in more than half a dozez campaigns, and who has vastly more of the *amor patriæ* in his soul than beard upon his face, " feels his keeping," shook off his blanket, flapped his wings, and crowed. Then a dozen others gobbled like turkey-cocks in an April morning, while at the same time some patriarchal owl, the head of the neighbouring generations, waked up the surrounding hills with a stirring whoop, when he was answered by his whole family of big-eyes in a language more distinct, and to us far more intelligible, than many Indian tribes we have known.

The roll-call continues. In the distance we heard "Old Kentuck," in his thundering bass, lumbering over his roll as if he was making a stump speech upon Salt River to all the political bipeds and quadrupeds in those parts. A little to one side of him was Jack Johnson. Jack is an old soldier—served his seven years in the United States army. Here is mathematics, and here is a cross to your name unless you answer the " first pop." Nearer still to us was the prince of orderlies : he would spring from his lair like a surprised deer, with a shrill, clear snort, which would penetrate to the inmost recess of the soundest sleeper, and then commence like a ready orator, " Tumble out here, boys, immediately, if not sooner,"

G

and go through his roll with as many variations of wit and humour as he had calls. This was Bob Waters, of the Fort Bend company. Bob is a small, active, quick spoken, and quick moving man, and wore a cap made by himself out of a skin which he took from a leopard-cat in a Brasos canebrake; and after a peregrination of two years in Mexico under the aforesaid cap, and performing in every calaboose from the Rio Bravo to the Castle of Perote, is again making cotton bales upon Oyster Creek.

These are the Texas substitutes for the regular army reveillé, which makes all wide awake, and which, unlike that reveillé, puts all in good humour. Good humour and emulation, in equal portions, with a few grains of ambition, go far to make both men and women do their duty.

Here is the commencement of a Texas campaign by citizen soldiers when not in the vicinity of an enemy. It is worthy of remark, however, that as the necessity of vigilance and discipline increases, no men ever conform more readily to that necessity; and, as evidence of which, the whole Texas Revolution does not furnish the first instance of Texians being surprised.

One thing we will here premise, and beg the reader to bear it in mind, that we do not hold it as indispensable to an efficient soldier in *American* warfare that he must be educated, and conform to the strictest rules of the scientific schools. The history of the campaigns we are about to record, as well as the whole Texas Revolution, furnish abundant proof that, as an aggregate, more efficient soldiers were never in uniform. European and American warfare—warfare in an open country with walled towns, and in American forests and swamps—should be as essentially different as if they were distinct trades. The Texas people are perfect in the latter, while they would be eminently efficient in the former, because they are the best marksmen in the world, and it is a cardinal point with them never to fire without covering the object fired at. The books teach us the different modes of carrying a fortification; here *tactics* is most needed, while in *American* warfare circumstances so often occur which no book-rule can cover. The draught, then, is upon the intellect, and he who can draw most heavily upon this source is most efficient. It is alone the natural intellect which teaches *strategy*, if we may be allowed the word. In Europe war should be the *science of tactics*, while in America, in contradistinction, it should be the *art of strategy*. Let us return to the Medina camp.

Thus, towards the close of this week of breeches-making and plenty, both the general and the artillery arrived, and orders were issued for immediate march.

CHAPTER VI.

General Somerville marches upon Laredo.—Gets into a Bog.—Taking of Lovedo.—Neglect to Ration the Troops.—Camp moved in the Direction towards Home.—Council of War.—First Texian Flag planted west of the Rio Grande.—General Somerville starts Home.—Camp without Water.—Much Discontent.—Another War Council.—Speech from the General.—200 Troops return Home, and the General marches with those remaining against the Enemy.—Cross the Rio Grande near Guerrero.—Get Sight of the Enemy.—Recross the Rio Grande for Home, and separate from the Main Body.

General Somerville, however, was too skilled in the art of strategy to let such a favourable opportunity escape him of surprising Laredo. So, after sending back the artillery which he had taken some two weeks to bring up, he suddenly makes a "left oblique" for the Laredo road, with an intention of surprising that defenceless town in six or seven days. The third and fourth days of this surprising march found the general in a most surprising post-oak bog about thirty miles distant. All persons who have once been in a post-oak region after a heavy rain, would again avoid so doing as a pestilence. This kind of land, with much appearance of firmness to the eye, and sufficiently firm to bear a man's weight, will let horses' feet through; and, after once through the grass sod, the soft quicksand beneath will soon worry the animal down. However, the glory of surprising Laredo put the army in this bog instead of carrying it a few miles around. Two days were employed in five miles of this kind of land, and during the whole time a scene was enacted ludicrous beyond all power of description. The whole seven hundred and sixty men, horses, and packs were scattered over the prairie as far as the eye could reach, some floundering and plunging forth; some with their bodies down upon the grass, their legs entirely out of sight, and their noses upon the ground in perfect quietude, as well as to say to their owners, "You put me in here, now get me out," while the owner would be standing by, giving utterance to all manner of curious oaths; some would be lying upon their sides, afraid to trust their legs under them; while the poor pack-mules, with their little feet, stood the worst kind of chance. The coffee-pots and frying-pans would go one way, and the *aparajos* and other camp appurtenances another. One horse, stronger or more used to getting through a bog than another, would call forth from his comparatively happy owner jests upon a more unfortunate comrade, which would be returned in curses upon their general. whom they dubbed all manner of funny names. Here one would strike a fire and go to cooking, as he would say, "while his animal could blow," while there a squad would be discussing the smartness of their general; some would conclude "they had seen enough," while others would say that "they had seen the elephant," and some, "if ever they got out of that place they would go home." When they got through about twenty did go home.

To a people less patriotic and less anxious to serve their country, this would have driven the whole of them home. They were determined, however, to let nothing dishearten them. Though they had the smallest confidence in General Somerville's ability as a leader, yet they ardently desired to be led against the enemy, believing that sufficient intelligence existed in the army to conduct it to a certain victory; and under this noble impulse they would have followed a crooked stick carried before the army as their general.

This "surprise" march against Laredo, instead of seven days, lasted seventeen. On the night of the 7th of December the Texian forces approached the town, and a most formidable preparation was made for attack. Had this peaceable and defenceless place contained the whole of General Woll's division, greater preparations could not have been made. After travelling all day, the men were kept mounted all night; the mysterious whisperings and grave concealments which the general frequently held, led the men to believe that they would have a fight at daylight, the appointed time. All were ordered to keep dead silence, and all was dead silence. Men never acted better, and a more perfect obedience to orders never existed in any camp. The writer was with the two advance companies of Captains Hays and Bogart, who were ordered to pass up the river bank and prevent any retreat in that direction, while the main force was to approach the town in the rear. At daylight we entered the city, where, instead of meeting an enemy worthy our steel, all our belligerent feelings were turned into shame for ourselves; for we met some women, children, and old men, who seemed as glad to see us as if we had been their near relations. All felt they were badly humbugged; and thus ended what the men, in ridicule, called "the siege of Laredo."

The authorities then conducted the army to a camping-place about one mile above the town, and promised to supply provisions. About noon, eight or ten beeves were driven to camp and butchered, which was bare rations for one day. They, having been promised supplies of bread-stuff and other necessaries, waited patiently that day for them, and when none, or but a very small and insufficient quantity was furnished, they naturally expressed dissatisfaction. In the evening of that day, the 8th, the general ordered the army down below the town about three miles, in the direction of the San Antonio road. The main road down the Rio Grande was on the west side, and the crossing at Laredo. "Why did the general not cross the river at that point, and take the main road?" was the inquiry in every one's mouth. No satisfactory answer was given, and I suspected, what the next day proved, that he was wending his way home! Feeling as others felt, that, if he did so, it would be a lasting disgrace upon our country and ourselves to return without crossing into Mexico, I took five men with me, crossed the river to the small town of Galveston, planted the Texian banner in the name of our country, demanded of the alcalde five good mules, which the boys took, and recrossed the river to camp. This place was the military station of Colonel Bravo, who was then secreted in Laredo, while his troops were still at that place. Upon my return to camp, I informed the officers that I had been among Bravo's troops, expecting, of course, General Somerville would send and capture them; but his mind was in other ways intent.

The next day, the 9th, still little or no provisions had been furnished, and the dissatisfaction among our men grew loud and determined. In this state of feeling, the men said that if the general was too great a friend of the Mexicans to feed them, they would feed themselves, and about three hundred marched into the town and took what they pleased. Much has been said by the partisans of General Somerville about the plunder of Laredo, giving that as evidence of insubordination in the army, and thereby wishing to excuse his hasty flight home. Though the writer would neither have advised or countenanced it, yet he cannot be blind to good reasons which the troops had for so doing. Most of these men had already been from their homes three months; they had been promised, time after time, to be led against the enemy; they had been promised that when they reached the Rio Grande they should have all necessary supplies. Had these promises been fulfilled in any particular? Was it right that the Texians should demand less of these people than the Mexican army invariably do? And was it not absolutely just and proper that General Somerville should have carried out his reasonable promises to them? The men saw plainly that their three months toil was to be swallowed up in the glory of getting a view of the Rio Grande, and then a hasty and disgraceful flight home, and without provisions to take them there. Under this state of things, a portion of them entered the town, and took, among absolute necessaries, many articles of a useless character. Though the unquestioned laws of war and of nature gave these men a perfect right to take all necessaries for their subsistence, did their general instruct them in what they consisted? No! when his own improvidence left the men to feed themselves, without such instruction, it was reasonable to expect they would also take useless and unnecessary articles. Had the general said to the men, "I have furnished you these ten beeves and these few sacks of flour; I can do no more, now look out for yourselves; here is a list of articles which you have a right by the usages of war to take, and, as Texians, it is expected you will take nothing else." Who believes that his instructions would have been violated? No one who knows anything of the Texian character. To lay aside all these good reasons, did

H

not the Texians have a clear right, by the *lex talionis* of war, not only to do so, but to lay every Mexican town upon the frontier in ashes? Did not the burning of our towns in 1836, and their subsequent plunder of Refugio and San Antonio give them this right? It clearly did! But a false magnaminity, which shielded Santa Anna at San Jacinto, seemed to possess General Somerville, as it doubtless did his *Mexican* advisers; and a greater interest was manifested by them for the "*poor Mexicans*," which was sung morning, noon, and night throughout the camp, than for our own men.

And to show with what willingness Texians will yield to council and authority, no sooner had they returned with these articles to camp, than they were told that in a council of officers thirteen out of fourteen captains had voted for crossing the Rio Grande, and that it was requested they should give up the articles taken from Laredo, to be sent back by the alcalde. They almost to a man did so. These articles were carried to the general's quarters, and he sent for the alcalde and delivered them to him, to be returned to their respective owners. Did this show more the love of plunder or the obedience of orders? The general, and those who were willing to follow him home, were deprived by this ready acquiescence on the part of the men of all plea of insubordination. Did he then follow the advice which had been so unanimously voted in the council of war—to cross the river, and proceed down it by the main road? No! but that evening started in a direction down the river on the east side, and proceeded several miles on this course, all believing, except his confidential *home* advisers, that he still intended to cross the river below, when suddenly the head of the line was turned to the left, into a dense and most difficult chaparral. For several hours the men were wound about through the prickly-pears and thorn-bushes, turning more and more in the direction of the San Antonio road, when, about 10 o'clock at night, from exhaustion, sore shins, and disgust, all hands came to a halt, without water and without supper. " What was the meaning of following so long in the direction of the north star, when our direction lay south?" was in every mouth; and it was not until some time after stopping for the night that it was known the army was on the march to San Antonio. This was so contrary, not only to the will of the men, but to the reiterated threats on the part of the general to punish the enemy in his own country, and in open violation also of the almost unanimous war-council of that day, that the indignation of the men burst forth in the loudest abuse upon their commander. General Somerville's eyes were then open for the first time to the dilemma in which he was placed, of crossing into Mexico and fighting the enemy, or of going home under a popular odium, which would, in all probability, overwhelm him. In every direction of the camp he heard himself ridiculed and abused the whole night. The next morning he remarked to an officer with whom he lay, that he did not sleep a wink that night. In such a quandary, what was to be done? He had in his confidence some who urged him forward to redeem the honour of his country, while the *Mexican* portion of his advisers persuaded him to retreat home. The former prevailed, and next morning the troops were informed that they would be conducted to water, and after getting something to eat, that another war council would be held. Accordingly, in about one mile water was found, and after getting breakfast, the officers were called together in council. Out of fourteen captains present, still eleven were for pursuing the enemy into Mexico, and giving him battle. The council adjourned, and the troops were accordingly again paraded. The general made a speech, in which he desired that all who were in favour of crossing to the Rio Grande would step to the right, and those in favour of returning home would go to the left; that if it was still their desire to pursue the enemy, he would lead them, but if not, his commission was in their hands, and he would cheerfully serve among the foremost in the ranks. Throughout his remarks were patriotic and cheering, and by acclamation he was elected, without one dissenting voice, their " volunteer leader." By the laws of Texas, the army had a perfect right to elect their commander, but heretofore they had not claimed this privilege, for fear it might create division, and furnish a pretext, as it had the spring previous, for thwarting the expedition. When, therefore, the proposition came from General Somerville to elect their commander, it was unanimously met by the men, in as magnanimous a spirit, by electing him. Of the 740 men present, about 200 voted to return; they were placed under the command of Colonel Bennett, of Montgomery, and did return, while the balance insisted upon being led against the enemy in the most enthusiastic terms.

Notwithstanding all the dissatisfaction which had been expressed previously as to the general's course, such was the patriotic enthusiasm of the men at the renewed prospect of service for their country, that all was hushed, and a more obedient and willing citizen soldiery never were assembled. The march commenced in a southern direction, so as to strike the river opposite Guerrero, at which place the men were informed they would be supplied with every necessary. From Laredo to Guerrero, by the main road, on the west side of the river, was two short days' march, while winding about in the chaparral on the east side occupied the army until the 14th, when they reached the river six miles from the city, and opposite an Indian village at the mouth of the Rio Salado. This tardy and zigzag march of General Somerville completely bewildered the enemy, and they took for a cunning military manœuvre what the tattered pantaloons and sore shins of our men too plainly told them was an unpardonable piece of stupidity and a cruel waste of time. Had General Somerville promptly crossed the river at Laredo on the 8th, and swept down it by the main road with a celerity befitting the occasion, he would by this time have taken every town down to Rhinosa, and created such a universal panic in that country as to have caused the enemy to evacuate Matamoras and fall back upon Tampico, leaving the former city entirely exposed.

Upon reaching the river, a portion of the Careese tribe of Indians, which occupied the village upon the opposite side, appeared greatly alarmed, and some started off to the city at full speed. It was perfectly clear, that if the enemy were in the city, one or two hours would bring them to the defence of the crossing, which even a small force might successfully do against two or three small boats, and hence the necessity of a rapid movement to occupy the west bank; but no orders to this effect were given, and after waiting several minutes in such expectation, the writer and Captain Charles K. Reese, of the Brazoria company, jumped into a canoe and went across, hoisted the Texian banner, procured a large boat, and returned with the two, when the troops commenced crossing their baggage and swimming their horses. After the two advanced companies of Captains Hays and Bogart had crossed, Captain Bogart and the writer mounted their horses to reconnoitre the road in the direction of the city. About two miles distant we met the

A "RUSE." 63

advance of Colonel Canales's "Defensors," numbering about three hundred mounted men, who gave us chase to within half a mile of the landing. The writer, being upon the slowest of the two horses, was left in the rear, and must have been captured had he not bethought himself of the *ruse* of unfurling the blood-red silk flag which he had in his hat. Being fully occupied in guiding his horse over a rough road, and carrying his rifle in his hand, he took the corner of it in his teeth, and no sooner did the enemy see it than they ceased the pursuit, doubtless supposing it was an intimation to an ambuscade. The enemy then flanked off upon each side of the road, and waited several hours, within a mile, for the Texians to attack them. Permission was refused so to do, and after dark they withdrew. Why was this permission refused? We had ample force already across the river to have beaten them. After several hours' delay, the general came across, but the writer has never heard any satisfactory reason why this insolent banter of the enemy was not met.

Early next morning the rear-guard of the army crossed, and a good portion of the day was employed by the general in guarding a fat hog, which, he said, belonged to "these good friends," and which hog our men cast wistful glances at. He, however, was not successful in his kind protection; for his eyes had hardly turned a minute before the animal was killed, quartered, and divided between several messes.

Colonel M'Cullough had been sent to the city to demand of the alcalde rations and other necessaries for the army. The alcalde returned a cheerful answer that everything should be forthcoming by the time the army arrived in town, where good quarters were prepared. That evening the army was marched in the direction of the town, encamping one mile from it, in an exposed situation, it being one of the most inclement nights ever witnessed. To this exposed situation the alcalde sent a few old hats and filthy blankets, some few beeves, and less than one quart of corn for each horse. The old hats and blankets should have been an insult to the general, as they were to the men, and the very insufficient quantity of rations more calculated to make men mad than to allay their hunger. Why did the general not go into the quarters provided in the city instead of exposing his men to such a cold rain? was asked throughout the camp, and no answer given. The next morning, when all were cold, wet, and hungry—having had no supper the night before—and expected to be marched into comfortable quarters in the town, the head of the line was again turned towards home, and the army marched rapidly back to the former crossing, to facilitate which the general made a detail, and carried down six large flat-bottomed boats, each capable of carrying one hundred men. A portion of the army recrossed that evening, and the remainder next morning.

MORE DISCONTENT. 65

Here the army found themselves again upon the Texas side of the river, and their faces fairly turned towards home, after getting in sight of the enemy and not fighting him. With a large majority of the men, strong discontent was manifested by this last attempt to run them home against their will and the interest and honour of the country. Something more was necessary to be done to appease this discontent and satisfy the men in following him home, and Captain Hays was then despatched with his company into the city with this order, " to demand of the alcalde five thousand dollars, or that he, the general, would sack the town." This order was delivered to the alcalde, when he returned to the camp with Captain Hays, bringing with him three hundred and eighty dollars, saying he had no more. Did General S. thus carry out his word, which, however proper or improper it was for him to have made it, as a Texian general he was bound to execute? No! and his reply to the alcalde was so ridiculous we forbear to name it. It was urged upon those in his confidence that still a brilliant opportunity was left him of doing a signal service; that his force was sufficient to occupy the river with the boats, while another portion could go down the river by land, and by thus acting in concert, occupying either or both sides at pleasure, the whole valley must necessarily submit; and with such choice of positions, his force would be more than equal to any enemy on the river. But no; home was the

I

word! and after giving *his* personal friends items of his intention, thereby allowing them opportunity of collecting mules, horses, mares, and colts, which they profited by, "*home! march!*" was the order. To secure a ready acquiescence on the part of the men to this order, General Somerville had, the night previous, ordered the fleet of boats to be sunk; but others, to whom the order had been given, knowing that his object was to destroy all means of operating against the enemy, and thereby force a compliance to his "home orders," moved the boats some miles below, and the general absolutely believed that the boats had been sunk until just before he started, when he was told that not one half of the men would follow him any longer; that he, and all who chose so to do, might go home, while the remainder would stay and fight the enemy. The general started home with two hundred and odd men, including his extensive staff, numerous enough for a field-marshal of France, while he left behind him three hundred and four men to do the fighting.

The march he had now to accomplish to Bexar was far more difficult than the one which had occupied him seventeen days to Laredo, in which he had used more than three hundred beeves; and though there were an immense number of beeves, sheep, and goats in the immediate neighbourhood of the camp, yet this difficult march was undertaken, as I have been informed, without his collecting any, trusting to the precarious chances of kill-

NEW TACTICS.   67

ing a wild cow or such game as good fortune might throw in his way. The consequence was, his whole command came near starving, many reaching home on foot, having to leave their horses broken down and bogged, the general's among the rest.

Upon General Somerville's arrival at home, he made an official communication to the war department of his doings upon the Rio Grande, which he closed by saying that, " having been eleven days upon the Rio Grande, he thought it imprudent to remain longer, as the enemy might concentrate." All the circumstances of this disgraceful flight home, and without rations, proved that in this declaration he was sincere.

We have many instances in the history of war of generals flying from their men during the rage of battle, when blood and death is calculated to terrify and unnerve; and we have instances of men running off and leaving their generals in the field; but this is the first instance of which we have any recollection of a general going home when in the immediate neighbourhood of the enemy, and leaving his men behind to fight. Some of General Somerville's friends have justified his so doing by saying that he acted under orders. If it be true that such were his orders, it is most certain that those orders were kept secret from the army, and he thereby permitted himself to be made a tool of by the President, to deceive that army and the country. If it be true that he received such orders from the President as to break up the campaign without fighting the enemy, why did his adjutant-general, Chief-justice Hemphill, read to the army, day after day, volumes of patriotic orders of his "glory, honour, and liberty?" If, on the other hand, he received no such secret orders, then he is chargeable with the grossest disobedience of public orders, and the nation have a right to be redressed therefor. The late election for major-general shows that the nation has stamped it with their most decided disapprobation; for out of some fifteen thousand votes, though General Somerville was brigadier of the first brigade, and a candidate, he received some hundred.

It is again said by some who returned home with General Somerville, and who wish to excuse that return, that the army was disobedient and unorganized. Justice to the whole army, and especially the gallant men of Mier, require that we should notice particularly these charges. The former one we have already shown how groundless; and we again repeat, that there never was a more obedient citizen soldiery assembled, in all things save in the one of running home without fighting the enemy. That they should have been disobedient in this, redounds to their own and their country's honour. If the charge of being unorganized was founded in justice, whose fault was it? Where was General Somerville, and what was he doing from the entry of General Woll into Bexar, on the 11th of Septem-

GEN. SOMERVILLE'S NEGLECT. 69

ber, up to the middle of December, when he left these men upon the Rio Grande? Was it not *his* duty to organize and discipline the troops, and did *he* make any attempt to do so? It is a well-known fact that he never, on the first occasion, drilled them, though he remained in Bexar weeks, and the men had nothing else to do. However, in our warfare, it is a popular mistake that our citizen soldiery should understand all the minutiæ of the regular army drill. It is important that they should understand how to keep in "*close order,*" and to "*wheel by column,*" and a few other important manœuvres, which may be taught in a very few days. The most important of all manœuvres we understand better than any other nation on the face of the earth, and that is, to "*look through the double sights with a steady arm.*"

It is painful to be under the necessity to make reflections either against General Somerville or any other gentleman, but duty to the army, to the service, and to the country requires us to say all, and perhaps more than we have said; and we surely do so without personal unkindness to any, and especially General Somerville, whose general kindness of disposition and social habits would disarm any one of such feelings.

CHAPTER VII.

Colonel Fisher elected Commander.—The Writer appointed Commander of the Flotilla.—Descent of the Rio Grande.—Capture of Carancawa Indians with a British Flag.—Occupation of Mier.—Requisition for Provision.—Arrest of the Alcalde.—Enemy's Appearance.—Council of War.—Order of Battle.

THE twelve hundred men who had been at Bexar one month previously, ready and anxious to pursue and engage the enemy, were now reduced down to three hundred and four.* After consultation with the officers and most influential men, it was agreed that Colonel William S. Fisher should be elected commander, he having been in the Federal War with Canales some two years before, and knew the country upon the Rio Grande better than any other officer present; and that the army had the *perfect right* to elect their commander, is evident from the law of January, 1840. The author was appointed to take command of the flotilla of boats, then numbering six large barges, each capable of transporting 125 men, and several smaller ones, used as tenders, and to proceed down the river *pari passu* with the land forces, the land and river forces usually meeting at night. The lamented George W. Bonnell and Dr. Richard F. Brennem, both of whom had survived the perils of the Santa Fé Expedition, who possessed the most exalted pa-

* See Muster Roll, No. I., in Appendix.

MIER EXPEDITION DESCENDING THE RIO GRANDE.

triotism, and who longed for an opportunity of retaliating their injuries upon the enemy, were appointed, the former first lieutenant of the Navy, as our flotilla was familiarly called, and the latter surgeon. Texas has met a heavy loss in the untimely end of these true patriots—they, in the prime of life, were brave to a fault, talented and patriotic upon principle—for the love of country and the love of liberty. We shall have occasion hereafter to speak more particularly of the manner in which they met their end, but on no occasion could their names be mentioned by us without an humble testimonial of respect for their worth. In the "Navy" other appointments were made, to wit, commandants to each boat, and Samuel C. Lyon sailing-master of the flag-boat, which was known by the *red* flag at the mast-head, the same which we had hoisted in Mexico opposite Laredo and Guerrero. Two of the large boats, with several of smaller size, were burned for want of men to occupy them, and the expedition proceeded down the splendid and heretofore imperfectly-known river Bravo.

In Texas, a popular opinion has prevailed that the Rio Grande was a rapid stream, full of shoals and rocks, subject to go almost dry in the fall, and fordable at any point. So far from this being true, we descended it at a low stage of water—on few occasions does it get lower—and never found any place at which it could be forded below Laredo, and it is, indeed, barely fordable there. It is a beautiful river, averaging four hundred yards in width, with high bluffs generally on one side or the other, and the opposite side always a fertile bottom. This river resembles more the Ohio, when in boatable order, than any we recollect to have seen, and is far superior for steamboat navigation to any other upon the Gulf of Mexico west of the Mississippi. The alluvion upon this river is almost exclusively upon the west bank, and is capable of the highest state of cultivation; while the eastern bank bluffs down nearly to the water's edge with high and precipitous hills. These hills are covered with a dense growth of trees and shrubbery, all bearing thorns in some shape or other, and forms what is called, in the Mexican language, the *Chaparral.* The immense number of stock which has fed upon these hills for many years having kept down the grass, has caused deep washes, with such precipitous sides that it is frequently with great difficulty that cavalry can proceed, and therefore makes this the most defensible country for Texian warfare, and especially the rifle. Both cavalry and artillery would be next to useless in these hills, and we hazard nothing in saying that, with the advantage of the water, stock, and contiguity to the towns and settlements upon the western bank, one thousand Texians could occupy it in perfect security against ten times their number. This river and the adjacent country were viewed, as well by the author as others in the expedition, with a military eye, in expectation of future campaigns; and we may congratulate our country that she is now in possession of information which, in such an event, will make her strength five times as available.

The flotilla proceeded down the river, capturing and burning between forty and fifty boats, and stopping at different settlements for provision sufficient for the troops; and we assert, from positive knowledge, that no unnecessary waste was either allowed or perpetrated by the destruction of any stock more than was necessary or barely sufficient as rations. The only waste which could not be prevented was by our horses when turned into the cornfields. The corn had been cut and stacked, and during the night the horses may have pulled down more than they ate, but this must have been inconsiderable. The first night after our separation from the *home* troops, the boats stopped at a rancho, where we met the tribe of Carancawa Indians, who had just previously to that time committed some depredations upon our coast about Live Oak Point, and fled for fear of punishment. These Indians protested their innocence, pretended great friendship for us, and expressed a desire to return to Texas. It was thought prudent to disarm them to prevent their joining the enemy, and all their implements of war, quivers, bows, arrows, &c., and with them a British flag, which they doubtless pilfered from some English vessel on the coast, were taken and placed in the boats.

K

A company of spies were constantly kept on the western side of the river as a watch upon the enemy, which the facility of crossing furnished by the boats made entirely practicable. As the different boats were governed by signals from the flag-boat, it was easy to direct their movements for this or any other purpose.

On the 21st of December, both the land and river forces encamped together upon the east bank of the river, about seven miles from the city of Mier, when Colonel Benjamin M'Cullough and some choice spies were despatched to reconnoitre the city, and ascertain if any troops were in the neighbourhood, their strength, &c. Colonel M'Cullough went into the city, conferred with the alcalde and some Americans living there, who informed him that Canales had just before evacuated the place, but that more troops were expected hourly. On the morning of the 22d, after a council of war, it was determined to march into the city and make a requisition upon the authorities for *necessaries* for the army, and that in no instance would anything like plunder be countenanced. So, after detailing a sufficient camp-guard, the troops were crossed over about 9 o'clock A.M., and addressed by Colonel Fisher in an appropriate manner. He called upon them to bear in mind "that they were upon an honourable service, and not one of pillage, and that their country would look to them for a soldier-like discharge of that service;" "that they had before them the recent plunder of Laredo, and the ill effects of that plunder; a plunder calculated to unfit a soldier in his duty, and to create anxious desires to go home." It is a singular fact in our physical constitution, that if we become loaded with gains either justly or unjustly, whether these gains be in the way of a caballada or *baby-clothes*, it increases a home desire to such an extent that none can resist it. In the fresh example of Laredo and Guerrero, it was manifest that in the few who indulged this way, their *amor patriæ* was lost sight of in their multiplied excuses to go home, for it is certain that they did go home. The troops responded to these sentiments as men and patriots who had a more exalted object in view, and they were marched into the public square and kept under arms without even attempting to violate orders in a single particular. The alcalde and principal men of the town invited Colonel Fisher and the author to the city hall, where they were informed that we wished a requisition of necessaries to be furnished to the army; that so soon as this was done the troops would withdraw, and then the citizens had nothing to fear from them. The alcalde expressed his willingness to comply in furnishing all necessaries for the army, and remarked that " he had it to do for the Mexican army, and could not expect to do less for us." Colonel Fisher requested me to make out the requisition, which I did. The following is a copy of the same:

" The alcalde of Mier will forthwith furnish and

deliver at headquarters upon the Rio Grande the following requisition for the use of the army, to wit: All the government stores of every kind, including cannon, small fire-arms, powder, lead, munitions of war of every kind, tobacco, &c.; also, 5 days' rations for 1200 men, to wit: 40 sacks of flour of 6 arrobas each, 1200 lbs. sugar, 600 lbs. coffee, 200 pairs of strong coarse shoes, 100 pair of do. pantaloons, and 100 blankets.

" By order of the general commanding," &c.

As is customary in cases of this kind, when a requisition is made upon the alcalde of a Mexican town, he apportions it among the different citizens in proportion to their ability to furnish, and they had nearly complied with the whole requisition, when the difficulty of transporting it to camp that evening presented itself, owing to there being no teams in readiness. Night was drawing near, and to return to camp without the requisition, and without any guarantee of its forthcoming, would have been placing undue confidence in a Mexican's word. Under this state of things, Colonel Fisher ordered the writer to take the alcalde to camp as a hostage to its fulfilment, which he promised should meet us the next day lower down the river, and opposite the town. Accordingly, the march was recommenced in perfect order, the alcalde being mounted and under a special guard. Here was a town, the largest and richest upon the river save Matamoras, in our possession all day without the least possible depredation being committed; and we think it a sufficient answer, as well as to President Houston's charge of robbery against the Mier men, as to those who returned home with General Somerville. At any rate, we will not dignify this malicious falsehood by any farther refutation.

The advance reached the river about dusk, when a melancholy incident occurred by the accidental discharge of a gun, and the killing one of the smallest boys in the army. This youth, by the name of Yocum, aged fourteen years, was one of the very few troops we had from the county of Liberty, was in a high degree manly for his age, and deserved a better fate.

The army recrossed the river to their camp, which was upon the second bottom above the landing. The alcalde was exceedingly anxious to go up and see the commanding general, and arrange with him, for he yet believed that the troops which entered Mier were but the advance guard of the army, and that the remaining portion of the twelve hundred were in camp. The writer informed him that he was under his special charge, that he had his orders what to do, and that he must be content until the requisition was complied with. He said that "the requisition would doubtless be down by the morrow, as such were his orders." After eating a piece of mutton, which we insisted he should join us in, we gave him part of our blanket, and, as the most respectful mode of guarding his honour, for he was a far more decent man than the majority of Mexican officials, we gently placed one of his legs between ours, and though there was no community of language between us, yet we seemed to understand each other's motions, for when one turned over the other turned, we always maintaining his leg in the same affectionate position. The night blew a heartless norther, which swept down the river with a most cutting effect, and the morning opened upon the most haggard countenance of Don Juan, for no less a personage was the alcalde.

On the morning of the 23d the camp was moved several miles below, to where the alcalde informed us the provision would be brought. That day passed without his promise being fulfilled, and he grew exceedingly restless. On the night of the 23d the norther continued to blow, and we again had the mutual honour of sleeping with each other in the same affectionate manner—we with Don Juan, and Don Juan with (as he called us) Commodore Verde, which means, in their language, *green*. Don Juan, not knowing what the non-compliance of his order as to the provisions would bring about, grew still more restiff. His dreams were anything but pleasant, if we were to judge from his nervous excitability, and sleeping exclamations of halters and bullets. His restlessness, together with the cold weather and the want of more blankets, failed to inspire us "with visions of an apple and a bee," which his wayward namesake brought to the downy pillow of the fair

Dudu, and I arose in the morning much worried by my courtly protection of his honour Don Juan the younger. Captain Baker and his spy company had been kept upon the west side of the river during this time, and on the morning of the 25th captured a Mexican and sent him into camp, who, upon being examined, informed our commander, that after the requisition had been started down in compliance with the alcalde's order, the troops of General Ampudia and Canales had arrived and stopped them; that they numbered about seven hundred men, with two field-pieces, and had taken a position upon the west bank of the river two miles below, to prevent our farther progress down. Upon the receipt of this information a council of war was held, when it was *unanimously* agreed to cross the river and fight them. Our troops commenced crossing about 2 o'clock P.M., Captain Baker and his spies in advance. At 4 o'clock all was crossed over and ready to march, when a brisk fire was heard in the direction of the enemy's position. In a few minutes a courier arrived from Captain Baker, stating that two of his most efficient spies had been captured, Samuel H. Walker, of Galveston, and Patrick Lusk, of Washington, and that he was in a position which he would endeavour to maintain until he could be succoured. Upon the receipt of this information a forced march was ordered to his relief, and upon our arrival in sight of the enemy they retreated rapidly in the direction of the city. Walker had proved himself a daring and efficient spy when General Woll occupied Bexar. After he was brought a prisoner into Mier, he was examined by General Ampudia as to our *numbers, intentions,* &c., and told in advance by the general "that if he told him a falsehood his life should pay the forfeit of it." Walker replied "that his life was in the general's hands, but that it was neither our *habit* or *nationality* to lie." After Walker's telling him that our effective remaining force was about 300 men, General A. says, "They surely have not the audacity to pursue and attack me in town." "Yes, general," says Walker, "you need not have any doubts upon that point; they will pursue and attack you in ——."

After the council of war had determined upon crossing and fighting the enemy, the writer returned to the boats to prepare for their embarcation. Here he found the alcalde asleep, and the most of the boats' hands cooking their beef and mutton. The surplus small boats were fired, and most of the troops crossed over before the alcalde awoke. He arose in the greatest possible alarm, asking what all this meant. He was told that General Ampudia and Canales had stopped our rations, and we were going to see by what authority they did so. He protested that, inasmuch as he had complied all in his power, they ought not to carry him into battle; that he had a dear wife and children at home. We told him that during the battle he could stand behind us, and that there was not so much danger there. This provoked a laugh at the expense of the poor alcalde, but did not make his countenance less dolorous. The writer, with a portion of his boat-hands, occupied the extreme right, among whom the alcalde was marched in file. Upon the retreat of the enemy to the city there was but one general impulse throughout the line, and that was to pursue and fight them, they having that day and the day previous taken five of our men who were believed to be in the city. Our march was pursued in the direction of the city, and about one mile therefrom we were hailed by a picket-guard, which fired into us and fled. This fire was answered by all the other sentinels in the neighbourhood, giving us a good opportunity to ascertain their position. Seven o'clock found us in midnight darkness upon a high hill on the east side of the Rio Alcantra, which separated us from the city, and *here* commenced the battle of Mier.

L

CHAPTER VIII.

BATTLE OF MIER.

THE Rio Alcantra is a small but rapid stream, about sixty yards in width, which forms a semicircle upon the east side of Mier, the city being built in the curve. The position which our troops occupied was upon a high hill, difficult of descent, and between the upper and lower crossings of the river. Here it was necessary to feel our way with great caution and profound silence. The night being dark and drizzling with rain, the troops were ordered to sit and protect their arms from the damp until more could be learned of the position of the enemy. While in this position, Captain Charles K. Reese, of the Brazoria company, with private Joseph Berry, was despatched from the left wing to fire into a picket-guard some two hundred yards to their left, for the purpose of extracting their fire and exposing the situation of their different pickets, while the author felt his way down the bluff in the direction of the lower ford. Here was stationed a strong force of their cavalry to defend this crossing, which he ascertained by the rattling of the cavalry gear when the horses would shake themselves. He returned to the position of our army upon the hill, and obtained permission of Colonel Fisher to take Captain Baker's spy company and some of the boatmen, among whom was the lamented Dr. Brennem, and thus open a scattering fire upon the cavalry below, while he could hunt out a crossing into the city between the two fords. Selecting a position for these men, protected by an embankment about three feet high, immediately opposite the cavalry, with the river only between them, the signal to commence the action was to be nine shots from his repeating rifle. The writer stepped to the water's edge and fired the nine shots in rapid succession into the enemy, which created some confusion in their lines, but was promptly returned, none of their's taking effect. The spy company and boatmen kept up the fire, which completely deluded the enemy, for they thought it was our main body which intended to force that passage. The opposite plan of Mier and its vicinity, the Texian camp, and their entrance into the city, will give the reader a more correct knowledge of the battle.

While this fire was kept up with galling effect upon the enemy, I passed up the river to hunt out an intermediate crossing. Feeling my way along the almost perpendicular bluff of the river, I found a place which could be descended with difficulty. Here I hung up a pocket-handkerchief upon a bush to designate the spot, while I returned and led the army down. In returning to the line, some delay was occasioned by the following unfortunate circumstance: Captains Reese and Berry, after firing into the picket upon our left, in attempting to make their retreat, the latter fell down a precipice about thirty feet and broke his thigh. Dr. Sinnickson and a guard of seven men were detailed for his assistance, who had to let down ropes, which he fastened around his body, by which means they drew him out and placed him in a house near by, where his wound could be attended to. We shall have occasion to speak of this small guard in detailing one of the most desperate and bloody conflicts which they had the next day with the enemy, and which the history of war can hardly parallel.

After this detail was made, the army followed me, in the most profound silence, to where the handkerchief was left, and then, in single file, slided down the bluff about forty feet to the water's edge, it being too perpendicular to walk down. We then passed up the river some hundred yards; the alcalde, being near the head of the line, was several times asked whether the river could be here forded, and his answer was "*Poco mas arriba*" (a little higher up). The cavalry below, being at this time severely galled by our spies and boatmen, were firing at random, and here we had two men, Allen and Oats, wounded. The anxiety which Don Juan seemed to evince in getting out of the reach of the cavalry shots made us suspect him of falsehood as to the depth of the river. At any rate, I determined to ascertain the practicability of crossing by first trying it in person. The head of the line was halted for this purpose, and, after wading through the rapids,

I was greatly rejoiced to find it not more than waist deep. Returning with this favourable report, Colonel Fisher and myself headed the line and effected the crossing with the same silence which had been previously preserved, and which was greatly favoured by the roaring of the river at this point among the rocks.

I had been appointed to the command of the right wing, and by the time the extreme left was across the river, the right was in immediate contact with a picket of the enemy, about fifteen or twenty strong. The constant fire below, which had been kept up between our spies and their cavalry, had so diverted the attention of this picket, that they did not discover us until we were almost touching, when the whole of them, in the greatest possible alarm, simultaneously hailed us. They received for answer to their "*quien viva?*" "Let them have it, boys!" when about one hundred shots from the right wing were poured into them. They never returned the fire, or ever kicked that we know of, and the only thing now to break the silence, save the firing down the river, was the thundering voice of old Colonel Ramires, some few hundred yards off, commanding the cavalry to charge us; but this order was given in vain. During this incident, which happened in less time than we have been relating it, the alcalde, favoured by the darkness of the night, fled. He had been placed in special charge of one of the boat-hands, the old sailing-master, a braver or better man than whom did not belong to the army; but his English blood had been aroused by the "*quien viva*" of the picket, and he had let them have the full benefit of his double-barrelled "Joe Manton." So soon as the report of our firing ceased, I spoke to the old sailing-master to look to the alcalde, and received for answer, "By my soul, general, he is adrift!"

We were now fairly in the suburbs of the city, and marching in the direction of the Military Square, which we had little doubt was the stronghold of the enemy. About fifty yards from the picket we entered a street at right angles, down which an officer, mounted and in full gallop, was passing. As he passed the head of our line, some dozen shots were fired at him, with what effect we do not know; his horse floundered, and passed out of our immediate path. The head of the line was wheeled to the right, up the street from whence this officer came, and proceeding about one hundred yards farther, it was necessary to reconnoitre the position of the enemy. Here a halt was ordered, when I passed the next corner upon our left, which opened upon a street that led directly into the square, and in which street was placed their artillery, around which a bustling preparation was making. Returning to the line, I informed Colonel Fisher of the exact position of the enemy, and obtained his permission to advance with the head of the right wing until it covered the street in which the artillery was placed, when we fired suddenly into them, passed the corner in quick time to make room for their "grape and canister," and repeated the fire alternately with them. This was done several times with deadly effect upon the enemy, while twice per minute their grape and canister shot would pour down the street, from whence our fire proceeded, with no effect upon us, we after each fire passing the corner to await theirs, and then returning to reoccupy the firing position again. By this manœuvre, while their artillery was playing upon a vacant street, our fire was sure and destructive. While the right wing was thus occupied, the left unfortunately exposed their situation by returning some random shots fired from the house-tops. This brought upon them a well-directed fire, which killed J. E. Jones, a brave and honourable man, an Englishman by birth, who had been one of the Santa Fé sufferers.

The night continued to drizzle rain, which made it more important that our troops should effect a lodgment in some strong stone houses, as well to protect their arms as to refix those already out of order, some of the men having fallen in the water while crossing the river. One of the strongest objections to the rifle is the ease with which it is put out of order, and the difficulty of refixing it; if the powder should get wet, the difficulty of unbreeching is far greater than the drawing of a musket-load.

The right wing was ordered to take possession

of a row of stone houses upon one side of the street, leading in the direction of the artillery, which they did by beating down the corner doors, and then, with the aid of an iron crowbar which they found inside, opened breaches through the dividing walls to within fifty yards of the artillery. A breach was ordered to be made in the upper end of this building, so as to command the artillery; and no sooner was it commenced on the inside than the artillery was directed against that point on the outside. The wall was thick and strong, and the twelve-pound shots driving against it in rapid succession tended greatly to facilitate our work by loosening the stones for us. No sooner was the opening made than it was filled with our rifles, which were unerringly destructive. Upon the left wing was Captain Reese's Brazoria company, and Captain I. G. W. Pearson's Milam company. They had been ordered to occupy a row of stone buildings upon the opposite side of the street, and had just completed their portholes, where the cross-fire from their position was equally destructive. After daylight, three times was the artillery manned and as often silenced, the last time sixteen out of seventeen falling, the commander, Captain Castro, a brave and honourable man, being the only surviver.

Our troops had now effected a strong lodgment nearly in the centre of the city, and beaten all opposition, with only *one* killed and *two* wounded. The same thing could not have been done in daylight against such odds with one hundred times the loss. In less than one hour after daylight opened upon us, their artillery was silenced and deserted, and the enemy had recourse to the house-tops, from whence they ventured to pour down upon the houses we occupied volleys of musketry. In the many thousand cartridges discharged at us an occasional one would take effect, and we had some valuable men killed and several wounded. In this situation, none but our best rifles and surest shots were brought into play, and they not permitted to fire except with dead rest and sure aim.* This explains why a large majority of their killed and wounded were shot in the head and breast, the only part exposed in firing at us. However, to obtain a better position for some of our picked riflemen, holes were made in the roofs of the houses we occupied, through which they ascended, and in that position we soon cleared all the houses within reach. Thus the battle continued until 12 M., and it was perfectly clear, from the manner in which their fire had slackened in every quarter, that they were badly crippled. One movement more on our part was necessary to complete the victory, and that was by commanding the public square, their stronghold. To effect this, a simultaneous movement—from the house occupied by the right wing, upon the alcalde's

* We might name many instances which came under our observation of astonishing marksmanship on the part of our men, by Colonel Wm. F. Wilson and others, but must refrain from so doing for fear of making this report too prolix.

M

office, about fifty yards distant, with a charge of Captains Reese and Pearson's companies upon a corner house just above them—was necessary. We obtained permission of Colonel Fisher to cross over to Reese and Pearson's building and give the order. The house which these companies were to occupy was still in possession of a strong body of the enemy, and it was necessary to make a charge upon it from different directions. One breach had already been made in the wall communicating with the back yard of said house; and Captain Reese and myself ascended a scaffold which still remained against the wall of a new house in our rear, to reconnoitre the enemy and see how that wall could be scaled. Here we were in the double danger of falling from this slender scaffold, fifteen or twenty feet high, as well as the fire of the enemy; and we occupied it but a moment, when we were driven below by a shower of musket-balls, fired by a platoon of the enemy at not more than forty yards' distance, which made the splinters fly thick about us. When I say that neither of us were touched, it will give the reader a fair specimen of Mexican marksmanship. We, however, determined that it would be better to make farther breaches in the wall than to expose the men to the enemy's fire by ascending such an elevation. To make these breaches required time; so we returned to Colonel Fisher with the report, while measures were taken to carry out the order.

Just about this time, private Cody, who has since perished in the mountains, stepped up to me, and said, "Look, general, yonder is the almightiest fight you ever did see." I turned in the direction to where he was pointing, and became an eyewitness of one of the most thrilling conflicts which the imagination can conceive. The guard which had been left with Berry the night previous, upon the east side of the Alcantra, occupied a small *adoby* house about six hundred yards distant, and on the declivity of the hill, which gave us a good view of their position. Here they had been impatient and anxious spectators of our battle for some seventeen hours, when a troop of cavalry, about sixty in number, passed near their house. This was too glorious an opportunity to let pass without their assistance; so their rifles and double-barrelled guns were brought to bear upon them with most deadly effect, killing their commander and eight or ten others, when the survivers fled in every direction. In a very few minutes after, several hundred cavalry and a field-piece were brought up. Berry's guard, well knowing that their adoby house could not withstand the force of the cannon-shot, determined at once to leave it, and charge through the lines of the enemy to our position. They accordingly charged, and broke the enemy's lines with the most dauntless bravery, each one killing his man, and some two, for several of them had double-barrelled guns. It was now three hundred yards to the river, to gain which point they would be safe, for the enemy would not venture closer than that to our fire. Finding now their guns empty and no time to reload, the enemy pursuing in overwhelming numbers, their only defence was the butts of their pieces. The multitude prevailed, killing James Austin, son of Captain Henry Austin, of Brazoria county; Joe Berry, of do.; Wm. Hopson, and J. Jackson, of Ireland, one of the Santa Fé prisoners. Richard Kean, of Washington, Dr. J. J. Sinnickson, and D. H. E. Beasley, of Brazoria, were taken prisoners; while Bate Berry and Tom Davis, of Washington, succeeded in reaching our houses with empty guns, and hatless. To see the unequal odds which these brave men encountered, without the power to succour them, was painful and exciting beyond anything we had experienced. Poor Berry was bayoneted in his bed.

After their cavalry had prevailed over these eight men, they manifested their joy by the most antic capers. They went through every evolution which is not in the books; they fired guns, shouted, and blew their trumpets long and loud, always taking care not to approach within four hundred yards of our rifles.

About this time a column of the enemy charged down a street upon the north of the building we occupied. Colonel Fisher being at that point, threw himself, with some twenty men, suddenly into the street, received their fire, which severely wounded several of his men, cutting off, also, the ball of his right thumb. They effectually returned their fire, when the party fled. Up to this time, for the last six hours, the artillery nearest us had been silenced, and no one of the enemy dared approach it. It had already, as we were afterward told, proved the death of fifty-five out of their sixty choice artillery company. To get it out of our reach, they had recourse to throwing a lasso over it from behind a corner, and dragging it off, in which they were more successful than in roping the steamboat Yellow Stone, as she passed down the Brasos River in 1836: this caused a yell of exultation from their troops. Just about this time they were blowing a charge in different directions. The writer was in the upper end of the buildings nearest the square, when he received information that Colonel Fisher was wounded: hastening to where he was, he found him vomiting from the effects of his wound.* The

---

* The effect of this wound upon Colonel Fisher was that of deadly nausea, which produced vomiting. Such, however, is usually the effect of gunshot wounds upon the nerves, which, unlike those from the sword or knife, show a fall of countenance and a corresponding depression of spirits. This physiological fact has been remarked, and I have often been struck with the truth of the following remarks of Lord Byron, in the fifth note to the "Giaour." He says: "It is to be remarked, in cases of violent deaths by gunshot wounds, the expression is always that of languor, whatever the natural energy of the sufferer's character; but in death from a stab, the countenance preserves its traits of feeling or ferocity, and the mind its bias to the last."

It has been said by some of Colonel Fannin's warmest friends, who survived the bloody butchery of Goliad, that after he received his wound at the battle of Coletto, his spirits sank under it, which had an undue influence upon the surrender. I am clearly of opinion that in future the advice of a wounded commander should be received with great caution, if at all.

lamented Captain Cameron and his gallant company had occupied, during the battle, a yard in the rear of our buildings. This yard had a low stone wall around it, which they had bravely defended, and from which they had done effectual execution. Here Cameron had seven men wounded and three killed, who had been brought inside the buildings. During this time, when the expected charge was looked for, Cameron came in under much excitement, and asked for a re-enforcement to defend his position. For the first time, here something like a confusion took place. Many were talking, and each one had his plan of defence, and the voice of each was drowned in the cabal. This was a critical moment. It was the first occasion which seemed to demand our whole united strength, for previously the *picked* riflemen had principally been in requisition. In this state of things, I mounted a table and commanded silence in the most peremptory tone, ordered a sufficent force to Cameron's position, and appointed the remaining force to the defence of the buildings. Suddenly, from a temporary confusion, no men ever behaved better. Each man went cheerfully to the post assigned him, without murmuring or the obtrusion of his farther opinion, and at this identical time they were in a better situation and temper to make effectual resistance than at any moment previous, for now they seemed more impressed with the necessity of it, when a white flag approached from a street leading east.

BATTLE OF MIER.

At this juncture, in the midst of victory, we date our misfortunes.

Dr. Sinnickson, who, of the eight, had been taken prisoner over the Alcantra, having been brought to General Ampudia's headquarters, was put upon his examination as to our force, &c.; it, however, fully corroborated Walker's statement. In General Ampudia's staff, as surgeon-general, was Dr. Humphries, a Scotchman by birth, formerly surgeon in the Texian army. In 1838 he was tried by the District Court of Brazoria county for the murder of Joseph Powell, from whence he broke jail, and made his escape to Matamoras, where he has since practised his profession The surgeon-general knew Dr. Sinnickson in Brazoria, and as soon as he communicated the fact to the Mexican officers, the cunning Canales and Carasco suggested, as a last alternative, that their old deception of a *white flag* should be tried upon us. At this time, so badly were they whipped, that we were told by Walker, Lusk, and the others of our men who were prisoners, and were tied at the general's headquarters, that the officers' horses were saddled, and held each by the bridle, and that the gate of the church-yard upon the Matamoras road was opened, and every preparation was being made for a flight, when Dr. Sinnickson was started to us with the white flag. Walker and others, who had been prisoners since the day previous, had witnessed the battle from where they were confined, knew the enemy was badly beaten, and knew their condition too well for either of them to be sent in to us. Dr. Sinnickson having just been taken prisoner, and knowing but little of the condition of the enemy, had no chance to communicate with the other prisoners, and on this account, as well as from his being surgeon in our army, he was selected to bring in the flag to us. At the time he started with the flag, the other prisoners believed it was for the purpose of asking terms from us, nor were they undeceived in this particular until they saw a portion of our men marching into the public square to lay down their arms.

Dr. Sinnickson was ordered by General Ampudia to say to the Texian commander "that he had 1700 *regular* troops in the city, and 800 fresh troops near by from Monterey, which would be up in a few minutes; that it was useless for him to contend longer against such odds, and that, if he would surrender his forces, they should be treated with all the honours and considerations of prisoners of war; that the Santa Fé prisoners should be treated so likewise, and that our men should not be sent to Mexico, but kept upon the frontier until an exchange or pacification were effected; and that, if these terms were not acceded to, we should be allowed no quarter."

While the *white flag* approached from the east, a column of the enemy's infantry advanced from the west, evidently with the intention of getting some advantage over us under the protection of the flag. By the time the flag reached Colonel Fisher, and before any communication could have been received from the bearer, the head of the column had approached within a few feet of the building where I was at that time. They approached without their arms being reversed, and in a hostile attitude, when I ordered a man at my side to shoot the foremost, which was promptly done. The next two shots I fired from my repeating rifle with equally good effect, when the remainder of the column dodged around a stone wall to their right. Our recollection is that these were the last two shots fired, and certain it is they were the last two which my faithful gun fired.

Some few moments elapsed between Dr. Sinnickson's first communication with Colonel Fisher and the astounding information which was communicated to our men, that it was a demand for us to surrender, for up to this time a general impression prevailed that they were asking terms of us. When this information was communicated to our men, it was promptly met by a general burst of disapprobation, "that they never would surrender their arms." The Mexican officers, who had been watching the reception which the white flag met, saw that it was *still detained*, and some discussion going on near it, and without any invitation or understanding upon our part, took occasion to slip clandestinely into our ranks from a direction different from that in which the flag had come. The officers who had thus, like spies, obtruded themselves into our lines without our permission, were General De la Vega, Colonels Carasco, Blanco, and one other, and the priest of Comargo, Padre De Lire. These officers, who had thus unwarrantably introduced themselves among us, saluted Colonel Fisher (several of whom were previously acquainted with him in the Federal War) with their hypocritical Mexican hug, calling him their dear friend, and pledging the straps upon their shoulders, with all the sanctity of honour and candour, that General Ampudia's terms would be fully carried out; the priest of Comargo, at the same time, pledging the holy Catholic religion to this observance, and in his fervency at deception, says to Colonel Fisher, with uplifted eyes, "My dear son, do not throw yourself away." During the Federal War Colonel Fisher had been confined at Comargo with the smallpox, when this priest administered *extreme unction* to him, for which reason he doubtless took the liberty of so familiar an address. I believed then, as I do now, and have done since the murder of Colonel Fannin and his four hundred, that no confidence could be placed in a Mexican's word. That these officers had forfeited their lives by introducing themselves as spies into our camp, and to let them return with their knowledge of our strength, situation, &c., would prove ruinous to us. My first impulse, under these reflections, was to shoot them for thus introducing themselves into our lines, and for, as it appeared to me, this most novel and unprecedented attempt to gull us into a surrender. Acting under this impression, I quickly brought my repeating rifle to bear upon them, when Captain William Ryan jumped before me, knocked it up, and begged that I would hold until more could be known of their propositions and intentions. They continued, in the most fervent manner, to pledge their good faith to Colonel Fisher, Captain Eastland, and some others of our officers, who were talking with them, when I ordered Captain Cameron to form his company near by, and be in readiness for farther orders, which he promptly did. Then stepping up to Colonel Fisher, I requested him to stand aside, so that Cameron's company could fire into them. Colonel Fisher peremptorily refused to do so. I then requested permission to take them prisoners, and march them unharmed, at the head of our column, to the camp, upon the east side of the Rio Grande, where, under any possible circumstances, we would be safe. This was also refused. Captain Reese, whose company was formed some forty yards still higher up, in the direction of the square, came up and requested the same thing; he was also refused. Under these circumstances, these officers returned to their lines with a full knowledge of everything concerning ourselves, and a full knowledge of all that was important for them to know; granting, before they departed, one hour for the matter to be determined.

This hour I believed of the most vital importance. Several of the officers and a respectable minority of the men had signified their willingness, some avowedly, and others tacitly, to accept the terms. I believed that it would be easy to convince these men of their error. I therefore went to the brave Cameron, and asked him "if it was possible that *he* was in favour of a *surrender.*" The bare mention of the word choked him: he was too full for utterance; but, taking me by the hand, he carried me into the building where our wounded were. Here he had seven of his *old* company, who had followed him for three years through many dangers and hard-fought battles. Most of these men called upon us not to leave them in language which would have wrung tears from hearts of stone. Some implored us, for mercy's sake, to blow out their brains, and ease them of their misery; while there were some, more iron-nerved than the rest, who rolled out withering imprecations upon the enemy, and called upon us, for the honour of our country, never to surrender. One of these brave fellows, whose thigh was broken, called me to him, and drew from his belt a pair of silver-mounted pistols, which he placed in my hand, with tears in his eyes, saying, "General, this is all I can do for you *now.*"* This scene was distressing beyond any power of utterance. Our twenty-three wounded, some with broken limbs, others shot through the body, and one poor fellow with both eyes shot out, lay scattered over

---

* This was young Bobo, of South Carolina.

the floor, interspersed with the dead, presenting a scene calculated to excite one's deepest sympathies over all other feelings. Cameron said, "General, what would you do?" My answer was, "Men, if by staying with you we could ease your pains or heal your wounds, the sooner my voice would be to remain; but you will have your own physician, and will doubtless be treated as well by our going as if we were to remain and surrender, for even then we would be separated." We passed out of the house, and I immediately sought the gallant Captain Ryan, of the Fort Bend company. He informed me that most of his company were for fighting it out; and while in conversation with him, Cameron returned, and in a voice of harsh determination, which his Highland Scotch accent rendered peculiarly impressive, said, "By God, general, me and the whole of my company will go it!" To the lasting credit of Captains Reese and Pearson's companies, the whole of them, to a man, were opposed to surrender. Thus was the hour spent by myself, Captains Cameron, Ryan, Reese, Pearson, Buster, Dr. Brennem, Judge Gibson, and others, in explaining to the men the entire practicability of marching in close order to where we the night before crossed the Alcantra, which was within three hundred yards, thence down the right bank about two miles to the Rio Grande, and so up the same to our camp. I informed the men "that under no possible circumstances could we lose more than fifty, and that our probable loss would not exceed twenty; for the precipitous right bank of the Alcantra would protect us from any cavalry charge, while we had nothing to fear from the infantry in a country so broken and so suited to our rifles; that I would head them in this attempt, and would pledge my life upon the result." The hour was about to close, when Colonel Fisher requested me to accompany him to General Ampudia's headquarters. Having from the first opposed the whole of their terms, my opposition had increased as I reflected upon the frequent times that we had been cheated by their cursed *white flag*, and I refused so to do. He went alone, where he remained some fifty minutes. Good use was made of this time by those who were in favour of fighting it out; and when Colonel Fisher returned, I do not believe that there exceeded twenty who were willing to surrender.

Colonel Fisher formed the different companies in the street to communicate the result of his interview with the Mexican commander, which was a reiteration of his former promises, and he concluded by saying that "I have known General Ampudia for years—know him to be an honourable man, and will vouch for his carrying them out; that if you are willing to accept these terms, you will march into the public square and give up your arms, or prepare for battle in five minutes; that, in any view of the case, your situation is a gloomy one, for you cannot fight your way out of this place to the Rio

Grande short of a loss of *two thirds*, or perhaps the *whole;* but if you are determined to fight, I will be with you, and sell my life as dear as possible." This speech was a deathblow to all farther prospect of fighting, for it at once determined half of the men to surrender, who instantly separated from the remainder, and moved off in the direction of the square. Among these were many of our oldest and most respectable fellow-citizens, and several who had heretofore stood deservedly high.

Now a scene commenced which defies description. In the countenances of those whom Colonel Fisher's speech did not induce to surrender, were disappointment, sorrow, rage: many shed tears, some swore, while others maintained a sullen determination, which showed that they were prepared for the worst. Those who marched off with the intention of surrendering showed in their countenances that they believed the act would purchase their lives. They did not pass Reese and Pearson's companies, which were still formed and nearest the square, without a shower of imprecations upon their heads. "Go!" says one. "I hope you may never enjoy the sight of your country and liberty again!" "Go," says another, "you —— cowards! and rot in chains and slavery;" and such like anathemas, which, from their solemn truths, seemed to fall heavy upon their spirits, for they returned no answer, but marched into captivity in silent obedience. In a feeling of rage and contempt which I was far from controlling, I pursued this party several steps, determined to exhaust the last shot of my repeater upon them, and take the consequences. Here I was met by an old friend, whose head was frosted by seventy years. He addressed me in a tone of feeling and friendship, which disarmed me of my intention, but possessed me of another feeling which absorbed my whole soul. I believed that we would be sacrificed, felt that I could stand it, and longed to see whether the others could. Under this feeling, I broke my arms upon the pavement, and said to them, "Now we will see who can stand shooting the best." In a few minutes I went into the square, where I found a group of officers in front of several companies of infantry. Among this group was the Mexican surgeon-general, Dr. Humphries, who knew me in Texas: he advanced and spoke to me cordially. I asked him to show me General Ampudia, which he did. Unhooking my naked sword-belt, I advanced and delivered it to him, announcing myself at the same time. I remarked to him, that, "having opposed the surrender in vain, I was prepared either for the prison or to be shot, and was perfectly indifferent in the choice." He received me kindly, and replied that "he appreciated the feelings of the brave, but mine was the fate of war; that his house and friendship were mine, and that he hoped I would consider myself his guest, and call upon him freely for any service in his power." I thanked him for his personal good feelings, and turned to look for the party who had preceded me, and found their rifles laid out in a row upon the ground, and two or three officers counting their *catskin and tiger-tailed pouches* with an indifference which showed they knew nothing of their value. This was a melancholy sight, from which I was relieved by some one calling to me from the iron grating of a window about forty yards distant. I approached the window, and found about one hundred of our men jammed into a small, filthy room; and the man who was calling to me wished me to "keep an eye upon the disposition of their arms, for," said he, "we find too late that you were right, and if we can get hold of our '*tools*' once more, we will go it with a looseness." Thus soon did their repentance commence, and long will it continue.

The balance of our men, as their arms were delivered up, were thrust into two other rooms, each distant from the other sixty or eighty steps. General Ampudia invited Colonel Fisher and myself to his headquarters on the opposite side of the square, adjoining the church. In this room was seated at a table the cunning *Canales*, drawing up the "Articles of Capitulation," which were soon after imposed on us for what they did not contain. On the floor, writhing in death-agonies, was the unfortunate Colonel Arsinal, adjutant-general of the enemy's forces. "There," said General Ampudia, with tears in his eyes, "is my son, the hope of the army, the

O

pride of the service. He has a death-shot through the kidneys, and must soon die." We replied that "it was the *fate of war*, and the brave in all ranks share our sympathy." This accomplished and unfortunate young officer was only twenty-six years of age, highly favoured by nature in his personal appearance, and had attained his elevated rank through wonderful proficiency in his profession.

While Canales was basely engaged in writing the articles of capitulation, General Ampudia had Colonel Fisher and myself served with coffee and chocolate, which were the more grateful, as we had been since the previous morning without refreshment. In the mean time the articles of capitulation were signed by General Ampudia, and his interpreter, by the name of Alderette, formerly a citizen of Victoria county, was called in to read them. The following is a literal translation from the original:

"Camp of the Army of the North,
1st Division.

"Agreeable to the conference I had with General William S. Fisher, I have decided to grant,

"1st. That all who will give up their arms will be treated with the consideration which is in accordance with the magnanimous Mexican nation.

"2d. That conformably to the petition which the said General Fisher has made to me, all persons belonging to the Santa Fé Expedition will receive the same treatment and guarantees as the rest.

"3d. All who desire to avail themselves of these

terms will enter the square and there deliver up their arms. PEDRO D'AMPUDIA."

When the interpreter read the first article, the words "*with the consideration which is in accordance with the magnanimous Mexican nation*" were studiously rendered "*with all the honour and consideration of prisoners of war.*" These latter words comprehended everything we had a right to claim; but, always doubting Mexican treachery, I suggested to Colonel Fisher if it would not be better for us to have our interpreter. He replied that, though he did not speak the language, he could read and translate it; and, after looking over the paper, he made no objection to it. At the door we found several of our captains waiting to hear the articles read. The interpreter then read them as he had done to us, which also satisfied them.

The aggregate number of Texians engaged in the battle were two hundred and sixty-one, our loss being ten killed, twenty-three badly, and several slightly wounded.*

The aggregate number of the Mexican forces engaged were twenty-three hundred and forty, composed of the Zapadores battalion, the Yucatan regiment, a portion of each of the seventh and twelfth regiments, and the artillery company of sixty men—regulars, in all twelve hundred and forty; also eight hundred mounted *defensors*, under Colonel Canales,

* See Appendix No. I.

and not less than three hundred citizens in and about Mier.* Their loss was between seven and eight hundred killed and wounded. The Mexican report of their loss on the evening of the surrender was four hundred and thirty killed and two hundred and thirty wounded. Canales, in his official despatch, in avoiding the truth, says, "*As every great good costs dear, the streets and gutters of Mier overflowed with valiant Mexican blood.*" All their officers that I conversed with admitted their loss to be rising of seven hundred. It is certain that only four hundred and sixty regulars marched back to Matamoras, myself and other officers counting them every day between Mier and that city; and I am informed by Dr. Sinnickson that none but killed and wounded were left behind. The regulars were so thinned that General Ampudia did not think them a sufficient guard for our two hundred and twenty-six prisoners, our wounded being left behind; and he required Canales with his mounted *defensors*, all of whom belonged to the upper towns, to accompany them. The loss of their cavalry must have been considerable at the lower ford, while those who attacked Joseph Berry's guard could not have been less than twenty. We were informed at Matamoras by the United States consul and several American and English gentlemen, who had it in

---

* The enemy's force has been variously estimated from twenty-seven hundred to thirty three hundred; but I have adopted an estimate still smaller, and one that I know to be under the mark.

BATTLE OF MIER. 109

confidence from the Mexican officers, that their loss exceeded eight hundred in killed and wounded. Their official report to the war department of the amount of ammunition expended in the battle was nine hundred cannon cartridges and forty-three thousand musket cartridges, besides three hundred rockets, &c., while ours was between fourteen and fifteen hundred of every description. There never has existed in any age a nation who understood so well as the Texians this important matter, "never to shoot without killing;" and this will explain why a larger proportion than one to two of our shots took effect in this battle.

With the permission of General Ampudia, I visited the church that evening to see our wounded, and carried them a quantity of bandages. Doctors Sinnickson, Brennem, and Shepherd were then attending them. All appeared to be cheerful, though most of them were badly, and several mortally wounded. I have never yet seen a calamity so great befall Texians as to prevent their making fun; and upon inquiry how they were off for rations, they replied, "Oh! we have plenty of brains, general." In the same building, one hundred and thirty-six of the enemy's wounded were stretched out on the floor, many of whom had been shot in the head, and their brains had oozed out, from the size of a marble to that of one's fist. It was a horrible sight, but will explain what our fun-making wounded meant.

The enemy were mostly wounded in the head

and breast, a large portion of whom died the first night. From many observations, I find that the lacerating effect of the rifle ball is far more dangerous than the smooth bore; and that the wound of a rifle ball carrying eighty to one hundred per pound is more dangerous, both from the lacerating effect the former has upon the flesh, and the small orifice it makes, which is insufficient to discharge the blood, and, consequently, the patient bleeds inwardly.

The evening after the battle Colonel Fisher addressed the following note to General Ampudia:

"Mier, Dec. 26th, 1842.

"Sir,—The forces which, through the chances of war, I now surrender to you, are composed of the most valiant and intelligent citizens of Texas. They have contended manfully against your superior force, and have yielded only when it was deemed folly longer to contend.

"Your well-established character as a brave and magnanimous officer is a certain guarantee to me that they will be treated as brave men deserve to be.

"I have the honour to be most respectfully yours,

"WM. S. FISHER, commanding.

"To General Pedro d'Ampudia, commanding Mexican army."

Thus ended the battle of Mier, the best fought of any during the revolution. To the brave men who justly won it, their inglorious surrender proved a sore defeat; but in all the moral and political consequences of this battle to Texas, a glorious triumph!

We repeat that the battle of Mier, in its moral and political consequences to our country, was a glorious triumph. It was there that the people of Texas demonstrated the entire practicability of conquering and holding that rich valley against immense odds. It was there that the people of Texas pursued and fought them nine to one, killing treble their own numbers, and proving themselves invincible to everything but duplicity and treachery; and it was there that the Texian made the name of his *rifle* and *death* synonymous terms throughout Mexico. Far from being of the least political advantage to Texas is the geographical knowledge acquired by our countrymen, both of the Valley of the Rio Grande and the situation of its towns, the river and mountain passes, and its defensible positions.

Though the survivors of the Mier men have suffered all the horrors of multiplied deaths, and many of their brave companions have gone to their eternal homes in all the agonies of human suffering, yet it was a tribute they freely rendered to their country's honour and liberty. It is for that country to say whether it shall prove a burnt-offering or a positive good.

CHAPTER IX.

White Flag.—Dr. Sinnickson's Statement.—Cavalry sent after our Camp-guard.—Camp-guard Escapes.—Major Bonnel's Death.—Return of Cavalry.—Preparation to march for Matamoras.—Dr. Sinnickson left in Charge of our Wounded.—Their Treatment and Escape.—March for Matamoras.—Suffering of our Men.—Triumphal Entry into Comargo.—Camp in a Cow-pen.—The Bull Comedy.—Camp in a Sheep-pen.—A new Comedy.—Triumphal Entry into Rhinosa.—Ridiculous Show.—Arrival at Guadaloupe.—Congratulations to Ampudia.—Visit of Tom and Esau.—Triumphal Entry into Matamoras.—Texas Negroes in Matamoras.—Our Incarceration in Prison, and Note to General Ampudia.

Much has been said of our improper surrender at the battle of Mier, and *now* all agree that it was not only improper, but wholly unnecessary. The reader will therefore see why it is that we have been seemingly tedious in our report of that battle. We have detailed facts apparently unimportant, for the purpose of affording opportunity to the reader to draw his own conclusion as to whom the wrong was attributable, if to any. There can be no difference of opinion that it was a radical mistake in not forcing the *white flag* off as soon as its object was known. Colonel Fisher says that he ordered Dr. Sinnickson to retire with it seven or eight times, and was not obeyed. Dr. Sinnickson is a gentleman long and favourably known in Texas, and, to do him full justice, we herewith connect his statement of this affair. (See Appendix No. IV.) On the other hand, it has been said, if Colonel Fisher, as commander, was not obeyed the first time that he ordered the flag off, he wore his sword to little purpose not to use it in so critical a juncture. Nothing can be more certain than that the whole of our command was both in better temper and order to make effectual resistance at this *identical period* than at any previous time during the battle. The second grand mistake was in permitting the before-mentioned Mexican officers and the priest of Comargo to introduce themselves at all into our ranks, and then retire with a full knowledge of all that was important to their success and our defeat. The third grand mistake was in our commander vouching for General Ampudia as a man of honour, and that his promises would be carried out, &c. These, however, I look upon as the mischances of war, and believe that no severer reflection should be made. I have never questioned the personal bravery of those who advocated the surrender, and certain it is that those who have expressed doubts upon this subject are not justified in so doing by a life of boldness, especially in Colonel Fisher, which has signalized him among the foremost in our revolution.

The evening after the battle, General Ampudia informed Colonel Fisher and myself that he would send his cavalry out to our camp upon the east side of the Rio Grande to bring in the balance of our men, horses, camp furniture, &c.; and, to prevent the farther effusion of blood, he would advise us to write to the men in camp to surrender and come in. We replied that we were *prisoners*, and they were

P

free; we could not, therefore, undertake to give such advice. I requested permission of the general for one of our men to accompany the cavalry, and to secure my baggage, the most important part of which was my journal, and manuscript maps of the roads, rivers, and the parts of the country through which we had travelled. Having obtained the permission asked for, I sent Sailing-master Lyon, with a *knowing* wink, to our boys in camp. The cavalry approached the river to within a few hundred yards, halted, and sent Lyon and a few men to " *Halloo across, and order our men to bring over the boats!*" Lyon being an indifferent Spanish, and the Mexicans with him worse English scholars, anglicized the above order thus: " *Boys, we are all prisoners, and several hundred cavalry are close by in pursuit of you. Take all the good horses and put!*" This advice was promptly acted upon, and all our camp-guard reached home in safety, with the exception of our lamented countryman, Major George W. Bonnel.

Major Bonnel, than whom Texas did not possess a purer patriot or braver man, in company with Dr. Watson and Mr. Hackstaff, when the army crossed the river the day previous to attack General Ampudia, then a mile below, were cooking our dinner, which consisted of a fat sheep, with a stick run through it, the ends of which rested upon the sides of a large canoe, with the fire in its bottom. We expected to have warm work with Ampudia, and ordered these gentlemen to float the canoe down opposite the battle-ground, hitch it to a bush, come up, take a hand, and then we could relish our dinner the better. As we have before explained, when we arrived in sight of the Mexican army, they retreated to the city at right angles from the river, leaving my friends and my dinner behind, they having no alternative then but to join the camp-guard. After the latter retreated, as Lyon advised them, some miles, Major Bonnel and one other man returned to camp for more of our horses, and was captured. Poor Bonnel was murdered, as his companion reported, who made his escape. Major B. was not only constitutionally brave, but, being a Santa Fé prisoner, he was doubtless stimulated to a more obstinate resistance, which could neither prevail over numbers, nor was calculated to inspire their savage breasts with magnanimity for such heroism. Thus fell a brave man and a pure patriot, without the last sad rites of burial. His bones now lie bleaching upon the banks of Rio del Norte. His spirit, if congenial spirits meet in heaven, will hold glorious communion with those of Milam and Travis, of Fannin, Grant, and Ward, of Bowie, Crocket, Brennem, Fitzgerald, and a host of other heroes who fell in the same struggle for liberty.

On the evening of the 27th, the cavalry which had been despatched to bring in our camp-guard returned with 320 of our most indifferent horses and mules, and a quantity of rubbish, consisting of old saddles, empty saddlebags, blankets, &c. Captain Alderette, the officer who had been sent in charge of the cavalry, as an excuse for not bringing in our camp-guard, represented them to be one hundred and twenty strong, and that they had retreated upon the best horses. General Ampudia expressed surprise that our men had not surrendered, and came in and informed Colonel Fisher and myself what the officer had said about their number. We answered that it was not in the history of our nation to surrender without fighting, and that the officer had told him a falsehood to screen himself for not fighting them. We informed General A. at the same time that our camp-guard were well apprized of our fate, and had selected all our fine American horses, and it would be idle to pursue them. He, however, started Colonel Carasco, with six hundred cavalry, in pursuit, who returned the fourth day deeply chagrined to confirm what we had said.

Preparations were now busily making for the march to Matamoras. Their dead were lowered from the house-tops by means of cords, which occupied all the day succeeding the battle, and their wounded were billeted about the town upon the citizens, according to their respective abilities to maintain them. Dr. Sinnickson was left in charge of our wounded men, and every kindness promised to be afforded him and them. From the doctor's report, none of these promises were carried out, but they were, instead, treated by the commandant in charge of them in a most brutal manner. Some two weeks after, eight of these wounded men made their escape to Texas (see Appendix No. I.), and the doctor, with the balance, were sent off to Matamoras.

December the 31st, General Ampudia took up the line of march for Matamoras in the following order: Colonel Fisher, myself, Adjutant Murry, and our four small boys, were kept with the general, under the special charge of Captain Clemente Castro, a brave, honourable, and good man, who had so miraculously survived his artillery company. We will ever feel grateful for the many kindnesses extended us by this officer, and rejoice to hear of his promotion, which he so well deserved. Our men were marched in double file, in the centre of the road, with artillery before and in their rear. On each side of them was a single file of infantry with fixed bayonets, and on the outside of them were cavalry. In the rear, also, a large body of cavalry was kept in reserve. In this order, the march was conducted at a rapid pace, without allowing our men to stop for water, for which they suffered greatly, not having means to pack it. They, not being used to walking, and having been shut up in a close room for the last five days previous, suffered greatly with sore feet and fatigue. That night they reached the Rio St. Juan, opposite the town of Comargo, and encamped, with but little fuel; consequently, they had small fires, and a most bleak norther blowing.

Our men suffered greatly here: all their blankets, worth taking, had been stolen by the cavalry; and when the fires would burn down, they, to keep themselves warm, would rake away the burning coals, and lay in piles in the ashes. We have frequently observed what an exhilarating influence the French language has upon men when in the worst physical condition. Those who understood that language would appear happy under its spirit-stirring airs, while our John Bull natures would compromise with nothing but full rations; and I believe that there are patriotic Frenchmen who would keep as fat upon a bottle of claret and the Marseilles hymn, as some of the English breed would upon the hind-quarter of a bullock.

January 1st. Our men were crossed over the Rio St. Juan into the town of Comargo, which is a beautiful place, containing about three thousand inhabitants, situated immediately upon the south side of the river, and six miles from its entrance into the Rio Grande. Here commenced the grand menagerie show of our prisoners, which was kept up during their zigzag march of fifteen hundred miles through Mexico. Our men were marched through the town and around the military square under the ringing of bells, firing of crackers and guns, and the "*vivas*" of the populace. A large number of small children, of both sexes, carried round the town, and in front of our men, long rolls of paper pasted together, upon which were painted the most bombastic and ridiculous mottoes, such as "Glory and gratitude to the brave Canales"—"Eternal honour to the immortal Ampudia," &c. Our men were placed in three separate prisons, where they remained until the next day. Colonel Fisher, myself, Adjutant Murry, and the small boys were quartered at the house of Don Trinedad, a kind and hospitable man, who showed us every attention in his power.

January 2d. Marched ten miles to a rancho, where our men were herded in a cow-pen for the night; and though they were suffering from sore feet, occasioned by the first day's march, yet there were some among them who would have their fun. Being herded in a cow-pen like so many cattle, the fun-makers were determined to complete the character. They would get down upon their all-fours, bow their necks, paw up the dirt, and low like bulls, to the no small astonishment of their captors.

January 3d. Our men were marched twenty-one miles to *old* Rhinosa, over a fine tract of country, and here herded in a sheep-pen. Here, too, the comedians had a new character to play, and it is certain they bleated more like sheep than any sheep in Mexico.

January 4th. Our men were marched eighteen miles to New Rhinosa, situated upon a high hill, about one mile from the Rio Grande, and containing 2000 inhabitants. Here great preparation had been made for the victor's triumphal entry. Triumphal arches, made of reeds bound together, and decorated with parti-coloured handkerchiefs, calico, and ladies' shawls and petticoats, were thrown across the principal streets through which we passed, and from which appropriate mottoes of *glory* and *honour* were suspended. To make our surprise the greater, and impress us the more with the wonderful resources of the *great nation*, just as we entered the town, riding in company with the general and staff, the warriors of the Careese tribe of Indians, naked, with the exception of the breech-clout, and painted after their war fashion, suddenly popped into our path, at the same time giving the war-whoop and firing their guns in our faces. Then suddenly wheeling off to reload, the same manœuvres were repeated several times. This excited mirth rather than surprise, and was followed by something more ridiculous still: about twenty little boys, between the ages of ten and fourteen, led by a little old man of sixty, who was not larger than a boy of twelve years old, all most fantastically dressed with different coloured handkerchiefs, and ribands fixed about them, with small mirrors fastened upon their heads so as to form an obelisk of four sides. Each held in his hand a long-handled gourd, decorated with blue and yellow paper, with small gravel inside. They were attended by several fiddlers, and suddenly appeared before us, led by their old leader, dancing in regular time to the music, first upon one foot and then upon the other. They so contrived, that while one foot was hopping to the music, the other was shaking to it, and the long-handled gourd and pebbles of each kept good time with the fiddles and the motions of the little old man. He would lead his little band close to our horses' heads, and as we advanced, by motion of his arms, his double file of juveniles would wheel off right and left, precede us thirty or forty yards, and perform the same manœuvres over, always keeping good time in step and motion. Thus were we danced to our quarters about half a mile.

We remained here the 5th. Through the intercession of Padre De Lire, the priest of Comargo, Dr. Wm. M. Shepherd was taken out of the prison and permitted to accompany our party, which was kept with the general. The padre was informed that Dr. S. prevented his being fired upon as he was coming into our ranks previous to the surrender at Mier, for which he felt grateful; and he often evinced his gratitude by taking from his pocket a flask of brandy, *vino mascal*, and taking a drink with us. Here we left one of our men, by the name of M'Dade, who shortly after died.

January 6th. Marched to church to witness the ceremony of mass, accompanied by the firing of cannon and crackers, &c.; then marched twenty-five miles, and again lodged in a cowpen. In passing a cornfield, a negro fellow, who had run off from Texas, looked over the fence, and, after giving his head a mournful shake, he said, in a still more

Q

melancholy voice, "Aha! white man, dey cotch you now; dey gib you hell!" This comfort was quite as good as their cowpen lodgings, up to their ankles in wet manure.

January 7th. Marched eighteen miles, and quartered in a cowpen. It was of much importance to get a cowpen to put our men in, as they were more easily guarded; hence the difference in the marches, which were suited to the locality of said pens. These pens were built by placing pickets close together in the ground, in an upright position, and fastening their tops with rawhide, to a horizontal timber. Around these pens their guards would be placed.

January 8th. Marched fifteen miles over a rich, flat country, well adapted to the cultivation of sugar, and camped again in a cowpen at the village of Warloupe. While at this place, many citizens of consequence came out from Matamoras to congratulate General Ampudia upon his victory. Among these were two of our acquaintances, *Tom* and *Esau*. These *gentlemen*, now of so much consequence as to ride three leagues in a coach to congratulate General Ampudia upon his *splendid victory*, were General Sam Houston's two barbers, so well known to the public of Texas. Tom treated us with marked respect and attention, spoke of his prospects in that country, his intended nuptials, invited us to the wedding, and said that General Ampudia was to stand godfather on the occasion. He remarked to

General Ampudia, upon meeting him, in our presence, " Well, general, I *told* you, before leaving Matamoras, that when you met these gentlemen you would catch it." He spoke much of Texas, said that he appreciated many gentlemen there highly, but that he could not consent longer to be the slave of such an unprincipled monster as Sam Houston, and regretted the necessity of leaving the country. Esau was more sulky, spoke in disreputable terms of his old master, and insultingly to some of our men.

January 9th. Marched nine miles to Matamoras; but, before entering the city, we were halted for the general to receive the congratulations of a large number of friends who came out in coaches to meet him. Many women and girls came out with joyous countenances to meet their husbands and sweethearts, but, alas for them, they had experienced the effect of the Texian rifle at Mier, and they returned with heavy hearts and bitter lamentations. A triumphal arch was thrown across the principal street through which we passed at every hundred yards; and, to make the grand pageant as imposing as possible, soldiers were stationed upon each side of the street about thirty feet apart, and what they lacked in soldiers they made up for the occasion by placing soldier-clothes upon citizens. We first accompanied the general to the church, which he entered to receive the blessings of the fathers; at the same time we were placed under the charge of Captain Castro, who hurried us along at full gallop to the general's quarters, to prevent the populace from offering insults. Thence followed our men slowly and solemnly up one street and down another, to give the brutal populace full opportunity to gaze at, and heap upon them dirty epithets, in which their language is so copious. Among the populace were a large number of negroes who absconded from Texas: these were among the foremost in their abusive epithets, and our men, without the power of punishing such insolence, would gnash their teeth in rage. At night a grand ball was given in honour of General Ampudia and officers, and we were turned over in charge of a new officer, who, to secure us the better for the night, conducted us to a lodging in an unfurnished room in the common prison. Here we were locked up without fire, bedding, or any article of furniture. This we presumed was done by order of the general; and it was so much at variance both with our former treatment and his gratuitous promises to us, that, after much persuasion, I obtained from the officer of the guard pen, ink, and paper, and addressed him a note, which was forthwith delivered, in which note we abused his Mexican perfidy and falsehood in the broadest terms. To our astonishment, in about one hour the doors of our prison were thrown open, and we reconducted to our former quarters by the general's aid-de-camp. We have reason to believe this was the more promptly done through the intercession of General Romola de la Vega and Captain Castro. Next morning General Ampudia, after apologizing for our treatment the night before, informed us that we must prepare for immediate march to the city of Mexico. He also informed us that Colonel Fisher and myself should be sent on in advance of our men, as hostages for their good conduct. We replied, that if we were denied the privilege of accompanying our men, which we most preferred, we would cheerfully go in their advance to Mexico, to endeavour to do them all possible service. We also desired a day to make preparations and write letters to the United States and Texas, which was granted. After our letters were written, they were submitted to his inspection, which he in the most gentlemanly manner declined, and endorsed a free passport upon them.

Matamoras is the only American-built town we saw in Mexico. It has many frame houses with shingled roofs, and is built of as combustible materials as most Southern towns in the United States. It is situated about half a mile from the Rio Grande, and thirty from its mouth, contains a population of about ten thousand, and is the most defenceless city in Mexico.

CHAPTER X.

Preparations for March to Mexico.—Our Friends J. P. Schatzell, Marks, and Strother.—Protest against ironing our Men.—March for Monterey under charge of Colonel Savriego.—Held as Hostages for the good Conduct of our Men.—Interview with them in Prison.—Arrival at Caidereta.—Bad Treatment.—Letter to Ampudia.—Arrival at Monterey.—Character of Colonel Savriego.—Quartered at Colonel Bermudez's.—His Character and Family.—Interview with Governor Ortega.

JANUARY 10th and 11th were employed in writing and preparing for our march. Several American gentlemen called upon us and offered their services, among whom we recollect with gratitude Mr. J. P. Schatzell, Mr. Marks, United States vice-consul, and Mr. Strother. These gentlemen were of infinite service to our men in furnishing money, blankets, and other absolute necessaries, without which they must have suffered much more than they did. While they have laid us under lasting obligations for such kindness, our country should not feel less proud of such friends, nor be slow to requite such services.

Having learned that it was in contemplation to march our men in irons to Mexico, and that they were in preparation to be placed upon them, Colonel Fisher and myself remonstrated against it in the strongest terms. General Ampudia, in answer, said that Colonel Canales, the officer who was to take charge of them to Monterey, insisted upon having them ironed, and that he would not undertake to guard two hundred and twenty Texians with less than one thousand Mexicans; but that he had overruled the order for ironing them as violative of his articles of capitulation.

January 12th. Early in the morning preparations were made for starting, and I applied to General Ampudia for permission to take with us our interpreter, Daniel D. Henrie, and my servant, Samuel C. Lyon. I will here remark that Lyon was not my servant in the ordinary meaning of the word, but that we had lived next-door neighbours for six years, and I knew I could greatly serve him by having him with me. I informed the general that such courtesies were common for us to extend to Mexican officers when our prisoners, and he gave the order for them to accompany us. Colonel Fisher, myself, Dr. Shepherd, Adjutant Murry, Interpreter Henrie, and S. C. Lyon, were each furnished a horse, and placed under charge of Lieutenant-colonel Savriego, who had under his command about forty cavalry. In the morning previous, not expecting the privilege of seeing our men, I addressed them the following note, in which Colonel Fisher joined me:

"FELLOW PRISONERS,

"It has fallen to our lot to become the captives of the nation with which we are at war. This is the fortune of that policy; and though our condition is incident to these privations, let us bear up under them with the fortitude of men. Let us nerve our souls in that impregnable armour which lightens the weary limb, and which the steel of our enemy cannot penetrate. That immortal spirit will make us superior to our condition, and triumph over our misfortunes. Recollect that the best nations of the world have battled with each other, and the best men have been in like condition with ourselves. Indulge, therefore, all reasonable hope in the magnanimity of our enemy, and in that justice which is the all-pervading providence of God.

"To-day, countrymen, it is the pleasure of our captors that we should be parted, and sent on in advance to the capital. A long and weary journey lies before us. The gloom of the prison and the fatigues of this thousand miles of space we embrace as pleasures in comparison to this cruel separation with you, who have so nobly battled for your country and shared every danger.

"The short time we have been permitted to remain at this place precludes the possibility of getting any assistance from our countrymen at home, therefore our means of pecuniary benefit to you are small indeed; but please accept with the warmest feelings of our hearts the small amount sent by Adjutant Murry for the assistance of the more unfortunate who may be sick on the road.

"Now, dear friends and neighbours, let us part, but with that hope which stimulates man to look beyond the present, and which, with God's pleasuse, will one day unite us again at our homes."

Just before starting, General Ampudia intimated to Colonel Fisher and myself that he was informed some of our men contemplated a charge upon their guards, and that we must go by the prison and inform them of the consequences to ourselves, should such be the case; that we would be held as hostages for their good conduct, and treated accordingly. Colonel Fisher desired Captain Cameron "to use his own judgment in the matter," if such was in contemplation. I implored the men, "as they regarded my friendship, their own condition, and the honour of the country, to let no opportunity slip in overpowering their guards and getting home, and to do so regardless of any consequences to myself." The men all testified by their burning tears that my advice should not be lost upon them.

We were escorted, rather than guarded, by Colonel Savriego and his troop to Monterey, a distance of two hundred and seventy-five English miles. We reached Monterey on the 22d of January, and were furnished quarters at the hospitable mansion of old Colonel Bermudez, the *mayor de la plaza*. The day before reaching Monterey we arrived at the beautiful town of Caidereta, containing a population of about ten thousand souls. Here, for the first time since we were under the charge of Colonel Savriego, we were treated badly. Great prep-

R

aration had been made to exhibit us, which Colonel S. refused to permit, and at night we were neither furnished bedding by the alcalde, nor permitted to hire the use of any with our own money. We understood this treatment was induced by Colonel Canales, who had written on to this place much to our disparagement. The following letter, which I wrote to General Ampudia, will fully explain not only his treacherous character, but the small cunning of one who has generally profited by such treachery.

"Monterey, January 23d, 1843.

"To General Pedro D'Ampudia,
   of the Mexican Army :

"Sir,—Having safely arrived thus far on our way to the capital, we desire to express to you our sincere thanks for the generous courtesies which, mainly through your kindness, we have met upon the road.* At Caidereta only have we been treated in a different manner, and this, we understand, has been induced by Colonel Canales. Of that treatment we do not complain; but when the colonel makes himself the HERO OF MIER, we feel much humiliation in

---

* What the writer has said of General Ampudia in his Journal, both candour and justice required; and while it gave him pleasure to speak that in his praise which he, in truth, could say of few other officers in Mexico, it has since been a matter of regret that General A.'s conduct towards the ill-starred General Sentmanat is infamous in the extreme. The capture and murder of that unfortunate "Federalist" should have satiated the vengeance of a despot, but the subsequent boiling of his head in oil was a vindictive refinement in cannibalism disgraceful in the vilest savage.

the imputation that we surrendered to *him*. We scorn such a reflection, for that gentleman had an opportunity at Guerrero, with three hundred troops, to meet fifty of us, and declined it. Colonel Fisher and officers join me in the hope that General Ampudia entertains a better opinion of their gallantry than to believe that such a thing could be possible to surrender to him who once deceived Texians.

"We farther desire to tender, through you, to Colonel Savriego, officers, and troop, who have thus far accompanied us, our heartfelt thanks for their soldier-like conduct and many kindnesses.

"With sentiments of the highest consideration and esteem, I am your obedient servant,

"THOMAS J. GREEN."

From having heard Colonel Savriego's name associated with some marauding expedition upon our frontier some years back, we had wholly misconceived his character. We had supposed him to be some rough bandit, who dealt in robbery and murder from habit or choice. Justice both to him and ourselves requires us to say that we have not met in Mexico a more intelligent, humane, and accomplished officer. The following note to him will give the reader a more correct knowledge of our estimation of his worth:

"Monterey, January 23d, 1843.
"To Colonel Savriego, Mexican Army.

"Sir,—Being about to separate from you on our progress to the capital, in justice both to yourself and our own feelings, we cannot do so without expressing our warmest gratitude for your kindness to us as prisoners of war, while under your charge from Matamoras.

"Your lofty and gallant bearing in the battle-field was a sure guarantee of what we have since realized in your magnanimous generosity, for such is the peculiar characteristic of the truly brave.

"When, sir, we met in the strife of battle, we did so as political enemies, each doing his duty for his country, since which, though it has been the fortune of war for us to be prisoners, it has been your better fortune to lighten our situation by the kindest personal considerations. We hope, therefore, that many years of happiness may be yours, and that good fortune may again unite us where our friendship may be reciprocated."

We remained six days at Monterey, which is a beautiful city, containing a population of about twenty thousand, situated high up on the Rio San Fernando, and between two elevated mountains. It is the capital of New Leon, over which Governor-general Ortega presided. At this city we were treated with every kindness which our situation would allow. Our table was supplied from the best French restaurant in the city; and our kind host, old Colonel Bermudez, was all the time apologizing for not having things good enough for us.

We call Colonel B. *old*, as the highest encomium

we can bestow upon him ; for, with one exception, and that one Colonel Terris, of the 4th regiment of infantry, we never met an *old* officer in Mexico who did not possess the highest sense of magnanimity and humanity. Colonel Bermudez is about sixty-five years of age, has seen much service, and is a gentleman of the old school model, of which I have a far better opinion than of the new. He has an interesting family, and several beautiful daughters. These amiable ladies, to beguile our heavy hours, would sing, and play upon the guitar and piano for us, and at evenings would invite the élite of the city, some of whom doubtless came to see us Texians, whom they would introduce as "*muy valiente,*" very brave. At these evening coteries we would endeavour to appear as if nothing had happened to us, and join in the dance as lightsome as any. The ladies would say, " What wonderful people you must be ! Here you are, prisoners in a foreign land, having already passed many dangers, and you must expect to fall into hands who will treat you unkindly—for all Mexicans are not what they should be— and still you appear as if nothing had befallen you."

How delightful it is to witness the salutations of Mexican female friends ! they trip across the room to meet each other with a gait superior to our women, and instead of grasping the hand, they embrace with a bewitching, gossamer, ethereal touch, which cannot properly be described. In their balldress they look like winged creatures, and the moscheto hawk, in stooping after its tiny prey, does not appear more lightsome than they when swinging through their delightful dances.

Most of the Mexican dances are exceedingly beautiful; there is a luxury in the music, and a fascinating swing in their women peculiarly winning. Nothing can exceed the grace of their quadrilles and contra-dances. Their waltzes and gallopades are too much of a good thing for my unsophisticated taste. Among their other dances, they have one called the zopilote, or turkey-buzzard dance. This is performed somewhat after the manner of the bull-dance in old Virginia, a dance well known to the young men of that good old state at the conclusion of their balls, after the retirement of the ladies. Their fandango is a lively operation, mostly danced by the more common people, in which the gentleman leads his partner to the centre of the room; here they move face to face, the gentleman beating his feet against the floor in admirable time to the music, while the lady faces him in a regular monotonous hitch-up and back-down step, as uniform as the oscillation of a pendulum. Thus it is kept up until each party is relieved by some other groups.

As the lady is thus relieved, her caballero, in compliment to her performance, serves her with either coffee, chocolate, or aquardiente and a cigarrito; the latter she invariably takes between the middle and forefinger, and occasionally indulges with infinite grace the luxury of inhaling its delicious aroma.

Unlike the prodigal Virginian, who puffs it out upon the high pressure principle, after keeping the smoke some time in her mouth, she suffers it to escape from her nasal organ with such quiet gentleness as to allow of the full enjoyment of its odour, while its fumes settle under the olfactories of her beau, giving him a second benefit of the well-nursed incense.

To one like myself, who had never smoked a cigar, this fumigation was made sufferable through the channel whence it came; but my politeness had been put to a severer test.

On one occasion, the fair senorita with whom I danced, seeing that I did not smoke, took from her reticule a cigarrito, lighted it with the one she was smoking by first placing the new one in her own rosy lips, and then offered it to me. Dreading the consequences, I commenced an apology, when my interpreter suddenly checked me by saying that it would be an insult to the lady not to smoke it. I received it with what good grace I could, although with something of a martyr spirit, well knowing the inevitable result. I resolved, however, to assume the best disguise I might; so I crossed my legs, and gently half closing my left eye, looked up to the ceiling with the little burning abhorrence sticking in my lips as if I was an old hand at the business. I was getting on with great proficiency, and had let off some half dozen tremendous puffs, when, reflecting upon the vulgarity of this tar-kiln operation, I attempted to squeeze it out through my nose. This required experience; for, instead of giving it vent through that channel, I forced it down both into my lungs and stomach, thus creating deadly nausea, which caused me to break for the door like a quarter-horse to relieve my distress. The ready wit of my interpreter rendered my desponding speech into a compliment; but when I suddenly left my seat for the door to relieve my sickness, and he explained that, in compliment to her beauty, it was the first I had ever smoked, she was greatly flattered, at what made me the more inveterate against a nationality so disagreeable.

In objecting to this national custom among the ladies, a very intelligent Mexican gentleman said, "It may, señor, appear very obnoxious to your nation, but the force of habit makes it look well to us. The men of your nation masticate tobacco; the Turks and Chinese chew opium; and these, to us, appear to be a very filthy practice; and in the court circles of England and France, the most refined nations upon the earth, the ladies use morphine for the same purpose, while in a portion of your happy country your own women mop with snuff. Thus, what the English and French ladies abuse in the Turks and Chinese, the refinements of fashion and taste furnish them in a different shape; and what your women abuse in ours for its public use, they take by stealth, and in a still more displeasing manner. It is all, señor, for the purpose of creating artificial excitement; and while I say that you object to our ladies smoking, we believe the most filthy of all practices is that of your '*snuff-dippers.*'" He continued: "On one occasion, señor, I was in the habit of visiting a lady in your country, whose time of life was verging upon the 'sear and yellow leaf.' She was in the neighbourhood of that unwelcome thirty-three, which concentrates to the eye-corners those hateful crow-feet, which from that time is so sure to ride the countenance to the grave. In the morning this lady showed all the languor of previous excess, and she was as uninteresting until she spent an hour with her snuff-mop as if she had just awaked from the excessive use of ardent spirits. I once, by accident, saw her mopping—and such a mouth! I never after that time thought of her, but what I saw. Oh! that horrid mouth, in all its licentious indulgence; teeth, tongue, and gums were filled with this cruel-looking lava, which had overrun the crater, and formed a sable periphery of most frightful extent. Ah me, I thought, how happy are our men, that we are not compelled to kiss such mouths! Do tell me, is it the mop which makes all your young ladies so entertaining? and believe me, señor, I love one of your pretty girls, but at every thought of the mop and her horrid dirty mouth I am taken aback." I assured the gentleman that this practice was confined to but few in our country, and I believed that every decent gentleman, both in Texas and the United States, looked upon it as far more odious than smoking. "I thank you, señor, for that fact," says he, "for my sweetheart is in Philadelphia; I hope soon to visit her, and you now make me the more anxious to do so."

I confess I was fairly beaten by this intelligent gentleman; but while he found in me no apologist for the "snuff-dippers" and snuff-eaters of my own country, he failed to convince me that it was right for a pretty girl to smoke. Though I have ever been opposed to matrimonial divorces as most destructive to the happiest state of society, yet, if I were a judge or legislator, and the abused husband was to set forth in his petition that his better half smoked and mopped, if I could not upon principles of law entertain his application, I would sympathize in his wrongs.

The third day after our arrival in the city of Monterey, Governor Ortega desired to see Colonel Fisher and myself at his quarters, he having been sick and confined to his house. He received us very courteously, and expressed his desire that we should be supplied with every comfort. Before leaving Monterey, we addressed the following notes to the governor and our good host Colonel Bermudez:

"Monterey, January 27th, 1843.
"To his Excellency General Ortega.

Sir,—Before leaving New Leon, over which your excellency presides with honour to the state and such happy benefits to the people, permit us to express our warmest gratitude for the kind reception and friendly entertainment you have extended to us.

"To be prisoners of war in a foreign land, far from our country, our homes, and our families, is melancholy enough; but that we have become so in doing the bidding of our own country is a consolation beyond all price. That you have lightened these melancholy reflections by the kindest considerations is still more honourable both to your heart and head; and rest assured, sir, that that great moral principle which now governs the civilized world is more omnipotent in its happy influence upon mankind than the most destructive engines of war.

"Allow us to hope that many years of happiness may be yours, and that you may long continue in the full enjoyment of deserved political and individual prosperity."

"Monterey, January 27th, 1843.
"To Colonel Bermudez, Mexican Army.

"Sir,—Since it has been our good fortune to be placed under your charge, such has been the kindness of your treatment, we beg you to allow us the present privilege of reciprocating that kindness so far as this humble testimonial of our hearts' offering can do.

"Your magnanimity of heart, as well as experience in the world, rightly estimates the situation and feelings of the brave, who, through the fortune of war, become prisoners in a foreign land. Such has been our fortune. In duty to our own, we entered your country as political enemies, and manfully performed that duty. Your conduct, and that of other Mexican officers, governed by the highest principles of moral bravery, does more in winning our admiration and affections, and in bringing about a right understanding between our respective nations, than the carnage of a thousand battles.

"In leaving your hospitable roof on our progress to the capital, we beg to tender you and your amiable family our warmest gratitude, with our hearts' best wishes that you may continue to enjoy many years of felicity in the exercise of that domestic happiness, of which, dear sir, you are so pre-eminent an example."

CHAPTER XI.

March for Saltillo.—Our Treatment.—Meet Captain Fitzgerald, Van Ness, and others in Prison.—Their Condition.—Arrival of Colonel Barragan with our Prisoners.—We march for San Luis Potosi.—Arrival at Salado.—Our Men arrive at Aqua Nuevo.—Captain Dimmit.—His Death.—Barragan arrives with our Men at Salado.—Concerted Attack upon the Guards.—The Charge and Victory at Salado.—Order to shoot us.—Narrow Escape.—Arrival at Cidral.—Narrow Escape from the Populace.—Narrow Escape from our new Guards.—Arrival at Mataguala.—Treatment there.—Report of the Battle of Salado.

JANUARY 28th. We left Monterey under charge of Captain Ugartechia and a troop of cavalry for Saltillo, a city containing about fifteen thousand inhabitants, and seventy-five English miles distant, where we arrived on the 30th. Both here and at Monterey we were treated kindly by several Europeans who visited us in our prison. Upon our arrival at Saltillo, we were first quartered at a miserable, filthy cavalry barracks, against which we protested in the strongest terms, when we were moved to an infantry quartel not much better. At this quartel we found Captain Archibald Fitzgerald, Mr. George Van Ness, Thomas Hancock, Norman Woods, Miblem Harrell, and John Higgerson: the three former were taken at San Antonio on the 11th of September previous, and detained at San Fernando as Santa Fé prisoners, by order of the government, to be shot; but, through the intercession of General Woll, were pardoned, and sent on with the three latter, who were badly wounded at Captain Dawson's defeat on the 18th of September. We found these men, and particularly Woods, in a bad condition, but by giving him warm clothes and good nursing he rapidly recovered. He must have died very soon without such assistance. Upon application to the governor, Van Ness was permitted to accompany our party as interpreter, and the other five turned in with our men, who arrived here on the 5th of February under charge of Colonel Barragan.

Captain Fitzgerald, Van Ness, and Hancock informed us that, while they were detained as Santa Fé prisoners at San Fernando, by order of the government, to be shot, the first news which they received of General Somerville's movements was from Henry Clay Davis, late of Kentucky, and a man by the name of M'Beth, who were put in the same prison with them. These two men had taken leave of us at Laredo, to return, as they said, to San Antonio, but instead of which deserted to the Mexican army at San Fernando, 140 miles north, carrying the Mexican commander letters from the alcalde of Laredo, and giving information of the Texian movements. General Reyes, the Mexican commander at that place, always doubting of treachery, incarcerated these renegades in the same prison with the above-named gentlemen, where they were kept eleven days, until he was assured of their fidelity by again hearing from the alcalde of Laredo and Colonel Bravo, the Mexican commandant at that place. Upon this information General Reyes released them, and gave Davis a ball, at which his health was drank as one who had seen the error of his ways by deserting the "Texian adventurers" and giving in his allegiance to the "magnanimous" Mexican nation. We have alluded to this circumstance as the first and last instance in our whole revolution where an American, born and raised in the United States, ever deserted our standard to join that of our Mexican enemy, and it should be a warning to others against a too intimate Mexican association; for, as ministers plenipotentiary are subject to be Mexicanized, so are humbler individuals. These young men had lived some time in San Antonio, and had acquired much of Mexican habit, with a consequent corresponding sympathy which outbalanced their Texian patriotism.

I have remarked that whenever a citizen of the United States resides long enough in Mexico to discard his suspenders, and tie up his pantaloons with a red band around the waist, cover his shoulders with a blanket, and eat a gill of red pepper at a meal—beware of him! he will both lie and steal; and while his new ethics teach him to filch from his neighbour's pocket, they would cause him, for a Judas reward, to sell the country which gave him life.

Our men, under charge of Colonel Canales, with six hundred infantry and cavalry guards, and one piece of artillery, took up the line of march from Matamoras on the 14th January, two days after our party had left that place. They proceeded to the pass Sacarte, upon the Rio St. Juan, without any incident worth noting. At this place a plan of charging the guards had been perfected, but, through some misunderstanding of Captain Cameron's order, it was not carried out. It was then determined to wait until they reached farther into the mountains. They arrived at Monterey on the 29th, one day after the departure of our party, and remained here until the 2d of February, when, under charge of Colonel Barragan and about two hundred and fifty guards, they marched for Saltillo. February 2d, camped at St. Catharine, twelve miles, and on the 3d at the *Rinconada*, twenty-four miles. Here they intended an attack upon the guards, and a more favourable place could not have been selected, but the increased vigilance of those in charge of them prevented it, and they supposed some "Judas" had betrayed their design to the commander. On the 5th they arrived at Saltillo, and were quartered at a different barracks from us. Colonel Barragan permitted several of our men to visit us in his company.

February 6th. Captain Ugartechia took up the line of march for San Luis Potosi with our party, and on the 7th Colonel Barragan followed with the main body of our men. Here Colonel B. increased his guards with a company of infantry known as the "Red Caps." Our march was interrupted with no more than the ordinary "incidents of travel" until we reached the hacienda Salado, forty leagues' distant. This road was over a barren country, very destitute of vegetation, and supplied from deep wells of brackish water, drawn up by mules working a very simply-contrived drum, with buckets attached to a broad leathern strap or hair ropes. This place we reached on the 9th, when Captain Ugartechia complaining much of his head and the want of sleep, Dr. Shepherd gave him some morphine. This had a singular effect upon him. He curled himself up in a corner of the room, would not speak above a whisper, concluded he must die, and sent an express back to Saltillo for his sister and another physician. In this situation he lay until the arrival of our men on the evening of the 10th, when we were turned over to Captain Romano; the main body of our men, under Colonel Barragan, having marched from Saltillo on the 7th, one day after our party arrived at the hacienda *Aqua Nuevo* (New Water), being twenty-four miles, the first day. This was another favourable place to charge their guards, and it was in contemplation; but from the soreness of the men's feet and other causes, it was again deferred.

This place is also worthy of note, from the fact that here our lamented countryman, Captain Philip Dimmit, poisoned himself, having determined so to act rather than die by the hands of his enemies. Captain Dimmit's name is too intimately connected with Goliad and our first effort at independence to be passed over with indifference. We knew him long and intimately as a brave man and a devoted patriot. When he was villanously abducted from his home, through the perfidious treachery of his own countrymen, the Mexicans knew the value of their prize too well to treat him slightly. Poor Dimmit knew full well that the "*Goliad Declaration of Independence*" would seal his fate. He and his few companions, with a heroism worthy the occasion, charged their guards, and, after three had fallen by his own hands, yielded to the superiority of numbers. His last act of defiance, after invoking his country's justice upon his betrayers and murderers in a strain of rare eloquence, was to die as he had lived, shouting for his country and liberty!

February 10th. Colonel Barragan arrived at the hacienda Salado with our men, where he found Captain Ugartechia sick, with our party. We had been quartered in a room opening upon a small courtyard, in which our guards were stationed. This courtyard adjoined a larger one on the south, from which it was separated by a dividing wall of about fifteen feet high, and in the latter our men were quartered. These quarters had no communication with ours except by the outer gates. Some few of our men obtained permission to accompany Colonel Barragan to visit us. Of these were Captain Ryan, Dr. Brennem, Captain Fitzgerald, Mr. Maxwell, and Edwards. Our men were highly elated at coming up with us; and the prospect of our uniting with them in an attempt to go home at once started the question anew of charging their guards. The men who visited us were requested to ascertain our opinions as to its practicability, &c. Colonel Fisher was opposed to the charge, but sent word to Captain Cameron *" to use his own good sense in the matter."* I was in favour of it, as I had uniformly been, and my plan of attack was freely communicated to Captains Ryan and Fitzgerald, and Dr. Brennem. They informed me that their plan was to charge at midnight. I opposed this hour, as being unpropitious for securing the horses of the cavalry, as they would most probably be out grazing, and recommended sunrise, at which time the horses would be herded. Captain Reese was opposed to the " break," as he informed me, because he thought we had advanced too far into the country. I told him I thought there would be no danger; that

ATTACK UPON THE GUARDS.

we should be strong enough to keep the road, and beat all the opposing force above Guerrero; that Fitzgerald and Van Ness had informed me the troops from San Fernando had been moved down to that point before they left the former place; that a few days rapid move on the main road would ensure success.

Our usual time of starting in the morning was half an hour after sunrise, and so soon as the main body of our men had succeeded in driving their guards, Captain Fitzgerald was to lead a party around the buildings, force our gate, and assist us, if necessary, against our guards. Captain Romano, contrary to our former custom, had started us about eight or ten minutes previous to sunrise. In this time we had proceeded about three fourths of a mile, when the sun made its appearance over the mountains. I was riding by the side of my old sailing-master, Lyon, and remarked, upon seeing the sun, that "if our boys were going to do anything, now was the time." I had barely made the remark when I heard the first gun. I knew what it meant, and exclaimed, "*We have them!*" The second, third, and fourth guns were fired before Captain Romano noticed it. He halted us, and sent his lieutenant, Aredondo, back to see what was the matter. Aredondo galloped back a few hundred yards, returned in great haste, and reported that the Texians had charged Colonel Barragan, and his troops were flying in every direction. This, however, we could plainly see: men, women, and children, infantry and cavalry, were scampering in every direction, hither and thither, leaving clouds of dust behind them.

Captain Romano ordered us on from the scene of action at full gallop, with his cavalry lances at a charge on each side of us. After going two or three hundred yards, we were halted and made to dismount. The firing had now become very brisk, and the excitement in our party intense: each had his speculations as to the result. I believed from the first that our men would prevail, with a loss not exceeding ten. Colonel Fisher believed that the attack was injudicious, and the whole of our men would be killed. Most of our party believed with me. At length a short pause was discernible in the firing; then it commenced brisker than ever, and in a few minutes another pause, which was quickly succeeded by a loud shout, which we knew to be Texian. This shout for the moment quieted our excitement, but it was to be quickly succeeded by one of more interest to us. At this time a lieutenant came up at full speed, with orders from Colonel Barragan to Captain Romano to shoot us and come immediately to his assistance. Both his countenance and actions showed determination to execute the order. He ordered his men to reprime their *escopetas* and make ready, which was instantly done. This was a critical moment, and it was necessary to be met with coolness and promptness upon our part. Colonel Fisher and myself asked him "if he was most bound to obey the orders of Governor Ortega, to take us to Mexico, or any subsequent order of Colonel Barragan;" and that we expected "we were in the hands of a gentleman and a soldier, not a murderer." His eyes were instantly lowered to the pommel of his saddle, and his countenance underwent hesitation, change, and satisfaction in as many seconds, when he raised himself in his stirrups, and, proudly clapping his hand upon his bosom, ordered the interpreter to say to the gentlemen "that they *are* in the hands of a *gentleman* and a *soldier*, and that *I* will carry out Governor Ortega's orders." Thus saying, our horses' heads were wheeled towards Mexico, and we forced on, at full speed, by the lancers on each side of us.

Our course was for many miles through a broad, level plain, with high mountains on each hand. Every dust rising in our rear—and we could see many miles upon our back road—made us believe that our lamented friend, Captain Fitzgerald, with a party of our men, were in pursuit to rescue us. This Captain F. had promised to do the previous night, in the event of our leaving before the attack; and the hope of which caused us to desire a slower pace, while the fear of it impelled Captain Romano forward. At this gait we were hurried twenty leagues to the town of Cidral, only stopping once for water.

We arrived at Cidral, which is a mining town,

containing about six thousand inhabitants, at four o'clock in the evening; and, notwithstanding the rapid gait we had travelled, the news from Salado preceded us. Most of the citizens we found in the street and public square, where we were halted several minutes. Here this dirty population heaped upon us their rich vocabulary of epithets: a favourite one was to call us "Jews;" for this ignorant population believe that every nation of white people who do not speak their language, and are not of their religion, had some immediate agency in killing their beloved Saviour. The only compassion we met was in the countenances of the females. In my intercourse with the world, I have had frequent occasion to observe that women were better than men; in Mexico this observation is forced upon you at every village.

To free us from the annoyance of the populace, Captain Romano ordered us to dismount and go into a room, around which he placed his cavalry to keep off the crowd. Here we remained for an hour, and were refreshed with some crackers, cheese, and a bottle of *vino mascal*, a common brandy made of the *maguey* plant, *Agave Americana*. Here Captain Romano determined to return to Salado, to assist, if possible, Colonel Barragan, and our party were turned over to the alcalde, to be sent immediately on to Mataguala, a city of fifteen thousand inhabitants, still three leagues farther ahead, as the town of Cidral would not be sufficient protection in case our men were to pursue us. We were hurried off under a guard of about thirty men, who were the most perfect savages we ever met before or since.

It was now night, with a fair moonlight, and from every demonstration these rascals intended to assassinate us before we reached Mataguala. On one occasion several of them cocked their guns, under pretence of shooting Sailing-master Lyon for not keeping in line, but were prevented by the interpreter saying that he was a sailor, and not used to riding. On another occasion they were in the act of thrusting their lances through Interpreter Henrie, when I caught his horse by the bridle and drew him up to my side. In this situation, Captain Romano and our old troop came up at full speed and relieved us. Captain R., learning the intention of these fellows after they had left Cidral, changed his determination of returning to Salado, and came to our rescue. Interpreter Henrie, knowing more of the language and intentions of these fellows, informed me that we were to be shot, and said that he wished to die as gloriously as possible, and therefore borrowed from the horn of my saddle a flask of *vino mascal*, into which he looked so long and deep that he had but little power of vision left, and would occasionally ride up against the guards. In this situation, they were about to spear him, when the timely arrival of Captain Romano prevented it. In coming up, our old guard, who, from two weeks' travel and intercourse with, had formed a warm attachment for us, congratulated us upon our escape from these fellows.

We arrived at Mataguala at nine o'clock at night, and found the whole population abroad to see us. We were hurried through the crowd, and quartered at a *meson*, tavern. Next morning old Colonel D. Matias d'Aquirre came to see us: this old veteran treated us with great kindness, ordered us to be removed to better quarters, and placed under special charge of a humane gentleman and an accomplished scholar, a lawyer by profession, D. Manuel Fernandez Palos. During our three days' stay in this city, we were furnished from the table of this gentleman with every luxury the city could afford.

We were here visited by all persons of distinction, among the rest the priest, a gentleman of superior intelligence and liberal feelings, who afterward sent us several rich viands from his table; also the Baron De Kawinsky, one of the travelling scientific corps of the Emperor of Russia, a gentleman of extensive acquirements, who has been for several years exploring the northern states of Mexico. This excellent old gentleman expressed for us the kind feelings of a father, and upon parting, insisted upon our taking some of his excellent tea, which we highly enjoyed during our trip to Mexico. Upon taking leave of him, we placed in his hands the following note.

"Mataguala, Feb. 14th, 1843.
" To the Baron De Kawinsky, of Russia.

" Sir,—As prisoners of war to the government of

Mexico, we beg to tender our warmest thanks for the kindness which you have manifested towards us during our short acquaintance.

"In prosecuting your scientific researches, should you find it convenient to visit our young republic, you will doubtless find many objects worthy of your notice, and the gentlemen of our country will be happy to extend to you the kind feelings of your humble servants."

On our first arrival at Mataguala, Captain Romano and troop went back to see what had become of Colonel Barragan, and we were turned over to the authorities of the place. On the third day after he returned with the intelligence that our men had defeated Barragan, dispersed his troops, took his horses, arms, munitions of war, and money, and made their way homeward.

In leaving Mataguala on February 15th, which we did under the escort of the first gentlemen of the place, we addressed Colonel Aquirre and Don Palos the following note:

"Mataguala, Feb. 14th, 1843.

"To Don Matias Martin D'Aquirre and Don Manuel Fernandez Palos and others.

"Gentlemen,—Before our departure from your city, we beg to express to yourselves particularly, and, through you, to the officers and citizens who have had us in charge, our heartfelt gratitude for the many kindnesses extended us during the few days we have remained here.

"To conquer in the field of battle depends much upon the chances of war; to temper that victory with generosity and humanity requires the exercise of those high moral qualities which constitute man superior to all other creatures. You, sirs, have given us a bright example of that superiority.

"It has been our fortune to enter your country, in solemn duty to the requirements of our own, as political enemies; we fought you as men, and since, through the chances of war, we have become your captives, we submit with the philosophy of men.

"Please, gentlemen, accept the highest considerations and esteem of your very obedient servants."

The good old colonel, to make the time of our party the lighter—for, says he, "I have three times been a prisoner"—sent us a bundle of English books from his hacienda, which met us on the road. To fall into the hands of such an officer is to rob war of its most rugged features; and if the young officers of the Mexican nation had half the sensibility, magnanimity, and humanity of the old ones, this war might have been conducted with the most high-toned spirit of chivalry; whereas, their repeated acts of perfidy, treachery, and brutality must force us to retaliate, as the only recource of justice and safety.

We return to the 11th of February, 1843, with a national pride which no other circumstance of our Revolution can inspire; and it should be an ever-memorable day in the history of Texian liberty,

TEXIAN CHARGE UPON THE CHAPPS AND VICTORY OF SALADO.

alike honourable to the country for the spirit in which that glorious movement was planned and executed. As our men advanced farther into the country, the more oppressive became the conduct of those under whose charge they were. On sundry occasions, the Mexican soldiers had been permitted to beat several of them: this was in such gross violation of our articles of capitulation, and afforded such a precious foretaste of "*Mexican magnanimity,*" that they determined not to let slip this last opportunity of regaining their liberty; and the prospect of having their officers with them in the glorious enterprise determined the blow. Among the privates foremost in the charge, as well as in bringing about the result—and to their lasting honour we record their names—were Dr. R. F. Brennem, S. H. Walker, J. D. Cooke, Colonel William F. Wilson, Patrick Lyons, and others. The officers were generally in favour of the attempt; and at the appointed time, the lamented Cameron, with a quiet coolness peculiar to him in trying emergencies, raised his hat, and giving it a gentle flourish in the air, said, in a distinct tone, a little mixed with his Highland brogue, "*Well, boys, we will go it!*" Thus saying, and suiting the action to the word, he grappled one of the sentinels at the inner door of their prison-yard, while S. H. Walker seized the other. It was the work of an instant to upset and disarm these, and get possession of the outer court, where the arms and cartridge boxes were guarded by one hundred and fifty infantry. These men were quickly driven out or made to surrender; and while our men were arming themselves and securing ammunition, the cavalry had formed in front of the outer gate, which was also guarded by the company of "Red Caps." In charging through this gate to drive this company and the cavalry, poor Doctor Brennem and Patrick Lyons fell, and several others were wounded. That portion of the cavalry which was mounted quickly fell back beyond the reach of our fire, while the "Red Caps" retreated round the main wall of the buildings to the south, through the gate into the courtyard which our party had just before left. A portion of our men pressed around to force this gate, believing still that we were in our quarters. Here Captain Fitzgerald received his death-wound, and John Stansbury, quite a boy, had his left eye shot out. The company of "Red Caps" soon capitulated, and gave up their arms; the only condition which our men required of Colonel Barragan, in releasing them, was, that our wounded should be treated kindly.

We had three killed, Dr. Brennem, Lyon, and Rice; Captain Fitzgerald and John Higgerson mortally wounded, and died soon after; Captain J. R. Baker, privates Stansbury, Hancock, Trehern, and Harvey, wounded. The enemy's loss was nine or ten killed, and many more badly wounded. From the difficulty of getting arms in the commencement of the action, it was not possible that more than one half of our two hundred and fourteen men, with the exception of those who fought with brickbats, could have been engaged.

When the main body of our men were marched from Matamoras, a negro fellow by the name of Sawney, who some years before had absconded from Texas, and taken up his abode in that city, seeing that it was a good chance for him to speculate off of his old acquaintances, followed them on to this place, and on the route swindled all who dealt with him for *chilé, tortillas, frijoles,* &c. No sooner, however, did the Texians charge their guards, than he exclaimed, "This is no place for Sawney!" and, very wisely, did not wait to suit the action to the words, for his double-quick time had already preceded his prudent conclusion; and well it did, as he would have paid dearly for his peculations and insolence had he been taken.

Thus it was that the Texians gave the world another evidence of their superiority over the Mexicans, when one hundred unarmed men charged three hundred with arms, beat them, disarmed them, and then turned them loose as harmless things.

CHAPTER XII.

Our Men take up the March for Home.—Departure from Plan of Retreat by turning into the Mountains.—Unexampled Suffering.—Killing their Horses for Food.—Many Die, and others Surrender.—Marched back to Saltillo.—March to Salado.—Decimation, and dying Words.—Our Wounded, and those who remained with them.—March from Mataguala. — Arrival at Count Zivyes. — Kind Treatment. — Arrival at San Luis Potosi.—Treatment there.—Correspondence with the Governor.—Notes to Captains Romano and Reyes.—The Valley of San Luis, Mode of drawing Water, &c.

At 10 o'clock A.M., one hundred and ninety-three of our men took up the line of march homeward, leaving eighteen behind, including the wounded, besides three killed. At 12 o'clock at night they reached the hacienda San Salvador, a distance of fifty-three miles; bought corn, and fed their horses: proceeded twelve miles farther on, and slept about two hours before daybreak. The remnant of the enemy's cavalry, under Colonel Barragan, which had escaped from Salado, kept in sight in the rear, but manifested no disposition to come near.

February 12th. They marched early in the morning, leaving the Saltillo road at 10 o'clock A.M., and bearing their course to the left for the Zacetecar road, which they struck in about ten miles; thence turning to the left for the purpose of obtaining water at a hacienda then in sight, they found the water-tank near the house, which was defended by a few regular troops, who hoisted a red flag, and commenced a fire upon them at about two hundred yards distant. Captain Cameron, having determined not to be detained by any engagement which could be avoided, filed to the right, receiving no other injury except having one horse wounded. He directed his course northward to a trail which he discovered leading over the mountain, which was very rough. In descending, found water enough for a drink all round, which was truly a God-send, as we he had been twenty hours without a drop. In six miles came to water at a rancho, where we found the men in arms, but did not molest them: inquiring the Comargo road, we proceeded on without any intention of taking it: continued our course west, and after descending a mountain into a deep valley, at 3 o'clock in the morning laid down to rest, and here took a Mexican spy.

February 13th. Marched early, taking the spy with us, course still west; at eight miles came to water, and thence proceeded on; struck the Montclova road, leading from Saltillo, about thirty-five miles from the latter place. Here we encountered a European, a friend of ours, who told our troops by all means to keep the road, directing them where they would be well received ahead. Had the advice of this man been kept, the whole party would doubtless have succeeded in reaching their homes; but our men, from sad experience, had been taught to believe that treachery was in every mouth in Mexico, and the more timid insisted upon leaving the road and taking to the mountains. At about 12 o'clock M. crossed a small creek, and sent Interpreter Brennem with our Mexican spy to buy some beef and corn from a rancho near by, where the Mexican was detained and Brennem ordered off, otherwise he would be fired upon. Cameron marched within a gunshot of the rancho, not molesting anything, when a woman came out and inquired "if any of *Jordan's* men were along;" and being told "there were," she replied that "if they would vouch for the good conduct of the rest, the whole should be accommodated at the rancho with whatever they wished." They, however, continued their course without returning an answer, when very soon after the proprietor of the rancho overtook them, and expressed regret that he had mistaken their intentions, and pointed out a good place near the road to graze and rest their horses. At sunset again they took up the line of march, but left the road at 8 o'clock to repose, when they were fired on by a small party of Mexicans. Proceeding a little farther, Captain Cameron was influenced to leave the road entirely and take to the mountains, contrary to his instructions and his own better judgment, as we have before stated, but induced to do so by the more timid of the officers and men.

February 14th. Directed their course through the mountains; travelled hard, making little progress, the country being too rough for the horses to get on, except with slow pace; found no water, and

camped for the night in a deep ravine. This day they passed a shepherd with a large flock of sheep, who informed them that they would find no water in the direction they were travelling, which should have been a sufficient warning to return to the road.

February 15th. Some of the men found water about one and a half miles from camp. Here they determined to kill their fattest horses and mules, jerk the meat for food, and take it on foot. The saddle flaps were turned into sandals to protect their feet from the rocks and thorns. Here was a scene of grand moral sublimity: freemen, who for the love of country and liberty had voluntarily reduced themselves to the last state of human sufferance, still cheerful under the bright hope of liberty; and when pressed by nature's extremest wants, putting their knives into the hearts' blood of their good horses with a melancholy regret which showed they had no option! So, having stationed sentinels upon the peaks of the highest adjoining mountains, they led their horses and asses down into the ravine, and commenced the mournful task. In doing so, no language can describe the feelings of these bold men—men who in battle had killed their scores of Mexicans without winking—when they stood with unsheathed knives beside their faithful animals, they found that their bursting hearts had unnerved their arms. Many turned from the effort and wept, while others, as much affected, performed the bloody deed in conscientious duty to their families.

X

their country, and liberty. The lamentable groans of the poor horses, as the keen steel would press to the heart's core, was distressingly painful to hear. Some, in the agonies of death, would squeal and flounder, while others would seem to look upon their masters in deep sorrow, and press against the fatal blade. This never-to-be-forgotten scene was the work of a portion of this day, as some built scaffolds with fire underneath to dry the meat, while others butchered, and some went with gourds still deeper into the ravine for water. At 3 o'clock P. M. the water was so nearly exhausted that the men could not fill their gourds, when the march was recommenced. At 10 o'clock P.M. camped in a deep ravine without water.

February 16th. The course of our men still north. This day several were left on the road exhausted for the want of water, and here they commenced, unfortunately, the use of the palmetto juice as a substitute.

February 17th. Marched early in the morning. At 12 o'clock M. discovered some Mexican spies in a large valley, the course of our men being northward across it. At 9 o'clock encamped without water, a number of our men keeping on, and bearing more to the eastward in hopes of finding some spring.

February 18th. No signal from any of the water-hunters: the course still across the valley. Now much dissatisfaction prevailed as to the course most likely to find water. Most of the men were now unable to travel, and halted to rest, when Captain Cameron, with about fifty men, continued on a short distance, bearing more to the west. They also had to stop during the heat of the day. At this time his party were also undetermined what course to take, as several parties had been left behind, and sent out in different directions to find water. The main body, as they scattered over the valley to screen themselves from the burning sun, would spread their blankets upon the thorn-bushes and get underneath them. They now would fain have drank

> "The stale of horses, and the gilded puddle
> Which beast would cough at;"

but neither had they: their good horses, too, had paid the tribute of their lives. In vain did they recollect Mark Antony's sufferings in the Alps, and the Arab tales of taking drink from the bowels of their faithful camels: it was but to augment their own sufferings. In the delirium of consuming fevers they sought

> "The roughest berry on the rudest hedge."

Some were chewing and eating negro-head and prickly-pear leaves, to produce moisture in their mouths, but these astringents greatly aggravated their sufferings; while others, with tongues so parched and swollen that they could not close their mouths, were scratching in the shade of bushes for cool earth to apply to their throats and stomachs;

yet, even yet, their sufferings were to be increased. Wild delirium seized upon those who had most freely used the astringent plants, and in their last agony they had recourse to their own urinary secretion. This was drinking living fire! and this they knew, for many were men of education; but still they drank and drank! Several expired, and all prayed for death to relieve them. To all who may chance to see these pages, and hereafter be in a similar situation, either by land or sea, recollect these facts, that it is far better to die without this last recourse, for the phosphate of lime contained in this liquid produces a consuming agony far worse than death without it.

At 1 o'clock P.M. discovered a large smoke to the right, and at first supposed it to be a signal from some of their water-hunters, and sent a messenger to Captain Cameron to inform him. At this time, most of the men, from pure inability to carry them, threw away their arms, and late in the evening started for the smoke. Some would stop to get the juice of plants to keep them from expiring, while every fifteen or twenty minutes others would have to rest. About 8 o'clock at night those in advance approached near enough to the fires to ascertain it to be a Mexican cavalry camp. They endeavoured to get around it, but found the pass ahead of them guarded by another camp of the enemy. It was now daylight, and our men, scattered, exhausted, and without arms, had no other alternative but to surrender to a force which, if they had kept the road, as was the original plan, they could have easily beaten; and had they pursued the original plan, at this time they would have been safe in Texas. Before, however, Captain Cameron surrendered his party to Governor-general Mexier, he demanded and received the positive promise that all should be treated as "*prisoners of war*," and, so far as he was concerned, they were so treated.

February 19th. The Mexicans continued to bring our men in by small parties. They remained here until the 22d, by which time they had one hundred and thirty four of our men prisoners, and then marched for Saltillo. These Mexicans showed humanity in not letting our men drink too much water, which, if they had permitted, must have proved fatal. They also furnished them with plenty of beef, and a small quantity of wood to cook it with; but, being tied with rawhide cords in pairs, and having the use of only one hand, they made but poor cooks.

February 23d, being the second day from the pass in the mountains, they reached a rancho, where they found Dr. M Math, Holderman, and Tawney. Here they remained on the 24th and 25th, when about thirty more of our men were brought in. The nights now being cold, the Mexicans having robbed our men of money, blankets, and clothing, they suffered greatly.

February 26th. Marched twenty miles, and

camped in a cowpen at a rancho. Now our prisoners had increased to one hundred and sixty, and the sick were permitted to ride upon "*burros*" (jackasses).

February 27th. Our men were whipped several times for untying the rawhide cords which sorely bound their limbs. Marched twenty-four miles to San Antonio, where the rawhide cords were exchanged for iron handcuffs. Notwithstanding this precaution, the Mexicans showed great apprehension lest another charge would be made upon them, for they would not allow the Texians to stand up in camp. Under all these cruelties, our men bore up with astonishing fortitude. They received their irons with smiles, promised a fair remuneration the first opportunity, and concluded the evening's entertainment by telling old tales and singing, to the utter astonishment of their captors.

February 28th. They marched twenty miles, and encamped at bad water. March 1st. Started early; got no water until they reached the suburbs of the town, where for the first time they were permitted to wash their faces, which were, as one may easily imagine, awfully dirty. Here they were halted for the governor to come up, while great preparations were making in the city to receive him. Our men were marched in under the ringing of bells, the firing of crackers, &c., and kept standing in the public square during the delivery of the victor's eulogium; after which they were marched into their filthy prison, infested with vermin, without anything this day to eat.

March 2d. Received their welcome breakfast at 10 o'clock. 3d. Waters and Torry were brought in and ironed together; also the two Sargeants, who had been several days in town. 5th. Ten more of our men brought in. On the following day received a donation of tobacco from a citizen—a most welcome present. 7th. Private Ackerman was brought in; had reached within sixty miles of the Rio Grande before he was taken. 9th. Petitioned the governor for more rations, and to one meal per day he added coffee. This evening, B. Bryan, an amiable young man and a good soldier, died from a cold received in sleeping without a blanket. 10th. Nothing important occurred, except the comet was discernible, which was at first seen a few nights previous, and which made the superstitious Mexicans very uneasy, for they are ever expecting something terrible to overtake their misdeeds. 12th. They were visited in prison by some Americans and Lipan Indians, who were not permitted to speak with the men. To-day five of the sick were baptized by a priest, and these men were afterward treated with more kindness by the citizens. They refused to render poor Bryan any assistance, because he would not be baptized by them, but let him die for want of necessaries. They now learned that an order had arrived from Mexico to shoot every tenth man, which the governor and citizens refused to execute, and petitions were sent back praying that they might be released, both on account of their magnanimous conduct at Salado and on their retreat. Captain Cameron was now treated with unusual kindness, the Mexicans in Saltillo declaring that they loved him for his bravery and magnanimity. 18th. Joseph Watkins and Wright were brought in, found near Montclova, having laid down to die for the want of water; were taken to the town of *Quarto Sinicas*, where they were treated kindly, after having been robbed of everything they had. On the 19th and 20th the examination of our interpreters took place about the attack at Salado, Colonel Barragan's conduct, &c., &c.

March 21st. The cavalry arrived from San Luis Potosi to guard our men to the city of Mexico. In the mean time, an order had reached Saltillo from Santa Anna to shoot the whole of our men, which was also disobeyed by Governor Mexier.

On the 22d they took up the line of march under command of Colonel Ortis. That night they reached *Aqua Nuevo*.

On the 23d marched fourteen leagues to San Salvador. Here their handcuffs were examined, being ironed in pairs, a right and left hand of each two closely fastened with large irons, and the sick also ironed. Now they began to suspect something wrong, but still hoped otherwise.

On the 24th marched eleven leagues. On the 25th marched early, and arrived at the Salado about

2 o clock P.M. Soon after they arrived, our men received the melancholy intelligence that they were to be decimated, and each tenth man shot.

It was now too late to resist this horrible order. Our men were closely ironed and drawn up in front of all their guards, with arms in readiness to fire. Could they have known it previously, they would have again charged their guards, and made them dearly pay for this last perfidious breach of national faith. It was now too late! A manly gloom and a proud defiance pervaded all countenances. They had but one alternative, and that was to invoke their country's vengeance upon their murderers, consign their souls to God, and die like men. Could these martyrs in liberty's cause, who so proudly yielded up their lives for their country, have known that their President had endorsed their execution by the most villanous of all falsehoods, declaring them brigands—great God! what would have been their feelings!

The decimator, Colonel Domingo Huerta, who was especially nominated to this black deed after Governor Mexier refused its execution, had arrived at Salado ahead of our men. The "*Red-cap*" company were to be their executioners; those men whose lives had been so humanely spared by our men at this place on the 11th of February.

The decimation took place by the drawing of black and white beans from a small earthen mug. The white ones signified *exemption*, and the black *death*. One hundred and fifty-nine white beans were placed in the bottom of the mug, and seventeen black ones placed upon the top of them. The beans were not stirred, and had so slight a shake that it was perfectly clear they had not been mixed together. Such was their anxiety to execute Captain Cameron, and perhaps the balance of the officers, that first Cameron, and afterward they, were made to draw a bean each from the mug in this condition.

The opposite plate, sketched by Charles M‘Laughlin, who was an eyewitness, and so fortunate as to draw clear, represents the gallant Cameron in the act of drawing first. He said, with his usual coolness, "Well, boys, we have to draw, let's be at it;" so saying, he thrust his hand into the mug, and drew out a white bean. Next came Colonel Wm. F. Wilson, who was chained to him; then Captain Wm. Ryan, and then Judge F. M. Gibson, all of whom drew white beans. Next came Captain Eastland, who drew the first black one, and then came the balance of the men. They all drew their beans with that manly dignity and firmness which showed them superior to their condition. Some of lighter temper jested over the bloody tragedy. One would say, "Boys, this beats raffling all to pieces;" another would say that "this is the tallest gambling scrape I ever was in," and such like remarks. None showed change of countenance; and as the black beans failed to depress, so did the white fail to elate.

The knocking off the irons from the unfortunate alone told who they were. Poor Robert Beard, who lay upon the ground near by exceedingly ill, and nearly exhausted from his forced marches and sufferings, called his brother William, who was bringing him a cup of water, and said, "Brother, if you draw a black bean, I'll take your place; I want to die." The brother, with overwhelming anguish, said, "No! I will keep my own place; I am stronger, and better able to die than you." These noble youths both drew clear, but both soon after died, leaving this last Roman legacy to their venerable parents in Texas. Several of the Mexican officers who officiated in this cruel violation of their country's faith expressed great dissatisfaction thereat, and some wept bitterly. Soon after, the fated were placed in a separate courtyard, where about dark they were executed.

Several of our men were permitted to visit the unfortunate previously to the execution, to receive their dying requests. Poor Major Cocke, when he first drew the fatal bean, held it up between his forefinger and thumb, and with a smile of contempt, said, "Boys, I told you so; I never failed in my life to draw a prize;" and then he said to Judge Gibson, "Well, judge, say to my friends that I died in grace." The judge, much affected at this last sad parting, showed it from his tears. The major replied, "They only rob me of forty years," and then sat down and wrote a sensible and dignified letter of remonstrance to General Waddy Thompson, the United States minister in Mexico; and knowing that his remains would be robbed of his clothes after his death, drew off his pantaloons, handed them to his surviving comrades, and died in his underclothes.

Poor Henry Whaling, one of Cameron's best fighters, as he drew his black bean, said, with as bright a look as ever lighted man's countenance, "Well, they don't make much off me, any how, for I know I have killed twenty-five of the yellow-bellies;" then demanding his dinner in a firm tone, and saying that "they shall not cheat me out of it," he ate heartily, smoked a cigar, and in twenty minutes after was launched into eternity! The Mexicans said that this man had the biggest heart of any they ever saw. They shot him fifteen times before he expired!

Poor Torrey, quite a youth, but in spirit a giant, said that "he was perfectly willing to meet his fate; that for the glory of his country he had fought, and for her glory he was willing to die;" and turning to the officer, said, "After the battle of San Jacinto, my family took one of your prisoner youths, raised and educated him, and this is our requital."

Edward Este spoke of his fate with the coolest indifference, and said that he would rather be shot than dragged along in this manner. Cash said, "Well, they murdered my brother with Colonel Fannin, and they are about to murder me."

J. L. Jones said to the interpreter, " Tell the officer to look upon men who are not afraid to die for their country."

Captain Eastland behaved with the most patriotic dignity; he desired that his country should not particularly avenge his death, but for her own honour he implored her never to lay down her arms until the most ample reparation and her unconditional freedom should be secured. He said, "I know that some have thought me timid, but, thank God! death has no terrors for me." Major Robert Dunham said " he was prepared to die, and would to God that he had a chance to do the same thing over again; that he gloried in the demonstration they had made, which showed Texians without arms to be more than equal to Mexicans with them." James Ogden, with his usual equanimity of temper, smiled at his fate, and said, " I am prepared."

Young Robert W. Harris behaved in the most unflinching manner, and called upon his companions to avenge the murder, while their flowing tears and bursting hearts, invoking heaven for their witness, responded to the call. I have the utmost confidence that this pledge, so solemnly plighted, will be redeemed.

They one and all invoked their country to do both them and herself justice. Captain Cameron, in taking his leave of these brave men, and particularly of Turnbull, a brother Scotchman, with whom he had been in many dangers, wept bitterly, and implored the officers to execute him and spare his men.

Just previous to the firing they were bound together with cords, and their eyes being bandaged, they were set upon a log near the wall, with their backs to their executioners. They all begged the officer to shoot them in front, and at a short distance; that "they were not afraid to look death in the face." This he refused; and, to make his cruelty as refined as possible, fired at several paces, and continued the firing from ten to twelve minutes, lacerating and mangling these heroes in a manner too horrible for description.

Our interpreter, who was permitted to remain with them to the last, says that "fifteen times they wounded that iron-nerved soul, Henry Whaling; and it would seem that Providence had a special care in prolonging his existence, that he might demonstrate to his enemies the national character they had to contend with; for he gritted his teeth at and defied them in terms of withering reproach, until they placed a gun to his head and blew his brains against the wall. Such was the effect of this horrible massacre upon their own soldiers, who were stationed as a guard upon the wall above, that one of them fainted, and came near falling over, but was caught by his comrades.

During the martyrdom of these noble patriots, the main body of our men were separated from them by a stone wall of some fifteen feet high, and heard

THE MEMORABLE 11TH OF FEBRUARY. 175

their last agonized groans with feelings of which it would be mockery to attempt the description. The next morning, as they were marched on the road to Mexico, they passed the mangled bodies of their dead comrades, whose bones now lie bleaching upon the plains of Salado, a perishing remembrance of exalted patriotism, but a lasting one of the infamy of their President, Sam Houston, who caused them to be falsely executed as robbers and marauders upon Mexico.

We repeat that we look upon the 11th of February, 1843, with unspeakable national pride; and had we been with our men on that occasion, I would have preferred, and it would have been vastly more to the honour of myself and country, to have perished in that attempt to regain our liberty, than to have tamely submitted to such slavery. Those who have denounced it as a "piece of moon-struck madness," perhaps in their judgments they are sustained by the uninformed, on account of our men departing from the original plan of keeping the main road home. The calculation both of success in battle and the reasonableness of reaching home were maturely made; and we repeat, without the fear of contradiction, that, had that plan of operation been pursued by keeping the main road, on the 19th, which was nine days after their victory at Salado, our men would have been safe in Texas. We knew the fact from Captain Fitzgerald and Messrs. Van Ness and Hancock, that all their regular forces at San Fernando had been marched down to Guerrero, and that before said forces could be informed from Salado, and then marched back to our crossing above the Precidio of the Rio Grande, our men would be far in Texas. We also knew the fact that it would be impossible to get any sufficient citizen force to attack them. These calculations were fully justified from the result that, 1st. Nine days after the battle, both Governor Mexier and Ortega had only four hundred and twenty men to intercept them, a force which, had our men kept together in the road, would never have approached them.

2dly. That on this road, and in sight of the city of Saltillo, Colonel Jordan, three years since, with one hundred and fourteen men, only ninety-three of whom were effective, fought General Vascus and one thousand five hundred troops, defeated him, and made good his retreat, in the face of this pursuing force, into Texas, with a loss of eight men.

3dly. That only two years since one hundred and fifty miserable Comanche Indians put the town of Saltillo under tribute, and were supplied with every requisition.

With these facts before us, will any except the "moon-struck" pretend to say that our two hundred and twenty-one men at Salado, who had performed such wonderful deeds of valour, could not do half what Jordan and his ninety-three did, or could not do what a few wretched Comanches had frequently done?

We return again to the battle of Salado, to inquire after our wounded and those who remained with them. Of the wounded, Higgerson died soon after our main body had taken the road home. Captains Fitzgerald and Baker, and privates Stansbury and Hancock, were placed in a rough cart and started to Mexico, with Captain Reese and those who were not wounded, but who refused to return home with the balance of the men. Fitzgerald died the second day, and was hauled from the cart before the vital spark had left his body, and thrown upon the prairie to the wolves and vultures.

We rarely knew so brave a man and so good a soldier as was Captain F., an Irishman by birth. He had served as captain in the "Peninsular War" under General Evans, where he had distinguished himself, and came to Texas, as he informed the writer, "because ours was the most just cause in which he could engage." He deserves the sympathy of all brave men, and the lasting gratitude of our country. The balance of this party, in all sixteen, were, under charge of Colonel Ortis, carried to San Luis Potosi, which place they reached the 26th of February, where they overtook our party, which had been detained here several days.

Captain Reese and his party have been severely censured by many of his comrades for not joining them in their attempt to reach home, and some have ascribed the worst of motives for his not so doing. Captain R. is too tried a soldier and devoted a patriot to allow a suspicion either of want of bravery or patriotism. It has been his good fortune, with his late brother, who fell fighting for Texas, to have been in every battle from the taking of San Antonio in 1835, in all of which they were distinguished for their bravery. The writer has been with him in several trying situations, and few men, on all occasions, have evidenced such cool bravery. Had he never given any other evidence than in his scaling the walls of Perote, and successfully making his way through an enemy's country many hundred miles, it would have been sufficient to have stamped him as a man of uncommon fortitude and daring. Captain Reese was opposed to the assault at Salado, because, as he says, he honestly doubted the success of the men in reaching their homes. But while the assault was going on, he exposed himself as much as any one in causing the Mexicans to give up their arms; and after our men were victorious, he determined to share their fate, provided he could get his younger brother William, who was quite a lad, to remain. William resolved he would follow him, and this determined the captain to remain; to which he yielded more on his account and that of his parents, who looked to him to take care of the youth, than his own.

Our party, under charge of Captain Romano, proceeded from Mataguala on the San Luis Potosi road, and on the 17th of February reached the hacienda of Count Zivyes. This gentleman has a large estate, lives in superior style, and treated us with the most bountiful hospitality. Instead of eating our humble fare of *tortillas* and *frijoles*, we were invited night and morning to his mansion, and had a dozen covers for our meals. This unsolicited, unexpected hospitality, to use a Texas expression, "looked so much like the white settlements" that it warmly attached this excellent gentleman to us. He took great pains in showing us through his extensive buildings, and all the appurtenances belonging to the establishment, particularly his farming utensils, which we found to be exceedingly crude, at least one hundred years behind Texas in this respect. He was a gentleman of liberal education, but educated in Spain, the wrong place to make a good farmer. He seemed sensible of this, and showed us several English works upon agriculture. Stock is the principal produce of this large estate of forty-five leagues. He showed us a large number of horses and mules, and some of the best native horses we saw in Mexico. He appears very anxious to improve them by fine American breeds, and seemed astonished at our knowledge of blooded pedigree. Upon inquiring as to the extent of his stock, he remarked that "there were many larger stock estates in Mexico; that he had twenty-seven hundred brood mares, which required sixty-eight stallions, and about fifty jacks to serve, as they did not allow more than twenty-five to each; ten thousand black cattle, and forty thousand sheep.

Stock of all kinds are very cheap in Mexico, and we fear we lost credit with the count by telling him the immense high prices at which our best bloods sold for in the United States; but perhaps we are in more danger now, by telling of his immense numbers. We parted reluctantly from the count, after extorting a promise from him to visit our country as soon as the war should end, and he desiring us to call freely upon him for every necessary in Mexico.

February 18th. Marched for San Luis Potosi, a distance of thirty leagues, which place we reached on the 20th; kept standing in the street, opposite the governor's quarters, in the hot sun, without permission to dismount, about twenty minutes, when we were marched off to a room in the hospital barracks. Being exceedingly fatigued, the sun having been excessively hot, and the dust in the road almost suffocating, we had procured a flask of *vino mascal*, when a corporal stepped up, and, in the most contemptuous manner, took it from us: this privilege had never before been denied us. In a few minutes we heard Colonel Terris order a sentinel to lock us up: this was done with as little ceremony as the taking away of our flask. Upon our remonstrance, the governor had our door unlocked, and promised a reprimand to the old brute. We remained in this city eight days, in which time the following correspondence was held with the governor:

"Prison, San Luis Potosi,
February 22d, 1843.

"To his Excellency the Commander-in-chief
of the Department of San Luis Potosi:

"Sir,—The letter addressed to your excellency on the 19th instant by General Fisher being unanswered, and no farther notice taken thereof, to the knowledge of the undersigned, than a verbal inquiry through an officer to know what was desired, makes it necessary that we should most reluctantly trouble you with another communication. We have a sufficient knowledge of the world to know how difficult is the approach to power in different countries; and in laying our complaints before your excellency from this uncomfortable prison, we make much allowance that the truth will always reach you, surrounded as you are by such a succession of officials.

"We should be recreant in duty to ourselves and to our own country, as well as to those illustrious governments which have formally acknowledged the nationality of Texas and the whole civilized world, to permit in silence a violation, in our own persons, of those wholesome laws which have been adopted for ages throughout all Christendom. And we most respectfully protest that being your prisoners of war, and incarcerated with all the indignity of state criminals, can in the least possible degree derogate from the character in which we capitulated, which we occupy in our country, and which the exalted governments of Great Britain, France, Belgium, and the United States recognise. At the same time, we do not pretend to assert that the violation of those laws are by order of your excellency; yet it is due that you should be correctly informed thereof, and we have the utmost confidence that such is not the desire of the illustrious men at the head of your government.

"Upon our arrival in your city, after a fatiguing ride of ten leagues beneath a hot sun, we were locked up in this prison, with the bare walls for furniture. We were about to refresh ourselves with a glass of "vino mascal," and even that was denied us. Some short time after we were favoured with the light of heaven, and permitted the use of spirits, for which was substituted quadruple guards within these high walls and without, so that we cannot, without intrusion, go one step to perform even the common offices of nature. Without a chair or bed to sit or lie upon, our apartment is made a guardroom, which bayoneted sentinels pace during the whole night, uttering every few minutes the most unearthly exclamations, as if the luxury of the brick pavement was too good a bed for us: these, with the "magnanimous" allowance of fifty cents per day for our support, is the situation in which we are at present.

"We protest that this treatment is wholly inconsistent with the magnanimity of any civilized nation under the sun, and we cannot believe it has the sanction of one occupying the exalted station of your excellency. Were such our belief, what a commentary would it be upon your high official station, that indignity, insult, and injury are heaped upon us because we had bravely done our duty to our country!

"We farther protest that it is not in the history of the English people, nor their descendants, the people of the United States, of whom we proudly acknowledge ourselves, that the honour of a general officer has been violated by breach of parole; and if your excellency rightly understands this national character, you will acknowledge this honour is more binding than the criminal's chains. We therefore most respectfully look to your excellency for an extension of those rights which not only our articles of capitulation, but the laws of civilized warfare, guaranty to us. In conclusion, we beg leave to inform your excellency, that when we left Matamoras it was under a positive promise from General Ampudia, to whom we capitulated, that we should be sent with all possible despatch, in advance of the other prisoners, to your capital. We doubt not, when your excellency is informed of a promise made with the representative of the Mexican government, you will take the earliest means of carrying it out.

"With considerations of high regard, we subscribe ourselves your excellency's obedient servants."

After we sent the above letter to the governor, we experienced much better treatment from our guards.

Before leaving the city, Captain Romano called to bid us adieu, and as a testimonial of his good conduct and kind treatment to us, we addressed him the following note:

"San Luis Potosi, February 20th, 1843.
"To Captain Herman Romano, Mexican Army:

"Sir,—Before separating with you, permit us to tender our warmest and heartfelt acknowledgments for the many courtesies you have extended towards us as prisoners of war since we have been under your charge.

It is a prominent part of the constitution of the brave to feel for the misfortunes of the brave: this feeling has marked you out, in our estimation, as eminently entitled to your government's confidence; for, at the same time that you have been kind and generous to us, you have performed your duty with firmness and dignity towards her. The coward has no feelings in common with the brave: their sentiments can never assimilate; they are essentially different; the one glories in generosity to a fallen foe, while the other delights in a tyrannical authority when placed beyond accountability.

"That you may meet with that honourable promotion which you deserve, and a safe return to your family and friends, is the sincere desires of your obedient humble servants."

While in this city we had been several days under the immediate charge of Captain Reyes, an old veteran, who, above thirty years previous, fought under Hidalgo, and from him we received also kind treatment, which we acknowledged in the following note :

"San Luis Potosi, February 28th, 1843.

" To Captain José Marie Reyes, Mexican Army.

" Sir,—Before leaving your city, permit us to tender you our warmest thanks for the kind and humane treatment we have received at your hands while prisoners of war under your immediate charge.

" One of your long experience, who has grown gray in the most honourable and chivalrous of all professions, can rightly estimate the feelings of a brother-soldier when his fortunes are reversed by the chances of war. Of this you have given us the most honourable proof, by which you have made us your debtors, and secured our lasting gratitude. Please accept our fervent and best wishes for your continued health and prosperity. Very respectfully your obedient servants."

The city of San Luis Potosi is a large and beautiful place, and the capital of the state of that name. Its population has greatly decreased since the commencement of the revolution in 1809. It is situated in an extensive plain, surrounded by high mountains, and the cultivation carried on, and the cattle watered from numerous wells worked by mules. These wells are usually deep, and dug in the form of a parallelogram; the mode of raising the water has been greatly improved since the Honourable Joel R. Poinsett travelled through this country in 1822. It is, however, exceedingly simple, and might be used with great advantage in many portions of the United States. A mule, blindfolded (for almost everything is hoodwinked in that country), is hitched to a shaft which turns a perpendicular spindle, to which is attached a crude vertical cog wheel, working a drum over which a leather band is passed, and upon which is attached small buckets, one foot apart, upon the plan of elevators in a flour mill. This band extends to the water, be the well deep or shallow. The water is consequently passed over the drum, and falls into a trough, which conducts it to an extensive reservoir, from which the cattle and farm are supplied. The hoodwinked animal works his day without a driver, and is then turned upon the common to recuperate, while a fresh one is hitched in his place, and thus a perpetual stream of water is poured forth from these numerous wells.

CHAPTER XIII.

MARCH TO THE CAPITAL UNDER COLONEL TERRIS.

Hacienda de Plata.—Bad Treatment.—Xaral, Marquis of.—Horses taken from us.—Made to walk over the Mountain.—Our Remonstrances with the Colonel.—Billy Reese and the Catholic Crosses.—Bugler, his Wife, and Sister.—Suffer for Water.—Punishment of a Soldier.—Dolores.—Hidalgo.—Calleja.—San Miguel el Grande.—Hacienda of the Jesuits.—Burned Hacienda.—Lodged in a Stable.—The Comet.—Superstition concerning it.—Mexicans meet Danger with a Prayer.—Cruel Treatment.—Mexican Officers.—Lasso.—Lice.—Fleas: Advantage of.—Locked up.—Protest.—Quartered in a Corral.—Villanous Conduct of the Colonel.—Valley of Mexico.—Arrival at Tacubaya.—Description of.—General Jackson's Birthday.—Friends visit us.—Mr. Cursin.—Captain West.—Mr. Packenham: Interview with.

MARCH 1st. Placed under charge of Colonel Terris, of the fourth regiment of infantry, and started for Mexico, in company with Captain Reese and his party of sixteen, who had arrived in San Luis Potosi a few days after us. To-day marched five leagues to a *hacienda de Plata*, a silver estate, which had previously been worked with much profit, but now, like a majority of the mines of Mexico, in disuse for the purposes of making silver. "Rich as the mines of Potosi" has long been a proverb; but if the proverb were now reversed, it would be more appropriate.

March 2d. Marched nine leagues to a hacienda, where we were halted about two hours, and kept standing in front of the buildings in the open road, and in the most intensely-burning sun, while the soldiers of the regiment had taken advantage of a few feet of shade upon the north side of a wall to repose for the time. As was customary with the savage old officer in command, he had sent his servant ahead and prepared dinner for himself and other officers, which they were enjoying within the cool and ample apartments of the building; after which they retired to their siesta, not only regardless of our comfort, but perfectly indifferent whether we ate or not. We gave the corporal of our guard money to purchase for us something to eat; after much delay, he brought a few eggs and *frijoles* (beans), not more for our eighteen companions than two could have eaten. After about two hours the officers made their appearance, refreshed from their siesta, and marched us five leagues farther to the hacienda Xaral, a large place containing about nine thousand souls, and one of many other, though smaller, haciendas belonging to the old Marquis de Xaral, who resided at this place. Here we were quartered in an unfurnished room in the *meson* (inn), and had the great satisfaction of buying with our own money enough to eat, which always came to us at two or three prices over and above what the Mexicans would pay for it; for frequently the officer of the guard, and always the orderly appointed to do our purchasing, had his profits to make.

As we expected, we did not see the excellent old marquis; for some of our companions, who the year previous had been with the Santa Fé prisoners, were most grateful for his benevolence to them on that occasion, as he has since been to the main body of our Mier men when passing his residence. Two of his sons, with many other citizens, came to our quarters and looked into our prison-room at us, with about the same amount of curiosity that people ordinarily look into a cage of monkeys or lions, with possibly this difference in their moral reflections: that it was strange that such heretics as we, so very ignorant of the Holy Virgin and the saints, should be braver and more skilled in war than they. With their supreme ignorance in most things, I have never yet seen a Mexican officer or soldier so ignorant as to doubt that superiority; and the very many with whom I have conversed think it no disparagement to their arms when *we* allow that they may possibly fight us five to our one.

The marquis has very extensive estates. We were told that he owned some twenty odd haciendas. We travelled several days upon his possessions. The principal income of his estates is in the sale of livestock. At the hacienda Xaral we were informed that he butchered ninety thousand wethers per annum. The slaughter-house was pointed out to us: an extensive establishment, with kettles arranged something after the plan of sugar-boilers, into which, after the sheep are butchered, and chopped up bone and flesh together, they are placed, and the tallow extracted. Both the tallow and the residuum form extensive articles of commerce: the former for candles and for other purposes, and the latter, being ready cooked, is generally kept for sale in the shops as an article of food, and much use made of it by the soldiery, it being always ready to be eaten.

The pavement in our prison-room being smooth, we slept soundly until awakened by the bugles at four o'clock. We were now informed that if we wished to ride any farther on our journey, we could have the privilege of hiring our own mules or burros. Up to this time we had been furnished horses, both by order of General Ampudia, and Governor Ortega of New Leon, and such was the order of the governor of San Luis Potosi, who had two days previous furnished us with the horses we rode to this place. We remonstrated with Colonel Terris against this act as violative of our articles of capitulation and the reiterated promises of General Ampudia, but to little effect. Our rations had been reduced by him from fifty to twenty-five cents per day, which, under the rascally imposition of our officers and orderlies, would not have been sufficient to sustain life, had it not been for our excellent friends in Matamoras insisting upon our taking some money to meet such emergencies.

We determined not to submit quietly to any imposition from the commandant, and told him that we would represent his conduct to his master at the capital; and after procuring a mule, upon which our blankets and sheepskins were packed, we were marched out on foot with a file of bayoneted guards upon each hand, under the repeated cry of officer, sergeants, and corporals, of "*dos-a-dos*," two and two.

MADE TO WALK OVER THE MOUNTAIN. 191

March 3d. Our road to-day lay in a southern direction, up the valley in which Xaral is situated, and five leagues brought us to a parallel chain of the *Sierra Madre*, the mother mountain, under the never-ceasing cry of "delante," forward, of our guards. It was the first day that we were compelled to march on foot— the first day on foot is always the most tiresome— and, having been hurried at a rapid gait to the foot of the mountain, the abrupt ascent of which for several leagues made us all wish for asses. To attempt to describe how tired one may be when broken down, but still forced on with the "*sharp sticks*," as our boys familiarly called the bayonets, at our backs, would be unintelligible to all except those who have experienced it. To be ordinarily broke down is bad enough, but to be broke down going up a steep mountain, too rough for any animals except mules or goats to travel, is the worst kind of fatigue: you experience a total giving way of the muscles of your thighs, and, however *willing* you may be to proceed, your legs will not respond. The greatest consolation we found in this fix was to gnash our teeth, and hope to see the day when we could balance this account.

Having proceeded several miles up the mountain side, I procured from one of the followers of the army the use of a mule to help me on. I rode but a few hundred yards, when I overtook my young friend Billy Reese, who begged me, "for God's sake, to let him ride some." I promised him that at such a pile of stones a short distance above he might take the mule. Upon reaching this place he blazed away with his walking cane, and knocking the Catholic cross from the pile, turned to me and said, "Now, general, I feel a *little* better; I think I can go another league;" so saying, our boys raised a shout, and pulled on up the mountain.

This very broken and stony mountain pass has been, from the first settlement of the country, more or less infested with robbers, and wherever they have murdered a traveller, on the spot is raised a cross, which the ignorant Catholic erects, not as the *memento mori* of our nation, but they believe it to be the key to heaven. Every good Catholic after, in passing the place, will cross himself in prayer, and throw upon the spot a pebble the size of a partridge egg, or larger, according to convenience. In proportion to the number killed upon the spot, or the character of the individual, and the time when murdered, so is the size of the pile. If the murdered was of high character or esteemed goodness, the greater the interest felt in redeeming him from purgatory, and, consequently, his pile is larger than that of the humble Péon. In this pass, at every few steps for several miles, the traveller will notice these pyramids of pebbles, from the size of a barrel to ten feet high, terminating in a cone, with a corresponding sized cross in the centre. Several of these crosses felt the weight of Billy's staff, to the unutterable horror of our black guards of the "true faith."

Young Billy Reese had more cause of complaint than most of us. He was one of the four small boys whom General Ampudia released from prison at Mier, and whom he promised to send home from Matamoras; but, when reminded of his promise, he said, "If I send you home now, you will be back upon the Rio Grande in three weeks, fighting us again:" so young Reese was sent on to the capital, where, through the influence of the United States minister, General Thompson, he was released. Billy was the largest of the four boys, and the downy evidences upon his upper lip, resembling a young frost, bespoke the confidence of sixteen. If our friend had less reverence for the mummeries of the "true faith," his Hotspur qualities made him the better soldier. This leads me to remark here, what my experience has long since taught me, that I would far prefer an army of boys to an army of men: the go-ahead qualities of the former will hardly fail to win, while the more calculating character of the latter make their movements too slow. Had our two hundred and sixty-one men at Mier been boys, I do not entertain a doubt but that I should have been spared the pain of recording their captivity, sufferings, and deaths.

Having ascended the mountain, we were marched several leagues upon the level table-land, extensively cultivated, and at the end of nine leagues we stopped for the night, and were crammed into a small, filthy room of an extensive hacienda, with several of their own miserable Péons, who were marched in our ranks and under the same guards, to be made soldiers.

One of these prisoner Péons was a bugler, and consequently, a prize of no ordinary value in the estimation of the Mexican commander; for the Mexicans, of all people, pride themselves most upon the empty show and pomp of the camp. In this skeleton of a regiment of less than three hundred men, there were more musicians than belong to a division in the United States army. On one occasion the Mexican officers asked us where our musicians were. We answered, "We are all musicians in Texas!" "Upon what instruments do you perform?" "Upon the rifle," we answered, when, suddenly, the muscles of their faces would elongate from the pleasant to the most inexpressible blank. On this and similar occasions, when we would quiz them—and we let no opportunity pass for so doing—they would always come to the conclusion that "we were a strange people."

In the wife and sister of this bugler prisoner we witnessed instances of female fortitude and devotion, which, if we were not to notice, we should be unjust to the purpose of these pages. This poor man, who had been kidnapped because he knew how to blow a horn, was kept in the strictest confinement. His wife and sister abandoned their homes, and followed the regiment on foot several hundred miles, packing water and provisions for him, and attending to his wants with a devotion I never saw surpassed. The sister, whenever the regiment would halt, occupied herself in making small paper segars, "cigarritos," which she sold both to our comrades and the soldiers, while the wife would buy gourds full of "*vino mascal*," and retail to us by the drink. The profit of their trades gave them the means of supplying the wants of the husband and brother. The conduct of these women, so pure, so unshaken in the interest of this unfortunate man, caused me to remark, what I have often before observed, both in Mexico and other parts of the world, how far superior, in the cultivation of the charities of life, does the female appear over the male portion of mankind.

The small, dirty room we had been forced into, with their own filthy prisoners, was barely large enough for our own party to lay down, and it opened into an inner court of the building, which was occupied by the regiment, into which we could not pass for the sentinel at our door. Here we were kept three hours without water, when it was but a short distance from us. The heat and dust almost suffocating us, added to our fatigue in being forced over the mountains at a rapid gait, made our thirst intolerable. The soldiers of the regiment had plenty of water near us, while we had to suffer all the tortures of the extremest want of it, until the Mexican officers had luxuriated in their national effeminacy, the siesta.

At length the lieutenant-colonel, whose name I

did not learn, but an officer vastly more humane than the colonel, made his appearance, and, upon our remonstrance, had the Mexican prisoners taken out of our room and a barrel of water brought us. In the mean time I purchased a tin cup of water, which had greatly relieved me; and while our men were drinking at the barrel, a dirty soldier of the regiment came in, thrust his gourd and hand into the water up to his wrist, and, when ordered out, replied in the most contemptuous manner that " we were nothing but robber prisoners." This was too much for my Southern temper under the chafings of that day. I smashed his gourd against the floor, seized the fellow by the throat, and kicked him out of the door into the midst of his regiment. As might be supposed, it was an insult to the whole regiment for a "heretic robber-prisoner" thus to treat one of the "magnanimous nation," and they showed strong indications of punishing it in a sanguinary manner, when the lieutenant-colonel came forward to quell the excitement. He inquired the cause of it, and was informed that I had kicked one of the soldiers out of the room, and would do so again when occasion required it, when he ordered that no soldier in future should be permitted to come into our apartment. My treatment of this fellow had this good effect: if it did not give us more bread, it gained us more respect.

March 4th. To-day, our feet being exceedingly sore from our yesterday's march over the mountain, we were permitted to hire a few mules, and eight leagues brought us to Dolores, a handsome town of several thousand inhabitants. We remained at this place all the 5th; it being Sabbath, the regiment had to undergo review, &c. This town is celebrated as the place where, in 1809, the priest Hidalgo first assembled his desultory forces and commenced the Revolution. We have already passed over the ground of his final defeat, where the king's troops, under Calleja, beat with great slaughter his mob-army, took him prisoner, and recaptured his immense spoil of many millions which he had taken from Guanaxuato and other cities. To this remarkable man is due the credit for the good or evil which has resulted to Mexico by a severance from the mother country. He it was that put the ball in motion, and though his life paid the forfeit, other and worse men have shared the spoils.

March 6th. We were marched ten leagues to San Miguel el Grande, a city of about fifteen thousand people, built upon the side of a steep hill, and bountifully watered by a mountain stream. Here we were quartered in a filthy, unfurnished room, upon the ground floor of an extensive cathedral, the upper apartments of which are used as a college, and which is celebrated as the institution where Hidalgo was educated. The name of Hidalgo seems to be held in great reverence here; we saw it inscribed in sundry places about the town. Our room opened upon a court in which a delicious *jet d'eau* fell into a large stone reservoir, where we had the luxury of washing our face and hands to our hearts' content. This luxury, almost as indispensable to Texians, or the nation from whence most of us sprang, as eating, is almost unknown in Mexico; we rarely saw an officer or soldier wash his face. To-day we were stopped to noon it at one of the confiscated haciendas of the Jesuits, in a delightful and well-watered valley, where there is an extensive and beautiful church, which, though built a long time since, the scriptural paintings upon the dome and outside are still brilliant. We were forced into a filthy alley, only a few feet in width, communicating directly with the *comûn*, the most horrible smelling of all places, where we had either to eat or fast.

March 7th. Marched eight leagues to the "burned hacienda," where we were lodged in a stable. This night, for the first time, we discovered the comet; and to obtain a clearer view, all hands had to mount the horse-trough. We had an excited argument among ourselves whether it was a comet, or what it was; and the warmth with which we debated the matter excited the curiosity as well as alarmed the fears of our ignorant guards. They inquired of us what it meant, and we told them that "it was a messenger sent by God, which foretold bloody war at the capital, for its tail pointed in that direction." This was a reasonable reply; for several days we had met news, all of which tended to show that a formidable outbreak was daily expected at the capital against Santa Anna, and that he was calling this, one of his favourite regiments, near his person in anticipation of some such event. The workings of the sentinel's lips, and the shy and rapid motion of crossing himself in prayer, soon showed that our tale had the desired effect: that night several of them deserted.

Let a Mexican be capsized in the middle of a river, instead of swimming he will stop to say his prayers. Let him be at sea in a storm, instead of laying hold of the ropes he will stop to say his prayers. Let any danger beset him on land, instead of applying himself to meet the emergency he appeals to his patron saint. I was informed by Lieutenant Taylor, of her Britannic majesty's navy, who was on board the Mexican steamer Montezuma, off Campeachy, when Commodore Moore first attacked them, that the whole Mexican portion of the crew fled below and went to prayers to supplicate the Holy Virgin to stand between them and danger. He gave it to me as his opinion that, had the breeze lasted for Commodore Moore to come to close quarters at that time, the Mexican navy would have fallen an easy prey. Extremely farcical and ludicrous as prayers at such a time must have appeared to a British officer, a repetition of them could not be submitted to when the reputation of a British officer was concerned. This officer then quitted that service with as much disgust as he, on the other hand, entertained admiration of the naval skill and gallantry of our commodore.

This day the officer of our guard proved himself to be a most finished young savage. On several occasions he refused us water when it was entirely convenient, for no stopping of our guard interfered at all with the movements of the regiment, we being kept far enough in the rear to have the full benefit of the most intolerable dust. In no country have I witnessed the dust comparable to the dry season in Mexico. At noon this day we were stopped for three hours in the road, exposed to the heat of a broiling sun, while the officers were eating and taking their siesta in the houses.

March 8th. Marched four leagues to a hacienda, where we were stopped at noon and placed in a stable, while the officers, as usual, were enjoying all the luxuries of the spacious buildings. In the evening the march was continued four leagues more, and we, with the Mexican prisoners, were lodged in a strong stone house, used as a granary. To-day our officer of the guard was more humane, and, from the small gold ring he wore in his left ear, it was evident he had been one of our San Jacinto prisoners. This mark of distinction, I was informed, is honorary, and observed by most of the officers who survived the perils of that day.

March 9th. This day we had the good fortune again to have another humane officer of our guard. He refused to let the guards follow us on occasions which need not be specified. He would stop with us at the pulque stands on the roadside and partake of that delightful beverage, and showed us all the kindness in his power. This night we were halted at the end of five leagues, and quartered in a strong stone granary.

March 10th. Marched five leagues to San Juan del Rio, a beautiful town of about ten thousand inhabitants. At this place Adjutant Murry was taken very ill, insomuch that we did not expect him to survive many minutes. When Colonel Terris came into our quarters, pretending to sympathize on the occasion, he was told by Colonel Fisher, Dr. Shepherd, and others, that it was his cruelty which had brought on his illness; that he had taken the old man's mule from him, and the rapid gait he had been forced in his lame condition was the cause of his attack. In fine, the abuse that we poured upon him was by no means measured, which caused the old monster to leave our quarters without ceremony.

March 11th. Marched ten leagues before we were halted to noon it, and placed in a stable with the horses, mules, and asses. This long march was exceedingly fatiguing, and we suffered badly for water. After much begging, I purchased one *medio* worth, while the Mexican soldiers were served with large caskfuls in our presence.

In the mean time, the officer of our guard retailed a barrel of pulque to our companions at an unusual high price. The settlement between him and the owner of the pulque explained that he was interested in its sale, and, as a more certain means of making us buy freely, we were kept from water. After the pulque was sold, and just as the march was about to be resumed, we were furnished water.

There is something so inexpressibly mean in this transaction, that a captain, wearing two epaulets, should be guilty of such low thieving, will be difficult of belief in the United States or any honourable service. The moral grade of honour governing the Mexican service may be better estimated from the fact that there were several officers who would borrow from one to five, and in one case as high as ten dollars from us, whose funds they must have presumed to be low, under, in every instance, the most solemn promise that at some place ahead they would return it. In no instance was a shilling ever returned; and though we loaned the money in no expectation that it would be returned, yet these loans were serviceable to us in two respects. The borrower looked upon it as an appeal to his better treatment of us, and it generally had that effect, while the amount loaned to different officers served to designate them. Thus, instead of using our vernacular English upon the hard Spanish names, we would, "*for short*," call such a one "Sergeant Ten Dollars," "Lieutenant Three Dollars," or "Captain Five Dollars," according to the amounts which they respectively borrowed.

Another characteristic peculiar to the "magnanimous nation" is, that they not only do not wash their faces, but they do not wash the plates in which they serve dinner. The sutler-woman, in bringing round to us for sale large earthen jars of hashed mutton, "chilé," and tortillas, would first serve to their own officers a saucer full generally for a *medio*, the sixteenth of a dollar, which they would eat with their fingers. There are only a few of the richest people in Mexico who own knives and forks, and the most of them handle them with as little grace as a cornfield negro would a rapier. The tortilla is a cake of bread made of Indian corn, about the thickness of upper leather, and quite as pliant. This cake not only serves the Mexicans as bread, but answers the triple purpose of knife, fork, and spoon: he with surprising dexterity will tear off a piece, and with his thumb and the two first fingers of his dexter hand, the fore finger being in the centre, so as to give it a spoon shape, dip up the red chops, and at every dip a new spoon disappears. The immense quantity of *chilé*, "red pepper," used in cooking gives everything cooked more the appearance of being submerged in a paint-bucket of oil and red lead than eatable gravy. Usually, after their officers, and frequently their dirtiest soldiers, would sop their saucers empty, not clean, our dinner would be served in the same without washing. On frequent occasions, the sutler-woman, for decency sake, would take the lately-used saucer, and, crooking the fore finger of her right hand in a half moon shape, run it round the inside of the vessel with surprising expertness, and then give the aforesaid semicircled finger a flirt to rid it of its contents, in readiness to serve the next.

On this occasion, a fat young sutler-woman brought into our stable a jar of this hashed victuals. After quietly sitting flat upon the ground, in the manner of United States tailors—the Mexican tailors sit upon stools*—she commenced fingering the lately-used saucer in the manner above described. Being hungry, and my temper not the most placid, on account of the pulque imposition, I ordered her to take her finger out of my saucer and wash it. "What does he want?" she said to the interpreter. When my order was explained, the good-natured creature burst forth into a laugh which made her fat sides shake; and all the satisfaction I could get was, "That you are the strangest people I ever saw; I haven't a doubt but that you have eaten many a peck of dirt before."

After the Mexican officers had finished their siesta, all except one old colonel came forth into the stable-yard where we were confined. Each had in his hand a lasso, with a running noose at one end

---

* I have observed that individual habit is not more inveterate than national, even in small matters. In Mexico, while working at their trade, the tailors sit upon stools, while the English race set flat upon a board, with their legs crossed under them. In Mexico the barbers turn their razors upon the edge in stropping, while ours turn theirs upon the back. Their barbers use their fingers to lather one's beard, while our people would consider it extremely filthy to have a fellow fingering about their lips. One of our petit inconveniences was in failing to find a shaving-brush for sale in all Mexico.

of it, ready for throwing. To catch a hog or a mule by the foot when running is esteemed by them a high accomplishment, and for a time they seemed to be proud of the amusement it afforded us, until they ascertained that we were laughing in ridicule of their national gymnastics. One of our men, whose wardrobe was not worth six cents in a fair market, told one of these gilt-laced gentry, " Why, sir, I would flog one of my negroes if he were guilty of such unintellectual stupidity as to throw a rope over a pig's head." " How, then," said the officer, "do you catch your cavallos and chickens?" "Well," answered the Republican, " the former we learn to come to the bridle; the latter, we cut their throats with the rifle, and we don't claim any that is hit on the head." " *Hai Dios!*" (my God!) he exclaimed, " what a strange people you are!"

Had I Santa Anna's power in Mexico, as it is his duty, and should enter deeply into his military glory, I would abolish in the army the extravagant use of chilé, and make it highly punishable for an officer to pack his bed or indulge in the siesta. These effeminate indulgences are more calculated to make women than soldiers. The extravagant use of chilé is as hurtful to energy as the too great use of ardent spirits. Before dinner, the slothful gait and languid countenance of the Mexican shows the absence of this stimulant, when, after dinner, its effects make the siesta indispensable. Santa Anna was enjoying the sweets of this evening sleep at San Jacinto when "that mishap," as he calls it, befell him; and experience should have long since taught him the force of these observations. I would also reduce that officer to the ranks who would be guilty of the low accomplishment of throwing the lasso. It has been said that "the Texian is born with a rifle in his hand," and with equal truth it may be said that "the Mexican is born with a rope in his," for at every Mexican settlement we noticed the children, from knee high and upward, with little ropes, catching the ducks and chickens. It appeared to be their only amusement; and they would throw them with remarkable certainty. The old roosters and drakes, that had been often taken this way, seemed to know how useless it was to attempt escape, and would squat to receive the rope when they saw it coming. In Mexico the lasso is used for catching every animal, from a wild bull to the tamest dunghill fowl; nor is its use unknown in recruiting "*their volunteers*" for the army. Our comrades used to say that "these blanketed, pepper-eating fellows would not believe a thing was caught at all unless it was done with a rope."

This evening we were marched two leagues to Arroyo Saco, and jammed into a subterranean room, covered with trodden straw, from which, whenever stirred, the most suffocating dust would fill the room. Added to this, the *pulgas*, fleas—not by the count, for there are not numerals enough in mathematics to give an idea of their number, but in bushels—the pulgas completely usurped the dominion of the *piojos*, lice; and the only advantage we experienced from them was, that their frisky activity made us for the time insensible to the slow, plodding operations of the latter. They acted as counter-irritants, for the same reason that a negro puts red pepper in his eye to cure the toothache.

What made this night the more insufferable was that, notwithstanding there were numerous unoccupied and comfortable apartments in this building, which we were not permitted to occupy, we were refused the privilege of sleeping in the open court upon the pavement. Colonel Fisher and myself addressed the following note to the colonel, from whom we received no reply:

"Sir,—We have been placed in a miserable barn, where the dust and vermin are insufferable, and we take this means of requesting the *gracious* privilege of sleeping upon the pavement in the open court. We have not time now to remonstrate against conduct which is in such flagrant violation of the articles of our capitulation and of every principle of civilized warfare."

March 12th. All hands rejoiced at the appearance of daylight, and the prospect of escaping from our most horrible lodgings. Four miserable small *burros* being furnished our sick and lame, we commenced our march after shaking off myriads of fleas.

After marching two leagues, Colonel Fisher and myself procured each a broken-down pack-mule, for which the owner exacted double price. At the end of seven leagues we were halted for the night, and the lieutenant-colonel had us lodged in two rooms, furnished with a pine table and a bench each. I saw but little furniture even in the best houses in Mexico. In fact, we usually see better furniture and more comforts in the most indifferent hotels of the United States than in the best in Mexico. There it is as usual for the traveller to pack his bed, as it is in the United States for the traveller to pack his saddlebags. The traveller, in stopping for the night, leases a room in the *meson*, inn, and pays for his provender according to the price stipulated and the amount furnished.

At ten o'clock this night the officer of the guard locked our door, which, when closed, was like an hermetical seal. Such a number, when confined in so small a place, had a reasonable prospect of suffocating. The suffocations in the black holes of India, and the prison-ships of England in the Revolutionary War of the United States, appeared to our imaginations in the full force of reality. Our little knowledge of the component parts of the atmosphere gave us no relief. We calculated how long the oxygen in a cubic foot would sustain life—how many cubic feet in the room—the number of persons in the room, and the length of time we had to occupy it. This calculation was the result of the instant, and it left a woful quotient for our consolation. We rose from our pavement, struck a light, and Colonel Fisher and myself addressed the following note to the commandant:

"To the Colonel commanding the 4th Regiment of Infantry, Mexican Army.

Sir,—We have been locked up in a small close room, where not a breath of air can enter except by the door. It is useless to remark upon this uncomfortable situation; but if by this order you intend to insinuate that it is our intention or desire to escape, we, as honourable men and officers, cast back the insinuation with that resentment which such gratuitous cruelty deserves.

" We have no hesitation in believing that *we* are far more anxious to reach the city of Mexico than *yourself*, where we may be placed in the hands of the high functionaries of your government, whose regard for the pledged faith and 'magnanimity' of the nation, it is *hoped*, will deal with us in a far different manner than has been your pleasure.

" Had it been our wish to escape, we had ample opportunities eight hundred miles nearer home to do so; but this we could not do without a violation of our words and honour, which we are taught in *our nation* to hold inviolable."

From the reiterated promises of General Ampudia in Matamoras, we believed that when we reached Mexico we would be able to negotiate terms advantageous to our fellow-prisoners, and we gave him our word that we would cheerfully go there in such hope. Though frequent opportunities of escape presented themselves previous to this time, we were influenced not only by the word we had pledged, but by the ardent desire of serving with our presence our countrymen at the capital. I know that no fear of consequences to myself, and I believe the same of Colonel Fisher, would have induced a forfeiture of our word. On the other hand, we did not believe the colonel commanding *overly*-anxious to reach the city. The daily news we met of revolution in that quarter certainly did not hurry him forward any.

After we had written the above note to the colonel, we gave it to the sergeant of the guard to be delivered. He returned in an hour, bringing back the note, with an excuse for not doing so.

March 13th. We were permitted to hire three worn-out pack-mules to help our party on, and started without breakfast. Five leagues distant we were marched into a *corral*, while the officers of the regiment were eating their dinner in the buildings. We sent out money to purchase something to eat, and just as it was about to be brought in, the bugle sounded the march. No breakfast, and after five leagues' rapid march, no dinner, put us all in ill humour: a hungry man can feel very ill; some swore, while the more religious would clinch their teeth in silence, their dilating nostrils showing that they felt no better than those who gave expression to their feelings. As we were marched forth from our cow-pen, the colonel rode out of the court of the building immediately to our left. This was the first opportunity I had for delivering the letter which the sergeant refused to do the night previous. I passed through the line of guards and presented him the note. In the act of doing so, Dr. Shepherd said, "That is right, general, give it to the old scoundrel:" he received it, and read but a few lines, when he called Mr. Van Ness to him, and asked him who that man was that cursed him, and to say to him that if he did so again he would have him shot: "that I am a man of but one word." The doctor replied, "If he wishes to shoot, let him shoot; I am ready to be shot." This reply so vexed the old fellow that he made an attempt to draw his sword, but putting it back, he rode up and struck the doctor upon the face, at which several of our party hallooed out to the doctor to give him his whip. Dr. S. told him that that was Mexican valour—*muy valiente*, very brave—to strike a prisoner, and that, if he was upon an equality of circumstances, he would not dare it. The colonel, who understood English well, seemed sensible of the rebuke, and rode off. Language fails me in expressing my contempt of a transaction so supremely mean and cowardly—that one wearing the insignia of honour and bravery should strike his equal whose hands were tied. Two leagues farther brought us to Tepec, where we were quartered for the night.

March 14th. Seven leagues to-day brought us to Guarticlan, where we were quartered, as usual, in a filthy apartment.

March 15th. At 3 o'clock A.M. the bugle sounded the march, and we had seven leagues to go before reaching Tacubaya, a small town upon an elevation in the Valley of Mexico, about four miles southwest of the city. At broad daylight we commenced descending into the Valley of Mexico, and the prospect was sublimely beautiful. It looked as if we were entering into Elysium. With tremendous high mountains surrounding the valley, which is a basin of about thirty by sixty English miles, and laid off in *labours*, beautifully ditched, and highly cultivated with the *schinus, osiers*, and other evergreens growing upon the ditches, and overlapping the roads with their luxurious foliage in every direction—with a magnificent city in the centre, and numerous smaller towns filled with spires, and scattered over the plain wherever the eye could reach, gave the view an air of enchantment, which to be enjoyed must be seen. When we reached the plain below, it was not difficult to imagine that we were on the highest and most choice spot upon the earth, surrounded by a tremendous high wall, for such is the appearance of the porphyritic mountain sides which surround the valley; but when we looked up to the eternal snow-mountains of Popocatepetl and Istazihuatl far above us, we could as easily imagine we were far into the earth's cavity. However, it is not for me to give life to this scene. I write "with a running pen"* and in a tyrant's chains; and though I may have viewed the ancient valley of Anahuac and the place of Tenochtitlan as did Humbolt, Poinsett, Ward, Prescott, Myer, and others, they were in better humour, and had more leisure to do justice to this classic panorama.

Thus, after years of fond hope that peace and competence would enable me to visit this place, so celebrated as the site of aboriginal refinement in the New World, and more celebrated still as the place of the most remarkable conquests in the annals of mankind, here am I a prisoner and in rags, treated with the contumely and cruelty of a felon, because we dared to war for our country, and fight her enemy in a manner she expected of us: thus, I say, to be compelled to view the city of the Montezumas—to be able to give but a passing glimpse at the aqueducts, calzadas, and teocallis of that remarkable people—to glance at the bloody paths of Cortes and Alvarado, is what I could not have preferred. However, it is a tribute which some have to pay to liberty, and it is as well that it should have fallen upon us as upon better men: it is the fate of war, and we bear it with the fortitude of men.

We reached the western suburbs of the city, where we halted a few minutes in front of a large church,

---

* I should have said, *with a pen running*. The common application of the *currente calamo* would betray a vanity which belongs not to this hurried scribbling.

and purchased some bread and fruit for our breakfast. From this place we veered to the right, and fell into a road which led to Tacubaya, which place we reached about noon, where the regiment were quartered in a portion of the archbishop's palace, which had formerly been used as a convent. This is an extensive building, adjoining a church, to which is attached a spacious enclosure of fruit-trees and evergreens. The portion of the building occupied by the regiment contained a great many rooms both upon the lower and upper floors, a number of which were appropriated to the use of the officers and soldiers. In the centre of the building was an open court, surrounded by a double corridor. The sides of this parallelogram, both below and above, were covered with large-sized scriptural paintings upon canvass, representing every stage of the crucifixion of Christ. The artist must have been a Mexican, for he has mixed in several of his pieces a rare combination of Mexican taste. In one piece, for instance, after our Saviour was nailed to the cross, and surrounded by the unbelieving Israelites, he has a Jew in full ranchero's costume, mounted upon a bushy-maned, long-tailed *mustang*, spear in hand, charging upon him. The blood flowing from his side, with forgiveness upon his countenance, and unrelenting persecution in the surrounding multitude, is a melancholy sight, and enough to make Mexicans hate Jews. The gray-bearded followers of the cross, looking down upon us in every direction, admonished how perishable are the things of this world, while the benign and angelic beauty of the Holy Virgin, just above, whose eyes appeared bent upon our lowly couch, seemed to pity our condition. Just beyond, one of the fathers is blessing the young Messiah, whose cherub beauty, surrounded by a halo of glory, showed that he was coming to illume a benighted world. The effect of these numerous paintings upon a Catholic population is calculated to inspire reverence for their religion: it made us Protestants feel like better men.

In the centre of this court is a water spout, emptying an ample supply of the delicious liquid, fresh from the aqueduct of Chapultepec, into a large stone basin, around which we drank, and washed our faces over and again. In this open court, upon this brick pavement, myself and companions were quartered.

It was but a little time before the candy-girls ascertained that we had money; and being greatly rejoiced, as we believed that this was the termination of our march, we luxuriated in sweet cakes and ice creams. Having procured a gourd full of *vino mascal*, we did not forget in our thanksgiving that, through the goodness of God, our distinguished countryman, General Andrew Jackson, had this day reached his seventy-sixth year.

This evening Mr. Cursin, bearer of despatches from the government of the United States, and Captain West, came into our quarters to see us. These gentlemen manifested the liveliest interest for our welfare. Hearing that we were approaching the city, they rode out on the San Christoval road several leagues to meet us; but, finding we had taken a more westerly route, they returned, and told us "that an order had gone forth several days from Santa Anna to shoot all our companions behind, and doubtless they would be, if they had not already been shot; that President Houston had written to Mexico, through the British charge d'affaires in Texas, saying 'that though we had entered Mexico contrary to his orders, and without authority of law, yet he begged mercy for us;' that our friends in the city thought us in imminent danger," &c. One less acquainted with President Houston than myself might have ascribed such a letter to some unaccountable misapprehension or to political stupidity. But, knowing his undisguised malignity and cold-blooded vindictiveness, not only to Colonel Fisher and myself, but others of the Mier prisoners, I lost not a moment in writing to my friends in Texas for evidence of his falsehood. I had too much respect for his personal and political astuteness to believe that he did not know what that letter would produce, and I knew that such *official* authority was the highest upon which the President of Mexico could desire to act. The evidence I wrote for to Texas came in due season, such as not only satisfied the United States minister, but even Santa Anna himself, of Houston's falsehood; and, without tiring the reader here with a recital of this melancholy, cruel, bloody tragedy, I refer him to the proofs of all that I have said in a correspondence published soon after my escape from prison in Mexico. (See Appendix No. VI.)

This evening William Reese visited General Thompson, the United States minister in Mexico, where this melancholy information of our prisoners was confirmed. The nights at this season of the year in Mexico are cold, and though there were hundreds of unoccupied rooms in this building, we were compelled to quarter upon the pavement in the open court with our thin blankets. We suffered much in body, but the anguish of mind was far beyond all bodily sufferance. To be butchered by wholesale as national marauders, by the perfidious, horrible decree of our own President, without the means of proving to the world his heinous falsehood, was to us a mental torment far worse than death itself.

March 16th. Mr. Cursin, Captain West, and several other friends came in to see us, and brought the welcome intelligence that, through the remonstrances of the United States and British ministers, President Santa Anna had countermanded the order for shooting our men. This evening I requested a friend living in the city to see these ministers, and desire them to call at our prison the next day.

March 17th. This day we were not furnished a

morsel to eat, and but for the little private means we had, should have consequently fasted.

The reason the officer of the guard gave for not furnishing our usual twenty-five cents each was, that "he had no money." General Thompson, the United States minister, sent us word that "he thought he could be of more service by not evincing too great anxiety in our behalf, and that everything in his power should be done for us." Though we were thankful for General Thompson's kind feelings, yet we were mortified at his position, which we feared in some measure compromised the dignity of his government. Mr. Packenham, the British minister, and suite came to our prison, and met us with the most unostentatious kindness. The representative of the British nation is no small character on any portion of this globe where the needle has ever turned. The colonel of the regiment, who, since the first day of our arrival at Tacubaya, appeared in all the ununiform, gaudy foppery of the Mexican nation, and who paid less attention to us than if we had been so many animals in a menagerie, when he saw the British legation in our prison, stood chapeau in hand, and looked as if he were in a superior presence. Mr. Packenham inquired for myself, and asked "if I desired to see him." I answered that "I did, and wished to make intercession through him for several English subjects, prisoners with us, among whom were Captain Ewin Cameron, Samuel C. Lyon, and others." Mr. Packenham said that "he would do everything in his power for these men, but that he feared much difficulty would interpose in this service; that these men, though they were British subjects, had made their own election in taking up arms against Mexico, and consequently had subjected themselves to all the penalties of the laws of war," &c. I replied, that "by the encouragement of the commercial policy of Great Britain, these men had become *sojourners* in Texas; that, pursuing *trades which their government had encouraged,* they had subjected themselves to the laws of Texas, which required all persons, citizens or sojourners, after a certain time, to take up arms in her defence. They had either to forfeit in Texas benefits which had accrued to them by their governmental policy, or submit to the *lex loci* where they were pursuing their English trades." I cited him the case of Samuel C. Lyon, then present. He was a shipmaster by profession; his father, mother, and family then resided in Liverpool, and were highly respectable; that, through the commercial laws and treaties of his country, he had been for a time in Texas, where he had acquired property and privileges, the fruit of his country's encouragement and his own industry, and that I must believe that there was a high obligation upon that country to protect and shield him; that, had the British government not countenanced and encouraged this trade, he would not have been subject to his present imprisonment.

Mr. Packenham asked us "how we were treated."

I pointed to our dirty blankets upon the open pavement as our bed, and requested him to be his own judge. He looked indignant, and replied that, "by the laws of war, as officers, we were entitled to our parole, and *doubtless* it would be extended to us;" but that "the same laws also required, as a matter of security, that the soldier prisoners should be kept securely." He left our prison with the same kindness of manner that he had entered it, and with our increased good-will and respect, the gaudy fops of officers who had charge of us standing aside for him to pass.

We have had frequent occasions to be mortified at the contempt in which citizens of the United States are held and treated abroad, and particularly in Mexico, when no Roman citizen in her palmiest days ever felt more pride and confidence in his citizenship than does at present the British subject. If anything is more calculated than another to lessen the respect and attachment for one's country, it is to be compelled to disown her and seek protection under another. Such, unfortunately, has too often been the case with citizens of the United States, who, speaking their mother English, and with an English parchment in their pockets, travel with impunity by denying that they ever were in the country which gave them life. The case of our friend Lieutenant C., of the Mier Expedition, is a striking instance. He was a citizen of New-York, and after his friends had in vain exhausted all their influence in trying to procure his liberation, his mother recollected that he was born at Halifax, "near the United States line," but came over when a few days old. This fact, made known to the English minister, procured his immediate release.

As I feel an abiding pride in that country which gave me birth, and in which are my earliest and dearest associations, I long to see her assume a more high-toned position in her intercourse with foreign nations. Heretofore, unfortunately, that government has too strictly estimated her honour by dollars and cents. If her flag has been insulted—if her citizens have been unjustly imprisoned and robbed—if her territory has been violated, the cost of redress is estimated with that cold, calculating, mathematical code so unworthy a great nation. Like some northern people when their wives or daughters have been violated, they send the case before a jury, who estimate their honour as a butcher would a pound of meat in market. If the meat be choice, the price is proportionately high, and *vice versa* if the article is poor. We feel no hesitation in believing that the honour of wives and daughters is in far better keeping in a thimble full of powder and one ounce of lead, and so, likewise, is the same conservative principle equally applicable to national honour.

To-day we were visited by several friends, who informed us they learned that on to-morrow we would be removed into the city; the officer of the guard also informed us the same; and I have reason to believe that such was the intention of the government, until Mr. Packenham visited us, and it was ascertained that much interest was manifested by the foreigners on our account. Then we were suddenly hurried off to a remote, and, as the government believed, an impregnable fortress. We had the precaution to send our original "articles of capitulation," signed by General Ampudia at Mier, to the American minister for safe keeping, with a request that he would furnish a copy to the minister at war. After the most unnecessarily wanton and savage treatment of us by Colonel Terris, of the fourth regiment of infantry, we represented it to the minister at war, and, from the continued favour which we learn has been extended to him, he seems to have received the thanks rather than the rebuke of his government therefor. What a commentary upon a government which in every breath speaks of its *honour*, *integrity*, and *magnanimity!* The days of that nation must be numbered whose "*punica fides*" enters into her most sacred obligations.

Having the privilege of going to the *común*, which is in the second story, we ascended to the *azotéa* of the palace, from which we had a splendid view of the city, Chapultepec, the snow-capped volcanoes of Popocatepetl and Istazihuatl, and the whole valley below, and a more charming landscape does not exist.

CHAPTER XIV.

MARCH FROM TACUBAYA TO THE CASTLE OF PEROTE.

Marched on Foot.—General Valencia, Wife, and Daughters.—Our Reflections.—Hire Asses.—Pulque-drinking Officer.—Pass the Volcanoes.—Germans.—National Character of the Germans and other Foreigners.—Puebla.—Bad Treatment.—Lieutenant Velarde.—New Officer.—The Execution of General Mexier.—Acahita.—The Death of Mexier.—Texian Talent for Drawing.—The Honest Mexican.—Arrival at Perote.—Meeting our Countrymen Prisoners.

MARCH 18th. At ten o'clock A.M., when we were in momentary expectation of orders to march to the city, a company of cavalry rode up, and the officer ordered us to bundle up our blankets to march to the Castle of Perote, one hundred and sixty miles east from the capital. We were told we would be furnished no horses, mules, or asses. We asked if we could have the privilege of hiring some to pack our blankets and sheepskins upon, and was bluntly answered "there were none to hire." Up to the moment of starting we had been told by our officer that General Valencia and family would be out to see us that day; and having learned that they had greatly interested themselves the year previous for our Santa Fé prisoners, we felt flattered at this information. How suddenly our fond expectation was changed! In a few minutes each of us had to roll up his dirty blanket and sheepskin, take them under his arm, and march down the street with a file of mounted lancers on each hand. We had proceeded but a few hundred yards when we met the splendid equipage—a Parisian coach and United States horses—of General Valencia, with himself, wife, and daughters. They were, in fact, as our officer informed us, upon a visit to the archbishop, it being some important saint-day.

From the manner in which they noticed us in passing, they seemed to know that we were Texians. This they may have easily inferred, both from our national costume—for we were too national to wear anything after Mexican fashion when we could avoid it—and also from our national *up-head* appearance. Freemen carry their heads higher than subjects, their hearts swell larger, and they are infinitely more proud.

Just at this time, when we met these beautiful young ladies—and they were of as fair complexion, dressed as fashionably, and looked as well as the best of our country—we felt all the elements of disgust, contempt, and bitter hostility for a nation so regardless of the obligations of truth and good faith. We now ascertained to our satisfaction that General Ampudia's reiterated and gratuitous promises to us were either made in bad faith, or that they had been wholly disregarded by his government; and when we passed these young ladies, whatever may have been our appearance, we felt like freemen. John Rodgers at the stake could not have felt more independent: we gave them a soldier's salute, and staggered on with our sheepskin bundles. Thus we trudged on half a mile farther, when the heart of our officer melted within him. He met a miserable *lepero*, leading a still more miserable mule, and permitted us to give four prices for the privilege of packing our bundles upon the poor animal.

Our road now lay east, and we had to pass through the southern suburbs of the city. In coming to Tacubaya we passed through the northern and western confines of the city, and now we were making almost a circle around it to reach the great stage-road leading to Puebla. When we reached the southern suburb we met some Péons with a number of *burros*, asses, returning from the city, where they had been packing charcoal to market. Our officer here discharged the *lepero* and his mule, and allowed us to hire some *burros*.

In Mexico they have but few wheel carriages, and everything is transported upon the backs of animals. In every part of the country we met immense numbers of mules and asses packed with every species of goods which constitutes the commerce of the country. The mules are usually fine. The best I have ever seen, either in Mexico or the United States, are the pack-mules between the capital and Vera Cruz; and what surprised us is, that both the horses and asses which produce them are small. The asses particularly are small; we do not recollect to have seen one which would have been considered a second-rate animal in Kentucky.

F F

Those used for packing by the poorer class of people are usually about the size of a badly-raised yearling of the cow kind. These small woolly animals, with hair usually as long as one's finger, and tremendous large bodies, and having no bridles, an *aparejo*, a kind of pack-saddle upon which is packed all kinds of produce, wood, charcoal, fodderstacks, &c., are driven to market in large droves. When the produce is disposed of, these droves of animals are driven home by the *arriero*, muleteers.

The *aparejo* is a large sack, made of the fibres of the maguey, and stuffed with straw, and when lashed upon the *burro*, is broad and flat upon the top— too much so to straddle. When mounted, we sat with our feet forward of the sack, like boys going to mill; and all the eloquence of our English was lost upon the long-eared brutes, for they would neither turn to the right or left, or quicken their pace, but huddle together as close as the sacks would allow, thereby giving us the better opportunity of cracking our jokes. When one would lag behind, the only persuasion he was sensible to was a sharp-pointed stick a few inches long, with which we would prick him just above his tail; this would drive him forward into a little shuffling pace to overtake his company.

We had gone but a few miles when our officer discharged this *arriero* and his asses, and coming across a fresh drove, permitted us to hire others at double price. Thus were we swindled three times this day in donkey-hire.

This officer was an ignorant man, with a face as red as cochineal, and exceedingly fond of pulque. In passing a pulque woman, we had only to flatter this lieutenant with the title of *Capitan*, point to the pulque, crook our elbow, turn our little finger over the thumb, give him, at the same time, a nod of the head, with a confidential kind of a wink, and he always drew up his horse with, *Bueno, señor*—enough said, sir. Our funny asses and exhilarating pulque put us all in better humour. We spoke of the beautiful Misses Valencias; we agreed that they were as white, dressed as fine, and looked as well as the best in the white settlements; and all said, "What a pity it is that such splendid-looking ladies should live in such a vile community!" This conclusion brought us to the eight-league stand, where we were quartered for the night.

March 19th. Early this morning the officer had stopped an unladen drove of pack-mules going in our direction, and gave us all the privilege of riding this day at fifty cents each, though our ration was only twenty-five cents. To-day we crossed the mountain, leaving the volcanoes Popocatepetl and Istazihuatl to our right, and descended into a deep cove to a stage-stand, called *Rio Frio*, ten leagues where we were halted for the night. The stage-house here is kept by a kind-hearted Frenchman and lady, who gave us supper at a low price, and the good woman divided all her husband's old clothes among our more destitute comrades. Here we met an unpretending, whole-souled German, a blacksmith by trade, who insisted upon giving us all his clothes except what he had on; and when our pulque-drinking officer refused to let us have more than one gourd full of *vino mascal,* because, he said, it would make Texians very dangerous, our German friend told him "he was a fool; that Texians had stronger heads, and could drink ten times as much as Mexicans, and still be men." This German philosophy procured us the second and third gourd full of the ethereal liquid, and all hands went to sleep praising the Dutch nation.

Of all nations, we found the Germans the most devoted to the interest of their fellow-countrymen in prison; next to them, the Scotch; next, the English; and last, our own Yankee nation. Mortifying as this acknowledgment is where my countrymen are concerned, truth requires me to say it. It is true, that in some instances we have met a whole-souled countryman, both from the north and south of our Republic, who would not only share with us his purse, but his blood. Such countrymen, though few, live in Mexico, and we regret most sincerely that we would do them a disservice by specifying their generosity; but, on the other hand, the bulk of our countrymen found abroad, and especially in that country, are a cold, calculating race; they go abroad for the purpose of accumulation; they have no sentiment beyond such miserable lucre, and they would permit a countryman to starve in a foreign dungeon just as they would at their own doors. The German does not wait to make the personal acquaintance of his oppressed countrymen: he asks their number in distress—feeds and clothes them, to the credit of their nation. Thus will also a Scotchman and Englishman do. We found many generous Frenchmen, though we had but few French prisoners. The old proverb, "When you cannot say anything good of your household, to say nothing," prevents me from instancing several of the most superlative meannesses of our countrymen.

March 20th. This morning we procured some of the most miserable *burros* we have seen, and eight leagues brought us to San Martin, a considerable village in a broad, cultivated, and well-watered plain. At this place our red-faced officer and guard returned to the capital, and we were turned over, March 21st, to two lieutenants; the oldest long, lean, and lank—a dyspeptic-looking man, who appeared always hungry—a fine specimen of ill nature and low breeding; the other quite a youth, but evidently the son of a gentleman: he was well bred, and exceedingly civil. They guarded us to Puebla, a large city ninety miles from the capital. This day we marched eight leagues, and were quartered in a horribly filthy room in a cavalry barracks. We asked our long lieutenant to " have the filth removed from our room—that we would pay the soldiers for so doing;" he replied in the most contemptuous manner to our request, when an exceedingly genteel officer came up and offered his services to us. He ordered the room to be policed, and desired to be useful to us. We could not fail to inquire the name of an officer capable of such unexpected and unsolicited kindness, and learned that he was Lieutenant Velarde, and was much pleased to find that he spoke English. He apologized in a handsome manner for the want of civility of some of their officers, and said that "they had never travelled out of Mexico, and knew little of the customs of other countries."

March 22d, we were placed under charge of a lieutenant and troop of cavalry. This officer was the most perfect savage we have before or since met. He was of middle size, and apparently about thirty-five years of age, with a sombre countenance, shrill, cracked voice, and eyes red with the dreams of his bloody deeds. His name I failed to procure, but understood that he was the sergeant who commanded the firing-party that shot the brave and lamented General Mexier, and for which act Santa Anna had promoted him to his present commission. His very gait and look bespoke assassination; he was the very impersonation of a murderer. Soon after daylight we were ordered by him to pack up and start. He refused to let us hire even a pack-mule, and we had, consequently, to leave some of our luggage. We were marched through the city, and attracted as much attention as if we had been a caravan of monkeys. One of our prisoners, Daniel D. Henrie, was exceedingly ill, and he was thrown upon a mule with as little ceremony as if he had been a package of goods. With great difficulty he made out to hold on to the mane of the animal for two miles, and in the act of falling was caught and laid upon the ground. I told the officer it was impossible to carry him in that condition, when he replied, "Let him die, then!" The word *die* had no pleasant sound to our friend Dan, who was not so far gone but that he knew its meaning, and after giving him water, we lifted him upon the mule, and one walking on each side to hold him on, we proceeded on our march.

At three leagues this officer stopped with his woman, who was accompanying him in a coach drawn by eight mules, to breakfast. He refused for us even to have pulque; "for," said he, "it will get in your heads, and then the devil will be to pay." At this place we hired some miserable poor *burros;* and Captain Reese, being mounted upon the most indifferent, was pricking it up with a sharp stick, when the owner came up, and attempted forcibly to take the stick from him. The captain drew back and threatened to give it to him, when our red-eyed brute of an officer rode up, and threatened to run Reese through with his sword if he struck him. Our only satisfaction was to curse him in the best of our poor Spanish. This night we reached the small town of *Acahita*, at nine leagues, where Santa Anna defeated and shot the brave General Mexier.

We cannot pass over a spot so sacred to liberty

without paying some small tribute to the memory of this deceased patriot.

General Mexier was strongly devoted to the liberty of his country, and, being one of the firmest adherents to the free Constitution of 1824, was banished the country by Santa Anna, and sought an asylum in the United States, where he remained several months. In the year 1835 he raised an expedition in New-Orleans, and made a descent upon Tampico, where he was defeated, losing a considerable portion of his force in killed and prisoners. Twenty-seven of these unfortunate prisoners were afterward shot by order of Santa Anna. General Mexier escaped the misfortunes of the day, and again reached New-Orleans. Subsequently he sailed with more success against Tampico, that place declaring for the Constitution of 1824. At this time the Governor of Puebla invited him to join forces and move against the capital. This treachery was concocted between Santa Anna and the latter; and when Mexier reached the mountain pass, a short distance from this spot, he found Santa Anna and his legions to oppose him. He made a determined resistance, but at length had to yield to superior numbers. Santa Anna offered him his life, provided he would swear allegiance to his central despotism. His answer was worthy of Leonidas himself: "No, sir," said he; "I will oppose you as long as I have an arm to strike for liberty." Thus fell this brave man, whose history I learned from an intelligent

United States citizen who had travelled subsequently in Mexico.

We were hungry and tired, and sent out to a *meson* to purchase supper, which was contracted for at twenty-five cents each for sixteen. After much delay it was brought into our prison, about enough for three hungry men, and from the whispering consultations between our red-eyed officer, it was clear that he divided our four dollars with the sutler.

Upon the walls of our prison-room we found inscribed many names of our countrymen, who had preceded us in the Santa Fé Expedition. In this, as well as in many other prisons upon our long march, we amused ourselves at our countrymen's genius for drawing. The "magnanimous nation" suffered whenever they could procure a piece of charcoal and a white wall. In all the caricatures the tyrant Santa Anna had a conspicuous place. At one time they had him crouched in a Texas prairie, hiding from the sons of freedom; at another they had him upon his knees, yielding up his sword with a most penitential phiz; and again they had him stalking forth upon his wooden leg, under a chapeau extremely ludicrous from its immense size, with a huge sword, dictating laws to his enslaved countrymen.

March 23d. This morning our assassin-looking officer had us badly swindled in the hire of some poverty-stricken *burras*, she asses. Our friend, Dr. Shepherd, happened to get the most fiery of these animals, which seemed to be known to our guards;

and when he was mounted upon the *aparejo*, without stirrups or bridle, and not suspecting any trick, one of the fellows speared the animal behind, which, with a sudden flirt, landed the doctor in the dust, much to the amusement of his comrades. He jumped up and made towards the fellow, evidently with the intention of striking him, who drew out of his reach; and though our brutal officer saw the whole transaction, he ordered the cavalry man to run him through with his spear if he touched him. We were halted for the night at a small village, having made seven leagues.

March 24th. This day we were marched ten leagues to a small town, and placed under charge of a tall, dark-looking officer, who treated us with much kindness. Here my companions had a hearty laugh at my expense. We sent out our orderly to purchase something to eat: the fellow had hardly turned his back before the sentinel at the door of our prison told us that that fellow was a noted rogue; that he would cheat us of the best half of our money; that it was a great pity the Mexican officers allowed us gentlemen prisoners to be so swindled; that in a few minutes his tour of guard service would be over, when it would give him pleasure to wait upon us; and that he would see we had the full benefit of our purchase. This fellow also told us he had been in the United States, and knew the difference between a gentleman and a *pillo*. During this speech, the fellow looked so very like an honest man that I handed him two bits as a premium for his honesty, he being the first honest soldier I had seen during my long march in Mexico. All my companions rejoiced in the opportunity of having an "honest man" to buy their food, gave him their extra bits, and this was the last we ever saw of the money or the fellow.

March 25th. We had five leagues this day to march before reaching the Castle of Perote. Upon our arrival at the village of Perote, in looking north about one mile we could see the massive walls of the castle, with its numerous portholes and dark-mouthed artillery. The great extent of ground covered by the castle wall and the earthen embankment around the outer "*chevaux de frize*" gave this fortification a low appearance, and, at first sight, we were not struck with the magnitude of its strength. Upon nearer approach, in making our way through its winding entrance, and across the drawbridge over the great moat, thence through an archway into the great *plaza*, fronting the governor's quarters, amid the bugle's blast and the roll of drums, the din of arms and the clank of chains opened our eyes to the reality of imprisonment, and showed us what abler pens than mine have described as the most approved fortification of the eighteenth century. Here we met, in rags and chains, fifty of our countrymen, who had been kidnapped from their homes in Texas, the September previous, by General Woll. There is a mutual sympathy in misery: we met as brothers, and I hope and believe we shall live and die as such.

CHAPTER XV.

IMPRISONMENT IN THE CASTLE OF PEROTE.

Three Days' Grace before Ironed.—The Castle.—Its Strength.—President Houston.—Orazabo.—Cofre de Perote.—Castle.—Its Situation.—Climate.—Description.—Bexar Prisoners.—Mexican Culprits.—Theft.—Rape.—Murder.—The Prisoner who killed a Priest for kissing his Wife.—Prisons of the Mier Men.—Their Treatment.—Ironed.—Mode of breaking off the Chains.—Tricking the Officers.—Santa Anna and the Blacksmith.—" Can't come it, Judge!"—Rations.—Ass's Milk.—Our Mess.—Cooking.—Best Way to make Coffee.—Ordered to Work.—Remonstrance to Minister of War.—To the Governor.—To the United States Minister.—Release of Judges Jones, Hutchinson, and Maverick.—Treason of Robinson: our Denunciation of.—Anniversary of the 21st of April.—Sentiments, Songs, Tecolote, and Old Guts.

There is a mockery in many things in Mexico, and now there was a mock mercy by way of three days' grace extended to us before our chains were riveted. During these three days we had the privilege of walking about in certain parts of the castle in the daytime, estimating its capacity, military strength, &c. We made in our minds many estimates, and, after all, came to the conclusion that, though this was one of the strongest places in the world before the improvement of the combustible shot, and though it reflected great credit upon the military genius of the last century, yet if Captain Stockton or John C. Stevens were to be placed upon a certain mountain elevation about two miles distant, with a few "peace-makers" pouring into it their death-dealing fulminators, these fellows would run out of this place as soon as hot water would drive rats from their holes. However, public expectation requires a more particular description of a place so celebrated in the history of the Mexican Revolution, and still more so from its being the prison-house of the best spirits of our country, where, through the cold neglect and vindictive hatred of their own president, they were permitted to dwindle out a miserable existence in chains and slavery, in rags and hunger.

Upon the north of this fortification, in the bottom of the great ditch which surrounds the castle, lie the mortal remains of many of the best men of our country, cut off in the prime of life, through their country's ingratitude and neglect. No! let me not do their country injustice; that country, when we speak of her citizens, has always been ready, willing, and able to supply their wants as well as to avenge their wrongs; but this generous spirit has been too fatally repressed by the injurious influence of the executive chief, reducing their country to beggary. Forbearing as are the people of Texas under the wrongs and usurpations of that executive, they yet possess the moral elements, as well as the physical power of self-government; and if much forbearance heretofore has marked their political career, it has been because they believed it better to suffer a while the evils that time and their invincible courage could alone redress.

The mariner, in approaching the Mexican coast

of Vera Cruz, is struck with the sublime magnificence of the Volcano of Orazabo, with its regular conical peak covered with perpetual snow, long before he can see the lower lands. Though this mountain is one hundred miles from the coast, yet so high and imposing is its appearance, it looks to be in the immediate neighbourhood. When at sea, off Vera Cruz, in casting the eye northward, the next most imposing peak is the *Cofre de Perote* (Trunk of Perote), so called from the rock upon its extreme summit having the appearance of a trunk. This peak, though frequently covered with snow, is not perpetually snow-capped. At the foot of this mountain, upon its north, and in a narrow valley, which separates it from another high mountain still north, is situated the Castle of Perote. Though it is built in a valley, apparently low from the extreme height of the adjacent mountains, yet it is about seven thousand feet above the level of the sea. Its contiguity to the snow mountains, its altitude, its position, such as the sun cannot reach but a few hours in the day, all render it an extremely cold place. The castle adjoining this mountain pass, as you ascend from the *tierras calientes*, the hot lands, has ever been the stronghold in Mexico of despotism or liberty, according to the whims of its inmates. The range of its artillery, bounded by the "Trunk of Perote" south, and the Mount of Pizzaro north, occupies one of the principal doors to the capital.

The castle is built principally of the volcanic

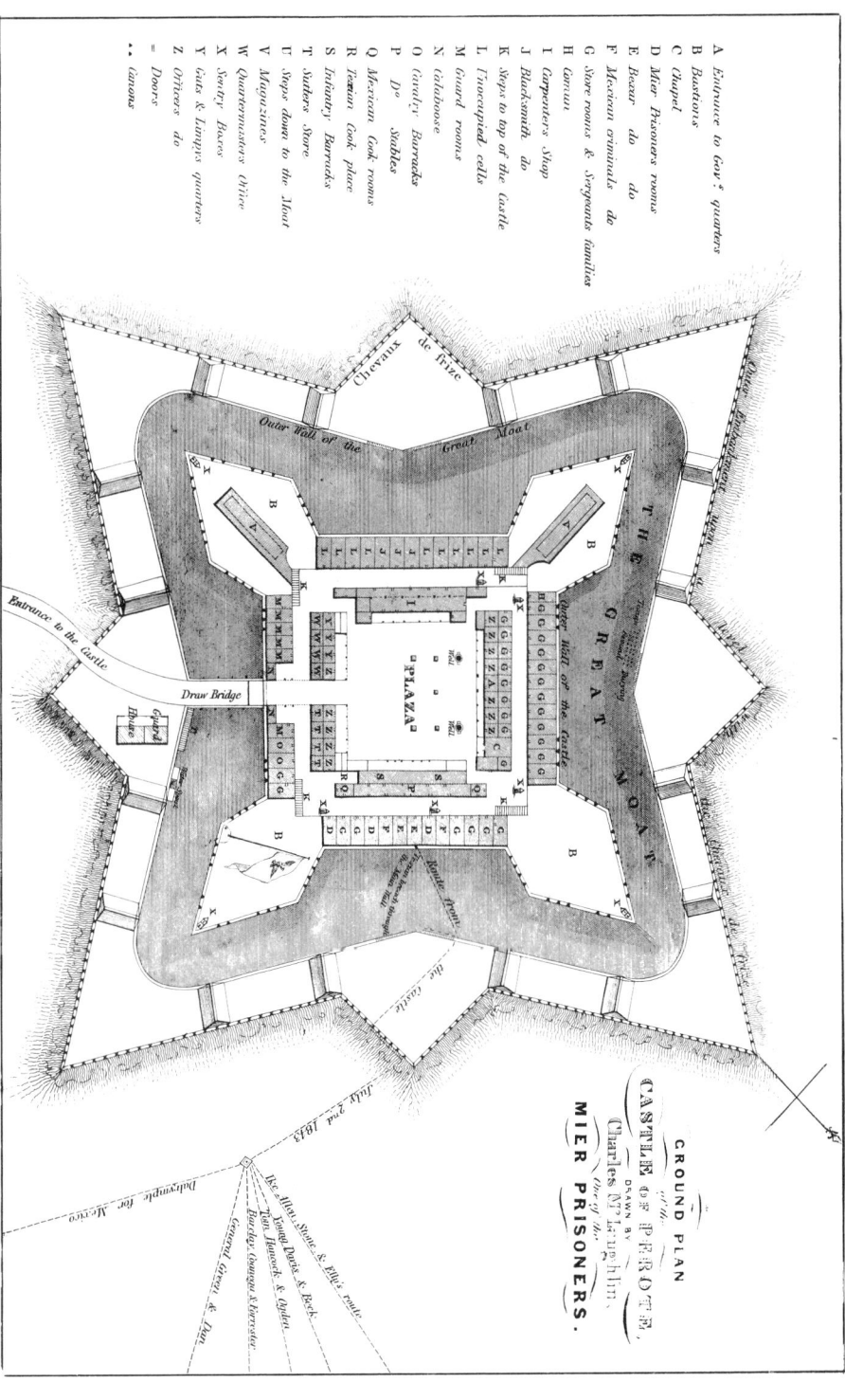

GROUND PLAN
of the
CASTLE OF PEROTE,
DRAWN BY
Charles McLaughlin,
(One of the)
MIER PRISONERS.

pumice stone, a dark, honeycombed cinder, which was, when first emitted from the volcanoes, in a state of solution by heat, but which has since become of such an extremely hard character that it will yield only by degrees to the hardest steel. The opposite plate is a ground-plan of the fortification, drawn from recollection; and though it may not be mathematically correct in all its proportions, it will give the reader a better idea of it. The main wall of the fortification is an equilateral quadrangle of about eight hundred feet on the insides, and about sixty feet from the top of the wall to the bottom of the great moat on the outworks. At each corner of the main rampart there is a bastion, extending outward, whose sides form an obtuse angle to the main wall, so that all points of the circle may be defended by guns bearing directly upon the point assailed. Around the main wall and bastions there is a moat, about twenty feet deep and two hundred wide. On the outside of the moat is a stone wall, while the main wall of the castle forms its inner side. About fifty feet beyond the outer wall of the moat is a *chevaux de frize*, built of squared cedar timbers twelve feet long, set upright in the ground: these are mortised through a longitudinal timber passing half their length. On the outside of this *chevaux de frize* is a ditch of about fourteen feet in width, the outer embankment of which is elevated so as to reach nearly to its top. The entire works inside of this ditch are said to contain twenty-six acres of land.

From the bottom of the moat to the top of the principal rampart the height is about sixty feet, upon which is mounted about eighty pieces of artillery, upon a flat roof seventy feet wide by the whole extent of the wall. This flat roof is supported by arches, adjoining each other, twenty feet wide by seventy in length, and each one opening with a door upon the inside of the castle. These arches, adjoining each other and extending entirely around the square, constitute the workshops, storerooms, and cells of the prisoners. These cells are regularly numbered, and when the castle was completed in 1773, *Ferdinando* VII. was inscribed over each door in large letters. The ruthless hand of revolution has run the paint-brush over the name, though it is yet discernible through the painting. Upon the inner side, and at each angle of the fortification, is a broad stairway ascending to the top. These stairways are secured by strong wooden gates about twelve feet high.

Upon the inside of this fortification, and sixty feet between, is another range of square buildings, two stories high, the upper apartments of which are used as officers' quarters, soldiers' barracks, &c. This building opens upon a centre court, which is reserved for the military parade. The courtyard is about five hundred feet square, paved with cement, underneath which is an immense water-tank, containing many millions of gallons, supplied by a subterranean stream of water as pure as ever flowed from the mountains: connected with this great water-tank are gates, by which, we were told, the moat may be flooded at the shortest notice. These works were the labour of many years; they cost many millions of dollars; and had not the improvement in the combustible shot formed a new era in the science of war, it would have been impregnable to assault.

We found our countrymen of Bexar occupying two of these long, narrow, dark archways, adjoining each other, in the eastern rampart of the castle. These arched cells are twenty feet wide by seventy long, with a door opening upon the inner side of the castle, and a loophole at the extreme end of the room, four by twelve inches, and widening through a wall eight feet thick to about two feet on the inside. When the doors are closed, which usually takes place at six o'clock in the evening, the prisoners are counted, and a sentinel placed at each door. The only ray of light admitted into this dark abode from without is through the loophole and a narrow grating over the door. The archways over head are fifteen feet thick, which support the artillery, underneath which are subterranean waterworks, magazines, &c.

Upon the left of our Bexar friends, the adjoining rooms were occupied by their own Mexican chain-gang, a large number of convicts condemned to different terms of service for every species of crime. One of these fellows boasted that "it was the fourth time he had been imprisoned for rape, and it would not be the last." Another, clapping his hand upon his breast, said, in the proudest tone, "I am no *ladron* (thief); I am placed here for murder." In Mexico they think murder more honourable than petit larceny, though a large majority of them would steal the value of a pin. The most genteel man among these illustrious convicts was in for killing a priest who was caught kissing his wife. This fellow I often pitied: he had been in good circumstances, but in killing a priest, such was the influence of the Church that all his money could not save him. He was brought there after our arrival, and his wife followed him to prison with a devotion not uncommon among Mexican women. He was a tall, graceful man, about thirty-five years of age, and his keen black eye and Roman nose bespoke a temper fierce as a lion: nor did they belie him. His first act in chains was to beat one of the turnkeys severely for treating him as if he were merely a common prisoner. Almost without exception, these culprits are sunk so low in human degradation, that even an outline of their crimes and modes of life would be incredible to those who had never been an inmate of a Mexican prison.*

---

* Mr. Myer, in his late work upon Mexico, gives the following graphic description of the "Accordada," one of the public prisons in Mexico, where a portion of our prisoners were confined: "Passing through," says he, "several iron and wood barred gates, you enter a lofty corridor, running around a quadrangular courtyard, in the centre of which beneath is a fountain of troubled water. The whole of this area is filled with human beings — the great congress of Mexican crime, mixed and

In the next room, and to the right of our Bexar prisoners, myself and fifteen companions of the Mier men were lodged. At 6 o'clock in the evening, all the prisoners were counted and turned into their respective cells, where they remained until 6 the next morning, when the doors were again opened. At 9 o'clock we were, as usual, counted, and turned over to the new officer of the guard, at which time our men were made first to take the filth out of the castle in handbarrows, and after that to pack in stone and sand to repair the fortification. The stone they had to pack from over a mile and a half from the mountain; the sand a shorter distance. In the performance of this labour, our men, being chained in pairs by the ankle with large log chains, and only about four feet between them, had to walk

mingling, like a hill of busy ants swarming from their sandy caverns. Some are stripped and bathing in the fountain; some are fighting in a corner; some making baskets in another. In one place, a crowd is gathered around a witty story-teller, relating the adventures of his rascally life. In another, a group is engaged in weaving with a handloom. Robbers, murderers, thieves, ravishers, felons of every description, and vagabonds of every aspect, are crammed within this courtyard; and, almost free from discipline or moral restraint, form, perhaps, the most splendid school of misdemeanor and villany on the American Continent." Mr. M. adds, "I did not see the prison for the women, but I am told it is much the same as the one I have just described."

In this prison was confined for more than two years our patriotic fellow-citizen, Colonel Antonio Navarro. When this gentleman was visited by Mr. George Van Ness, he assured Mr. V. that he never left the small apartment which, by courtesy of the officers, he was permitted to occupy, for fear that these horrid wretches would commit upon his person a most unnatural crime, common among themselves, but never heard of among the English or their descendants, and too execrable here to be named.

very close together, and on each hand was a file of guards with fixed bayonets to keep them in order.

At nine o'clock of the fourth day after our incarceration, the Mier men were ordered to stand aside to receive their chains, a full ton of which had been brought out and laid in a heap, with a corresponding quantity of cumbrous, rudely-made clevises to fit around the ankles. Here stood the fat old officer in charge, a Captain Gozeman, who, from the immense protuberance of his abdominal region, our boys dubbed "Old Guts." This genius was exceedingly civil at times. He desired Fisher and myself to make choice of our chain. In fact, there was no choice between them, the lightest weighing about twenty pounds; and even if there had been any difference, neither of us was in a temper to make the choice. I felt that placing those irons upon me would make Mexico greatly my debtor, which some day I would cancel with a most usurious per centage. We held forth our feet, the one a right, and the other a left foot, and the son of Vulcan riveted us together as though we had been a pair of unbroken oxen just being introduced to the yoke. It is the habit of soldiers, in walking together, to step at the same time with their right foot, and then with their left. These chains subverted this well-established and strictly-observed custom, for one being chained by the right, and the other by the left ankle, those even and odd had to move together, or they would pay the penalty by a severe jerk. Colonel

Fisher and myself being first ironed, we laughed at the "jewelry," as the boys called the chains, but it was the laugh of a consuming vengeance. We thought, with King Lear's fool, that these were "cruel garters! Horses are tied by the heads, dogs and bears by the neck, monkeys by the loins, and men by the legs." We started to our cells, but the inconvenience of being coupled so closely together, and our un-Siamese locomotion, determined us to separate, and, upon reaching our apartment, we looked out for the means of breaking so large a chain. Texians are a most ingenious people, and are usually equal to the emergency. We soon found means to accomplish our purpose.

In our prison-room lay a loose stone, about one foot across, on one side of which it was slightly concave. In the room we also found a six-pound cannon-shot. We sat flat upon the floor, with the stone in our laps, the concave side up, and covered with a blanket as a non-conductor of sound, to prevent the alarm of the sentinel at the door; then placing the middle link of the chain across the concave surface of the stone, and another fold of blanket over the link, we commenced hammering upon it until it came to fit the stone, turning it over and beating it back until it also fitted the other side, and thus, after twenty turnings of the link, it parted, leaving each about five feet of chain. When we had occasion to leave our apartment, we would take the broken ends of the chain in the same hand, and walk past the officer with the same indifference of manner as though the chain were not parted.

Our companions, in turn, were all ironed, and many were the devices they resorted to in order to free themselves from their chains when not in the presence of the officers. In that horribly cold place, sleeping upon the cold pavement, and with the still colder iron for your bedfellow, is no very enviable situation. Some would bribe the blacksmith to make them leaden instead of iron rivets, which, when blackened with charcoal, had much the appearance of iron, while they could be easily taken out or reheaded. One *medio* would buy a leaden rivet; and for some time this *ruse* was practised. Frequently, however, when the officers would suddenly enter our cells, they would find our comrades without chains, and as suddenly every fellow would jump to his "jewelry," and clamp it on with a magic celerity which entirely bewildered the senses of the officers, and then as suddenly put on a demure, inoffensive countenance, after the manner of schoolboys cutting up their juvenile antics upon the sudden appearance of the pedagogue. Our old friend with the large corporation, after much fretting about our not wearing the "jewelry," told the governor "that it would require as many blacksmiths to keep us ironed as there were Texians in the castle."

One of our companions, who belonged to the Sante Fé prisoners, the year previous told us a similar anecdote, which then happened in the city of

Mexico. Santa Anna sent for the blacksmith, and gave him a severe scolding for not keeping the chains on the prisoners. The poor smith, trembling with fear in his mighty presence, replied, " I know not how it is, sire; I place the best and largest irons upon them, but no sooner do I turn my head than the irons will be laying upon the ground, and they will do '*just so*' at me: they surely must be kin to the devil."

What the poor smith meant by "just so," in which he suited the action to the word, was the "*you-can't-come-it-Judge*"-motion—à la Kendall. This motion is performed in the following scientific manner, to wit: place the extreme end of the thumb on the tip of your nose; then lock the little finger of your left hand into the thumb of your right, and with the four digits of the said right, give a quivering motion, as if you were performing upon the piano variations to the *Battle of Prague;* give a comical wink, and pronounce the talismanic words, "*You can't come it, Judge*," and you have it. This is what the Mexicans cannot comprehend; and you see them frequently practising it at one another with as imperfect a knowledge of its meaning as a Texian has of the *rationale* of animal magnetism.

Respecting our rations, they were such, even without labour, as would hardly have kept soul and body together. We fortunately had a small balance of funds still by us, which had been so kindly furnished us by our friend J. P. Schatzell, and Mr. Marks, the United States vice consul in Matamoras. So long as it lasted, our room-mates made out pretty well. A *medio* each of lard, onions, and red pepper, cut fine, put into our rations of poor beef, and re-cooked over a small earthen stove of charcoal, made quite a savoury meal for several. We also purchased sugar and coffee, and every day, at twelve o'clock, from the milkman, a gallon of *leche de burra*, ass's milk. When we had the means, all of our mess took a hand at cooking. Our old sailing-master, Lyon, did the outdoor catering, browned the coffee, and superintended its grinding. A soldier's wife would grind it upon a flat stone, for which she would receive toll. Daniel Drake Henrie, of whom we shall have to speak more hereafter, usually called *Dan*, for short, sat upon the stone with a small Indian fan, and blew the coals, while he sung "*Long, long ago*," and the "*Soldier's Tear*." Colonel Fisher would hash up the meat; Captain Reese would stand by Dan, spoon in hand, and stir the milk, to keep it from boiling over; Lieutenant Clark would beat up the peppers and peel the potatoes, while I would cut up the onions and mix in the condiments. After frequent tastings, when I would pronounce the thing right, all hands agreed that "this was the very best dish we had yet cooked." Thus a keen appetite made each last dish the best. Each of the mess, like artisans in a pin factory, had his separate office to fulfil, but the fulfilling of that office depended upon his first washing his hands; for as yet we were not so accustomed to the voracity of the vermin as not to make war upon them.

The *burra's* milk is very far superior in richness to that of either cow or goat; and the following recipe will make better coffee than was ever made in any other manner by the best cooks in Paris:

Take one pint of ground coffee, after being well browned, and not ground too fine; mix it up with the white of two hen's eggs, to which add two quarts of good water, and enough loaf sugar to make it as sweet as desirable; boil this fifteen minutes; to which add, after boiling it long enough to take off the "long-eared" smell, two quarts of ass's milk: take care that the milk does not burn.

This beverage, prepared in this manner, is so delicious, that the most fastidious will forget the "long-eared," *comico* gravity of the animal which produces it: for our countrymen, Colquhoun and Bradley, both Virginian epicures in coffee-drinking, pronounced it better than anything they had tasted, "even in the Old Dominion."

A short time after we were ironed, our fat friend very politely informed us we must prepare to go to work. We very politely replied that, as we were Texian officers, we would do no such thing. He went with our reply to the governor, when Colonel Fisher and myself addressed the following letter to the minister at war:

"Castle of Perote, March 31, 1843.
"To his Excellency General Tornel,
  Minister of War and Marine:

"Sir,—Having seen it published in your public journals that we surrendered at '*discretion*,' and judging, from the treatment we have received since we were placed under the charge of the commandant of the 4th regiment of infantry, that such an impression still exists, we beg most respectfully to enclose to your excellency a copy of the articles of capitulation entered into at Mier on the 26th of December ultimo.

"Of this treatment we do complain as violative of the pledged faith of your government, and highly abusive of her 'generous magnanimity.' That this complaint may not appear unfounded, we beg to state, that, with few exceptions, we have had a right to complain; and since we are not the less grateful for good than sensible of bad treatment, we enclose to your excellency, as we have nothing to disguise from your government, a full copy of our correspondence with the several officers under whose charge we have been.

"It would, indeed, be tedious, and perhaps unprofitable, to enter into minute details of the treatment which has been, and still is, imposed upon us, so completely opposed to the spirit of our articles of capitulation, as well as of all civilized warfare, and the magnanimity of a great and generous nation. And we protest, in the name of the civilized world, that the imposition of this treatment upon us, as subjects of a '*revolted province*,' is arbitrary, and not justified by the circumstances of the case. Seven years since the people of Texas lost the character of '*rebels*' by demonstrating their ability to maintain themselves as a nation, and have been so recognised by the most enlightened nations of the earth; and whatever may be the opinion of your excellency upon this subject, we are bound, as candid and honourable men, to assure you that, although that ability is greatly increased, yet the people of Texas are not the less anxious for an honourable peace.

"The unnatural and predatory warfare which for several years past has been carried on upon the borders of our respective countries, has been reprobated by the most intelligent of our country.

"But when we understood that your government, last summer, declared that she would thereafter conduct the war upon the '*principles of civilized warfare!*'—and the invasion of Texas by General Woll was believed to be in accordance with that declaration—the undersigned took the field under the orders of their government. The consequence is well known to your excellency. We met General Ampudia's division in honourable combat, and while success crowned your arms, we have not discredited our own. We capitulated under the most solemn promises, made through the honourable and chivalrous General Romolo de la Vega and Colonels Carasco and Blanco; they pledging the straps upon their shoulders that we should be treated '*with all the honours of prisoners of war.'* To add greater assurance to this promise, one of the fathers of your Church, Padre De Lire, the priest of Comargo, came forward and pledged the holy Catholic religion for this observance.

"Our credulity accepted the terms, when still we possessed means of resistance; and what is the consequence? Let these dirty prison walls and the criminal's fetters that now bind our limbs answer. We refer to what follows of our remonstrance with feelings of deep mortification and shame, not for ourselves, but for that authority which adds insult to injury. *We are now ordered out with your criminals as scavengers of nameless filth.* There is, however, a limit of endurance, beyond which, as humble representatives of our own country, we are not permitted to go.

"We furthermore solemnly protest, that if peace with Texas be desirable, she cannot, with honour to herself, in any possible manner entertain the question during the continuance of such treatment. However, it is not for the undersigned to suggest to your excellency the impolitic tendency of such treatment; of its injustice the whole world may judge.

"We have the honour to be, very respectfully, your excellency's obedient servants."

April 6th. Our corpulent old friend returned to our prison, and said that he had positive orders from the governor to make us go to work. Colonel Fisher, Captain Reese, and Lieutenant Clarke, the only Mier officers present, pledged themselves to me that they would be shot down sooner than submit to the order, and so we informed him. We then addressed the following note to the governor:

"April 6th, 1843.
"To his Excellency the Goveror-general of the Castle of Perote.

"Sir,—We have been ordered out by your officers to perform unusual and degrading labour. In the name of our country and the whole civilized world, we, as officers, solemnly protest against the imposition of this degradation.

"We farthermore respectfully protest, that, even were we willing tamely to submit to such a disgrace, for the honour of our country we never would.

"We herewith enclose your excellency a copy of our articles of capitulation.

"Very respectfully, your excellency's obedient servants," &c.

General Durand, governor of the castle, though a weak, is not a bad man. Upon the receipt of this note, he sent for Colonel Fisher and myself to his quarters, to argue us into the propriety of working, and the unavoidable necessity of his performing his duty. He said such was the orders of his government, and he had no alternative; that we were not entitled to protection under our articles of capitulation, &c., &c. We replied that such a declaration was in accordance with "Mexican magnanimity," but that "we knew our duty to our country, and nothing should drive us from it." He said then that "he would communicate again with his government upon the subject." This day I addressed a letter to the United States minister, from which the following is an extract:

"To his Excellency Waddy Thompson,
United States Minister, near Mexico.

"Sir,—It is for him, the President of Mexico, to do me justice, or exercise cruelty over my body at his sovereign will. I ask nothing for myself which the laws of civilized warfare do not guaranty to me, and must believe that upon reflection his excellency will concede this much, not only for myself, but my brave companions in arms, whom the fate of war has made prisoners with me.

"When his excellency Mr. Packenham, the British minister, visited our prison near the city of Mexico, he led the officers to believe that we would have our parole according to the laws of civilized warfare; instead of which, we have been treated with every species of indignity, insult, and, in some instances, with inhuman cruelty.

"At present we are occupying a filthy prison, chained together with cumbrous log-chains, lying upon the dirty floor for a bed, and ordered about by a brutal soldiery as if we were their own miserable Péons. To-day we are ordered out as scavengers of the filth of this whole garrison, and are told that for refusing to disgrace ourselves and our country by a tame obedience of this infamous order, we will be incarcerated in a dungeon in solitary confinement. Be it so; yet the duty we owe respectively to our Creator, country, and ourselves, we never can abuse.

"Can it be that those governments, yours among others, which have formally acknowledged our nationality, will longer permit a violation of those laws which are common to the whole civilized world? We hope not; and as your government claims friendship with ours, we most earnestly trust it will not. At the same time, we are grateful for the interest which your excellency has manifested towards us as kin and countrymen, and we beg to tender you our warmest acknowledgments for the same; at the same time, we solemnly protest that the open violation of this law is no less an insult to those who claim to be our friends than it is upon ourselves.

"With considerations of the highest regard, I am your excellency's obedient servant,
"THOMAS J. GREEN."

Time passed heavily, and though we were repeatedly told that we must go to work, yet the order was not attempted to be enforced upon us. The balance of the men, with the exception of those who had been excused, from inability or other causes, were, however, compelled to work in the manner before described.

About this time our countrymen the Hon. Wm. E. Jones, S. A. Maverick, and Judge Hutchinson were liberated, through the intercession of General Thompson. They had been ordered from Perote to Mexico, where they were delivered over to General Thompson, and now, while on their way home, they called to take leave of us. This afforded our companions good opportunity to write home, which many eagerly embraced.

We were told also that Judge James W. Robinson, one of the Bexar prisoners, previous to our arrival at the castle had opened a correspondence with President Santa Anna, in which he represented a general feeling to prevail among the Texian prisoners, as well as in Texas, for returning back to the Mexican fold; that this correspondence, with a promise from Robinson to use his utmost endeavours to accomplish this end, had procured his release. So far as Robinson's falsehood concerned himself, his companions in chains were perfectly willing that he should humbug Santa Anna out of his liberty; but they were unwilling to be under the imputation of disloyalty to their country even at the price of their liberty. Many wrote letters to Texas, and several to Santa Anna, denouncing the falsehood and the traitor.

Up to this time we had been five months from our homes. We knew but little of what was going on there, and that little obtained through the newspapers. It was of the most melancholy and foreboding character, and contained in President Houston's many messages and proclamations, the last of which had just reached us, in which it was stated that a portion of our country was in a state of civil war, on account of his violent attempt to remove the public archives from the seat of government. No wonder, we thought, that Santa Anna should believe Robinson's statement, when he saw under the sign manual of our own president such evidence of national disruption. He therefore concluded, as did many intelligent men in Mexico, that the people of Texas, to escape from such a state of anarchy, would cheerfully return to the Mexican family.

Had we been as little acquainted with President Houston and his habitual disregard for truth, such possibly might have been our conclusion. We knew him better; we knew the people of Texas better; and there was but one sentiment with our fellow-prisoners, which was, "that we would rather rot in these walls, ere Texas, by any act, directly or indirectly, should acknowledge the supremacy of Mexico, or do anything on our account which would compromise her dignity and honour."

The following extract of a letter which I addressed to the United States minister on the 5th of April, will show the feeling which possessed every Texian, whether in sickness or in health, in chains or rags: "It has been rumoured here that James W. Robinson obtained his liberty from the President of Mexico upon a promise that he would use his influ-

K K

ence to bring Texas back into the Mexican family. If he has done so, he has *lied* to obtain his liberty. I tell you, in perfect truth and candour, that it is worth his life, and every other person's in Texas, who will dare intimate such a thing. I say again, that, notwithstanding the dolorous forebodings and infamous slanders of our country by our drunken, opium-eating president, Texas is much stronger than ever, and *never* will entertain such a proposition."

During this time, when not presiding as chief *cocinero* (cook), much of my time was employed at the desk, which I had erected by propping up an old door in one corner of the prison. Here I employed my hours in writing letters both to Texas and the United States, and in keeping up a correspondence with General Thompson, the American minister, who evinced the liveliest interest in our welfare.

My health declined so much on account of the coldness of our quarters and want of proper food, as well as the chafing of the mind under such restraint —added to which, the bitter mortification at what seemed to be my country's neglect—that the chief surgeon of the hospital ordered my irons to be removed. This was fortunate both for Colonel Fisher and myself, as it afforded us the privilege of walking about the castle uncontrolled.

The anniversary of the Texians' triumph over Santa Anna at San Jacinto found my finances reduced to the last extremity. Was this day to be passed in silence, though the wheel of Fortune had placed that tyrant at the top and ourselves at the bottom? No! And though I might have never expected to own another ounce, we would have rejoiced in our country's triumph; so *that* last doubloon was devoted to our country's jubilee.

We purchased seven gallons of *vino mascal*, and as many of ass's milk, thirty dozen eggs, a large loaf of sugar, and appropriated all our cooking utensils and water jars to the compounding of egg-nog; and such egg-nog as never before was seen or drank under the nineteenth degree of north latitude.

Colonel Fisher, Captain Reese, and Lieutenant Clarke beat up the eggs; the old sailing-master, Lyon, pounded the sugar, which operation he accompanied with one of his best "*yarns;*" *Dan* stood by, and was peculiarly eloquent in singing his favourite ditties, "*Long, long ago,*" and the "*The Soldier's Tear,*" while I presided over the synthetical operation of stirring in the requisite ingredients. When *I* pronounced it right, they all said, "It is exactly the thing."

We went around to the prison rooms, and summoned all hands to attend the thanksgiving. When these noble fellows stood round the bowl in rags, with their "jewelry" riveted upon their ankles, brought up and tied around the waist with a cord hanging in a graceful festoon between each pair, the sight filled my heart to overflowing. Though the body was oppressed, they looked like caged lions, and every face bespoke the invincible spirit of a freeman.

"Fill your cups, boys!" was the word; and they did fill them, for many had not tasted "a drop" for months.

"The day we celebrate, and the liberty of our country:" three cheers, and "Will you come to the bower?"

Drank standing and uncovered; they had neither seats nor hats. All hands pronounced it better than the nectar of the gods, for *that* they understood to be pure, unmixed, and unadulterated "mountain dew," while this had the "body;" for while the juice of the agave inspired the soul, the ass's milk filled the stomach.

"Our wives, children, and sweethearts:" three cheers, and the "*Soldier's Tear*," from Dan.

"A fair field, and no more white flags:" three cheers, and "*Hail, Columbia!*"

"*Old Peg-leg*, and his yellow nation: we owe *thee* much:" groans, three times three.

Thus we were getting along swimmingly, when our liberty shouts rose high above the walls of the prison, and alarmed our keepers. They supposed that we intended to swallow them and take the castle. When our fat captain came round with the guard to know the cause of the riot, we told him it was a mode we had in our country of celebrating our saints' days, and hoped he would not disturb us in our mode of worship, as we did not disturb him in his. He replied, "*Bueno, señor*— Very well, sir," and started, when we gave the wink to Trimble.

Trimble, poor fellow! has since paid the debt, and in the prime of life too, which many of our best countrymen have also paid, and which the best men must pay for the want of bread, caused by the criminal and treacherous conduct of our own president, who could have relieved him at pleasure. The poor man has left a destitute family to mourn his loss.

Trimble could mimic the look of an owl, and twist his head, and whoop, far better than the most eloquent owl upon the great Mississippi. This poor fellow, thus having the wink at the time that the guards came up, squared himself, rolled his eyes entirely over in the sockets, twisted his head " clean round" on his shoulders, and gave a whoop that beat the best of owls.

Our burly captain turned round, frowned, and then hesitated whether to be mad or pleased, whether to laugh or swear; and, after a moment's hesitation, with a vacant look, he burst forth in an exclamation, " Tecolote," and moved on. The universal roar of laughter from our companions hurried him forward. "*Tecolote*" in native Mexican means "*screech-owl*," and thus poor Trimble carried the soubriquet to his grave.

CHAPTER XVI.

IMPRISONMENT IN THE CASTLE OF PEROTE.—Continued.

Our fat friend.—Commissariat.—Statement of Rations.—Jake upon Cowology.—Snake-bitten old Cow.—Guts in Caricature.—Old Limpy: his Character.—Lousing.—Simeon Glenn.—Louse-racing.—What is an Old Soldier?—How to select the Racers.—An Argument in favour of Phrenology.—General Austin in the Accordada.—The Old Sailing-master's Pipe.—Longing for Brandy.—Sutler, Wife, and Daughter.—Shifts to get Brandy.—Surprise of Senorito.—The Sergeant's handsome Wife.—Dan: his "Soldier's Tear."—A United States Midshipman.—How he avoided Work.—A Favourite.—"Long, long Ago."—His Heresy lost him Favour.—His intellectual Improvement.—Mr. Black, United States Consul.—Billy Reese.—Shooting of Captain Ewin Cameron.—Reminiscence of Captain Cameron.—George B. Crittenden.—O. Phelps.—Letter to President Tyler.—Letters from United States.—Letter to Mr. Calhoun.—Preparation for Emigration to Texas.

Our fat old guard was so corpulent, that, when standing still, he had often to rear back to preserve his equilibrium, on which occasions his abdominal prominence formed a huge semicircle from his chin to his hip-joints. When moving forward, to preserve his balance, his epicurean preponderance impelled him along at a railroad speed—a kind of running pace; and, though he was the largest man, yet he was the fastest walker in the castle. When he would be coming round in the direction of our prisons, the word "Guts," sung out by some wary sentinel, told us that we had no time to lose in adjusting our "jewelry."

If any department of the Mexican service is worse managed than the pay department, it is the commissariat; as evidence of which may be mentioned the fact, that though this castle is considered the stronghold of the powers that be, yet, with the exception of water, there is not one day's rations of provisions in it.

The government nominally allows both the soldier and the prisoner twenty-five cents per diem for rations. This amount is not paid to the prisoner, but, as a matter of favouritism, is allowed to some officer to draw and furnish the rations. From avarice—for none but the avaricious seek such offices—he puts the poor prisoner upon what will barely sustain life, and frequently it falls short of even that.

The fat man referred to was the *comisario*, who received our pay and furnished the rations; and it would be difficult to imagine any human being more penurious. He had lived to an age when avarice absorbed his whole soul; but all this was in some degree excusable in his case, as he had three daughters to support, whose *proportions* at *this* present writing but too much resembled that of their worthy sire.

The rations of the Mexican soldiers are not subject to the like abuse as in the case of the prisoners. The former have officers to whom they can complain to prevent such outrageous swindling, while the foreign prisoner is insulted in his complaints, and unpitied in his misery.

The estimate of the cost of the Texian rations did not exceed eight cents per diem, with a reservation of three and a quarter cents per day from the twenty-five, making forty-seven cents paid over to each man once in two weeks: the balance was, consequently, clear gain to the old cormorant referred to.

The reader may form some estimate of the quantity and quality of our food from the following statement, which I furnished to the American minister: "7 o'clock A.M., our cook brings us in a large tin kettle of coffee, 'the devil's broth,' to wit: 13 ounces of a burnt substance, so called, boiled in about five gallons of water, and two and a half pounds of brown sugar, 'pilonci,' a fraction over a half pint each. This amount is also served us at 5 o'clock P.M. At noon, the rations about four days out of each eight are sixty-two pieces of beef, chopped up with the bone, there being sixty-two prisoners. These pieces average, with bone, about fourteen ounces. The beef is much poorer than I ever imagined would be served for food; much worse, generally, than is served to their own soldiers; in some instances, too poor to walk, the animal having been brought in upon hand-sticks. These sixty-two chunks, wholly destitute of anything like fat, are boiled in water with six ounces of *manteca*, lard, with a sufficiency of salt and red pepper. At the same time, eleven pounds of good rice are boiled with one pound of lard, and a small quantity of onions. The other four days of the eight we have no meat of any kind, the lack of which is supplied either by Irish potatoes, or *frijoles*, beans, which last are most generally of an indifferent quality, and not sufficient for any except the very smallest eaters."

After we left the valley of the Rio Grande, we saw no beef that would be considered even tolerable in Texas. About Perote it is much inferior to any we found elsewhere. These poorest of poor cattle, whose years of service had long since passed, had been turned upon the common to die; they, consequently, could be purchased *cheap*. These supplied the beef upon which the ill-fated Texians had to feast themselves. What rendered the beef the more intolerable was, that the night previous to the morning on which they were butchered, these poor old grandmothers were brought into the castle, and tied to a certain post at our prison door, where we could all see and pity them. Our boys would gather round these poor old creatures, count the rings upon their horns, and ascertain their years accordingly. One of the animals numbered seventeen rings: she was nearly blind from age, and would roll her glassy eyeballs around upon her heathen spectators with the demure and quiet gravity of appeal as to what the strange procedure portended. Jake, a heretic brave, who has followed cattle long upon the Texian prairies, and was deeply versed in cow-ology, knew well her meaning. Though Jake had killed his score of Mexicans with less compunction of conscience than if they had been so many vipers, he was deeply affected; his heart swelled with emotion, till, with a choked utterance, he turned from the scene, exclaiming, "Boys, she looks so much like my poor old grandmother in Texas, I'll be sworn if I taste a mouthful of her!"

On another occasion, when one of these venerable mothers had laid herself down to die, having been snake-bitten on the neck, which caused a swelling even to a larger size than her body, and rendered the poor creature wholly unable to stand upon her feet, she was in that condition packed into the castle upon hand-sticks. In remonstrating against such an atrocity, the only satisfaction we obtained was a surly reply; for, after the old fellow had reared back into one of his semicircle attitudes, in a most complacent manner, after a deep and thoughtful look, with his right hand upon his chin, and his fore finger pointing up above his mouth, he said, " Well, I'll not give you the snake-bitten part."

We had our revenge upon this old brute by caricaturing him upon the castle walls, to the great amusement of his brother officers. We had a prisoner with us, a German, by the name of Voos, about whom a book of stirring incidents might be written. Voos was the man who, in 1835, fresh from Germany, and on his way to join our liberty army, rode smack into San Antonia when the Texians lay before that place, and asked for the Texian general's headquarters, when he was shown into the calaboose by General Coss; he was subsequently taken prisoner with Colonel Fannin, and escaped that horrible massacre by passing himself off as a physician, being retained to heal the wounded. He has since seen a great deal of frontier service, and been in many Indian fights: he is a man of education, and has fine taste for drawing. Upon the sunshiny side of the walls of our prison, Voos, with charcoal, could give a lifelike sketch of the corpulent individual so frequently referred to. On one occasion he made him fishing up the beef's bowels from our cook's kettle upon a flesh-fork, saying, "*These are very good guts, Texians.*" The likeness was so good that all the Mexican officers recognised it, and the more they laughed, the more towering Guts's passion rose, until serious fears were entertained of an explosion of his ire.

He was too much absorbed with avarice, however, to be greatly disturbed by any other passion; and had his senior officer been a better man, perhaps Guts would have been a kinder master. This senior officer, who watched him so closely that he had to watch us with like diligence, was the *Mayor de la Plaza*, and next in command to the governor.

When Admiral Baudin turned loose his French crackers upon them at Vera Cruz in 1838, it is said that this officer, in scampering out of danger, ran against a stone corner and knocked off his knee-pan, from which his leg has never since straightened. He walks with a staff, and upon the tip ends of his toes, which gives him a gait uneven as that of the kangaroo. This old chap, whose temper, if possible, is more uneven than his gait, and whose mother entailed upon him the misery of a name that Texians never could pronounce, for short we called "Old Limpy." If we met worse men in Mexico, we certainly never met so mean a wretch as "Limpy." He would slip round the corners, and take all the low, eaves-dropping turns upon us of a mean negro. He would, by every means in his power, endeavour to curtail our liberties and comforts, the greatest of which was, after a cold night, to get on the sunshiny side of the wall and kill the vermin.

This operation in Mexico occupies a large portion of the daylight of that nation; and I am told that from long habit, vermin-killing is almost as necessary an excitement to the vitality of this race as bread and meat is to ours. "There were lice upon man and beast," and it would be difficult to imagine that there could be a greater number in the country, even had the dust of the earth been "smote with the rod of Aaron."

There were certain hours between the opening of our prison doors and the "turning off of the guard," when our men would seek the sunshine, spread out their blankets, and down upon their all-fours, not to hunt the vermin as a matter of amusement, but to make upon them *flagrante bello*. The rays of the sun would start these night-walkers from their hiding-places, and their motion would make them the more easily seen. The Texians, for decency's sake, called this operation "driving:" nor did they ever drive in vain. At times, when one of these animals showed himself particularly fleet of foot, he would be captured and saved for the races. How greatly does early education influence our lives! the early prejudice against crushing this hideous insect between the thumb nails always operated adversely upon my appetite; and I do confess that I can maintain a better stomach at the killing of a Mexican than at the killing of one of these prison-associates after the above manner. Though I frequently scalded and swept my " 3 by 6" sleeping-place, and changed my clothes almost every day, yet, upon an average, each morning I would have from thirty to forty of these provoking bedfellows upon me. In one thing I was peculiarly fortunate.

In the same prison-cell with me was Simeon Glenn, one of my "old '36 brigade." He felt all the attachment for me which an old soldier feels for his superior officer, and volunteered to do a service which was calculated to shorten my breakfast. Simeon was a good fellow and an old soldier in more than one sense. When he was first ordered out to work, he told our sentinel that he had the hernia, and that the American doctors told him "never to stoop down and lift up anything." This was sufficient, as the opinion of American doctors was regarded as of the highest authority in all human maladies, and Simeon was permitted to remain in prison. This indulgence afforded him ample opportunity to war *ad libitum* upon the *piojo*. Most of the time since 1836 Simeon had lived with the Mexican population of Bexar; and while his residence did not make him the better friend of the Mexican, it confirmed his decided hostility against these vermin.

The first thing in the morning after the turnkey would open our prison door and let in the light, I would get up and call for Simeon. I generally prefaced handing him the shirt by saying, "Glenn, I had a very disagreeable night of it." Taking the shirt, Simeon's sympathy would as often respond, after turning down a plait in the collar, "No wonder, general! look here at this cursed old sow with her litter of pigs!"

Simeon lost nothing by this operation, for he usually came in as one of our mess; and when he assisted as cook, it was not until the formal proclamation of the irrevocable law of "*soap and water:*" no law of the Medes or Persians was ever more strictly enforced when we had anything to cook.

This very delicate pursuit of louse racing has long since been known in Mexican prisons as one of the very few amusements of those dull regions. The races come off in the following manner: The Mexican prisoners draw a circle upon a beef's hide about eighteen inches in diameter, inside of which they draw a smaller one, and in the centre of this they make a *holy cross:* even to this vile purpose is that emblem of purity prostituted! The racers are placed on the outside of the inner ring, and the one that first crosses the double ring, and arrives at the holy goal, sweeps the *plata* or *soap*, as the case may be. We have witnessed the most ludicrous scenes around these pools.

As the tiny animals start, their owners become as much excited, doubtless, as the owners of Fashion and Boston at their great race. They jump and climb over each other to get a better view: it is, "Hurra for the white," and "Well done for the red," and many such expressions, accompanied with the most antic capers, each countenance being expressive of different degrees of hope and despair, according to the locality of their respective coursers. On these funny occasions, we have stood off to watch the countenances of the parties interested, and have witnessed grimaces which would have shaken the pencil from the hands of Hogarth. The only thing comparable to it is the negroes around a cockpit on a Whitsuntide in Virginia or North Carolina, a festival of ancient fashion in those good old states, where the negroes are as free of constraint as were the slaves of Rome on their *Saturnalia*.

The Texian prisoners thus simplified this mode of racing: they drew a charcoal circle upon a plank, in the centre of which the racers are turned loose at a given signal, and the one that "first crosses the black ring is winner."

Soon after pay-days, when each man is flush with his *forty-seven cents in cash*, I have known a whole "*medio*" bet upon a race; but the most usual bet was *an old soldier*. An "old soldier" in this sense is not the absolute war-worn veteran, covered with honourable scars and long years of service, but a chew of tobacco, which has from time to time undergone mastication from friend to friend, with the same kindness which one would loan another his knife or comb. These "old soldiers," after losing all the virtues of the "weed" from long grinding, are dried and smoked in a pipe; the latter operation coming as near the idea of the destructibility of matter as philosophical analysis will allow.

There is much skill to be exercised in the selection of your racers. At the same time that you would avoid the selection of an epicurean-built animal as you would an overly fat horse, it is not always that the most Cassius-looking fellow will win. Those who had watched more closely the natural history of the animal, soon discovered that they have as much love for their young as animals of a larger size. Thus those of our countrymen most skilled in the zoology of this troublesome little creature won the most "old soldiers." They would select a mother, which had lately deposited her young, around which she would hover with the devotion of a hen over her brood. When the mother of the young family was turned loose, her philoprogenitiveness impelled her forth, and doubtless she felt all the keen, though instinctive anxiety for her offspring which wiser animals feel. Whether her organ of locality could safely direct her back to her household after such abduction is more than was ascertained. This is certain, that she usually reached the goal first. Had Pindar been an inmate of a Mexican prison, he would have enriched his " Lousiad" with a more accurate knowledge of his subject. And might not Mr. Combe, or some other phrenologist, strengthen their theory by subjecting the head of a mother louse to microscopic inspection? Or, would it be a strong argument in favour of this fascinating science should the bump of philoprogenitiveness be larger in a louse than in a flea? for the latter deposites her young and hops off with all the ball-room gayety of a coquette, leaving the " little ones" to make the best of their way into the world.

The lamented General Austin once told me, that when he, by order of Santa Anna, was so long incarcerated in the Accordada in solitary confinement, a mouse was his only companion; and that it became so very gentle as to feed from his hands. Until I witnessed the interest which prisoners take in smaller things, I could not realize *that* interest which, he assured me, in the absence of man or books, he took in his little companion. " Often," said he, " when reason was nearly dethroned, and hope sunk into despair, this little animal would come as a special messenger sent by Providence to recall my senses; and—would you believe it?—I have laughed at his antic miniature comedies, and talked to him for hours."

Lord Byron makes the prisoner of Chillon thus beautifully express this feeling, and it has in it even more truth than poetry:

> " With spiders I have friendship made,
> And watch'd them in their sullen trade;
> Had seen the mice by moonlight play,
> And why should I feel less than they?
> We were all inmates of one place,
> And I the monarch of each race;
> Had power to kill—yet, strange to tell!
> In quiet we had learned to dwell:
> My very chains and I grew friends.
> So much a long communion tends
> To make us what we are."

It is constitutional with mankind that his desire increases for the thing inhibited to him. I have seen many striking illustrations of this fact. I have known men who could well do without tobacco where it was plenty, but when they could not get it would long for it with the intense feeling of a woman for some particular fancy when in the most interesting state of nature. I have known men who rarely or never drank ardent spirits when it was easily to be had, so soon as the use of it was denied them, they would put themselves to the greatest possible shifts to procure it. Above all others, the most inveterate habit was the use of tobacco, and those of us who had never used it were truly fortunate, as it was a contraband article, and difficult to procure.

The old sailing-master was a great slave to the weed, and it was always gratifying to meet his good-natured face when his pipe was well filled and protruding full two inches from his contented countenance. Then his happy looks made one feel better; but on those occasions when he could not fill his pipe, both his face and his gait reminded us of a funeral procession, and made us feel sad. Much, however, as he loved his pipe, he did not love it so well but that he would stop, no matter how great his hurry, and let a comrade take a pull at it— half a dozen long, strong pulls. As liberal as he was with his tobacco, still, at times, "the boys" would depredate upon him.

Near the head of his sheepskin, where he slept, there was a crack in the wall, into which, after the lights were blown out, he would carefully transfer his "old soldier," when frequently those best "at crawling" would ease it out of the crack and regrind it. If they failed to replace it in the crack, the first thing in the morning we would hear the old sailing-master sing out, "By my soul, boys, my old soldier is adrift;" but should he find it in the crack, and fresh from the mill, his song would then be, "By my soul, boys, some of you have been foul of my old soldier." Then, after igniting a loco foco, he being "quarterlero ocho," would commence and sweep up the decks; the conclusion of which operation was always with the grateful acknowledgment, "Now, by my soul, I have got a good 'presperation,'" at the same time wiping the exuberant drops from his benevolent physiogomy.

On certain days we had the privilege of buying brandy at the *tienda*, shop, a kind of sutler store, kept by the wife and daughter of a superannuated lieutenant. The old man was a dried-up octogenarian, who had served under Napoleon in Italy. He occasionally looked after our men at work, and was not a bad man. His wife was about thirty years his junior, and weighed two hundred and thirty pounds, and was the most stingy *fat* woman I ever knew. The daughter was twenty years her junior, and twenty pounds her senior: her face was marked with small-pox: she was, however, one of the best-tempered women of *her* size. She made but slow progress in English, yet always met us with a smile.

Her venerable sire still called her *Niña*, by the fond name he did thirty years ago, which means child. We called her *Señorita Niña;* others of our boys, who made as slow progress in Spanish as did *Niña* in English, called her *Señorita, muy bonita*, with a low bow, the English of which is, *Miss, very pretty;* but the low bow gave it the undefinable touch. There were still other Texians who were not up to this, and who employed a language which all seemed to understand and no one could explain. They would tip *Señorita Niña* Mr. Kendall's admirable "can't-come-it-judge" motion with a low bow, and the sight of a picayune, and the good creature never failed to wet their whistles.

The high estimation in which these people generally held Texians may be known from the fact that many of us could get credit for a dollar's worth, some even five, without a pledge of any kind, when they would not trust one of their own officers without he left his straps, sword-belt, or something in pledge corresponding to the amount purchased. *Senorita Niña* frequently invited Colonel Fisher, Colquhoun, Ogden, Van Ness, myself, and others, into her back parlour to drink our *vino mascal,* and would frequently remark, when she would return from the store, "What a very strange people you are! I can leave you here by yourselves, and you won't steal a thing."

There were certain days that it was *positively* against orders to sell us brandy. On these occasions many were the shifts resorted to for procuring it. One of their soldiers, in going to town, would cut off about three feet of the bowels of a beeve, tie up one end, fill it full, tie up the other, and then curl it up like a snake in the top of his cap, bring it in the castle, and retail it to us at a usurious profit "per suck."

There also lived in the castle a frisky, laughing, handsome little woman, the wife of a sergeant. She hated to see the *poor* Texians suffer, and would smuggle it in a beeve's bladder, out of which many a time we have drank to "*the glory, honour, and liberty of Texas.*"

On these occasions, under the pretence of looking after our washerwoman to get a light-coloured shirt, we would step in, and after giving her the "can't-come-it-judge," we were always answered by the pert little woman, first taking the forefinger of her right hand, placing it under the right eye, and pulling down the skin until you could see the red of the ball. This meant, "Look out for the officers while I pour out of the bladder."

This good little woman had also a high opinion of our integrity: in her front room she kept for sale fancy articles upon her centre-table, which we would take up and examine with Yankee curiosity while she would be in the back room exhuming the bladder. Frequently, when she would return, after casting her eye quickly over the table to see that all was right, she would hold up both hands, with her pretty round face elongated into expressible surprise, exclaiming, at the same time, "What a very strange people you are! I can leave you here by yourselves, and you won't steal a thing. Why, I would not trust the governor here by himself!"

Our friend Dan, on these and similar occasions, would make himself useful. He, though a rare bird, was not after Ovid's description, "*rara avis in terre, nigroque simillima cygno,*" but was of the gayest plumage and the most eloquent discourse. Often, when he has made these good women cry by first translating and then singing the "Soldier's Tear," they would wipe away their tears and pity our sweethearts.

Dan was formerly a midshipman in the United States service, and attached to the Brandywine on the Pacific station, where he learned the language of these people; but, like several other brave and generous spirits, he quitted that honourable service to fight for the liberty of our rising star. As midshipman, he had taken early lessons in the arts of the "Old Soldier." He was a proficient in raising a chew of tobacco, and sung himself into many a glass of *vino*; but his genius never showed the true intellect until he was ordered out to work.

One day at this rural sport of packing volcanic stones from the mountains was enough to satisfy his curiosity, and he wisely concluded that, inasmuch as he never put any of these stones on the mountains, "he would be shot if he took any away."

How was this to be avoided? He took a steel pen from my writing table in the corner, scratched his legs from his ankle to the knee, wrapped them around in many folds of old shirts and blankets, and quietly awaited the second order. When the order came, his legs were in a high state of inflammation from their superabundance of clothing, so much so that the surgeon had the irons taken off his ankles. The consequence was, that Dan's first day of packing stones was his last. Afterward it was easy for him to increase the inflammation upon inspection days.

Dan's knowledge of the Spanish, and exemption from work, made him a kind of moving oracle among this ignorant population of Mexican soldiers and sergeants' wives. For a long time he was a favourite among the latter, to whom he generally paid our washing bills, and to whom he would, as usual, first translate, and then sing, "Long, long ago." When he would come to

> "Now that you've come, all my griefs are removed,
> Let me forget that so long you have roam'd;
> Let me believe that you love as you loved
> Long, long ago—long, long ago,"

he would throw into the "long, long ago" such a pathetic physiognomy that he rarely failed to melt his fair hearers.

Alas! everything on earth is mutable, and Dan's favour met a check from which it never recovered.

If there are any people more than others tenacious of their religious tenets, it is the Catholics of Mexico. These women had a number of sprightly children, who became very fond of Dan. He had nothing to do, and could talk Spanish to them. They all had their Catechisms, and held the opinion that *we* had some immediate agency in killing their beloved Saviour, and not a very long time since; but Dan persuaded these little fellows that we were not the people who killed their beloved Jesus—that it was the Mexicans themselves: "for," said he, "do you not see that they have crowned him with a wreath of thorns? we have no thorns in our country: and do you not also see *that there*ранchéro spearing him in the side with a long lance? we have neither ranchéros nor lances in our country: we fight with the rifle." So soon as these good mothers found what an inroad Dan had made in the "young idea," he lost all favour; and when he would come about afterward, they would call in the little chaps with the most anxious care, and stand between them and Dan like an old hen between a hawk and her brood.

If anything exceeded the horror which Dan's heresy inspired in these ignorant people, it was a scene we witnessed in the commencement of the campaign. While our volunteer army was collecting about Bexar, preparatory to the march upon the Rio Grande, a portion of them were encamped near the Mission Church of San José. Around the door-facing of this church, as most churches in Mexico, there are a number of scriptural images cut in stone, and among them one of the fathers with the infant Messiah in his hands. On this occasion, one of our buckskin Republicans, who had struck for liberty, rode up, and not finding a convenient swinging limb to hitch his "critter" to, he threw the larieta over the head of the young Jesus. Very soon the animal took fright, pulled back, and carried away the head. At the sight of which, the men, women, and children, old and young, swarmed around the desecrated image, crossing themselves in prayer, showing by their countenances a degree of grief, indignation, and horror which it would be impossible to describe.

The first care of our liberty-man was to secure his horse, and then he went up to the old woman who held the head, and appeared, if possible, more distressed than the balance, and said, "Ole 'oman, now it ain't no use to make such a fuss about the thing. I didn't know that the 'tarnal critter was goin' to pull off his head: you have got d—n mean stone about here, anyhow." This speech the Republican considered the *amende honorable*, and went his way whistling, leaving the group in prayer to propitiate the calamity.

A gentleman of Dan's leisure now required intellectual recreation, and among his other teachings he persuaded the ignorant Péon who sold us ass's milk that "it was the richness of the milk which made their ears so much longer than either those of the cow or horse," and that the length of their ears respectively was in proportion to the substance of the milk; "for," says he, "don't you see that corn will grow higher in rich than in poor land?" There was no resisting this argument, and this poor fellow left the castle a wiser man than any other dealer in ass's milk.

Mr. Black, the American consul in Mexico, humanely sent us a trunk of clothes and a blanket each, for which we were sincerely thankful. Captain West, formerly of Philadelphia, also sent us from Mexico a trunk of clothes and some writing materials, for which we acknowledged many obligations. Also, Dr. ——, and Señor Conzalvi,[*] sent us a package of English books, which rendered our confinement more tolerable, and for which we shall long remember them with gratitude.

[*] August, 1845. A few days since, in passing up Canal-street, in New-York, I met at 118, where he keeps a coffee-house, this excellent man, Señor Conzalvi. His disinterested friendship in furnishing my destitute comrades clothing, bread, and medicine became known to the Mexican authorities, and he had to fly. He is a Corsican by birth, deserves the lasting gratitude of Texians, and the good-will of all just men.

Young Billy Reese, who had just recovered from a dangerous illness in Mexico, was on his way to Texas, and came by to see us. He confirmed the melancholy intelligence of the decimation of our seventeen companions at Salado. This intelligence threw a still darker gloom over our imprisonment. When, a few days after, we heard of the shooting of the heroic Captain Cameron, and the more than heroic manner in which they all met death, all of us shed tears to their memory—we trust, not tears of forgetfulness.

After the horrible murder of our seventeen countrymen at Salado on the 25th of March, the main body of the survivors were marched on the road to the capital, a distance of five hundred miles, under sufferings the most cruel, which killed several; and many others, being unable to travel, were left in the hospitals of San Luis Potosi, Dolores, and San Juan del Rio, from which miserable sinks but few ever returned. It would be swelling this journal beyond all reasonable bounds to detail the actual suffering of these men; indeed, language would give the reader but a poor idea of these sad recollections. Thus, after thirty days' march, they arrived at the village of Huehuetoca, seven leagues from the city of Mexico, where they were all crowded together in a room too small to permit of their lying down, and into which not a breath of air could enter when the door was closed. In a very little time the air became so impure, from the exhaustion of the oxygen, that the candles went out, and respiration became exceedingly difficult. They in vain appealed to the guards at the door to let in fresh air, and when death the most cruel stared them wholesale in the face, as a last alternative they had recourse to cutting holes in the door with their pocket knives, and alternately breathing at these small orifices.

This was, indeed, as the Mexican soldiers called it, *la noche triste*, "the sad night." Their march of many leagues the day before, through an insufferable dust, a burning sun, the want of food and water, and then at night not even space sufficient of the stone floor to lie upon, and a suffocating atmosphere to breathe, was not their full measure of wo. About eight o'clock at night a menial murderer, with a pair of epaulets upon his shoulders, and a guard of about one dozen mounted men, under broad-brimmed hats, arrived with orders from the tyrant Santa Anna to shoot the bold and beloved Captain Ewin Cameron.

Captain Cameron was unchained from his partner, Colonel Wm. F. Wilson, and, with his interpreter, Alfred Thurmond, taken out of prison, and kept under a separate guard until morning; and when informed that he was to be shot, wrote a manly and dignified letter of remonstrance to the British minister against such a cold-blooded murder of a national enemy and a British subject. The writer regrets his inability as yet to be able to procure this last letter.

The next morning, after our men were marched for the city of Mexico, he was taken out in the rear

SHOOTING OF CAPTAIN CAMERON.

of the village to the place of execution. A priest, the usual attendant of Mexican executions, was in waiting, and when he was asked if he wished to confess to the father, he promptly answered, "No! throughout life I believe that I have lived an upright man, and if I have to confess it shall be to my Maker." His arms were then tied with a cord at the elbows and drawn back, and when the guard advanced to bandage his eyes, he said to his interpreter, "*Tell them no! Ewin Cameron can now, as he has often done before for the liberty of Texas, look death in the face without winking.*" So saying, he threw his hat and blanket upon the ground, opened the bosom of his hunting-shirt, presented his naked breast, and gave the word "Fire!" when his noble soul in a twinkling passed into another, we trust a better world. Thus fell Ewin Cameron! Long, long will the patriotic of his adopted country cherish the memory of one whose bosom was bared to every danger, and whose life was sacrificed to liberty.

As we have before said, he was a Scotchman, and a more honourable or bolder Scotchman never left his native land. He was about thirty-six years of age, tall and well proportioned, weighing nearly two hundred pounds, and of extraordinary physical power, which was in perfect keeping with his manly countenance and lion heart. We recollect him well at the battle of Mier, defending with his gallant company one of our most exposed situations. He wore a bowie-knife at his side, and held in his hand a tremendous rifle which carried ten balls to the pound; and it was certain death for an enemy to cover his sight at three hundred yards. On one occasion during the action, a column of the enemy charged so near upon his position, along a low stone wall four feet high, and not having time to reload, he thundered out, in his ever-memorable, glorious Highland brogue, "*Boys, to your stones!*" No sooner said than a shower of fifty well-aimed pebbles, about the size of one's fist, saluted the assailants, knocking down many, and scattering the remainder to the four winds. This sensible man, with an intuitive forecast which he could never have picked from all the books of all the wars, previous to the charge ordered his company, stationed along the before-mentioned wall, to "pile up good-sized throwing-stones," and keep them in readiness as a *corps de reserve*. They proved to be as effective as if they had been hurled by steam-power; for the fact was ascertained after the battle that several of the enemy were found dead without having their skins broken, such was the effect of this novel repulse.

Lieutenant George B. Crittenden, who had been also released by order of Santa Anna, came by to see us. He was permitted to remain locked up in prison with us one hour, and by him we sent home many messages to wives, sweethearts, and countrymen.

Orlando Phelps, who had also been released by Santa Anna, came by to see us, which afforded us another opportunity to write home. The release of Phelps shows that the President of Mexico is not wholly destitute of gratitude. When he was confined a prisoner at Orozimbo, in Texas, the seat of Dr. Phelps, in 1836, and failed in his attempt to poison his guards, he was ironed by Captain Patton, the officer in charge of him. This threw such a gloom over his destiny, that in a fit of despondence he determined to drink the poison prepared for his guards. Dr. Phelps succeeded in pumping it from his stomach and restoring him, for which he generously released his son, and furnished him means to return home.

Owing to Santa Anna's personal hostility to myself, I had nothing to hope from his clemency, and but little to desire. With my letter of the 25th of April to the President of the United States, of which the following is a copy, I had done everything in behalf of my unfortunate countrymen which my situation would allow, and I determined to migrate to Texas, where I could prosecute the argument in a *different* shape.

"Castle of Perote, Mexico, April 25th, 1843.

"To his Excellency John Tyler,
President of the United States of America:

"Sir,—This will inform your excellency that I am one of two hundred and forty-eight Texians who were taken prisoners of war by General Pedro d'Ampudia, of the Mexican army, on the 26th of December ultimo, at Mier. On the 11th of January, with the permission of General Ampudia, I addressed you a hurried note from Matamoras upon the subject of our captivity, and not hearing whether said note ever reached its destination, I am induced to write again. In the above-named note I solicited your intercession, as the head of a neutral and friendly power, in our behalf, and in the then hurry and limited time of writing, suggested only one ground for your intercession, which I then thought, and still believe, tenable. Since which, other and stronger reasons have occurred to my mind in favour of your doing so, which you will please permit me to state more fully.

"In my note of the 11th of January, I assumed the position that a seven years' maintenance of our nationality, which is recognised by the most enlightened and powerful nations of the earth, has taken from us the character of a *"rebel province,"* and this consideration entitles us to all the tolerations of civilized warfare. I was more confirmed in this position when I understood that the Mexican government last summer declared that on their part the war with Texas should hereafter be conducted upon the strictest principles of civilized nations. This declaration I understood to have been made to the foreign minister resident near Mexico, with the farther declaration that "no farther interference upon their part should be allowed in favour of the subjects of their respective countries who should be found in arms with the Texians, but that they would be treated as prisoners of war." This principle, so boldly avowed in the proclamation of Major-general Arista, commanding the army *del Norte* of Mexico, was widely distributed in Texas last spring when invaded by General Vascus, under his (Arista's) orders, and also when General Woll invaded Texas he made a like declaration.

"If, then, the seven years' maintenance of our nationality, either with or without this declaration on the part of Mexico, entitles us to this consideration, which I am bound, in respect to those governments that have so recognised us, to believe, let us see how far it has been carried out.

"Last spring, when General Vascus invaded Texas, the sacking of San Antonio and the plunder of a very large amount of private property was the consequence. The fall following, under General Woll's invasion, not only was private property taken without remuneration to the owners, but fifty-three of our best citizens, who had, in the hurry of the alarm, risen from their beds in defence of their immediate homes, to oppose, as they believed, a band of robbers, were taken and carried into captivity— truly and literally abducted. Those Texians who fought the battle of Mier consisted of some of the most valuable citizen soldiers of our country, who assembled under the laws of that country to *repel* an invasion thereof, and surrendered prisoners of war under the articles of capitulation herewith enclosed, with the most solemn and repeated verbal promises of their observance and good treatment by the general in command of the Mexian forces. How far these promises have been carried out we will hereafter inquire.

"In my note to your excellency, as above referred to, I stated, that if this principle of civilized warfare was to be observed, the Mexican nation was still debtor to Texas, in way of exchange or liberation of prisoners, about five hundred; that Texas had unconditionally liberated about eight hundred Mexican prisoners, and that Mexico had only liberated three hundred Texians; that, therefore, upon every principle of exchange of prisoners, we were entitled to our liberation. Since, however, writing the above-named note, I have reflected, that inasmuch as the Texians had suspended hostilities against Mexico at your excellency's special request, and while at their respective firesides, in the peaceful pursuits of their avocations, some were abducted from their homes by that country who, unlike us, had refused respect to that request, and others who, in obedience to the highest of all laws, had assembled to repel invasion, that there is an obligation of the highest national character upon your government to relieve us from a situation in which an obedience on our part, and a want of respect on the part of our enemy to said request, has placed us. The request I allude to is dated by Mr. Webster, secretary of state of the United States, as well as I now recollect, in July last, to the Honourable Mr. Eves, chargé d'affaires near the Texian government.

"I will not stop here to argue, nor do I believe it necessary with one of your national dignity and enlightened wisdom, how far friendly nations may interfere to enforce the observance of those customs which the long practice of civilized nations has made a law, but respectfully solicit of your excellency a full consideration of the Texian and Mexican question. In the absence of all authorities upon the subject, being shut up with my brave companions in this uncomfortable prison, loaded with irons, and treated with all the indignity of state felons, much allowance should be made for the opinions of one so directly interested. Candour impels me, however, to say, that in my humble judgment the immediate vicinage of your nation to the powers in dispute fully authorize your interference. If the compromising of your commercial relations and the interest of your border citizens by this protracted war of nearly eight years' duration—a war more in name than in any bold attempt by Mexico to subjugate Texas—if the bold and fearful avowal on the part of our enemy for the abolition of slavery in the immediate vicinity of your slave states—if the conduct of this war, wholly deceptious, uncivilized, and cruel, justifies such interference, to say nothing about our near relationship—that we are of the loins of your manhood, that we are of the same language, religion, and laws, and that we are striving to the maintenance of the same character of government as yours—then ought you to interfere.

"Your excellency will indulge me in concisely summing up the history of this war:

"In its commencement in 1835, the province of Texas did not rebel against the old established government of the mother state, but against a new one then sought to be established. In 1836, the close of the Mexican invasion with the battle of San Jacinto demonstrated her ability to maintain her separate independence, which the government of the United States recognised in March, 1837. Since which period, every other nation to whom we have applied, including France, England, and Belgium, have done the same, and Texas has continued an unprecedented growth in settlement and population. On the other hand, Mexico has continued a predatory war upon the borders of Texas, without once attempting to resubjugate her by a *formidable* invasion. This predatory warfare has been marked by treachery and cruelty on the part of Mexico unprecedented in the history of civilized nations. She has captured our minister plenipotentiary returning home under his passports from the government of *your* country, and incarcerated him for months in a vile prison. She betrayed the lamented Colonel Benjamin Johnson, under the protection of a flag of truce, and murdered him in a brutal manner. She in cold blood put to death Colonel Fannin and four hundred brave men, in violation of his articles of capitulation. She betrayed the Santa Fé command into a surrender, and violated the most solemn promises made to them. Last spring she summoned the city of San Antonio to surrender, and plundered her for obedience to said summons. Last fall the Anglo-American citizens of San Antonio were taken from their homes, because they thought fit to defend themselves against, as they believed at that time, an unauthorized band of robbers. Last fall, after Captain Dawson's company of Texians had surrendered to the Mexican army, four fifths of them were put to the sword, after their arms were given up. To the shame of humanity I have to record the basest perfidy on their part yet. At the battle of Mier, on the 26th of December last, after the Texians had fought them for nineteen consecutive hours, killing and wounding more than double their own numbers, the Mexican commander sent in a flag of truce, summoning them to surrender, and promising in the most solemn manner, through his leading officers and one of the fathers of the Church, that "we should be treated with all the honours and consideration of prisoners of war." These officers, among whom were General De la Vega, and Colonels Carasco and Blanco, pledging with uplifted eyes the straps upon their shoulders, and the priest of Comargo, Padre De Lire, pledging the holy Catholic religion to their observance. The Texians, ever credulous, as brave men are, surrendered, while still they had formidable means of resistance in their hands. The result of that surrender produced from the general in command the enclosed articles of capitulation, which were read to all of our officers by *his Mexican interpreter,* "*with all the honours and considerations of prisoners of war,*" we not being allowed our interpreter at the reading. We afterward learned the true reading of this article to be, "*with all the considerations consequent upon the magnanimous Mexican nation.*" As representatives of a people unused to such low cunning, and believing that with any civilized nation the obligation of good treatment would be as binding under this article as under the one which had been so solemnly promised, we were for a time content, and the more so under the disposition which the Mexican commander, General Ampudia, evinced in carrying out his promises. Soon after which we were sent to the capital of Mexico, from whence we have been incarcerated in this prison, coupled together with cumbrous iron chains, and made to do not only the servile labour of policing the filth—*not* of *our* creation—but doing the work of mules and oxen in packing in stones and sand about one mile, and upon the most indifferent rations. The greatest infamy is still untold! When General Fisher, myself, Captain Reese, and Lieutenant Clarke remonstrated against the performance of degrading labour, we were gravely told by the governor-general here that we were not *prisoners of war*, and could claim nothing under our articles of capitulation. Let me tell the worst! I have just learned that seventeen of my brave companions have been lotteried for, and shot in cold blood.

" If this catalogue of human outrage on the part of our enemy, and their sending, time after time emissaries into your country to stir up the Indians to their murderous warfare upon our borders, with other and numerous good reasons too tedious for rehearsal in this letter, can claim your interference, then let me beg it in behalf of my unfortunate and brave companions. Our desire is that we should be liberated, because it is just that we should be; and then that the war should be conducted upon principles of civilized warfare, because we are too brave to retaliate by such dastardly perfidy and cowardice. Let this be done, and we are willing, anxious, and able to carry on the war. I have the honour, very respectfully, to be your excellency's obedient servant,
" THOMAS J. GREEN."

I received many letters from the United States expressive of the anxious solicitude of my friends in my welfare, all of which I acknowledged with the warmest gratitude. I am particularly indebted to President Tyler, the Honourable Messrs. Mangum and Haywood, senators, and Mr. Graham, late senator from North Carolina; the Honourable John C. Calhoun, and others, for the warm interest they manifested towards me. The usefulness, however, of my friends was impaired, from the fact that my political connexion with Texas prevented them from coming under pledges of my not taking up arms against Mexico. The following extract from my letter to Mr. Calhoun defined my position: "Eight years of the prime of my life, and a considerable portion of my fortune, have been spent for the establishment of liberty in Texas; therefore my friends must see that I am too closely identified with her to take *my* liberty upon conditions which may compromise my political relations to her, and I hope they will avoid any promises of that kind." So long as the war shall continue with Mexico, those who know me will require no assurance that I shall be found in the foremost ranks of her enemies.

CHAPTER XVII.

ESCAPE FROM THE CASTLE OF PEROTE.

Preparation to Escape.—Procuring a Map of the Road.—Deceiving the Officer with Shaving Tools.—Work upon Breach in the Wall.—Letter to our Prisoners in Mexico.—Santa Anna's Birthday.—President Houston's Orders to Colonel Snively prevents our Liberation.—Commodore Moore off Campeachy.—Prosecution of the Breach in the Wall.—Laying in Provisions to Travel.—Last Visit to " Guts."—Quarterlero.— Voos, his Rheumatism, and Grunts.—All decline the Escape but Sixteen.—Left Papers with Colquhoun.—Note to Santa Anna.—Take Leave of our Friends.—Turnkeys.—Mode of Counting.—Locking up.— Deceiving the Sentinels: mode of.—Monte Bank.—Bull-dance.—Commence going Out.— Toowig.— Ike Allen: his Fall.— Character.— Beeve's Bladder.— Aguardiente.—Governor.— " Guts" and the Dialogue.—Stone hung in the Hole. — The Herculean John Young. — Passing the Sentinels.—Their Hailing.—Our Response.

Now that my usefulness either to myself or my fellow-prisoners was at an end, I determined to return to my country, or perish in the attempt. To escape from this strong place, guarded as it was with the most unremitting vigilance, was considered impossible by the Mexicans, and the project required the greatest caution, coolness, and calculation. I made known my determination to Captain Reese, who agreed to join me in the enterprise, and also to stake his life upon the issue.

Our first plan was to scale the different walls, the height of which we could carefully estimate by the eye, during some stormy night when the sentinels could be most easily passed. We accordingly set about making arrangements.

Our ignorance of the country, and the insurmountable difficulties of so mountainous a region, rendered it first necessary that we should have a map to travel by, and this could only be obtained in the city of Mexico. I accordingly wrote to a friend to procure the article. He returned for an answer that on a certain day he would pass Perote in the stage on his way to Vera Cruz, and that I must meet him at the stage-office, if it were possible to procure the governor's permission. The stage passes Perote three times per week on its way to Vera Cruz and back. The stage-office is in the town of Perote, about one mile from the castle; here the stages meet, one running from Vera Cruz, and another from the city of Mexico; this is the stopping-place for the night. They arrive usually about four or five o'clock in the evening, on which days it was usual for the governor to permit one, and sometimes two of our men to go out under a strong guard to get our papers and letters. I went to the governor, and asked permission to go to the stage-office, which he granted, sending an officer and six soldiers as a guard. When I reached the stage-office the coach from Mexico was already in, and my friend waiting my arrival. We were old acquaintances, but neither appeared to know the other. He had in his pocket the map I was so anxious to procure, but how was that to be given to me? The officer did not leave my side three feet, and the soldiers stood single file upon each side of the door.

After some minutes, my friend, who spoke the Spanish language well, stepped up to the officer, and pointing to me, he said, " Is not that a Texian prisoner?" " Yes!" replied the officer. My friend walked around me, and eyed me from head to foot as a thing of much curiosity; then turning to the officer, remarked, "Well, such is the fortune of war: will you join me in something to drink?" There are very few Mexican officers who will refuse a drink of *aguardiente*, if it cost them nothing, and he readily consented. My friend, again turning to the officer after taking the drink, said, " Shall I offer the poor prisoner some?" "If you please," was the reply. I stepped up to the counter, and while taking a drink, received a hunch from the elbow of my old friend. In a little time he again asked the officer to drink, and again his invitation was accepted, the officer taking a " stiff pull" each time. He soon became good-natured and loquacious; was eloquent in giving this stage-passenger a history of the Texians, their mode of warfare, &c.; said that we were very daring, and could shoot out one's eye at three hundred yards with our big rifles, and wound up by depicting my character, performances, &c. He said that I had had Santa Anna prisoner once in my country; I ought, therefore, to be closely watched, as there was nothing too daring for these people to undertake. This *new* stage-acquaintance stepped into the adjoining room, and returned in a few minutes with a razor, hairbrush, and comb, so folded in a rumpled paper that their ends plainly shown. He remarked to the officer that " that poor fellow looks as if he would be the better of a good razor: can I have the privilege of giving him these shaving tools?" " Certainly," replied the officer. He handed them to me, with a wink which I well understood. I carelessly took the package in my hand, and walked back to the castle by the side of the officer, he little dreaming that the rumpled envelope was a lithographed map of the country between Vera Cruz, via Perote, and the City of Mexico. This survey had been made a few years since by order of the government for a railroad; the rivers, mountains, and passes were plainly marked. When I reached my prison safe with it, one important difficulty was surmounted. My friend Lodovic Colquhoun, being a good draughtsman, made several copies of it.

Passing in and out of the castle to the stage-office, I had estimated the height of the walls from the bottom of the great moat to the top of the bastion. This I was the more easily enabled to do from counting the number of layers of squared stones, and multiplying that number by the thickness of each. This ascertained, the next difficulty was to procure a rope of sufficient length to tie to the carriage of the artillery, pass over the wall, and reach to the bottom. The rope could be purchased in town, but the difficulty was the getting it in the castle. This we accomplished by sending time after time, and purchasing short pieces, that it might not attract notice. These several pieces once in our prison-room, were easily made into one by the sailor experience of several of our companions. It is about as easy for the old sailing-master to *splice* a rope as it is for a landsman to cut one in two.

Our preparation had progressed thus far with entire success, but yet there were many difficulties to overcome, one of which was to elude the vigilance of the officer at *lock-up time*.

At six o'clock in the evening we had to be counted before being locked up for the night. If we were out of the room, how were our places to be supplied? This we could do by getting our interpreter to say that "there lie two very sick," pointing to our mats, carefully folded over some baskets, and our hats laying as if they covered our faces. The probability of the officer taking it for granted was the risk we had to run. In the mean time we would be in a stable opposite our prison-room, and concealed with our rope under some straw. At a few minutes before nine, having chosen a stormy, cold night, we could crawl past the sentinel upon all fours, and then climbing up against the gate, and one standing upon the shoulder of the other, could reach the top; then descending upon the opposite side by the rope, the first holding one end for the other to descend by, one being over, he could hold the rope for the other to ascend by, and thence to the shoulders of the first. This operation would place us upon the steps, which would ascend to the top of the castle, and by carefully crawling past the upper sentinels, and tying one end of the rope to the wheel of a cannon, we could descend to the bottom of the moat.

With all our arrangements completed for our migration, we were yet prevented from so doing at this time, on account of the following circumstances:

In the centre one of our prison-rooms, which contained thirty-six of our countrymen, a few lion-hearted fellows determined also to make the attempt at escaping. They had commenced the operation of going through an eight feet wall, and if Captain Reese and myself escaped by scaling the walls, which we now considered pretty certain of accomplishing, it would, consequently, break up all farther chances of others doing so by any means whatever. We then determined to join in the plan of going through the walls, and all escaping at the same time.

The breach was in progress of being made, several weeks having been spent at work on it, and all who determined upon the hazard were in high spirits, when we were informed, through General Thompson and several other sources, that we would be released on the 13th of June, Santa Anna's birthday. Indeed, our information appeared to be so authentic we did not doubt it, and consequently knocked off from our work upon the breach in the wall. General Thompson wrote down to us to make preparation for going home; and, knowing that the yellow fever was raging at Vera Cruz in its most malignant form, I feared that our countrymen would go to that place in advance of any preparations for sailing, and fall victims to the disease, as did many of the Santa Fé prisoners the year previous. I addressed the following note to our countrymen in Mexico:

"Castle of Perote, June 5th, 1843.
"To Captains Ryan, Pierson, Baker, and other Texian Prisoners of War at Mexico.

"Friends and Countrymen,—Since our separation I have heard of your difficulties and trials, at which my heart has sorely bled; at the same time, we have not been without ours. If we have suffered much, it will be a consolation beyond all price that it was for our country, and in the cause of liberty and equal rights; and while we mourn the loss of one fifth of our brave companions, let us believe that our country and posterity will do them and us justice. We are taught to believe that justice, eternal and all-pervading, is the peculiar province of God; and under this bright hope the time *must* come, when, in recounting our wrongs, we may point with pride to the *debit* side of the account.

"We are informed from various unofficial sources, besides through the letters of the United States minister in Mexico, that we are to be liberated on the 13th instant. To see you all safely landed at home once more is my weightiest care; and, knowing that but few of you have the means, I have taken some steps to procure a vessel at Vera Cruz, by the time of your arrival, for your transmission. Should we be liberated on that day, I have advised our companions here to stop at Xalapa, about thirty miles distant, until I can go to Vera Cruz and perfect an arrangement for their sailing, as it would be very dangerous for them to remain in that place, where the yellow fever is already bad. I also advise you to come to that place, where you will join your comrades, and where I hope to meet you with the arrangements for sailing.

"I beg, my dear friends, that all and each of you will accept my warmest feelings for your happiness and welfare. THOMAS J. GREEN."

The 13th of June drew near, and every officer we met told us that "in a little time we would leave that place and return to our country and friends." The soldiers, by way of congratulating us, in their mixture of Spanish and English, would make a flourish peculiar to the Mexican people, dash their right hand through their left in the direction of Texas, and say, "*Poco-tiempo Texas*" (Texas in a little while). Even this from the most stupid soldier flattered our desire; but still, the 13th came and went, and no liberation. The next day it was promised, but the next failed of liberation. The next, and still the next, came and passed under a like promise from our officers, bringing with each successive day the chagrin of disappointment to take the place of joyous hopes.

In a few days, however, letters from the capital explained the secret of our detention. President Santa Anna had changed his determination of liberating us as soon as he was informed that President Houston had sent out a party under Colonel Snively to rob the Santa Fé traders. In Houston's order to Snively it was stipulated that "*the spoils should be equally divided between the government and the captors.*" Thus, after his open and violent denunciation of the conduct of General Somerville's command at Laredo, *he stipulates* that the Republic of Texas shall be a party to this robbery, and a recipient of the stolen goods. This news cast a still darker gloom over our destiny; we felt it keenly, because in it we saw our government officially degraded. That influence which President Houston had exerted in suppressing the national enthusiasm of avenging our wrongs—in keeping back Generals Rusk, Mayfield, and other gallant spirits from striking boldly upon the Rio Grande for our liberty—was now employed in the *petit larceny* of waylaying the road, and robbing a few harmless traders of their handkerchiefs and calicoes.

With this disgraceful intelligence from our country all hope of speedy liberation vanished, and we again set to work upon the breach in the wall.

One circumstance, however, cheered us on in our work, and lightened our country's accumulated disgrace: that was, that every mail brought us news that our little navy, and the gallant Commodore Moore, was off Campeachy, and had beaten and blockaded ten times his naval force. Our correspondent in Mexico sent us private word that Moore had taken the Mexican steamers, and such was the belief for many days in Mexico. This was glorious news, and it exhilarated our spirits to the highest degree. We made all the inquiry in our power to ascertain the practicability of reaching Moore at Yucatan by land, but found it impracticable, from the many hundred miles we would have to perform, through both a mountainous and a swampy country.

As the reader has been previously informed, our arched cells were twenty feet wide by seventy long, with a door at one end opening in the castle, and a loophole at the other opening upon the outside, underneath which is the great moat. This loophole is a small aperture, upon the outside about four by twelve inches, and gradually widening through the eight feet wall upon the inside to about two feet. Could we have pursued this aperture by widening it, our labour would have been less; but soon we found, from the hard character of the stones, and the secure fastenings immediately around the hole, difficulties which, with our poor means of operating, were impossible to surmount. We consequently struck off to the left, leaving these difficulties entirely to our right, and prepared to bore through the solid masonry.

To avoid discovery, both from the sentinel at the door and the officers when they came in the room upon inspection, a careless rap upon the door or post by our *look-out* man was sufficient for the operator in the hole to *lie low*. These men engaged in the work alternately, as only one at a time could operate, and he was secreted by the shutter enclosing the loophole, and blankets carefully hung about it. The labour was extremely tiresome, as the hole had to be made horizontally through the wall, and consequently required the operator to lay upon his abdomen, and rest upon his elbows, which position, after a few hours' work, became very painful. After working his tour, he would gather up the fragments of stone and mortar which his labour had detached, and bury them under some loose stone and brick in the floor. As the quantity thus buried would raise the pavement too high, it would be taken out under our blankets, and emptied into the *comûn*, privy.

The tools with which we operated were narrow, inferior carpenter's chisels—the Mexican tools were generally of an inferior kind, which our carpenters would bring from the shop. Some of our men were carpenters and wheelwrights, and were employed in the carpenter shop making artillery carriages; and as they would have to come to their meals, and sleep in the same prison-cells, they would smuggle the chisels out of the shop under their blankets. The reader will understand that our men had to wear blankets over their shoulders as an essential portion of their wardrobe; and as they despised Mexican fashion too much to give it that peculiar *à la Mexicana* sling about the arms, they wore them *à la Texas*, by first suspending the blanket over a string, then tying the ends of the string round the neck; and he who was so fortunate as to have a warm one felt as proud as a Roman senator with his ermined toga. The Texas mode, however, of wearing the blanket, though different from that of the "blanketed nation," afforded both comfort and ample means of smuggling.

As a water-drip will wear away the hardest granite, so the breach in the wall gradually grew deeper under our incessant labour. This work was principally accomplished by drilling holes into the stone and mortar with the chisel, and prying off small pieces; and frequently, after a hard day's labour, not more than a hatful could be disengaged. The greatest difficulty, however, was, that as the hole grew deeper, it grew smaller, and the position of the operator rendered it next to impossible to avoid this difficulty; so that when the hole reached the outside of the wall, it had a funnel shape, the outer end being reduced to ten by fourteen inches. On the first day of July the hole had been drilled down to a thin shell on the outer side, which could be easily burst out, after the final preparation was made for leaving.

For some weeks previous to our escape, those who intended to go were busily engaged, every safe opportunity, in completing their arrangements—fixing their knapsacks, saving all the bread they could procure, laying aside every cent to purchase fat bacon and chocolate. Having been furnished money by a friend in Mexico, I was enabled to supply several with sugar, coffee, and bacon, which compensated for my lack of work in the hole.

We considered it imprudent to start with less than two weeks' rations each, as we calculated to be all of that time in the mountains before venturing into a settlement to replenish our stores. To buy so large a quantity at one time might lead to suspicion as to what purpose we wanted them for, as heretofore our purchase had been of the smallest character. To avoid this suspicion, we had been for weeks buying a little at a time. At length, Sunday, the second day of July, opened upon us with a favourable symptom. This day we had an officer of the guard who was considered less particular in counting and inspecting us at lock-up times; and though we wished to celebrate the sixty-seventh anniversary of our forefathers' independence by our emancipation from the prison, yet we considered this too favourable an opportunity to lose. We passed the word for all who intended to go to be in readiness by night.

I went round to old Guts's quarters and purchased my last bacon, chocolate, and sugar. I found the old fellow exceedingly polite, and when I laid his money upon the counter, he insisted upon crediting me for the amount, saying that I might have use for the money. I told him, "Short settlements make long friends." He thanked me for my custom, and hoped that I would continue to deal with him. I replied, that the next purchase I made *in the castle* should certainly be from him. So far I have kept my word.

In each of the prison-rooms one of our men were detailed and exempt from work, whose duty it was to sweep the room, receive the bread, count it out to each man, and be responsible not only for the general police of the room, but also for the safety of everything in it. This officer was termed "quarterlero," and Voos held the appointment for the centre room.

About an hour before we were locked up, I met Voos with his head and jaws tied up, and limping along with the greatest apparent difficulty. "What is the matter, Voos?" said I; when, after turning his head very carefully upon his shoulders, and rolling his eyes up in the sockets with the graceful affectation of a sick maid, then turning round and surveying well the premises, he replied, "General, I am quartelero of the centre room, and it is very necessary for me to have the rheumatism and go to the hospital before you leave, or I shall catch it to-morrow." At this moment an officer hove in sight, and Voos hobbled on. It was the officer of the guard bringing in the surgeon of the hospital to examine Voos's rheumatism. He pronounced it a very bad case, and in a few minutes four soldiers brought in upon their shoulders a palanquin, upon which Voos was carefully laid, when they bore him from the castle in the most tender manner under the reiteration of the most doleful grunts.

This witty Dutchman passed me with a cunning wink, but did not forget to grunt; and, until he was shut out from our sight by the outer gate, these lugubrious sounds came back to those who were in the secret to excite their risibility at the best comedy of the season.

It was considered the safest plan, after getting out of the castle, to pair off, and not more than two or three go together, as, the smaller the company, the more easily they could secrete themselves, the whole not being sufficient to carry on either offensive or defensive operations to advantage.

Under this arrangement I had selected Dan, mainly on account of his speaking the language of the country. I had a pair of saddlebags, which we divided and made into two knapsacks, which were filled with fat bacon, a bag of ground coffee and pounded sugar, with several cakes of chocolate, and one hundred dollars in silver. I divided out my blankets, sheepskins, and clothing among my companions, putting on the most indifferent upon which my name was not seen. Our countrymen who worked in the carpenter's shop had made each a walking cane of the *sapote* wood, which is very heavy and strong. These canes, and a pocket knife each, were our only weapons of defence.

Several, who had previously determined to come, from prudential motives now declined it, as they considered, and very rightly, that getting through the walls of the prison was the least difficult part of the undertaking. To escape several hundred miles through an enemy's country, speaking an unknown tongue, was a difficulty which could not be too cautiously weighed. If retaken, all calculated to be shot; and we farther calculated the chances of success greatly against our reaching our country in safety.

Knowing President Santa Anna's personal hostility to myself, and believing that all he wanted was some reasonable pretext for having me shot, I believed it was worth my life to be recaptured, and the chances of escaping were ten to one against me. Some of my friends have considered this attempt rash, but these were the questions I had to settle with my own conscience, and which I did, divested of all passion : Could I be of more service at home to my unfortunate countrymen prisoners? and was it more honourable to myself and my country to draw in such a lottery, and perish in the attempt, or longer live the life of an insulted slave? My conscientious duty pointed me to hazard, and I embraced it without fear.

Sixteen of our number finally determined to make the effort. Of the sixteen, Richard Barclay, R. Cornegay, John Forester, John Dalrymple, Thomas Hancock, Isaac Allen, John Young, Davis, Stone, Beck, and Elley, were inmates of the centre prison-room, through which the breach had been made. John Toowig and D. C. Ogden belonged to the right-hand room; Captain Reese, Daniel Drake Henrie (Dan), and myself, belonged to the room on the left. To transfer ourselves from the outside rooms to the one in the centre, and get some of the inmates of that room to supply our places and elude the vigilance of the officers at lock-up hour, was a ticklish business and required much address.

I left my papers in charge of my friend Ludovic Colquhoun, who, in expectation of a close search after it was discovered that we were gone, carefully buried them. Several weeks after he forwarded them through Colonel John Bradley, who was released by Santa Anna through the intercession of General A. Jackson.

I left a note upon my table for President Santa

Anna, which I desired Colonel Fisher to hand to the governor at counting time next day, in which I exculpated the officers of the castle from either knowledge of our going, or neglect of duty in closely guarding us. Justice to these officers required me to say thus much; and I here repeat that not a living Mexican in the castle knew anything of it until after our escape. I also stated to Santa Anna that, "not having been trusted upon my parole, which neither the love of life nor fear of death could have induced me to forfeit, and the climate of Perote not suiting my health, I should, for the present, retire to one in Texas more congenial to my feelings."

At half past five I took leave of my friends, and a sad parting it was. Most who remained believed it was a voluntary sacrifice of ourselves, and few believed it possible for us to escape. I never shall forget that hour. As we grasped each other's hands, most believed for the last time, the big tear filled the eyes of those brave men, and they wished me success with an utterance which showed their hearts were overflowing. Said they, "God grant that you may reach home in safety, for then we know we will be fearlessly and truly represented." Colonel Fisher said, "As you have determined upon the hazard, though the chances are greatly against you, God grant that you may reach home in safety. I know you will do us justice, and will be of infinitely more service to us there than here." We left our prison room and passed into the centre one, from which three of its inmates passed into ours. Two from the same room also changed places with Toowig and Ogden.

At 6 o'clock we heard the turnkey, with his ugly load of securities clanking their dull music to the blast of many bugles in the great plaza. It was a moment of intense excitement, as a discovery of one man out of his place would blow up the whole plot.

The evening was dark, and there was a cold rain, which was the most fortunate circumstance, as the officer would not require us to form in front of our prison doors. The men were ordered to form in our respective rooms, the back ends of which were measurably darkened. At the remote end of the lines from the doors, those who had changed places had taken their stations, with slouched hats, and their blankets well muffled about their faces. In such positions, and on so dark an evening, it would have required a close inspection to have told each one from his face. Still it was deemed prudent that Captain Ogden and myself should lie upon the floor, with our blankets drawn close around us, and when the count commenced, to have one of our men standing by to say, "Here are two fellows *muy malo*" (very sick). In the event that the officer should inspect us still closer, we were to muffle our faces, and grunt as if we had the stomach ache; for *frijoles* were very excellent to give one pains in those parts, and such pains were not uncommon among us.

We selected places upon the floor near each other, and continued to crack our jokes even in this excitement. I thought, in the event of our discovery, our situation would not be so ludicrous as that of Prince Talleyrand, when, at sea, he assumed the apron, greasy face, and flesh-fork of the cook, as an English cruiser hove in sight. The captain of the vessel said that the great diplomatist "could stand as much like a cook, hold his flesh-fork as much like a cook, and look as much like a cook, every way, as if he had been born and raised in a caboose." With such an example, could we fail to represent the *frijoles* pains?

The count commenced in the right-hand room, and presently we heard the heavy doors grating upon their hinges, with the shaking of the keys, which told us, so far, "all's well." The next moment they were in the centre room; the turnkey with his huge bunch, the counting sergeant, and the officer of the guard, with the quickly-repeated order "*Formarse, formarse*" (to form). The count was made, and two were missing, when our lamented friend, "Tecolote," sung out, with an admirable mixture of confidence and sympathy, pointing, at the same time, to Ogden and myself upon the floor, "Here is two *muy malo*." "*Bueno*" (very good) was the quick reply of the officer, and the next moment they passed out, pulling the door after them with a heavy crash. The like operation of shutting the door in the left-hand room told us that thus far we had succeeded to our most sanguine expectations.

We had now to divert the attention of the sentinel at the door, as he could, by standing tiptoe upon the sill, look in through the grates at our operations. This we managed to great perfection.

We first made the fellow good-natured by giving him *vino mascal* through the grates in an eggshell: nothing larger could be passed through. Next, some of our men, who were not engaged in getting out, spread a blanket down nearest to the door, on which was placed two candles, and four or five engaged in a game at *monte*. We had provided the players with a hatful of "*clacos*," square pieces of soap about one and a half inches each, with the stamp of the state, or person issuing them, upon the sides, and worth one and a half cents each. Here was a brisk game kept up, to the greatest possible interest of the sentinel, and, to enlist him still more, the players were ordered to give him some "*clacos*" to bet. He would pass his soap through the grates, and direct upon which card they should be bet. Of all nations under the sun, the Mexicans are the most inveterate gamblers; and though the monte bank was well calculated to divert him, yet the necessary noise we had to make in passing through so difficult a hole in the opposite end of the room required other precautions.

Next to the monte bank, some eight or ten were engaged in a "bull-dance," being the only one we could perform in our "jewelry;" the twenty pound festoons which coupled the partners not being well adapted to the "*chassé*" and "*balancé*," they had to *go it* "*dos-a-dos*." They danced to poor "Tecolote's" music, who, at the conclusion of every set, would either give his inimitable owl-whoop, or "flap his wings" and crow, very like the gamest cock that ever graced a pit. When the dancers would tire, there were others ready to join in a chorus which drowned all our noise. Between our breach and the door blankets were also hung up, which more effectually hid our operations.

At seven o'clock we commenced our final preparations before emerging from the room. This was to remove the shell of the wall yet upon the outside, then to make one end of the rope fast inside of the room, and pass it through, by which we would have to let ourselves down to the bottom of the moat. When this was done, it was found that the breach was too small upon the outside to admit of any but the smallest of our men passing through it, and required two hours hard work to scale some pieces of stone and mortar from one side of it, so as to permit the larger ones to pass. This required until nine o'clock.

All things being now ready, John Toowig, a gallant son of the Emerald Isle, got into the breach feet foremost, and, drawing his bundle after him, inch by inch squeezed out, and let himself down hand over hand about thirty feet to the bottom of the moat.

The depth and smallness of the hole rendered this operation exceedingly slow. Another and another followed, and at half past twelve, after three hours and a half hard labour, all of the sixteen had safely landed.

As Isaac Allen (Ike, for short) made his appearance upon the outer aperture, he said, "Stand from under, boys; I can't say whether these hands are gwine to hold;" and no sooner said than the laws of gravity landed Ike in the midst of us. The sand being about ankle-deep, it was an easy fall, and he rose as if nothing unusual had occurred.

Ike previously had the contents of his gun passed through both hands, which weakened his hold, and was the cause of his falling. He had seen much service fighting for liberty in Texas, had been in many Indian hunts, and had met danger with as little fear as any man. It was one of his chief delights to hate the Mexican nation, and if he had a greater pleasure, it was in telling the Mexicans of it. On account of the crippled condition of his hands, he had been separated from his partners, as he told them that "his hands would not pack stones," and he was permitted to wear his chain single. He, on one of the days when it was positively forbidden by the governor to sell us *aguardiente*, had paid his devotions too assiduously to a certain bladder we have had occasion to speak of, when, feeling keenly his own and his country's wrongs, he strutted forth in front of the governor's quarters, singing at the top of his voice, "*Viva la Texas!*" (long live Texas!) The old governor came out in the greatest rage, and sent for "Guts" to know what that *land robber* meant by insulting him in that manner; and threatened "Guts" severely on account of his getting brandy. Old "Guts," full of wind and wrath, brought out his guard at a charge bayonet, and rushed Ike off to the solitary calaboose.

"Now," says Guts to Ike, "you bloody robber! I will keep you here until you rot, unless you tell me where you got your brandy from."

"Well," says Ike, "I got it from you."

"You audacious rascal!" says Guts, "how dare you say so? Don't you know it is false?"

"Yes," says Ike, "I know it is false, Guts; but I will tell the governor I got it from you; he knows how far you will go for a *medio*, and will believe me; and I will swear it, too, on the largest cross upon the Bible."

"Not," says Guts, "upon the holy cross?" his eyes dilating with horror at Ike's heresy and the fear of the governor.

"Yes," says Ike, "I'll be —— if I don't, Guts; and, what is more, the governor will give you —— for selling me the *aguardiente*."

Ike's rhetoric was convincing, and this *experimentum crucis*, though bold, was entirely successful. Guts swelled with anger, then thought of the governor, then paused, and then opened the door of the calaboose, and said to Ike, "Go out of here!

I'll not have anything to do with such a heretic." What tale Guts concocted for the governor we know not.

Ike was no less a găl'lant than a gallánt man. He was tall—women, in general, like tall men best—and wore an air of confident nonchalance, which bespoke his boldness—and women like bold men best. It was not strange, therefore, that Ike should have been a favourite with the ladies, for with them he had more credit than any man in the ranks. The luxurious Niña would always credit Ike, and any sergeant's wife in the castle would trust him for the washing of his camīsa. On these washing days, Ike, having but one shirt, would fold his blanket close about him *à la* Mexican; on the other days his Republicanism made him wear it *à la* Texas.

On one occasion Ike went into the dormitory of his washerwoman for his clean shirt. She had boiled it so well—boiling was necessary to prevent the incubation of the *piojos'* eggs—and she had ironed it so smooth, that a man of less gallantry than Ike could hardly fail expressing his profoundest gratitude therefor. So, after sundry bows, he commenced, "*Concédame, Señora, esta gracia*" — Madam, grant me this favour; and, suiting the action to the words, impressed a tender kiss upon the cheek of the *cabo's* wife. She, thankful for the condescension, commenced replying, "*Lumbre de mis ojōs*"— Light of my eyes, when in popped the corporal, her husband, with a shoemaker's awl in his hand,

and, not waiting for an explanation, ran furiously at Ike, and "socked" it in the thick of his back "smack up to the handle."

Ike, never so little dismayed as in the heat of battle, seized this petit officer by the collar, and dragged him forth in front of our prison rooms, calling at the top of his voice for Lieutenant Gomez, the officer of the guard. Gomez came quickly up, and all of the Texian prisoners gathered around Ike to know the difficulty. He was in a tremendous passion, and soon explained that the corporal had stabbed him in the back.

"What for?" exclaimed twenty of his indignant countrymen.

"Nothing under heaven," says Ike, "but my returning thanks to his wife for the washing of my *camisa.*"

"How returning thanks?" repeated a dozen of his comrades.

"Why," says Ike, with a thundering oath, "can't *you* thank a body for a thing?"

"Yes; but is that all you said?"

"As God is my judge!" replied Ike, with increased emphasis, "all except kissing her."

This last explanation of Ike's filled us all to overflowing with laughter, but still we kept it in, not knowing the extent of his wound.

The officer of the guard was still not satisfied, and Ike continued in his most passionate tone, half Spanish, half English, and swearing that he would take satisfaction himself of the corporal unless he was duly punished.

Lieutenant Gomez still wanted ocular demonstration of the injury, when Ike, loosening his belt, let fall his pantaloons to the ground, and stooping down, first the lieutenant, and then we, inspected his wound. Instead of finding a knife or sword cut, we saw the blood oozing from an orifice the size of a brister-shot, which for the first time explained to us that he was stabbed with a cobbler's awl; and, turning to the affrighted corporal, still in the clutches of Ike's left hand, saw that the awl had only gone in up to the handle, and not more than two inches deep at that.

This discovery, and the farce which preceded it and was still going on, proved a matter of rare mirth with the Texians; and Gomez, to appease Ike's wrath, had to march the disconsolate corporal off to the calaboose, leaving the wounded caballero behind to explain with Señora Cabo how innocent a thing it was " to return thanks for the washing of a camīsa."*

---

* Since writing the above, poor Ike has paid his last debt. After being liberated by Santa Anna with the other San Antonio prisoners, he landed in Galveston with the yellow fever in June, 1844, from on board the United States war-steamer Poinsett, which terminated his eventful life at about thirty-five years of age. Quite a volume might be written of the most stirring incidents about this fearless man. He had some good qualities in a high degree. His love of country was no less remarkable than his love of friends. On one occasion, when he had a friend killed in Bastrop county, Texas, he determined to avenge his death; and while the person charged with the killing was upon trial in open court, Ike went in and fired a pistol-shot at his head, which, though not proving

John Toowig was a son of Old Ireland, a small, energetic man, and a true-hearted Republican. His size and energy both befitting the operation in the hole, he had done more than his share of the work. He was the same who, in the spring of 1842, at San Antonia, put a match to a keg of powder and blew up his store, with several thousand dollars worth of goods, rather than they should fall into the hands of the Mexican General Vascus. It was less difficult for him than some others to get through the perforation in the wall. I found much difficulty in passing through, though I was now reduced from one hundred and sixty pounds, my usual weight, to one hundred and twenty. The gradual funnel-shape of the breach made it like driving a pin into an auger-hole, for the deeper we went, the closer the fit. The smallest of us having gone through first, for fear that the largest might hang in the hole and stop it up, it now came to Stone's turn, who was a large man.

He hung fast, and could neither get backward nor forward. In this situation, being wedged in as fast

---

fatal, wounded more than one. On another occasion, at San Antonio, in 1837, Dr. G. picked a quarrel with Ike, which resulted in the death of the former. Though public opinion did not justify the manner of the killing, yet little sympathy was felt for G., who had just previously wrongfully charged young Lawrence, of New-York, with stealing his money; and when L. demanded satisfaction for the injury, killed him in a duel by forcing upon the party challenging the use of the rifle, of which he knew nothing. The death of the highly-injured and amiable young Lawrence, who fell in so manly a defence of his honour, was much regretted when it was afterward known that the real thief was his second in the duel.

as his giant strength could force him, our friends on the inside of the room, who had been assisting us, had to reach in the hole, tie ropes to his hands, and draw him back. This operation was very like drawing his arms out of his body, but did not satisfy him. "I have a wife and children at home," says he, "and I would rather die than stay here longer: I will go through, or leave no skin upon my bones." So saying, he disrobed himself: his very great exertion, causing him to perspire freely, answered nearly as well for the second effort as if he had been greased, and he went through after the most powerful labour, leaving both skin and flesh behind.

John Young, if anything, was a larger man than Stone, but was much his junior in years: he was as supple as a snake, and no Roman gladiator ever exhibited more perfectly-formed muscles: nor was his determined temper in bad keeping with his physical conformation. He was the last that came out; and while the balance of us sat under the side of the wall, we feared that it would be impossible for him to get through. Presently, with the aid of a dim sky above us, we saw his feet slowly protruding, then his knees, and when he came to his hip joints, here for many minutes he hung fast. When this part of his body was cleared, the angular use of his knees gave him additional purchase to work by; but still our boys said, "Poor fellow! it will be impossible to get his muscular arms and shoulders through." We sat under him with an agony of feeling not to

be described, while he ceased not his efforts. His body was now cleared to his shoulders, but still he hung fast. Having the full purchase of his legs, he would writhe, first up and down, and then from side to side, with Herculean strength; and when he disengaged himself, if it was not like the drawing of a cork from a porter-bottle, it was with the low, sullen, determined growl of a lion.

Being now through our greatest difficulty about the castle, we adjusted carefully, though silently, our knapsacks and blankets, passing orders from one to another in low whispers, which were interrupted alone by the almost perpetual cry of "*centinela alerta*" of the sentinels above us, both upon the right and left bastions, and between which we had now to pass. The moon had gone down at 8 o'clock; and being favoured by the darkness in the bottom of the moat, through which the sentinels overhead could not penetrate, we slowly crossed over to the outer wall in Indian file, then felt along the wall until we came to a flight of narrow steps eighteen inches wide, up which we crawled upon all-fours. When we reached the top of the wall, which formed the outer side of the moat, we passed on to the *chevaux de frize*, which was about twelve feet high, of pointed timbers set upright in the ground. These upright timbers passed through a horizontal sill about six feet from the ground, which we could reach with our hands, and then pull ourselves up, from which we could then climb over the sharp points of the upright posts, thence down to the bottom of the outside ditch, up the outside bank of which we crawled, it not being walled. When we reached the top we breathed more freely, for we were now in the wide world, and felt more like freemen; and as the sentinels drolled out their sleepy notes of "*centinela alerta*," we jumped up, and cracked our heels together three times, as a substitute for cheers three times three.

CHAPTER XVIII.

RESIDENCE IN THE MOUNTAINS, AND ENTRY INTO JALAPA.

Two hundred Yards east of the Castle.—Separation.—Parting Speeches.—Pass the Powder-house.—Meet with Reese and Toowig.—Divide Rations with.—Take to the Mountains.—Residence and Sufferings in.—Return to the Valley.—Charge of Cavalry and Escape.—Separation from Toowig.—Narrow Escape from a Precipice.—Make Coffee.—Approach to Jalapa.—Our Distress from Sore Feet and Thorns.—Entry and Peregrination in the City.—Our Location in the Suburbs.—Re-entry, mode of.—Don: his Wife, and warm Supper.—Meet Toowig.—Residence in City.—Kind Treatment.—Robbers employed, and we delivered over to them in a dark Hollow.

As the castle bell tolled "half past twelve," we were in the open common, about two hundred yards east of the outer ditch. Here we had to await the return of Ike Allen, who had gone ahead with Captain Reese, Ogden, and Toowig, on the following account:

Reese, Ogden, and Toowig, who were more flush

ESCAPE FROM THE CASTLE OF PEROTE.

of funds than the balance of us, had, previous to leaving the castle, perfected an arrangement, through a friend living at a considerable distance from Perote, to have a confidential guide and three extra horses near by on this night. The guide was to kindle a fire as a signal, one mile east of the castle, between the hours of ten and one, at which fire they were to have met; then to ride with relays of horses, and get into Vera Cruz ahead of the alarm. The guide, as we afterward learned, came to the place, but owing to some shepherds astir in the neighbourhood, they failed to kindle the fire through fear of discovery. Ike had accompanied these gentlemen to the appointed place to meet a second guide, who was promised just previously to this time to be there on foot, and to conduct us a blind way through the mountains to the seacoast near Vera Cruz, at a place where vessels occasionally anchor off to water. Here the balance of us were to be secreted until our sailing arrangements were complete. The signal-fire failing, Ogden and Ike returned, leaving Reese and Toowig still in search of the promised guide.

We were now thrown back upon our original plan of escaping in pairs, and after shaking hands, and wishing each other a safe, if not a pleasant journey, we separated in the following manner:

Little Tom Hancock and Forester were considered the best walkers in the crowd. Tom was a great woodsman; he had the organ of the honeybee in a high degree, and facing himself to the northeast, then looking over his left shoulder to the north star, so as to form an acute angle to that luminary, he pointed his sapote staff dead ahead, and said, "Boys, this will bring me to the Gulf of Mexico, and then I shall know where I am. I will have nothing to do but to follow round the left of the pond to Texas." Thus saying, Tom and Forester started, and Captain Ogden, being disappointed in his horse arrangement, went with them.

Ike, facing a little more north than Tom, but still keeping the north star upon his left, said, "Boys, this will bring the Rio Grande, where I am well acquainted with every path and crossing, and about this time my cattle and mules are in good driving condition, so God bless you all." Thus saying, he moved forward, his two comrades following.

The Herculean John Young, who stood well built and six feet two under a slouched hat and thirty pounds of fat bacon, split the difference between Tom and Ike. He was a man of but few words, and saying, "A thousand miles this course will reach Texas—that's nothing," he and his chums started.

Dick Barclay had much of the polarity quality in his composition. His frequent Indian hunts in Texas had well tested his locality organ, and he struck a course still east of Tom, his comrade following in silence.

Dalrymple was left alone, his partner having de-

clined coming; he said, " Well, boys, here is for the city of Mexico," and obliqued to the right for the main stage-road.

Myself and Dan took the other end of the road for Vera Cruz. My plan was to pursue it rapidly until daylight, and then turn into the mountains of *Cofre de Perote*, which lay upon our right.

In leaving the castle, our friend Major Bugg promised to fold up a dirty-looking blanket, as near the colour of the wall as possible, and so fill in the hole, as the breach upon the outside could not be easily discovered. Thus we had every confidence that our escape would not be known before counting time at nine o'clock next day. Consequently, I pursued the road with no fear of arrest that night; the only probability was that we might meet with some robbers. We passed along the road at a brisk walk, occasionally stooping low, surveying the horizon to see whether any one was moving. When we reached the powder-house, as the " *molino de polvora*" was called by us Texians, which was three miles from the castle, many dogs of " low degree" flew out as if they would certainly take us. From experience, we knew how cowardly were the Mexican dogs, and kept our way, only balancing our sapotes in our hands in case of necessity.

About five miles farther on we came to a brisk little creek, running over a bed of round pebbles. Here we laid down to drink; and while quaffing the pure mountain liquid, we heard a noise in the road

T T

from the direction in which we came as though some persons were in pursuit. Having the advantage of the horizon, from our stooping position we could soon see two figures approaching to within a few feet of us, and as I gathered a round stone in each hand, and was in the act of throwing, one of them hailed in English, "Who's there?" We at once knew it to be Reese's voice, and was greatly rejoiced that he spoke so soon, as we intended *first* to fire, and *then* to tail. It was Reese and Toowig, who, having been disappointed in finding the guide and horses, were now thrown upon their own resources, and without provisions, for the guide was to have furnished them.

Very fortunately, Dan and myself were supplied with twenty days' rations each, and we divided with them. We pursued the road several miles farther, passing a large hacienda, and every variety of "barking dogs," until we heard a noise ahead. Stooping down, we saw some persons in the road, and it being near daylight, concluded to turn off to the right and make for the mountains.

The only kind of shoes we could procure in the castle was a thin kind of goatskin slippers, only fit to be kept dry and worn in the house. In a little time, walking through the wet grass, they would stretch and come to pieces. Our feet not only suffered from the sharp mountain stones, but we had become greatly enervated from our prison life, and our fatigue was excessive. Those who had labour-

SUFFERINGS IN THE MOUNTAINS.

ed in the castle could stand the fatigue much the best. Before it was fairly light we had ascended the mountains so high that we left all the settlements below, and a brisk rain which had fallen had not only thoroughly drenched us, but it also rendered our pursuit impossible, by obliterating our tracks. After we had got so high into the mountains as only here and there to see the traces of the shepherd, or the sign where some Péon had burned his charcoal for market, we selected a dark cove and lay down to rest.

With the assistance of our map and a pocket compass we knew our general course, and started before sundown, but the almost bottomless ravines and inaccessible mountains succeeded each other so quickly that our progress was slow and fatiguing beyond anything we had yet experienced. Winding around the base of a mountain, the perpendicular sides of which it would have been impossible to ascend, we would come to an abyss, down the sides of which we would have to feel our way, inch by inch, with the greatest caution, which much retarded our general progress. This was the work of evenings, nights, and mornings. At length our provisions were becoming rapidly diminished, and we determined to descend into the lowlands.

This was during the " rainy season," for in Mexico it rains nearly all the time from June to October; consequently we were nearly all the time wet. If we caught enough sun about the middle of the day to dry us, it was to be succeeded by another drenching at night, which, in that snowy region, made us suffer intensely from cold. The constant rains made the mountain sides nearly as slippery as soap; this made our way still more difficult. Where such heavy labour was performed, much drinking of water was necessary, and the rains furnished this blessing in abundance. We would drink at every brook, and fill our gourds, which would last to the next.

Having descended many miles the valley of a bold creek, which, from our map, we judged to be the head of a river leading through the Valley of Jalapa, we crawled into some bushes after daylight to sleep. Here we were first aroused by a heavy rain and several shepherd boys, who came so near that it would seem impossible for them not to have seen us. We lay as close to the ground as if we had been so many snakes, but watched closely their countenances: had they discovered us, we would have emigrated sooner than our regular hour. We were in a valley which now rapidly descended, and about sundown we again took up our march. Soon we struck a path, but its precipitous descent and rich black soil, made in the highest possible degree slippery from the continued rains, rendered our descent, if possible, more fatiguing than the ascent. Our feet and legs skinned, swelled, and excessively sore, with the general stiffness of limbs, "rusted with a vile repose," and a great want of muscular action from cold and rains, we had but little power of holding back, and frequently slipped and fell with great violence.

At daylight we were in the immediate neighbourhood of a thick settlement, and took lodging in some bushes and weeds upon an elevation, from which we could see below us people cultivating their fields. Here we waited until near night, when we again set forth. Descending into the valley still below, and crossing a small field, we met a Péon with a hoe upon his shoulder, returning from labour. This poor fellow was exceedingly alarmed, but after our assuring him that we intended no harm, we asked him the way to Jalapa. He commenced a difficult direction, when we determined to take him with us as a guide at least part of the way; then ordering him to go ahead, he led us down a bold creek about two miles to a crossing, and then told us to take the right-hand end of the road, which would lead us to the *molina*, and thence to the city. We gave him a piece of silver, and he took the other end, much relieved from his alarm, which our outlandish appearance occasioned. The right-hand end led immediately across the creek and through a gap, with a high mountain on each hand. We had proceeded but a few hundred yards, Toowig and Reese in advance of Dan about fifty yards, and he in advance of me about fifty yards, my feet being badly swollen and skinned, and distressingly sore, and I hobbling on at a tedious gait, when I discovered four ranchero cavalry emerging from the gap in the mountains through which we had to pass, and coming immediately towards us. I hallooed to my comrades to look to the front, but by this time they had met, saluted the caballeros with apparent confidence, and passed on. Dan did the same, and I followed suit with the best of my poor Spanish. I kept my eye well over my shoulder to watch their motions.

When they had passed about one hundred yards, they wheeled their horses' heads together, and, after a hurried and very excited consultation, dashed back upon me in full charge. I called my comrades to return to my assistance—that these fellows were charging upon me, at the same time facing them, and mixing up in an angry tone the worst Spanish and English oaths. The only weapons I had upon my person were my tongue and sapote walking-stick; the first I freely used, and the other I held in reserve for close quarters; but, as Providence would have it, the fate of war had now halted me in the midst of a rich supply of throwing-stones, and I did not consider the odds very unequal. Had I turned my back upon these knights, I should have fallen an easy prey under their cutlasses; this I knew, and I determined to fight it out upon the spot. The foremost of these fellows had by this time reached within fifteen or eighteen steps of my position, and the instant I expected the battle to commence, he filed suddenly to the left, the others following at full speed. They dismounted in great haste at a house some hundred yards opposite me, as I judged, for the purpose of procuring re-enforcements.

I turned to look after my comrades. They, not understanding what I said when I called to them, and believing that these fellows were the advance of a stronger force, had dashed into the thick mountain brush, Toowig upon the right, and Dan and Reese upon the left of the road. I hurried on, and went into the same place where I had seen the two last enter. Here I found them, and we scrambled up a precipice too steep for cavalry to follow, and lay down under some thick bushes to rest. Dark came on before these fellows could complete their preparations for pursuit; and after resting, and giving our private whistle for Toowig, whom we could not bring up, we set out in a different course, leaving the Péon's direction to our right.

Our course this night was over an excessively broken country, alternate mountains and valleys of exceeding height and fearful depth. Briers, thornbushes, and sharp stones impeded our progress, and made the labour of the foremost much the most difficult. Accordingly, we alternately took the lead. When it came to my turn to lead, we fell into a path comparatively level, which we pursued several hundred yards, the end of my walking-stick always ahead of me about two feet, feeling the way. At length I felt no bottom, and from habit stopped as quick as thought, not making another step, at the same time speaking to my companions behind to halt. Stooping down where I stood, with my walking-cane I reached as far as my arm would allow, but still I found no bottom; and, after laying down and straining our eyes, we discovered the appearance of tree tops far below. Changing our course, we felt our way down a steep descent of at least one mile to a valley, the creek through which washed the base of the dangerous precipice we had just escaped. How inscrutable are the ways of Providence! One step more, myself, then Reese, and then Dan would have fallen a thousand feet—for no alarm from the foremost would have reached the next—leaving no one on earth a knowledge of our destiny.

Having passed through several cultivated fields in this dark valley—for, when we looked back upon our frightful escape, we likened it to the "Valley of Death"—daylight found us again lying under our wet blankets in some thick bushes. We rested a few hours, being much exhausted, and suffering greatly for want of refreshment. We had coffee and chocolate in our knapsacks, but for fear of raising smokes we had only on one occasion used any. Hearing the roaring of a cataract at some distance below, we determined to get water, seek a dark and secure place, and make coffee. We traced the roaring of this waterfall, and found it at the bottom of a dark and deep hollow, overlapped with a thick foliage. From the brink of the hill no one could be seen below, while we below could easily discover the approach of any one from above. Here we made a small fire, and, with the assistance of our pint tin, we made cup after cup, until we were greatly relieved. The roar of the waters prevented our being heard, and we, after bathing our feet and legs, luxuriated in a good chat, for most of our intercourse had been carried on by signs and low whispers, which had become irksome.

From the distance and general course we had travelled, we believed that we were not many miles from the city of Jalapa, and the paths all converged in the direction which we believed the city lay. Before night we left our cooking place, and skirted along the cultivated fields, avoiding the paths, as we expected the different entrances to the city would be guarded. We had not gone many miles before the ringing of the city bells could be plainly heard; and having understood that the city lay in a valley between two mountains, which were now plainly seen in the bright moonlight upon our right and left, we for the first time understood our precise locality. Our plan was now to leave the city to our right, and follow round the base of the mountain to our left; strike into the valley of the river, which our map showed led to the seacoast, thence follow it down.

We bore to the left to avoid the city, and crossing many stone fences covered with prickly-pear and briers, which surround the little cornfields, were sorely lacerated. The more we tried to avoid the city, the thicker, it appeared to us, became the settlements; and a succession of these small fields and stone fences for several miles exasperated us to a degree which made us indifferent to the consequences. We determined then to strike south into the heart of the city, and play our game boldly.

Of all nations, the Mexicans are most devoted to bells, to which they attach much superstition, their cities being filled with them, and of which they make a perpetual use. Their constant ringing during our peregrination in the neighbourhood told us how the city lay, and we had no difficulty in striking through its centre. By Indian file we passed up one street and down another, under our broadbrim ranchero hats, with our shoulders and knapsacks covered with our darkly-variegated blankets, which we had been careful in procuring before leaving the castle. To the frequent "*quien viva*" of the sentinels we made no reply, but kept our course in silence. It appeared to us that there were more dogs in this town than we had ever before seen at one place; and though they barked in an angry tone, as if they knew us to be strangers, yet they kept at a respectful distance from our sapotes.

We had been reconnoitring the city for three hours, and as daylight drew near we determined to go a short distance south and select a lodging for the next day, which would overlook the whole place. In the southern suburb of the town we found a position admirably suited to our views. It was an insulated conical mound, such as are frequently seen in the valleys of Mexico, rising out of this valley to several hundred feet, and covered with high weeds and brush. Upon the apex of this cone we took our lodging, not judging, from the appearance of the weeds, that it was often ascended. Here, in our wet clothes and blankets—for we had just had the benefit of a cold, drenching rain—we lay down upon the wet ground, as close together as we could get, and spread our wet blankets over us, covering us entirely up. The steam which our respiration created under the wet blankets soon warmed us, and the greatest distress we experienced was in turning over; for in laying together as compact as three spoons, this had to be done at one time, and by common consent. In these turnings the cold air would rush in, and the change it would produce in our feelings, if not a good illustration of the collapsing of a steam boiler, explained the philosophy of some of the northern nations wetting their coverings to keep them warm at night.

We remained in this situation until ten o'clock next day, when we rose to take our position to survey the city below. Here we studied its geography until night, many persons passing near the foot of the hill, but no one ascending it. As soon as it was dark we started into the city, and coming to a dilapidated church upon the right of the street, around which grew some high weeds, Reese and myself seated ourselves by the side of the wall in the weeds, and sent Dan ahead. He was to pick up some *common* looking Mexican, and give him a *real* to conduct him to the house of our friend. Dan had not proceeded far before he employed a suitable guide, which his knowledge of the language rendered easy. In reaching the door of our friend, he, with a cunning wink, said to Don ——, as he opened it, "I have brought your watch, which your brother sent up from Vera Cruz." "Ah," says the Don, "come in ;" and, shutting the door after him, a word explained who he was, and that myself and Reese were by the side of the old church. The Don put on his blanket, and came down with our concerted signal; he gave the true sign; we followed him in silence, and when we entered his house, found his good señora preparing a warm supper, with a most delightful toddy ready mixed.

Those, and those alone, who have experienced like suffering, may form a reasonable estimate of our present happiness: once more under a kind roof, with a smoking supper before us—what inexpressible felicity!

We were conducted after supper to a secret hiding-place, where we found Toowig carefully ensconced, having gotten into the city one night ahead of us. This was the first intelligence we had of him since we separated in the mountains three nights previous. Here we remained five days, and were treated with a kindness by these good people we never shall forget. Mexican women are kind-hearted to a degree, which makes their goodness contrast singularly with the vices of the men. Our feet and legs were bathed and poulticed; and we sent out and purchased good shoes, and all the paraphernalia of the *mountain ranchero*, preparatory to our farther journey. Here we luxuriated in a great variety of tropical fruits grown in the neighbourhood, and by the sixth night we had become so far resuscitated from our mountain fatigues as to be able to proceed.

Don ——, whose name we regret the impropriety of mentioning, as it would doubtless occasion him persecution from his government, was known to us from a long negotiation. No one knew better than he the country and its inhabitants, from Santa Anna down to every mountain robber of decent reputation. His pride was greatly enlisted in our success, and he had ample means of assisting us.

At 10 o'clock of the sixth night, the Don said to us, " Prepare to follow me, and ask no questions." We did so, and he led us through the city into a dark valley about two miles off, and after telling us to hide in the bushes, he went about one hundred yards farther down the hollow, and bringing a shrill whistle, a tall, well-made, active man, about thirty-five years of age, came to him. A very few words were passed between them, they having been together the night previous, and perfected all arrangements. The moon shone bright; they came in the direction of where we were concealed in the shade of some bushes, and called to us to come forth.

"This man," said the Don, "you must follow, but ask no questions. My express ahead will complete every arrangement for you in Vera Cruz, and be under no alarm as to the result; this man knows his business." Both the place and circumstances wore much the air of mystery: it looked like "treason, stratagem," and murder; and to our question, "Might not this fellow betray us for the reward?" "No," says the Don; "*I* have looked to that. He," pointing to our conductor, "is the most noted robber and murderer in Mexico, and is in more danger of losing his head than you. He dare not show himself to the authorities." Thus saying, we took affectionate leave of the generous Don, he returning to the city, and we following our silent conductor down the hollow.

CHAPTER XIX.

FIVE NIGHTS' JOURNEY TO VERA CRUZ UNDER CONDUCT OF ROBBERS.

Head Robber.—Coming to the Horses.—Signal.—Silence.—Winding around Precipices.—Narrow Paths.—Sure-footed Animals.—Puente Nacional.—Rio Antigua.—Lying in Swamp.—Hot Breakfast.—Lodged in vacant House.—Gray-bearded old Man.—Meeting Robbers.—Enter Antigua.—Cavalry Officer and the Gray-bearded old Man.—Narrow Escape from the Officers and Guards.—Crossing the Ferry, and deceiving the Officer.—The Gray-bearded old Man's Exultation.—Taking the Road to Manga de Clavo.—Secreted for the Night.—Head Robber goes into Vera Cruz.—Our Location next Day.—Vessels at Sea.—Sand Storm.—Head Robber arrives with Don E.—Start for the City.—Storm and Separation.—Arrival near the City Gates.—Suspicions of the Head Robber.—Bad Night.—Don E. finds us next Day.—Our Entry into the City.—Parting with Robbers.—Valedictory of the Gray-bearded old Man.—Our Hiding-place.—United States Friends.—Dick Barclay.—Recapture of our Comrades.—A Look into the Castle after the Dénouement.—Surprise, Wonder, and Astonishment.—The Governor, Guts, and the Children.

SILENTLY, and in single file, we followed our dark-looking conductor down the hollow, and in a dismal-looking place, in a second ravine, we came upon his companion, holding by the bridle five mules and horses. A whistle and an answer told that all was right. The head man placed a bridle into each of our hands without saying a word, then drew from his goatskin bag a bottle, out of which he drank, to satisfy us that it was not poison; then passing it to us, we all drank, and returned it. Stowing it carefully away, he turned to the east, and placing the fore finger of his right hand perpendicularly across his lips, which was a caution for silence, pointed in the direction he faced, and gave the sign to mount. We mounted, and followed on a narrow, winding path, leading through deep ravines and broken cliffs until daylight, not one word passing between us during this long ride. At the appearance of day he turned off the trail, and went into the hollow of a mountain covered with thick shrubbery. Here he dismounted, and giving us the sign, we did the same. Placing by our side his goatskin bags filled with provisions and a gourd of water, he told us that night precisely at 8 o'clock he would come, and we must answer a particular whistle which he then made. So saying, he and his comrades led away the horses and mules. After eating, we laid ourselves upon the ground, and slept soundly until near night.

At eight o'clock P.M. we heard the concerted whistle, and answered it, when our robber stealthily approached, with the never-failing caution of his fore finger across his lips. He made the sign to follow, which we did, and after winding us through a very rough tract for about a mile, another whistle and its response discovered to us his companion, holding our animals.

At the given sign we mounted, and followed this night, as we had done the last, under that dead silence, which made our journey the more oppressive. Our rugged and winding way through the mountains, which caused us frequently, in the same hour, to travel to every point of the compass, showed that our conductor knew the country well. Our faithful animals, so well used to that mountainous region, were astonishingly sure footed. Frequently, in passing around almost perpendicular cliffs, in paths exceedingly stony and frightfully narrow, with a dark abyss on the one hand and a perpendicular mountain on the other, the thought of our animals stumbling would make our hair stand on end. Those, however, who are used to these paths seem not to apprehend danger, and they have the utmost confidence in their animals, which pick their way with a loose rein, and seem to know the necessity of a sure foothold.

Nearly the whole of this night we rode in a heavy rain, and for two hours in the most tremendous storm. About one hour before daylight we approached the Rio Antigua, near the *puente nacional*, and across the great road leading from Vera Cruz to the capital. Keeping the river to our right, we travelled through a flat, marshy bottom until daylight, when we were told to "dismount and lay low." We had been drenched the whole night with a cold rain, and had now to repose in water ankle deep, which covered the bottom. Excessive fatigue soon brought sweet sleep to us, from which we were aroused at noon by the known whistle of our guide.

He had under his blanket a delightfully-cooked chicken, eggs, and *tortillas*, smoking hot, which showed that he was in the vicinity of his accomplices. We never enjoyed a meal better. After we had finished eating, he threw around his shoulders his dark-coloured *serape*, and with his usual sign of silence disappeared through the bushes.

Everything in this life is good by comparison. We had slept several hours, and a sumptuous meal made us feel vastly more comfortable; but yet we were deprived of our dessert, for Dan could neither sing " Long, long ago," or the " Soldier's Tear." After whispering to one another our anecdotes, we slept several hours more, when our well-known whistle again started us. Our guide approached and beckoned us to follow him. After half an hour winding us through a boggy bottom, we came to an unoccupied hut, built of bamboos, and covered with palm leaves. Here he told us we might sleep this night, as he must rest his horses; that he had some friends at hand, and if any alarm should be given, we must disappear in the thick bushes near by.

In a short time he again returned with a new friend, a long gray-bearded, though athletic old man. The old man greeted us very kindly, with many professions of devotion to our interest, and from his signs we readily recognised him to be a brother in the same cause as our guide. We gave him two dollars to procure us supper, and, after an absence of an hour, he returned with one smoking hot, which we the more enjoyed, as our clothes were now measurably dry. The old man lived in the immediate neighbourhood, and, true to his promises, he and his family kept a close watch over us that night and the next day.

At sundown our horses were brought up, and an additional one for the gray-headed old man, who, with all his travelling paraphernalia, showed that he meant to see us safe through our journey. This veteran, with all the pride of many years, mounted upon a gay, plaited-tailed charger, rode ahead of the party. He was a man of ready words and many compliments; next to him came our head man, of much less address, who knew that our greatest difficulty was yet to encounter. This night we met frequent companies of smugglers and robbers, but the gray-bearded old man passed them with as much ease of address as one could speak to his neighbour upon a court green. We would follow in our dark robber costume without saying a word, and doubtless passed as citizens in the same trade.

Our course still lay down the River Antigua, and on the personal estate of Santa Anna, through a dense forest of large trees, many of which were new to our northern raising. Among the most remarkable was the celebrated banian-tree, of the fig family (*Ficus religiosa*), which has been so long regarded by the Hindoos with religious veneration. This tree has the singular quality of extending long horizontal branches from the trunk, about twenty or thirty feet above the ground, and throwing out roots from these branches, which will continue to grow downward through the open air until they reach the ground, take hold, and themselves become trunks. We observed a vast number of these trunks, covering a large extent of ground, all united in one common covering of dense foliage, and each trunk giving the like support to the others, as well-set and well-braced pillars in an edifice would to its aggregate of strength. An immortal bard makes this the kind of fig-tree from which our first parents procured their first aprons:

> "There soon they chose
> The fig-tree; not that kind for fruit renown'd,
> But such as at this day, to Indians known,
> In Malabra or Deccan, spreads her arms,
> Branching so broad and long, that in the ground
> The bended twigs take root, and daughters grow
> About the mother tree a pillow'd shade.
> * * * * * * * *
> * * * * * Those leaves
> They gathered."*

The undergrowth consisted of limes and other tropical fruits. It was necessary that the Antigua should be crossed before reaching Vera Cruz, and the only practical point of so doing was at the small town of the same name near its mouth. This place, which we entered about ten o'clock at night, has been for many years a noted place for smuggling. Vessels anchor off the mouth of this river under pretence of getting fresh water, which affords them a good opportunity to carry on the contraband trade. The wide and dense bottom which lay upon each

---

* See Book IX. of Milton's "Paradise Lost."

side of this river, interspersed with circuitous paths, known only to smugglers and robbers, affords ample shelter for this illicit trade. Here our old man was well acquainted; and when we entered the town, he drew up his horse opposite a store, with a light burning on the counter, where a Mexican cavalry officer was writing at the desk. He whispered to us not to dismount; that he would go in and buy some cheese and crackers for our supper, and see "how the land lay."

Upon entering the house, he appeared to be well acquainted, and rolled out his salutations with his usual volubility. The cavalry officer first addressed him, "Who are those upon their horses in the street? I have been sent here with my troop these two weeks, with orders to send every foreigner without passports to the Castle of San Juan de Ulloa. Do you know that sixteen of those daring Texians have escaped from the Castle of Perote, and several of them are yet abroad?" Before the old man had time to reply, the officer added, "As soon as I finish this note, I will examine their papers."

The old man, with his ready wit, replied that "they have all got passports, and from the English minister at that, and they are going home," at the same time setting a large tumbler of *aguardiente* before the officer with many compliments. He drank to the venerable old man, and resumed his writing in much hurry, so as to examine our passports.

The old man continued talking with his usual vivacity, and threw another dollar upon the counter for more brandy, and before the note was finished the officer had to stop and take another drink. Watching his opportunity, the old man slipped out into the street and spoke to the head robber to "put off in haste, and cross the ferry as soon as possible," while he would stay and drink with the officer. The ferry was at the other end of the town, about four hundred yards distant, and we made as little delay in reaching it and getting into the boat as possible. We had barely started from the store before the officer came into the street to examine our papers, when the old man remarked that he expected we would wait for him at the ferry. The old man now feigned to be highly excited with drink, and mounting upon his fiery horse, swept by them as though he could not control the animal. He reached the ferry just as we were getting into the boat, and the shortest explanation showed the necessity of our hurry.

The old man had no sooner spoke to our head robber than he threw his lasso over a limb of a tree which stood upon the bank, and ran back to meet the officer. He knew that one minute of time was of the last importance to us; and meeting the officer about one hundred yards from the ferry, he said, "They are waiting for us," and drawing his bottle of *aguardiente* from his goatskin bag, he passed it to the officer; then *he* took a drink with a long speech

of salutations, and begged the officer to let him pass it to his guards. This was granted; and it gained us those few minutes of time necessary to our liberty. When they arrived at the ferry we were half way across; the old man appeared in a towering passion, and bawled out to us " to stop upon the other bank until he came over;" he then turned to the officer and said, " Señor, you need not trouble yourself farther about those foreigners: *I'll vouch* for their passports; but if you would rather, go over with me and examine for yourself." In the mean time, while the boat was returning, the bottle was freely passed between them, the old man feigning both to drink and to be drunk. It was no sham with the officer, for by the time the boat returned for them, he was willing to take the old man's word for the passports.

As soon as we had crossed, we put off in the direction of Vera Cruz, and stopped upon the roadside to wait for our good old friend, and to keep a bright look out who was with him.

In a few minutes the boat recrossed, and we discovered that only one passenger was in it; and as the old man galloped up to where we awaited him, he proudly clapped his hands upon his breast and said, "It is useless for young boys to try their wits with me; I have been too long in the service."

The old fellow strutted to and fro, and recounted the adventure with the self-satisfaction of a Wellington after the battle of Waterloo. He concluded his speech by turning to us and saying, "Now, *ca-*

balleros, you have but one more danger before you, and trust this old head for that." So saying, we moved on.

We were now fifteen miles from Vera Cruz, and just ahead of us the road forked, both leading to it, the one *via* the seacoast, and the other *via Manga de Clavo*, the seat of Santa Anna. By mistake, the old man took the right-hand road, which led by Santa Anna's house. He had gone but a few hundred yards before he stopped, and, after a thoughtful look, turned to us with that slow wave of the fore finger peculiar to that nation, and said that "it was not good for us to travel that road," and after shaking his jolly sides with a good hearty laugh, he wheeled to the left, and soon fell into the one leading by the seashore. This road we travelled about five miles, until we reached the mouth of the river, where we crept into the bushes and slept till daylight. The head robber, when we stopped for the night, informed us that he would go to Vera Cruz and arrange for our entry, and that we must remain under charge of the old man and his companion till his return.

At daylight we changed our lodging by crawling into a cluster of bushes upon the top of a conical sandhill, which commanded a view of the river, sea, and road. Here we lay all day, saw several vessels pass in and out from Vera Cruz, one of which, we afterward found, contained our friend Toowig, who had reached that place just as she was in the act of sailing. Many persons passed the road at a short distance from us, but the moveable sands had obliterated our tracks, and we felt secure.

About noon our junior robber brought us something to eat, and a gourd of water. In the evening a sand storm came over us, which wellnigh buried all hands.

Our anxiety for the return of our guide now grew intense, as it was near night, and no news of him. About one hour before sunset we discovered two men riding at full gallop down the road from Vera Cruz. Watching them closely, we recognised both the horse and clothes of our guide. Not knowing our exact locality, as we had changed it after he had started for the city, he and his new companion rode upon a bald sandhill, and made a sign with a handkerchief. We answered it by tying one upon a stick, and running it up above the cluster of bushes where we lay, upon seeing which they came to us. A few words of explanation told them where the old man and his partner kept the horses. They soon brought them up, and we started for the city.

This new friend of ours, whom justice to himself forbids me to introduce to the reader in his proper person, had been for weeks looking for us to make our appearance about Vera Cruz. It must suffice when I say that this friend, Don E., was a warm-hearted, whole-souled man, and I regret to say that there are few such Mexicans in that whole nation. He had provided us safe quarters, and from him our robber guides were to receive a certificate of our safe delivery before they would be paid the balance due their contract upon their return.

Upon leaving our hiding-place at the mouth of the Rio Antigua, in company with our three robber guides and Don E., we rode at a rapid gait, as it was important to reach the city before nine o'clock, at which hour the city gates would be closed. When within three or four miles of the city, a violent blow coming on, Don E. and the gray-headed old man being a short distance ahead, got separated from us, and search after them was wholly vain.

The other two robbers kept on with us till within a mile of the city walls; here our dark-complexioned head man stopped and said that "he would go no farther; that there was some rascality afloat with our Vera Cruz friend; that he did not like his countenance; that he would doubtless, if he could, betray all hands; and," says he, "where would my neck be if he did?" We remonstrated with him to no purpose; we begged him to take us to the city gates, where our friend would certainly come, as the force of the storm had separated him from us without his desire. But no; he said we must dismount here, and creep into some bushes near by, and next morning he would make his way into the city and find out all about it. We had no alternative but to comply, and a more disagreeable night we have rarely spent. A cold rain fell in torrents upon us the whole night.

True to his promise, our head man went into the city next morning in disguise, and after ascertaining through some friends that Don E.'s intentions were honourable, and that he was greatly distressed at being separated from us, he sought and informed Don E. where we had been left.

Don E. and the old man having kept up the whole night watching, and next morning having procured a fresh horse, they rode around the town in every direction, in hopes of finding us, when they met the robber, and learned where he had left us over night.

Our Mexican friend, Don E., came to the spot where we had dismounted the night before. We had moved our lodgings some two hundred yards, though we recognised him, and hoisted a flag from the bushes where we lay concealed. He knew it, and came to us. This was about noon. He told us to leave our blankets, and follow him at about two hundred yards distant, and let that distance intervene between each of us, and to look as if we belonged to the city. This we did: he went ahead; Reese, Dan, and myself followed through the crowd, each whistling, with as "don't care a look" as can be well imagined. We passed through the city this way, making it convenient to stop into a Frenchman's drinking-house to warm the "inward man."

We regretted to hear that no vessel would sail for the United States, and our friend Don E. conducted us to a small private room upon the second floor, where we were fed from a restaurante.

After we had been safely ensconced in our hiding-place, our three faithful guides came to take leave of us. They did so in the most feeling manner. The gray-bearded old man made the valedictory. He congratulated us upon our extreme good luck in falling into the hands of "*honourable* men," for, says he, "as humble as your apparel appears to be, you must know that there are thousands in this country who would murder you for that dirty jacket," pointing to the one I had on. "I thank God," said he, "that as long as I have worn this gray beard I have never forfeited my word of honour."

During this speech he strutted across the room with the utmost self-satisfaction, slapping his hands upon his bosom whenever he spoke of a *man of honour*. When he had finished his speech, we drew from the waistband of our pantaloons several ounces of gold, which we had been careful to keep dark until now, and distributed among them as a gratuity over and above their contract. We thought this precaution would seal their allegiance, as we had been often told that the *most honest* collectors of customs in Mexico will say to the importer, "That, as thin as is a doubloon, no man can see through it."

We had taken particular pains upon the road to exhibit our small store of silver, which they supposed was all we had. When they saw the gold come forth from its hiding-place, a look of surprise was exchanged; and when they fingered the yellow stuff, their countenances beamed with renewed devotion to our interest.

We certified in writing that they had been true and faithful to us, and the tall, dark-skinned robber, after first kissing the paper, carefully stored it in a secret place under his shirt. Upon taking leave, the old man, after several facetious jokes " how we would surprise our sweethearts when we reached home," embraced us with a Mexican hug both long and strong. In Mexico, one's regard for another is graduated in proportion to the length and strength of the embrace. Thus each of these robbers embraced us, and thus we returned it; for if we found in all Mexico the most fearless devotion to our interest while in misfortune, it was in our three robber guides.

Cooped up in this situation we remained thirteen days, and it was anything else than pleasant. Our lodging was in the midst of the infected district, where scores died daily of the *vomito*, the worst kind of yellow fever, and where we we were constantly under apprehension of discovery. A small window opening from our hiding-place into the street gave us a full view of every passer-by, among whom were several officers of the Mexican army that we well knew, and among them Captain Santa Anna, son of the President, whom we had seen passing Perote. Here in this death's hole we had to lay and sweat out the last days of hot July. We would long for the approach of night, that we might walk forth, as recreation both of mind and body; for during the eternal tolling of the church bells over the dead and dying, we could fancy the dreadful malaria coursing through our veins.

After night it was my habit to go to a hot bath a few squares distant, where an hour's bathing was succeeded by a profuse perspiration, which was of great relief to me. On one occasion, after coming out of the bath, I stepped into a drinking establishment for the purpose of keeping up the perspiration, and while taking a drink at the counter, two Mexican officers came in and drank by my side. One of these officers I knew; and as my disguise prevented his recognition of me, I concluded compliments were unnecessary. I am sure the free use of the bath kept me from taking the disease; for my companions, contrary to my advice, not making such constant use of it, were both taken down, upon reaching home, with the severest cases of fever.

During our seclusion here, several seafaring men from the United States, then in port, found out where we were hid, and came to see us and offer their services. Among them was my old friend Captain F——, and Captain H ——, and Captain ——. These gentlemen were of the most essential service to us, and I regret that it might be doing them a disservice by returning thanks to them by name.

The good Donna E., to while away our time, frequently sang for us, and her charming voice, like balm upon a wound, soothed our spirits, and made our confinement more tolerable. This good lady never seemed tired of serving us, and long shall we cherish the kindest remembrance both of her and the Don's goodness.

In her absence we had two room-mates in two loquacious parrots. The younger of the two had much to say. He rolled the drum and blew the bugle after the manner of the guards. He imitated the bray of the *burros*, sang the chorus to several of the Donna's songs, and at times was exceedingly wicked, and would swear outrageously.

The other was an old housekeeper, and entirely blind. She would sit upon the door for hours together, occasionally muttering to herself like some superannuated grandmother, who fancied that she was neglected by the rising generation. No sooner, however, were our meals brought in, than her worn-out nature seemed to reanimate; and, unless she was quickly served, would bawl out in the most emphatic and indignant tone, "Here am I, old and cross-eyed, and you don't care a —— for me." This rebuke never failed to procure her a breakfast. Indeed, in the absence of more dishonest bipeds, we found much company in these birds.

After we had been several days in our dark room, looking into the street one day, who should pass but Dick Barclay. Dick was the first of our escaped companions we had seen: we called him in, and learned the following account of the balance:

It was now one month since we left the prison walls of Perote. During this time, Dick, with his chum Cornegay, had kept in the mountains, occasionally venturing into the huts of poor people to purchase supplies, and had most ingeniously worked his way into this place under assumed characters: that the night after our separation at the castle, the Herculean John Young had fallen over a precipice in the mountains, and badly crippled himself— so much so that he was taken back to prison in a most helpless condition: that Beck and Davis, his comrades, were also retaken by the pursuing cavalry: that Tom Hancock had also been retaken in venturing into a rancho to buy supplies: that Captain Ogden was retaken entering into Jalapa the night we left it: that Ike Allen, Stone, and Elley were still afloat, and he expected, by this time, "herding their cattle upon the Rio Bravo;" and that Dalrymple was flourishing in the city of the Montezumas. Toowig had already sailed, and here we six were in anxious expectation of so doing.

Let us for a moment look into our late prison abode at the castle.

The night of our escape, and the next morning up to the counting time, as might be expected, our late companions were under the most excited apprehension, not only on our account, but also what the discovery might cost them. Under this excitement, things remained quiet as usual, for no one in the castle except themselves knew a breath of it. At nine o'clock next morning, Guts and the new guard came around to the prison rooms with the sharp and often-repeated order "*a formen, a formen.*"

This order was well understood by our countrymen; it meant "to form," and that in front of the prison doors, as usual, in the morning; but still they held back, and were slow to come out of the cells. Some made one excuse, some another; Guts stormed at their tardiness; he went into the cells in person to look where the absent were, and found them not; he inquired of the balance; one says, "Perhaps they are at the *común;*" another says, "They are at the *tienda:*" these places were sent to, but they were not to be found. Our boys said among themselves, "We will put them off to the last minute, for every minute is important to them, as they can get the deeper into the mountains." During this time Guts swelled and raved: "Where are they?" he thundered out to the interpreter; when some of them said, "Well, Van," to Van Ness, "it is no use to put it off any longer; let him have it." Van replied, "*Deiz y seis faltan*"—sixteen deficient. "Where are they gone to, and how did they get out?" bawled Guts, in a still louder tone. "*Quien sabe?*"— who knows? was the reply. Then commenced the greatest possible row: the whole castle was alarmed—officers and soldiers turned out—the governor came forth with death-like horror upon his countenance—officers and guards flew all over the castle; examined every nook and corner—the top walls— went round the great moat, but still did not discover the breach, the hole having been so carefully stopped with the blanket. The last place where they thought of looking was in the prison cells, and after much useless search, one of the officers pulled back the small shutter in the centre room which covered the loophole, and found, to his inexpressible horror, our breach obliquing to the left. "Who could have thought these daring Texians would have undertaken such a task? they *surely are* kin to the devil: this castle has stood these hundred years, and no one ever dared such a thing before;" these, and many such exclamations of wonder and astonishment, burst forth from men, women, and children, officers, soldiers, and culprits; for they all, from the governor to the smallest child, came to satisfy themselves of what their astonishment mixed up with miracle.

While the best-informed Mexicans will admit our superiority in war, both in daring and the use of arms, the more uninformed entertain the strangest notions of us. Many believe that we have magic power, and have near kinship with the devil. Others believe us to be northern barbarians, of one of two tribes of white Indians, who form the connecting link between mankind and the other world.

The northern Mexicans have frequently thus inquired of different Texians, "Do you belong to the tribe of How-do-do's, or the God-damn-me's?" this being the first English which they are apt to learn of our people. They are generally answered that "my mamma was a How-do-do, and my daddy was a God-damn-me." Thus pedigreed, the Texian is looked upon by them with far more astonishment than the Kentuckian who was sired by a steamboat and come out of a penitentiary.

My letter to Santa Anna was handed to the governor, with a request from me that it should be forwarded immediately to his excellency; and as it exonerated the governor and officers from any neglect of duty, he was not slow to comply in sending it by an extraordinary courier.

The surprise which our escape had created caused another hour to pass before the cavalry were mounted and sent in pursuit. They traced us to where we had the night before separated, but could follow no farther. Then they separated in different commands, and took different roads and mountain-passes.

We have already given an account of those recaptured, and as they were brought back to the castle, they were locked in the dark calaboose, except poor John Young, who had fallen over a precipice and was badly crippled: he was sent to the hospital in the village, where, after the most excruciating sufferings, his iron constitution survived his injuries.

The balance of our countrymen were reironed, and all huddled together in one room under double guard and increased vigilance. The officers now thought that nothing was impossible with Texians; and one of my friends, writing from the castle, said that "they even believe that we will escape in a letter."

After our escape, some of our friends circulated the report that we had gone, under the conduct of five Mexican robbers, to join Commodore Moore, in Yucatan. The consequence of this report was highly beneficial, as the greatest search was made after us in that direction.

Santa Anna, as I learned, pretended not to believe my statement, and very unjustly arrested all the officers of the castle, the governor, Limpy, and Guts inclusive.

CHAPTER XX.

EMBARCATION AT VERA CRUZ FOR HOME.

Preparation for Embarcation.—Captain Loyd and Steamer Petrita.—Pass Officers on the Mole.—Sup on board a U. S. Vessel.—Hailed by War Steamers.—Board the Petrita.—Meet my Companions and Dr. Sinnickson.—Mexican Officers come on board.—My Berth under the Boilers: its Temperature.—Dialogue with Steward.—Passage and Arrival in New-Orleans.—Once more in the Land of Liberty.—" Tom and Jerry," " Hail Storm," and " Sherry Cobbler."—St. Charles Hotel and a Soft Bed.—Sail for the " Lone Star."—Land at Velasco.—Reese and Dan.—Our Remaining Countrymen in Mexico. — Their Destitution, Sufferings, and Deaths.—The Cause, and Treasonable Armistice with Mexico.

UPON inquiry, our seafaring friends ascertained that the steamer "Petrita," formerly the "Champion" of Mobile, would be the first vessel sailing for the United States; that her captain had recently died, and she was now in charge of the mate Loyd. Loyd was an old acquaintance of mine, and a true-hearted American; and it is easy to imagine that, both from personal feeling to me and duty to his nativity, he readily came into the plan of assisting myself and companions home. So, on the night previous to the morning upon which he sailed, my friend Captain H——, of New-York, called for me at my hiding-place. Between sundown and dark we started for the mole, where the captain's boat lay. I sauntered along in his rear a few paces without baggage, and while the officer of the customs was examining a portly Englishman, upon whom they found a wallet of silver more than he had given in, and which seemed to create a dispute between them, we walked past with as much apparent indifference as though the Mole and all the tax-gatherers belonged to us. Upon reaching the place where the captain's boat lay, we kimboed our arms and talked loud, pretending to be in no great hurry. In a few minutes it grew more dark, and we got into the boat and pulled to his vessel in the offing, lying near the Mexican steamers *Montezuma, Gaudaloupe,* and *Dublin City,* which had that day arrived from Yucatan with General Ampudia's retreating army. Here we partook of a warm supper, a good glass of wine, and discussed our " father-land."

Just before nine o'clock the captain and myself slipped down the side of his vessel into the boat waiting to receive us. He steered past the war steamers, and was hailed by the sentinel, to which he made no reply, and coming alongside of the Petrita, about one hundred yards still farther on, my good old friend Loyd was ready to receive us with open heart.

On board I found Forester and Cornegay, who had shipped as firemen, and who were standing below, with smutty faces and red flannel shirts, as though they had been brought up to that business. Also Captain Reese, Dan, and Dick Barclay, with English names and English protections in their pockets, and who looked as independent as wood-sawyers. Also Dr. Sinnickson, who had been released by President Santa Anna at the instance of General Thompson. Captain Loyd told me that there would be no danger that night, and in the morning he would stow me safely below when the boarding-officer came alongside.

We had a good sleep this night, and early next morning the captain told me that he would go ashore with his boat, and when the officer started to come on board he would make a signal, and then I was to go below and crawl under the boilers. The boat's hour for sailing was 8 o'clock A.M., and her steam had been up half an hour when Loyd made the concerted signal from the Mole. I went below, and crawled into the darkest and hottest place this side of the infernal regions. Every five seconds I had to turn over to keep from burning to death. I was willing to take a good scorching, as I had settled it in my mind never to be taken back to prison alive. The hour which the officer occupied in examining the passports and vessel appeared to me to be a year, and being nearly exhausted, I determined to come out and meet the consequences. As I reached the front of the fireman's hole, the officers were getting into their boats, and Loyd called to me.

Being helped out of the hole by the firemen, with much difficulty I reached the cabin, and called to the negro steward, " For God's sake, to give me a bowl of water."

My inferior wardrobe and dirty appearance, covered with sweat and coal-dust, speaking thus to the *head* steward, stirred up his aristocracy. He slowly turned his head over his shoulder, and eyeing me with the most significant contempt, said, "Look here, stranger, you cabin passenger?" " Yes," was the reply; when, giving another look at me, he said, " I doubt it d—nably."

I replied, " My good fellow, you have a perfect right to doubt it; but ask that man," pointing to the captain. He went to the captain, and pointing to me with increased contempt, said, " Captain, is *that* fellow a cabin passenger?" The captain chucked him in the side, and whispered, " Yes; that is General Green, of Texas; and get him what he wants."

The poor steward came to me with the most contrite physiognomy imaginable, and after poking his face close to mine, and peeping through sweat, dust, and beard, he discovered behind these uncomfortable companions an old friend and acquaintance.

"Good God!" says he, "master, I know you now;" and from that time this deeply-mortified black man smothered me with kindness. He had been steward of steamboats in the United States, and I had travelled often with him before.

We were now at sea, with a clear sky and fair prospects, and having fair weather during the passage, we landed at New-Orleans on the eighth day, at 11 P.M. With feelings which do not often occur in one's life, we once more leaped upon freedom's soil; and as we required neither clearance or porters, we wended our way up town, and called into the first open "drinkery."

Here the scene changed. These very men, I among the rest, who, a few short weeks before, would have given a pint of their blood for a gill of the most miserable brandy ever distilled, now want, one a "*sherry cobbler,*" one a "*Tom and Jerry,*" and another a "*hail storm;*" and all concluded that a little rose water round the edge of the cut glass would make it go the better. How comparative is human happiness!

Having taken our drink, we passed on to the St. Charles Hotel, and called for a bed each with the most Republican independence. The barkeeper, on ringing for the servant to show us rooms, seemed to be impressed with some of the steward's misgivings, and as we started off, said, "Gentlemen, it is a rule of the house to pay in advance for tumbling the beds." We replied, "All right, landlord: we are a suspicious-looking set," and threw him a dollar each. The next day Colonels Wm. M. Beal and Durochea generously gave me money to ration my comrades, and in two days after we were again upon the " deep blue sea" with Captain Furgarson, sailing for the " Lone Star."

The sixth day we landed off the Brazos, where, soon after, Captain Reese and Dan were taken down with the severest kind of fever, which they had contracted at Vera Cruz, and with great difficulty recovered from, while my fellow-citizens elected me to the more pleasant excitement of the Congress Hall. Reese has since married a charming lady, and is making cotton-bales upon the banks of Cedar Lake; while Dan, true to his first promise, is again upon the Mexican frontier with Captain Hays, ready to take his change out of the "blanketed nation."

Let us now turn to inquire after the main body of our countrymen-prisoners; and we do so with feelings of mournful sorrow, with a heart overwhelmed with sadness. We go back to the prisons of San Luis Potosi, and find them covered with rags and filth, loaded with vermin, and worn down with hunger and all the multiplied cruelties of their captors. We trace their bloody path south three hundred miles, through the scorching plains of Mexico, by the unburied bones of many noble souls who sunk under a task more than human. We see the brave and dauntless Cameron taken out upon this path and murdered for no other cause than his bra-

3 A

very. We see the remainder herded together like beasts of burden, and driven forth into the streets with sticks and bayonets by brutal overseers, as scavengers of filth too horrible to contemplate. We see their manly frames worn down by an insufficient allowance of the offal of a rotten population. As the opposite plate will show, which was drawn from life by our indefatigable fellow-prisoner, Charles M‡Laughlin, we see them heavily ironed, working upon a pavement in front of the archbishop's palace at Tacubaya; and what was still more grating to their feelings was to be gazed upon from their coaches by the yellow, pepper-eating, demi-savages, as if they had been so many hyenas. We trace most of the survivors, naked and emaciated, two hundred miles east, to the dark, cold dungeons of Perote; the balance to San Juan de Ulloa, to be offered up as a certain sacrifice to the *vomito*, that universal malaria of death. We follow around the massive castle walls of Perote upon the north, and in the bottom of the great ditch find newly-stirred earth. Here, underneath the loose sand, without a plank to cover their bones or a stone to mark the place—without the last sad rites of burial, in a spot not only unconsecrated, but cursed by a fanatical priesthood, lie the remains of the best spirits of our country. Here, in a foreign land, in a priest-ridden nation, and in full view of the eternal snows of Orazaba, repose the bones of fathers, brothers, husbands, and sons of Texians—here we helped to deposite

Booker and Jackson, Trapnal and Crews, Saunders, Gray, Trimble, and a long list of others. Peace to their ashes, and a nation's gratitude to their memories! But oh! how the heart sickens at perfidy the most unparalleled, when we trace these bloody murders, starvation, and deaths to the President of our own country! I would to God that a due regard to truth, as well as justice to the memories of these brave men, would allow me to throw the mantle of eternal darkness over the sequel; if so, I would bury this most horrible conclusion in lasting oblivion, for my country's credit. It is, however, my task to register this bloody tale, and I have no option but in truth; and when President Houston has been charged as the cause of the sufferings and murder of our countrymen, for our country's honour it has been too clearly proven. (See Appendix Nos. II. and VI.)

We still look after the surviving half of the brave band of Mier, and find them in the cheerless cells of Perote, living skeletons, without clothing enough to hide their nakedness; and what language do we hear from them? Though they feel mortified and indignant at their president's denunciation of them, and his heartless usurpation of the laws of their Congress in withholding their supplies, yet there is but one sentiment, one language among them, and that is, "*The honour and liberty of their country.*" At all times, all occasions, and under all circumstances, when hunger has pressed them most, when

Death made no sham visits to their gloomy abodes, boldly did they publish this sentiment. Time after time did they write home to their countrymen, "Let no consideration of us forfeit your country's honour. Let us rot in these dungeons ere you concede one inch to these coloured barbarians." And when there was one recreant slave among them, who fostered a coward and a traitor's heart so servile as to beg his liberty at his country's dishonour, he was denounced by the others with universal execration.*

I believe that I may safely assert, from my intimate knowledge of the Mier men, that two among them could not have been found who would not have preferred the most cruel death to signing, as the representatives of their government, the late infamous armistice acknowledging Texas a "DEPARTMENT OF MEXICO." And though owerwhelming public opinion in Texas has driven President Houston to disavow any such authority on the part of *his* commissioners, yet it is perfectly clear that this commission *was created by him* and sent into Mexico, based upon the propositions which "*the lawyer Robinson*" bore from Santa Anna, and no other.†

Yet these are the men of whom President Hous-

---

* This was "the lawyer Robinson," one of the Bexar prisoners, whom Santa Anna despatched to Texas to bring her back to acknowledge the "*supremacy of Mexico.*"

† *Vide* Correspondence upon this subject between Santa Anna, his minister of War and Marine, Tornel, and the Honourable Mr. Doyle, the British minister in Mexico. Appendix No. III.

ton caused a part to be murdered, and others to starve, by violently withholding from them the bread which the representatives of their countrymen liberally voted them, while he, in open violation of the Constitution, dipped his hand into the public chest, and furnished *his* commissioners means to go to Mexico to acknowledge that we were no longer a sovereign nation, but "*the Department of Texas.*" (See Appendix No. VI.)

* * * * * * *

On the 25th of March, 1844, precisely one year from the date of the bloody black-bean lottery, the following sixteen of our Mier prisoners made their escape from Perote, out of the same cell from which we escaped on the 2d of July previously: A. B. Laforge, Cyrus K. Gleason, John Johnson, Edward Kean, Richard Kean, Wiley Jones, William Moore, T. Smith, E. D. Wright, Francis Arthur, John Toops, William T. Runyan, John Tanney, William H. Frensley, Stephen Goodman, and William Wynn. The first-named nine succeeded in reaching Texas, and the remaining seven were recaptured and carried back to prison.

An account of this escape is the best commentary upon the character of our people. Their daring is only equalled by their never-tiring perseverance, and their capability to overcome the most appalling emergency.

From the time of our escape in July, the officers were constantly upon the *qui vive*. They would a dozen times per day enter the cells of our men, and examine the walls with the most minute care, not thinking it possible that there could be any other mode of escape. In this they were much mistaken. During that terrible malady of *hard work* and *starvation* which swept off so many of our men, the governor granted the survivors permission to cover their pavement floor with heavy boards, being softer to sleep upon than stones. They then conceived the plan of sinking a perpendicular shaft through the pavement of their floor some forty feet deep, and tunnelling underneath the main wall so as to reach the bottom of the great moat upon the outside. Tremendous an undertaking as this was, these bold men completed it in forty nights, for they could not work upon it in the daytime.

This work, which was worthy of an experienced engineer, with all the implements for sapping, they commenced by sawing a trapdoor out of one of the boards upon the floor with a piece of tin, which fitted so exactly that the officers never discovered it, though they often stood directly upon the place. From this trapdoor they commenced digging the perpendicular shaft with sharp sticks and small knives, and as they proceeded downward, the disengaged earth was elevated by a hair rope being tied to one of their small provision baskets. This earth, when drawn up, was so nicely distributed under the board floor as to raise them all equally, and thereby not attract the notice of the guards.

One great difficulty they had to encounter wellnigh defeated their enterprise. This was, that after they had descended to a considerable depth, the carbonic acid gas, which was generated from the coal fires used in the castle, being heavier than the atmosphere, descended into their pit, in which no one could labour but a very few minutes before he had to ascend to prevent suffocation. Notwithstanding this serious impediment, there was always a fresh hand to supply the place of the last labourer. Thus the work progressed for many nights, when the volume of this destructive gas became so deep that it would nearly exhaust one before he could reach the bottom of the shaft. In this situation, when the work progressed by fractional parts of inches, it would seem that a kind Providence directed the course of the tunnel so as to intersect with a gopher hole, which communicated with the bottom of the great moat upon the outside, and through which this deadly gas escaped, thus affording the sappers power to push the work with greater energy.

On the night of the 24th they were nearly through, and all their preparations being made, the following night they passed out and ascended the outer wall of the moat, and crossed over the *chevaux de frize* as we had previously done. Thus did these heroes celebrate the first anniversary of the "decimation," and make the 25th another memorable day of their captivity. On the 25th we had crossed the Rio Grande, and drove Ampudia's legions behind the walls of Mier: on the 25th, the most cold-blooded murder of the nineteenth century was perpetrated upon our seventeen decimated countrymen: on the 25th we entered the gloomy cells of Perote; and on the 25th the noble Cameron was murdered.

The morning after the escape, the remainder of our prisoners, who looked upon it as another triumph of Texian prowess, did not wait for the guards to find it out, but ran to Guts, and said that "another sixteen of the Texians have gone, señor."

"*Hai Dios! Diez y seis falten? Carajo!*"— My God! Sixteen missing? O villains! was his first exclamation; but at the thought of the gloomy dungeons of San Juan de Ulloa which stared him in the face, he burst forth into a roaring cry. The tears rolled swiftly down his fat face and fell upon his still fatter belly, which laboured like a bellows, to the no small amusement of the Republicans, who wellnigh split theirs with laughter. Had Heraclitus been a prisoner, one peep at Guts would have made him laugh.

The whole castle was instantly in an uproar. The governor came around to assure himself of a work which all said the devil had a hand in. When he saw it, he exclaimed, "*Mucho trabajo*"— much work, and consoled himself by saying that "they had a finished engineer to conduct it."

The remainder of our men were put upon their examination as to the time they were at work upon it, and testified that they were forty nights in completing it. These forty nights were rendered to the government as three nights, for the longer time would have procured both the governor and all the other officers quarters in the dungeons of San Juan. As feasibly as this escape was accounted for to the President Santa Anna, some one had to atone for it; and Captain Peneder, one of their most humane officers, was sent prisoner to San Juan, where he soon fell a victim to the *vomita*.

It was this escape which Santa Anna, in his letter to the United States' minister, called "abusing the generous confidence of my government." Thus casting from their limbs, each, twenty pounds of iron, eluding the vigilance of multiplied guards, and escaping through the walls of the strongest fortification in his empire, from the menial service of slaves and brutes, was abusing the "*generous confidence*" of his government! Was such a perversion of truth ever perpetrated by the head of any other nation?

Time rolled heavily on, and our remaining prisoners were treated with increased cruelties, when a ray of hope beamed in upon them. This was the reported annexation of Texas with their father-land. This news caused great joy, and it was manifested in more ways than one. Our charcoal sketchers drew upon their prison walls the "lone star" of Texas surrounded by the constellation of the northern republics. This put the Mexican officers in the greatest rage. With true Quixotic boldness, they charged this mighty galaxy sword in hand, and after cruelly belabouring the plastering, had it whitewashed over. No sooner had these bold caballeros turned their backs, than another and another flag sprung from the deathblows of the last, until they found it worse than useless to war upon this Phœnix-like spirit.

Heavy time brought with it another disappointment, but hope revived with the return of Santa Anna's birthday, which was succeeded by disappointment still worse.

The United States minister, General Thompson, was upon his return home, and Santa Anna, in parting courtesy, placed the Bexar prisoners at his disposition, denouncing the others, at the same time, in all the eloquence of his court abuse. This was adding insult to misfortune, and they had redress from neither but in the bold speech of freemen: they both wrote and published, regardless of all the refinements of his cruelty.

The United States legation was left in charge of the young, accomplished, and talented Benjamin E. Green, who deserves the thanks of all Texians for his bold advocacy of their rights, and the many kind courtesies extended to their suffering countrymen.

In the latter part of the summer of 1844, Governor Shannon, the present minister from the United States, reached Vera Cruz, and upon his arrival at Perote, though in the night, obtained permission from the governor of the castle, went into each of the cells where our prisoners were confined, and made the most critical inquiry into their condition. This conduct was highly praiseworthy, and at the same time that it manifested the warm feelings of a countryman, it showed a boldness worthy of his country and his station. He promised our prisoners his devotion to their interest, nor was that promise neglected. His first official note was to President Santa Anna, asking for their liberation: to which note the President returned the following answer, which we here insert, as the most finished compendium of hypocrisy, vanity, falsehood, and malice to be found in the annals of diplomacy.

"National Palace, September 5, 1844.
"Wilson Shannon, Envoy, &c., &c.

"Much esteemed Sir,—I have received the very friendly and attentive letter which you addressed to me under the date of the 30th ult., respecting the liberty of the Texian prisoners confined in the fortress of Perote.

"In reply, I have the honour to inform you, that, as well for the efforts made on various occasions by the members of Congress of the United States, as through respect for Messrs. Jackson, Thompson, Clay, and others of respectability, I have liberated many of the Texian prisoners who were captured in various actions and encounters between the Mexican army and the adventurers, and now only those are retained in prison who, abusing the kindness extended them, have attempted to escape by assassinating the Mexican soldiers who guarded them.

These criminals deserved death, and nothing but the *mildness and magnanimity natural to the Mexican character** has prevented its application. Justice, however, demands that they should be treated with

---

* The following incident, related to the writer by Captain S. C. Lyon and Mr. Harvey, gentlemen of unimpeachable veracity, is strikingly illustrative of Santa Anna's vindictive hatred to the Texians. After their liberation on the 16th of September at Perote, they were making their way, via Vera Cruz, to take shipping home, and had proceeded twenty leagues below Jalapa, when they stopped at a house upon the roadside for a drink of water. At this place they saw a coach which had just previously stopped to change mules, accompanied by a guard of about twenty lancers. In the house was an individual in citizen's dress, with a gold band around his cap, who, upon Harvey's entering with his hat off, asked if he was a Texian. "Yes, sir," was the reply. Turning quickly to Captain Lyon, he said, "Are you likewise?" "Si, Señor," the captain politely replied; when the great unknown, no less a personage than Santa Anna, the President of Mexico, aimed a blow at his head with his walking-cane, which was promptly caught upon the arm, the captain at the same time stepping out of the reach of a second; whereupon Santa Anna turned against Harvey, who was still uncovered inside of the door, and violently assaulted him. The President's vengeance possibly found some pretext at Captain Lyon's replacing his hat after the meeting salutation, but those who are acquainted with the natural urbanity of this gentleman can find no excuse for conduct in the Mexican despot which would be a disgrace to the veriest tyrant of Arabia. After thus wreaking his vengeance upon two unoffending, worn-down prisoners, whom his " MILDNESS AND MAGNANIMITY, NATURAL TO THE MEXICAN CHARACTER," had starved two years in dungeons, he drove them off, under the most vulgar oaths, without one drop of water. At the same time that the reader's indignation cannot fail to be greatly provoked at such a brutal outrage, language suitable to it would, perhaps, illy become these pages.

In the face of these and a thousand other brutal outrages committed by the dictator, as well upon English subjects as others, such is POLITICS, that the Queen of Great Britain considers him a fit representative of St. George's cross. The enlightened throughout the world will concur in the opinion that this proud and most honourable badge was most unfitly bestowed.*

* See Appendix No. IX.

greater severity than those who have not aggravated their faults by stabbing the innocent soldiers who guarded them. This is all that I ought to reply to your esteemed communication; and in having the honour to do so, I have the satisfaction of subscribing myself, for the first time, your most affectionate, attentive, and constant servant,

"Antonio Lopez de Santa Anna."

Governor Shannon did not despair of success even at the receipt of this vindictive tirade, but wrote to our prisoners to "be patient, and wait a while longer," until he made another trial. In a few days thereafter they received the joyous news of their liberation; and on the 16th of September, the governor of the castle, representing the "magnanimous nation," and acting under instructions "natural to Mexican magnanimity," gave each of the Texians ONE DOLLAR to bear his expenses to Texas, being a distance less than two thousand miles, and then turned them upon the open common as if they had been so many herbivorous animals. One hundred and twenty was the aggregate number released, of whom there were at Perote 105, Vera Cruz 10, Mexico 3, and Matamoras 2. (See Appendix No. V.)

In solemn, melancholy duty, we again turn to inquire where are the balance of that brave band who fought at Mier and Salado? My heart sickens at the answer. Their bones are strewed from the banks of the Rio Bravo to the bottom of the great sewer of

Perote—they are washed by the grand river of the north, and widely scattered in the mother mountains—they are bleaching upon the battle-fields of Mier and Salado, and whiten the commons of Vicario, Potosi, St. Miguel à Grande, Dolores, and San Juan del Rio. Peace! peace be with their ashes! Eternal honour and gratitude to their memories!

SUPPLEMENTAL CHAPTER.

Reflections upon the Present Political and probable Future Relations of Texas, Mexico, and the United States. — Annexation.—Abolition.— Southern Boundary.

It is not my purpose to enter into a detail of the present condition either of the government or people of Mexico. Prescott, Mayer, Kendall, and other late writers, whose opportunities have been far greater than mine, have so recently and so ably occupied this whole field, that were I to attempt it would but be to weary the public with an oft told, and, maybe, a worse told tale.

The late radical change in the government of Mexico from a seeming republicanism to an avowed military dictatorship;* her position to Texas, and that of Texas both to her and the United States of America, as well as to other nations, forces upon me some general remarks, which may not be out of place at this interesting juncture in the politics of

* The reader will recollect that this was written (1844) during Santa Anna's dictatorship.

these several governments. From what I saw in a zigzag march of more than fifteen hundred miles through many of the Departments of Mexico, these reflections were convincing to my mind, and I offer them to the public as I received them.

We entered the northern boundary of Mexico at the 28th degree of north latitude, and meandered the magnificent Rio Bravo several hundred miles to its mouth; thence through Caidereta, Monterey, and Saltillo; thence across the Sierra Madre, *via* Mataguala, to San Luis Potosi; thence *via* Dolores, San Juan, Miguel à Grande, to the capital; thence *via* San Martin, La Puebla, and Perote, to Vera Cruz; and what do we behold? A geographical area capable of supporting three hundred and eighty millions of souls, with seven thousand five hundred miles of seacoast, and every variety of soil and climate, from the 15th to the 42d degree of north latitude, containing a mineral wealth unknown to any other portion of the globe, and a capability of agricultural product which has not yet entered into political estimate.

In this vast circumference of the most choice portion of God's earth, we find a population of seven millions of souls, scattered here and there, without the moral ability to appreciate the unequal boon. Of this seven millions of people, we find twelve out of each thirteen in a state of squalid misery, wretched ignorance, and want, rarely known, and never before paralleled in the history of the world where the elements of competence were so abundant; we see a small fraction of the remaining thirteenth holding, in a most unjust and unwise proportion, benefits which should be more diffuse as the aggregate happiness of the whole is desirable; we see the bulk of this population, sparse and well located as it is, since the days of the Conquest uniformly sinking lower and lower in the scale of human degradation, without one scintillation of energy to foretell a change; we see this population, in the last twenty years—unlike its great and prosperous neighbour of the north, doubling its numbers—absolutely reduced in the aggregate twelve per cent.; we see their boasted eight millions at the completion of the Revolution reduced to a small fraction over seven, with increased taxes, with diminished product of metals, with an agriculture which has gone back from bad to worse, with ninety millions of public debt, the most of which is due a foreign creditor with the will and the power to force its payment; we see an unwise accumulation of wealth in the priesthood, who hoard from a fanatical laity with a mania which increases with age; we see a foreign commerce, the profits of which is a perpetual drain upon the body politic, with a government of bayonets, the support of which is death to the citizen: in fine, we see a nation of abject ignorance and slavery, without a Constitution, and governed with the sword. Thus it is we see Mexico, without the hope of advancement, and everything receding to a state far worse than aboriginal simplicity, because in its backward march, without the virtues of the primitive man, it carries with it the vices and corruptions of civilized artifice.

If we are asked to what these things are attributable, it would be an unsatisfactory answer to say that such is the history of the Spanish colonies. Let us look beyond.

Upon the discovery of the new continent, the bright metals allured a court, then governed by the fanatical dogmas of the Romish Church, to a belief of unceasing wealth. That court, in extending its colonial government over such untold treasures, as well from the religious fanaticism which governed the sixteenth century as from an equal desire to possess itself permanently thereof, threw its government into the control of a priesthood, whose long-settled policy has been to govern by the suppression of the Bible, and through the ignorance of the governed. This policy, adhered to with such unceasing aim for three hundred years, at the same time that it made the court and the Church the recipients of the wealth, sunk in a reverse ratio the subject both in ignorance and want. A system so erroneous in its commencement could have no cure short of universal dethronement of the power first instituting it; and how was that power to be reached, when it was the moral soul of the governed?

The Church in Mexico, whose existence depends upon its unchanged policy, is the moral soul of the people; and were it to allow learning to the million, it would permit a transfer of that great moral lever by which it governs. Thus, while its fanaticism debases, its cupidity impoverishes the many. With its hundreds of millions of wealth, it teaches the strict doctrine that upon your conduct depends your redemption from purgatory, and *without my will you cannot enter heaven.* Is it strange, then, that people under such a belief should be patient under worldly sufferings? The whole history of the Mexican Revolution will show, that where the priest excited opposition to the mother state, it was for the purpose of concentrating more power in themselves, to do which they invariably made use of their holiness as the surer and more effectual means. If the policy of the Church, as it has the power to prevent it, is thus opposed to change, where is the remedy? Certainly not in those whose souls have to reach heaven through that channel. The history of many nations in time past answers the question; some other people, more skilled in the arts of war and the science of government, ambitious of the possession of so choice a portion of the earth, will extend their arms and government over it; for where there is so much to tempt national cupidity, a pretext for war is never wanting. Here this question presents itself.

Is the present moral and political condition of Mexico already so low as to justify such a measure?

The present degraded state of Mexico is perhaps a sufficient answer to this question; but in this age, when the "moral opinion of the world" is so frequently talked of, and possibly more respected than formerly, it would require a reasonable pretext in a foreign nation to assume such a position.

Great Britain, for instance, would, upon the refusal of Mexico to pay her sixty millions of debt to English subjects, and to extend a full protection to the hundred millions of English manufacturing and mining capital, have a better pretext to extend her laws over Mexico than she had in most of her East India conquest, or in forcing opium upon the Chinese.

France, perhaps, would have as good a pretext, if the late arbitrary act of the Mexican government against the French subject is in contravention of existing treaties, as it is grossly violative of that *comitas inter gentes* which should ever exist.

The national vicinage between the United States and Mexico, that great and leading neighbourhood policy which has the right to keep off a stranger who possibly might be troublesome, certainly would give the former the right, if it did not make it her imperative duty, to possess herself of that which a stranger might. This policy, called "*American*," belongs as much to the New, as that called the "*balance of power*" does to the Old World.

If a decent regard for the "moral opinion of the world" be wanting by other nations to make such a conquest of Mexico, it is not so wanting on the part of Texas; a nation, though small at present, but whose destiny will extend south and west as surely as that has been the course of former conquest.

All history teaches that the general course of conquest has been from north to south. It was so in the days of Tamerlane, of the Goths and Vandals, and, from the best evidence upon the subject, it has been so already with Mexico herself. Physiology also instructs us, as a general law, that animals are more daring and ferocious in high than in low latitudes; that as the cold climate makes it the more difficult of subsistence, it nerves the system to an energy commensurate to the want; that while the perpetual produce of the warm climate renders such energy unnecessary, it enervates the system and debases the mind. Nothing can be more true, and a knowledge of the people of the United States and Mexico is strikingly illustrative of the fact.

Let the present condition of the former nation, whose population has increased from a unit to twenty millions, with her improved state of agriculture, with her hundred millions per annum of foreign exports, with her commerce upon every sea, with her vast strides in literature and science, with improvements in the art of war, which makes an era as important as the invention of gunpowder, compare with the latter nation, occupying the most favoured location upon the new continent, fronting upon both seas, with a climate adapted to vastly more extensive produce, with her hills and mountains filled to overflowing with the useful and precious metals, with her population less in numbers and worse in condition than in the beginning, and we have a strong evidence of the truth of this remark.

When we look more closely into the individual habits of the people, the remark is still more convincing. The people of the first are of stouter frames and more enduring constitutions, and, upon an average, sleep only *one third* of their lives, while those of the latter, of smaller persons, whose constitutions and minds, from generations of slothfulness, have been enervated, for want of mental occupation sleep *two thirds* of theirs.

Let our experience follow them to the camp, where we have met, and contrast their habits with the people of the northern nation. Here we see the Mexican soldier wrapped in his blanket, and shivering in the sunshine, while the Texian, in his shirt sleeves and open collar, thinks the weather pleasant. We see their officers with a cumbrous cortège, and all the paraphernalia of the boudoir to invite sleep; while the Texian officer, with his saddle-blanket as a cover and his saddle for a pillow, indulges only when Nature can no longer resist. The Mexican officer looks upon his huge load of bedding as essential among the munitions of war as the Texian does upon his dry powder and well-placed double sights. That which is considered so essential to the one, is looked upon by the other as a womanish effeminacy which would be his disgrace. The former rises in the morning, and, with a piece of sweet bread as large as one's thumb, drinks his half a gill of chocolate, which serves him until dinner, when the enormous quantity of red peppers he eats stimulates him into a siesta, which he looks upon as necessary to his existence, while the latter rises from his solitary blanket ready armed and spurred, stows away his couple of pounds of beef, either with or without bread, as the case may be, and is ready to meet the consequences of the day, be they pleasant or otherwise.

These are the nations which have been eight years warring against each other. Mexico, with her seven millions of people, whose course has been unproductive of favourable result in this war, and whose tendency has been more downward than at any former period in her history, is still pertinacious in her vain desire of reconquest; while Texas, with her twenty thousand souls, threw off the yoke—has increased her population eight or ten fold—multiplied her exports beyond her imports—has a surplus of corn and beef vastly more than the wants of her people, and cheaper than in any other portion of the civilized earth. With this rapidly-growing power, already strong, and bidding so soon to wield a giant's strength, her course has been temporizing and weak beyond measure. When Mexico has vainly threatened Texas with annihilation—when she has violated every principle of civilized warfare by a catalogue of cruelties the most unparalleled—when she has, time after time, plundered and burned our towns and farmhouses—when she has kidnapped our citizens and carried them into foreign bondage—when she has offered up in cold blood our best citizens to satiate the bloody vengeance of a despot, it has been the misfortune of Texas, the most of this time, to have in her executive chair one who had neither the energy nor the will to punish these cruelties. When the nation called upon President Houston to do so, she was answered in deception, and by him the enemy were falsely told that "*we have no means of prosecuting the war.*" Then comes his denunciation of his gallant countrymen of Mier; then his proclamation of piracy against his gallant navy; and, lastly, his thieving copartnership with Colonel Snively's expedition. This executive, without either the energy or the will to do that which the honour and interest of the country required, instead of boldly meeting the enemy and punishing "his aggressions," commences a compound negotiation of diplomatic frauds as disgraceful to the nation as they were stupid in their author.

At the same time that the Texas executive was begging the mediation of Great Britain, whose price was beyond his gift,[*] he had commissioners beyond

[*] The "*abolition of slavery*" was, then, the price, and however covertly the Texas executive may have connived at the measure, he dare not openly advocate it. More recently the British government has varied her conditions of mediation, and it is but a variation. She seems just now tenacious of the separate nationality of Texas, well knowing that her Constitution is a rope of sand; that in six months, under that Constitution, a preponderance of European paupers may be introduced, with all the rights of citizenship which belong to that few whose patriotism

the Rio Grande, entering into a disgraceful and treasonable armistice with Mexico; and while he would promise benefits to other nations, the public will of his countrymen, which he could neither control nor resist, offered political union to the confederated Republics of the North.*

It is not my purpose to argue the good or evil which might result from such a union. It is sufficient that an immense majority of my countrymen desired it, and, whatever may be the result of their application, duty to Texas requires me to defend her against the slander of her executive, and demonstrate her entire capability of defending herself successfully against the united and concentrated power of Mexico. What I have already said upon this subject might, with good reason, be considered a sufficient demonstration of this position; but the history of this whole war is a history of proofs of this fact.

and blood won the country; and that, when thus introduced, and thus equally vested with the rights of suffrage, they can uproot the Constitution and abolish slavery with that legal dictum which is not unfrequently the despotism of the majority. No sooner did the British government fail by a direct attack to carry an institution so closely identified with the welfare of our present population, than she commenced another assault by a political strategy, which, if the people of Texas are true to themselves, will likewise fail. If they take, as it is their first duty to take, early measures to amend their Constitution, and guarantee themselves against European mendicancy, then, with or without annexation, Texas will be safe against such strategy, and English sappers and miners will meet as signal a defeat in their present subterranean movement. The people of Texas cannot be blind as to the extent of English friendship, when that government proposes, through her mediation, that "Mexico shall acknowledge Texas's independence upon condition that the latter remain a separate nation."

* See Appendix No. VIII.

REFLECTIONS. 393

In the year 1835, the battles of Conception and the "grass-fight," where large odds were driven from the field by Texians—the same year, when three hundred Texians stormed the city of San Antonio, and compelled General Coss and eleven hundred Mexicans to surrender—in 1836, when one hundred and eighty Texians in Alamo, under the command of Colonel Travis, held out thirteen days against Santa Anna at the head of eight thousand opposing forces, and every Texian falling after killing five times their number—in the same year, when Colonel Fannin and four hundred men, at the battle of Coletta, in a three hours' engagement, beat off thirteen hundred of the enemy under General Urea, though the next day he was deceived into a surrender—in the same year, when seven hundred Texians, of their *own spontaneous* will, charged and routed fifteen hundred of the enemy, under General Santa Anna, at San Jacinto, killing and capturing the whole—in the same year, when Deaf Smith, with twenty Texians, charged and routed one hundred and twenty of the enemy—in 1839, when one hundred and four Texians, under Colonel Jordan, beat one thousand of the Mexicans at Saltillo, and made good their retreat into Texas, in the face of such odds, with the loss of only four men—in 1842, when Colonel Caldwell, with two hundred and ten Texians, repulsed General Woll and thirteen hundred of the enemy at Arroya Salado—in the same year, when two hundred and sixty-one Texians

3 D

drove ten times their number into Mier, fought them for nineteen hours, killing and wounding three times their number, though they were deceived into a surrender, and cheated out of their victory—in 1843, when two hundred *unarmed* Texian prisoners at Salado charged twice their number of *armed* guards, beat and dispersed them—in the same year, when Commodore Moore, off Campeachy, silenced ten times his naval force, and compelled them to seek shelter—in fine, let us go back to Mina's expedition in Mexico, and follow him through his bloody campaign, and nowhere will we find that the Mexicans have stood the charge of the North Americans and the descendants of the English, and good reasons teach that they must be regenerated before they ever will. A small knowledge of the Mexican's raising, his habits of life, and his mode of enlisting, will prove this assertion.

The Mexican army is composed of the veriest dregs of their population, having been raised in the most abject degradation and slavery, without ever being permitted the use of fire-arms: they are forcibly taken from the *criminals' prisons*, the *unprotected Péons*, and the *houseless leperos*. These wretched creatures are tied together like brutes, without their will, and without the power of remonstrance, when they are forced into quartels, where for many months they are drilled like machines, then placed in uniform, and given a bright musket, which his greatest punishment is to be made to fire. In the Mexican army we see no targetfiring, and upon inspection days the *inside* of the gun is not looked to, when it is the especial duty of the soldier to keep the *outside* bright. Their army, with a gay, peacock uniform and bright arms, under the exciting notes of the bugle, has, to an inexperienced eye, a formidable appearance. The soldier goes through the "*manuel*" with a stiff, uniform, machine-like motion, while the company and regimental drill is taught as horses are taught to perform tricks which they cannot know the meaning of. Such soldiers, thus recruited, are called *volunteers*, and the army the "*defenders of liberty!*"

With such mockery of truth, such destitution of principle, is it to be expected that such an army can cope with freemen, who in the nursery are taught that they have no superiors and but few equals—who go forth from their mother's watchfulness with the rifle in their hands, and by the time they are entitled to breeches, emulate their bold sires both at the target and in horsemanship? While the chief accomplishment of the Mexican is in throwing a rope over a pig's head or a mule's foot, the Texian fires at the target with the most scientific estimate of the strength of his powder, the weight of his shot, and the placing of his sights. His first lesson from his father is, "Never to touch his double trigger until his double sights are right;" and from this important lesson no circumstance can drive him. He holds in contempt the empty show and gewgaw pomp of the camp, and looks upon it as the shadow rather than the substance of power. It is this feeling which has been called by foreigners the *ultra* democracy of the nation: it is a conscious superiority in themselves which gives confidence to the action.

If a Mexican commits theft or other crime, he is sent to prison therefor, where he takes the highest degrees in human vices, which, it would seem, in the estimation of that government, perfects him for the soldier, and from whence he is turned into the army, while one upon the suspicion of theft in our army would find his head shaved and himself drummed out of the ranks, to the music of the *Rogues' March.* "*An honourable discharge*" from our army is the highest boast of its owner; he prizes it as the richest jewel he can leave to his posterity; and while with pride his heart swells over it as a matter of patriotism, it is the foundation of his land-title. Not so in Mexico; neither land nor patriotism enters into the account; *honourable discharges* are not known; and while a bad criminal is kept in the service as a punishment, a good soldier is too valuable to be spared the service. In their ranks, good and bad alike wear out a premature existence upon a scanty pittance, which poorly serves him from day to day; and without the expectation of future reward, he seeks every opportunity of deserting from this unthankful service.

Nowhere, upon my long march through Mexico,

except in the valley of the Rio Grande, was the least sign of improvement, either public or private, either in building or agriculture. The withering hand of decay appears to be fastened upon the land; everything seems to be in its downward tendency, as fast as time and neglect will carry it. The subject, so long debased, is sinking lower and faster, if possible. Their ages of vice and misery have entailed upon them diseases, which follow from generation to generation, sickening to contemplate, and disgusting to behold. Lunacy, blindness, deformity, and many libidinous diseases are the hereditary entailments of the multitude, and carry off thousands yearly when in the prime age of manhood.

At San Luis Potosi I was quartered in a hospital, and in the room adjoining that in which I was confined there were forty out of forty-three of its inmates inflicted with lewd diseases, most of whom were considered to be incurable. During my short stay at this place, several died the most horrible deaths. This, I was informed by an intelligent Mexican officer, was a fair proportion of the diseases of the country, and that it was hereditary in families. When, with astonishment, I asked him if the disease extended to the better classes of society, he replied in the affirmative, but said " that people, of late, were getting more particular, and now its *non*-existence entered into the marriage contract: that it was one of the first inquiries of parents before they bestowed the hand of a daughter, and *vice versa* with the parents of the son." What a monstrous state of society! and how shocking it must appear to the public ear of the United States! that community which looks with such horror at the possible existence of it, even in the very small proportion of the lowest dregs of a city population.

I saw families, a large proportion of whom were blind, and one, in particular, wretchedly deformed, without any other use of their legs than to crawl upon their all fours, with a kind of jumping gait, much resembling the motion of the mud turtle. These miserable creatures, who appeared as destitute of reason as of physical power, were huddled together in the greatest destitution, and seemed to move and propagate by instinct. There can be nothing more certain than that these diseases and infirmities are propagated. One instance came under my observation strikingly illustrative of this fact: it was in the person of one of the camp followers, a most unwise proportion of whom pursue the Mexican camp. He was a man apparently of about forty-five years of age, with a full-sized, well-proportioned head and body, but whose legs, from his hip joints to his feet, did not exceed one foot in length, and his arms were in proportion to the length of his legs, thus giving him the height of a boy of seven years of age. This little man was of the most enduring constitution, and would toddle after our regiment in a brisk run thirty miles per day. When the regiment would halt for the night, the little fellow would dance either for *clacos* or *aguardiente*, of both of which he was very fond. He told us that he had a very tall wife and eight children; that four of them took after their mother and had long legs, and four of them after himself and had short ones. Many other instances of *lusus naturæ* came under my observation, and I was informed that an alarming proportion of the population were afflicted with these wretched entailments.

In the Valley of the Rio Grande only did we see anything resembling improvement. Here the people are infinitely superior in condition and intelligence to those more south: here were new fields being opened, and some cotton plantations under way, with the border towns from Matamoras up to Laredo, which, during this war, have doubled, and some quadrupled their population. What a volume this single fact speaks! that upon the immediate border between the two belligerants is the only improvement in the one claiming to be "mighty and magnanimous." Can there be a stronger argument of the irrevocably lost condition of Mexico, than that the only improvement in her mighty empire is in that immediate district which has borne the burden of the contest? And why? Because that district is contiguous to a race of improvement—that, notwithstanding all the burdens and calamities of an eight-years' war, their intercourse with Texians, even in hostility, has opened their eyes to the improvement of their neighbours. If, then, this often ravaged border is the only portion of all Mexico in a state of improvement, what would be not only its condition, but that of the whole country, under the benign influence of peace and good government?

What we have already said of the recruiting of a Mexican army, and the character of that army when recruited, is the least difficult part of their war establishment. This army, after a long and tedious drilling, is turned into a flaming automaton, without the thought necessary to meet a sudden emergency, and hence always subject to surprise and panic; but, machine-like as it is, it requires to be supported, and, from its size and duties, a support larger than the resources of the government. Even without foreign war, the whole immense extent of the Mexican territory has to be watched, to do which a large army establishment is necessary. The presence of bayonets alone can keep down a people goaded to desperation with onerous exactions under unwise laws. Withdraw this threatening power, and the people are at once in arms: the presence of the bayonet is essential to the existence of the despotism, and their support is the consumption of the people's substance. If, then, a necessary peace establishment at home requires more than the income of the government, how is it possible to increase it so as to wage a successful foreign war? Let her withdraw the peace establishment to prosecute a foreign war, an enemy at once rises up at home which subverts the existing government. Her army has to be fed, clothed, and armed alone from the public chest, and without such support from day to day, it must certainly dissolve. They have no provident commissariat, which looks ahead to emergencies, and the soldier's support is consequently a *daily* drain upon the army chest. The government, without manufactories, has to seek her arms from abroad, and the refuse of other nations, both from their cheapness and the ignorance of the Mexicans in the daily improvements of the age, are bought up. How is it with Texas?

Here is a whole nation of soldiers, from the twelve-year-old boy to the grayheaded grandfather, not shut up in walled quartels, as ready instruments to enforce the exactions of tyranny, but each soldier occupying his own armed castle with his true and faithful rifle ever in readiness, and his water-proof shot-pouch always filled; here, in one hour's notice, these guardians of liberty can be in their saddles, in readiness to meet wherever danger threatens, and prepared to stay from home according to the emergency; here no man is too poor to buy one dollar's worth of powder and lead, which will serve his rifle through a bloody campaign; and should there be such a one, his more able neighbour cheerfully supplies him; here is a surplus of corn and beef throughout the land always in readiness for those in the service of the country; here is a skill in the use of arms unknown in any other portion of the world, and an intrepidity of daring which frequent dangers have made commonplace : in fine, here is a moral principle controlling the action which no circumstance can subvert. Thus it is that we see Texas, with an army of twenty thousand citizen soldiers quartered throughout the country, always in readiness to meet a foreign foe, and without the cost of one dollar to the government.

When the called session of the Texian Congress of 1842 urged upon the executive to prosecute the war, he, in his message to the Congress, makes the frequent assertion that the nation had no means of doing so. Not only was that message published to the enemy, but the same executive again reiterates the assertion, time after time, in the many speeches which his extraordinary conduct made it necessary for him to make to justify himself, without ever once adverting to the fact that, of the many thousand volunteers who took the field in that year, not one required either pay or rations of the government. The whole campaign of that year has plainly demonstrated the fact, that it was unnecessary to furnish either pay or rations. The ample pay which the soldier looked to was the consummation of that liberty for which he at first struck; nothing more did he desire, nothing less would he have. His sustenance was to be found upon every prairie, the free use of which was his welcome privilege. Thus we find Texas a nation of soldiers, brave in war and skilled in arms, with all the munitions of a campaign in readiness, and with a moral purpose which despotism can neither control nor check.

When the timid and weak-headed of our own, and the speculative and uninformed of other countries, have expressed doubts as to the ability of Texas to maintain herself against Mexico, these doubts were the offspring of ignorance and fear. A people like the bulk of the Texas population, born in and reared under the principles of free representative government, will not even entertain a question of change. That proposition which purposes to send them back to despotism can get no hold upon the popular thought, and the occasional recreant who would harbour it in his own bosom dare not utter it. Effeminacy, licentiousness, and corruption, after the slow and gradual inroads of ages, may undermine a nation's political morals, as will indulgence an individual's. What months and years may do to the individual, requires ages and centuries to effect with the nation. Thus it has been with those representative governments which have preceded us: the constituents had first to be corrupted one by one, and when all the members were affected, then the body sunk. Such may ultimately be the destiny of Texas; but, with the lights of the world before her, there can be no just fear that her course of freedom will be short of any nation which has gone before.

Can a nation born and raised in such principles long practise a *neighbourhood comity* with one whose principles are in such diametrical opposition?

History has given a negative answer to this question. It was not so in the days of the Grecian Republics or the Commonwealth of Rome, and the short life of representative government in France has fully demonstrated its entire impracticability. The lamb might as well be caged with the hungry wolf in the hope of living in friendship. Such nations, to keep in peace, must either be separated by long distance or by some difficult natural boundary, the surmounting of which will be equivalent thereto. They cannot commingle in the same trades, and practise rights common to both in quiet. What may be the policy of the one may prove the bane of the other, and we could with the same hope make virtue and vice assimilate: thus, for instance, the subjects of the present slavish despotism of Mexico holding, in common with the citizens of Texas, the free navigation of the Rio Grande, with the high tariff, contraband laws, and government monopolies on the one side, and the low tariff and free trade principles on the other. The interference of the former with the rights of negro property of the latter, and many other opposite interests, would keep up between the two perpetual excitement, which would result in perpetual war.

In Mexico, for instance, none but a licensed few, who pay high for the privilege, can raise tobacco, and that, when raised, is to be sold to the government at a price far below its value. In Mexico, none but the government dare make a segar, and no man, woman, or child dare smoke one except it has the government stamp upon it, while every man, woman, and child in the nation smokes. The valley of the San Antonio River in Texas is capable of making more tobacco at a cheap rate than the wants of all the northern states of Mexico, and it is preposterous to say that this would not be done, and carried across the border, in defiance of all the laws of Mexico, even had she an army upon that border twenty times her ability to maintain.

So it is with the articles of raw cotton and spun yarns. Under the unwise management of Mexico, her manufactories are languishing, with the latter at sixty-two to seventy-five cents per pound, while the cotton can be grown, spun, and transported from Texas into Mexico profitably at less than half that price. What possible circumstance can prevent this from being done, when the soil of Texas produces double the quantity of the raw article per acre which is reared in the United States—when, from the larger size of the Texas cotton-bolls, fifty per cent. more can be saved per day—when the length of the picking season is longer and better—when provisions are cheaper than in any other portion of the world, and where a superabundant water-power costs nothing?

Two nations so contiguous, so opposite in their policy, and every way so unlike each other, can never live in friendship with a border which invites both to its advantages. The Rio Grande, from its head to its source, from the forty-second to the twenty-fifth degree of north latitude, is capable of maintaining many millions of population, with a variety of product which no river upon the north continent can boast. This river, once settled with the enterprise and intelligence of the English race, will yearly send forth an agricultural export which it will require hundreds of steamers to transport to its delta, while its hides, wool, and metals may be increased to an estimate which would now appear chimerical.

If annexation of Texas to the United States of the North succeeds, this boundary can exist but for a short period; and though there seems to me to be a destiny in the womb of time which marks her southern boundary at the extremity of the north continent, where the two great oceans of the world will unite under a genial sun and a smooth navigation, yet her more *immediate* southern boundary must extend to the *Sierra Madre*, that great Chinese wall which separates the people of the Rio Grande from those of the more southern table-lands. Can this be considered a greedy desire upon the part of the mighty northern nation, when her facilities of communication with those people from her capital in twelve days are superior to their present means of communication with the capital of Mexico in thirty? We say not. This age has merged distance in time, and the people of the Rio Grande at present are as near neighbours to the capital of the United States as Boston was to Philadelphia at the promulgation of President Washington's inaugural message to the first Congress.

Should annexation not take place, this will be done, and sooner done by Texas. Both the government of the United States and Texas are founded upon the same political code. The same political sentiment enters into each. They have the same common origin—the same language, laws, and religion—the same pursuits and interests; and though they may remain independent of each other as to government, they are identified in weal and wo—they will flourish side by side *pari passu*, and the blight which affects the one will surely reach the other. The unity of the Texian government, her immediate contiguity to Mexico, and her multiplied causes of quarrel therefrom, will cause her arms to extend south and west sooner than would those of the United States. In the later government of such a confederacy of republics there are many heads to consult and many interests to accommodate. These numerous sectional interests, whether real or fancied, must be accommodated, and by an action necessarily slower than that of Texas.

As I have said before, it was not my purpose to discuss, at present, the question of annexation. That has been often and ably done, and much has been said on both sides; but as a Texian, feeling a proper degree of pride in her nationality, and an absorbing interest in her welfare, whatever may be her destiny, duty requires me to deny a position which seems to have grown up with the argument, to wit, that most or all the advantages of union would result to Texas.

If Texas has been the applicant for this political copartnership, she has not been insensible to the fact that she would enter the firm as a junior partner, bringing with her into the concern more than her *pro rata* of capital; she has not been insensible to the fact that she voluntarily abandons her own freedom to take a junior position in that mighty national confederation which will give her but a feeble voice in the general direction of affairs; she has not been blind to the fact that, by entering into the union, she makes herself a party to the many quarrels of conflicting interest which perpetually excites that great national family; that by this step she voluntarily leaps into the questions of bank or no bank; of free trade, high tariff, and protection; of abolition and disunion; she is fully aware that she gives to the Northern States all the benefits of her carrying trade, to the injury of her own citizens, and taxes herself with northern manufactures at least thirty per cent. higher than she could procure like articles from other nations; she is not insensible to the fact that after this current year a ten per cent. *ad valorem* tariff, without direct taxation, will be ample for the support of her government, when, by coming into the Union, she voluntarily taxes herself four times that amount; she is not insensible to the fact that she offers to the confederacy four hundred miles of seacoast, with all the advantages of the rich valley of the Rio Grande, including sixteen degrees of latitude, from its source to its mouth, with more than one hundred millions of acres of public domain. And for what are these mighty surrenders made? Does Texas receive a *quid pro quo* in having her coffers filled for the purpose of carrying on what ought to be her brilliant destiny even as one of the states? No! She receives just enough of the proceeds of her immense domain to pay a debt, not a tithe of its value. And to whom is this debt paid but to the citizens of the United States, most of whom have bought it upon speculation? Texas is none the better off for this, save in the protection of that national faith, which she prizes as an honest nation should. If this debt were paid to her own citizens, it would be that much towards her individual state wealth, whereas not one dollar in fifty comes to those citizens. It goes into the hands of foreign money-shavers and broker-gamblers, who care nothing beyond for her prosperity, because such people have no feelings except in the usury of coppers.

Thus it is that Texas would denude herself by abolishing her Constitution—by dismissing her foreign ministers—by cutting short her acquaintance with an enlightened world—by surrendering her separate independence, and committing national suicide—to submit to a high protective tariff, and resort to the grinding operation of a direct tax for the support of her state government, and then sink to an obscure corner in the constellation of states for that proud feeling which a majority of her citizens claim in their nativity. The United States can not, must not, therefore, view her as the only beneficiary to the contract.

This feeling of nativity must be strong indeed which would voluntarily make these mighty surrenders; and to him who cannot feel that pride of birth which most of the people of Texas feel, these surrenders must appear truly astonishing. It is an exalted feeling far above all calculations of dollars and cents; and truly may we exclaim, in the language of a distinguished Roman, "*Nescio quâ natale solum dulcedine cunctos ducit, et immemores non sinit esse sui.*" If the sordid interests of money were to enter into the calculation, it would appear as reasonable for a son who had received a competent outfit from a father, and taken upon him all the duties and pleasures of a household, to seek to surrender everything back to that father when he had subsequently married a termagant stepmother.

Since the establishment of Texian independence, she cannot have viewed, but with regret and mortification, the rapid growth of principles in her fatherland, which no circumstances under annexation will cause her ever to submit to. At the establishment of Texian independence, a fanatical few preached the doctrine of universal equality between the white and black man, between the master and the slave. Then this few received the countenance of but few —then the many abhorred them as unprincipled disturbers in the large and happy household; no man of character gave countenance to the unnatural associations of such disgusting doctrines. How altered now the case? The contagion of fanaticism, however absurd, is like the contagion of physical maladies, which communicate by contiguity. It spread first to the ignorant, because they were in nearer contact. When it found a lodgment in the multitude, it met a response in the demagogue of higher standing; then found apologists in the Senate; next, advocates among the most talented, and now the election of President is bending to its influence. When the son proposes to give everything back to the father, he finds that father wedded to this unnatural mother, with whom he never intends to live in friendship. Still, the son insists upon giving back all his wealth to be divided among the offspring of his mother, the young half-bloods, who are taught from their cradle to despise him. The boast of the son is in his father's name: he feels that there should be a common destiny between them, and he makes the wonderful sacrifice of interest a tribute to his pride. He sees his wealth divided among the large family, trusting to the precarious whims of his parent, now under alien influence, not only for justice, but for bread. Texas is a stronger case: from her father she went forth into the world penniless, and now offers her hundred millions of acres and her boundless resources, which is the fruit of her own industry, sweat, and blood.

Are these all the advantages which would result

to the United States by such a union? No, indeed! Many others might be enumerated; but, in connexion with the question of southern boundary, I will only notice two, which seems to have been overlooked by most writers upon the subject. 1st. The possession of the shortest and most practicable route to the settlements and commerce of the United States on the Pacific; and, 2dly. A boundary in connexion with the question of the amelioration and ultimate destiny of slavery in the United States. First, The annexation of Texas to the United States, with the Rio Grande as the consequent immediate southwestern boundary, would necessarily, by treaty or conquest, extend to the *Sierra Madre*, and, as a protection against the northern tribes of Indians, should cross to the Gulf of California about the 28th degree of north latitude. This would be the shortest and most expeditious route from the United States as well to her Oregon settlements as to her other numerous interests on the Pacific.

Taking New-Orleans as the most convenient point of embarcation from the United States, we will find that sixteen hundred miles of steam navigation to the mouth of the Rio Conchoes, upon the Rio Grande, can be made in about the same time, and, taking the year round, with the same facilities, that Cincinnati can upon the Ohio; and from the head of steam navigation upon the Rio Conchoes, across the *Sierra de Carcay* to steam navigation upon the

Rio Hiagui, a distance of three hundred miles by railroad, the port of Guaymas, upon the Gulf of California, could be reached in eight or nine days; saving a distance of four thousand miles, and twenty additional days steaming, *via* the Panama Canal, provided that was completed; and saving a distance of twenty-four thousand miles, *via* Cape Horn, and the average economy of one hundred and twenty days sail, steaming such a distance being too expensive. It would save a four months' travel the present route across the country from steam navigation of the Missouri waters to Oregon.

This short and expeditious route to the growing, and soon to be the important settlement of Oregon, and, at present, many other interests in the Pacific in the event of the acquisition of this country by the United States, would be the smallest reasons for the accomplishment of this route.

The most desirable portion of this continent lies between the 28th and 42d degrees of north latitude upon the Pacific. It presents more than a thousand miles of seacoast, with the important ports of Guaymas, San Diego, San Gabriel, Monterey, San Francisco, and many others, with a soil and climate of unsurpassed capability for grazing and agriculture, and a mineral wealth supposed to be equal, if not superior, to any in the world. This vast country of more than one million of square miles, lying due west of the settled portion of the United States, between the frozen regions of the north and the vertical sun of the south, between the gentle influences of the Pacific Ocean and the great backbone of the continent, capable of giving wealth and happiness to a hundred millions of souls, is now in possession of roaming tribes of unhoused Indians, and a few settlements of less than two hundred thousand Mexican subjects.*

If Oregon is important to the United States, this country is a thousand times more so. The extreme northern lines of the states of Pennsylvania, Connecticut, and Rhode Island only reach to the 42d degree of north latitude: that latitude cuts in two the states of Massachusetts and New-York, and Lake Erie and Michigan, while the 28th degree is north of the United States settlements in Florida, and nearly three degrees north of Texas, at the mouth of the Rio Grande. While it is due to the United States that she should not permit this important country to fall into European hands, it is equally due to her that she should possess it by any and every means necessary thereto.

Let the United States apply, if necessary, the usufruct doctrine of her possession of this country, which Old England and Old Spain practised towards the aborigines upon the discovery of this continent—a doctrine of common sense and sound reason—of

---

* It will be perceived that I have spoken in round numbers of the population of this country. Both Forbes and Mayer make the population much less, but their remarks are applicable to Upper California, while mine extend to the 28th degree of north latitude.

human necessity and justice. If the Author of the universe intended the earth for the support of the few, to the exclusion of the greater number, the reverse of this doctrine is true, and then it is right and proper that a very few should hold this country, of which they can make no adequate use, to the exclusion of many millions in other portions of the earth, who may be dying for the want of space to live in. When Spain claimed title and possession to this vast tract of country under this doctrine, that the aborigines had no title in the soil, but only a temporary right to the use and occupancy thereof, such only as the buffalo enjoys, she was justified in such possession only by applying it to a better use. Three hundred years have passed, and neither herself nor those claiming under her have applied it to that better use, and she holds it without such ability so to apply it, to the exclusion of others who have, and whose necessities require it. England, France, or any other nation, whose population is greater than her means of subsistence, has a right, derived directly from the Maker of the earth, to occupy it with her redundant people; and it alone is a question of policy or power whether its present claimants or nearest neighbour will permit it. This era, so marked in the improvements of agriculture, machinery, and navigation—in the knowledge of geography, and the increased necessity of the case, will not allow a perversion of the use of this country. For many wise reasons, the United States should extend her settlements over it; but should she, by a different policy, fail to do so, the all-seeing eye of Great Britain will not let slip such a golden opportunity in possessing herself of this desirable middle ground between home and her vast Eastern possessions. Besides, if the Oregon settlement is important to the United States, without a harbour sufficient for the entrance of her smallest vessels of war, the port of San Francisco, or some other port in the south, is absolutely necessary for her.

It may, however, well be questioned whether either Spain or the present government of Mexico has ever had any other than a nominal possession of this vast region; for only here and there, in a very few isolated spots, has she had a few people in real possession, and those few shut in by fortifications as protection against the aboriginal occupants. If, therefore, she has no power of absolutely possessing herself of this country, her declaration of ownership to it was arbitrary, and the act not justified by her means; and with the same propriety she might have claimed, to illimitable extent, that which she neither had the use of nor power of using, depriving millions of the earth's population of support and the proper uses thereof.

While I hold that it is both just and proper that any nation with an overgrown population may settle these vast wastes with her redundant people, I repeat again that it would be short-sighted policy in the United States to permit it. That nation, with her twenty millions of people, in the ordinary course of events, in fifty years, will have eighty to provide for, and a large country will be necessary for so many within the lifetime of numbers now busy in the politics of that country. With such an acquisition, the United States would not be larger than Brazil with her six millions of people, and about one third of the size of the present British dominions. With such an acquisition, the United States would contain but a fraction over three millions of square miles, and without Texas that would be cut nearly in twain by a narrow slip extending to the 42d degree of north latitude, which is the parallel of Boston. If it be wise policy, and the United States extends her dominions to the 28th degree upon the Pacific, then Texas becomes absolutely necessary to her. Then the *Texas wedge*, making into the centre of her square and compact surface, will appear obviously wrong. It would be a severance of her entirety, which few would be willing to reconcile; and without a union of the two countries, a conflict of interest would inevitably grow up between the separate nations, detrimental certainly to one, and probably to both. This conflict would beget countervailing laws, such as are at present in the bud, and would produce estrangement to the advantage of European powers, which would profit by the quarrel.

Secondly, This boundary, viewed with reference to the amelioration and ultimate destiny of the negro population of the United States.

Though I believe that so good a political institution does not exist in any nation for the government of its poorer or more dependant population as slavery in its general character in the south and southwestern portion of the United States and Texas; and while I believe that it is the reverse of either a "moral or political evil," viewed as it is at present, yet the day may come, and probably in the lifetime of that generation now coming into the world, when, either from individual interest or public policy, the white and black man can no longer occupy the same soil. Does it not, then, behoove the politicians of this day and time to cast about for the solution of that difficult problem before which all other questions of public policy must sink into utter insignificance? What is to be done with the black? is that difficult problem.

In the solution of this question, I hold it to be self-evident, that the abolition of slavery in the United States will not take place till it becomes the interest of the owner, and not then until there is a separate country to locate them upon.

Both those who advocated the re-colonization of the black race in Africa, and the fanatical abolitionist who preached the doctrine of equality in its broad sense, were far ahead of the question—the colonizationist, because of its impracticability, and the abolitionist, because neither public justice nor public safety would permit it. The first commenced the work without a due estimate of its cost, and the latter without regard to the political safety and moral operation of the measure upon those immediately concerned. While the first met the approbation of many leading political philanthropists of the country, all the means which their most sanguine expectations could hope for would not transport to their native country a tithe of the blacks' increase; and from fanatical impulse, the latter looked to the successful precedent of the Northern States as their strong argument, without ever estimating the vast dissimilarity of circumstances between the North and the South.

In the fifteen free states and territories of the American Union, containing a population of 9,557,055 whites, there are only 172,892 people of colour; that, at the time the abolition of slavery took place in these states, but a small fraction of that number existed, and their labour had become comparatively profitless. How altered is the case now! In the fifteen slave states and territories, with a white population of 4,632,053, there are 2,701,566 blacks, being 385,540 more than half of all the white population of those states. This was the population of the United States in 1840, and at present the blacks of those states are more than three millions. Let us, then, strain a supposition that it was to the interest of all concerned that these three millions of people should be manumitted and turned over to the Colonization Society to be sent home to Africa: it would require ten thousand of the largest class merchant ships, supposing each to transport 300 souls, and $150,000,000, allowing the moderate expense of fifty dollars each to collect them together and transport them across the Atlantic Ocean. This is an amount entirely hopeless even to the most zealous infatuist. Again, let us allow, as we know to be the case, that it is not the interest of those concerned to give up this large amount of property without a just remuneration; yet it cannot be expected that the government should undertake to pay this remuneration, which, at their present value of $300 each, would require $900,000,000 in addition to the $150,000,000 necessary to carry them to Africa: an amount which the wise will not contemplate, and which the ignorant cannot estimate.

We will again suppose that the government had both the will and the credit to create a *par* stock to the amount of the purchase of this property: is it fair to presume that the owners ever would consent thereto, unless the immediate *cash* outlay of the $150,000,000 for their transportation was incurred?

Experience, the wisest of teachers, in recurring to the past and present condition of the free coloured population of the United States, has given an unequivocal negative to this inquiry. There are, in proportion to the number, seven times as many deaf and dumb, blind, insane, and idiots among the free coloured population of the Northern States as among the slaves of the South. This fact, united with the startling disproportion of crime among the former

over the latter, would forever prevent the abolition
of slavery, when the emancipated slave is to sit
down by the side of his late master in the enjoyment of the same political rights, to create nurseries
of vice and misery. That the two colours can occupy the same country without degradation attaching to the one in a greater degree than to the other
is supremely absurd. The degraded cast, deprived
of the honours and emoluments of office, and feeling their unequal station in society, would become
the natural enemies of the more favoured one, which
would result in all the horrors of bloodshed. The
stronger party would argue that their safety was in
the annihilation of their enemy, which would be the
inevitable end either of the white or black community in any other than in their present relations of
master and slave. In this relation, the master is not
the enemy, but the friend and protector of his slave.
He is so from interest, and, from long habit of protection and friendship, is so from choice. He is the
lawful guardian of these dependants, and interest,
feeling, law, and public morality require him to be
so—to provide them with food and raiment, to nurse
them in sickness and in health, to govern them with
humanity. In an immense majority of the slaves of
the United States, they value this protection; they
feel proud of their master's friendship; they partake
of his character with all the feelings of birth or aristocracy to which he may have been raised, or to
which pride, circumstance, or ambition may cause

him to aspire. With such feelings, millions of white and black do live in friendship; sever these ties, and you make them enemies by arming each with political jealousies which must prove the injury of both, and certainly the destruction of one.

Let us look into those countries of Europe where the labouring classes are said to be the best off—in England, Scotland, France, and some of the German states—in those countries where the more social names of lord and tenant are used instead of master and slave, as in the United States; and where do we find the owner responsible under all circumstances for the food and raiment, the medicine and physician's bill of the operative, but in the United States and Texas? In these countries, the law makes it the master's duty, and both interest and attachment to the needy and afflicted makes it his pleasure. In these countries, the physician who visits the master also visits the slave; he serves each with the same medicine out of the same spoon, and charges the identical rates per mile for visiting the one as the other. In these countries, if from drought or flood, or other calamities, dearth ensues, it is the master's duty to look abroad to supply the deficiency. From the first settlement of the English American colonies to the present day, there cannot be a solitary instance cited of a slave perishing for the want of food. We do not believe that the same can be said of any other nation, in this or in any age, where the peasant is dependant upon the landlord for hire, and where he has no resource in case of misfortune or calamity to fall back upon save that hire. In the United States the dearth falls upon the master; in Europe, it falls upon the peasant. In the former countries the master is the responsible commissariat of his establishment; in the latter, the land-rents must be paid, or a new tenantry substituted, and the greatest want will be endured by the tenant sooner than the loss of home. Here, if a tenant die for want of bread or medicine, a surplus labour of a like kind supplies his place at as cheap a rate.

It is very true that in most European countries their poor establishments might furnish the simple article of medicine necessary to *check* disease. This is the most inconsiderable item towards *complete* cure. The mode of giving it, nursing, watching, supplying a thousand wants, and answering as many whims of the sick man, complete the cure. Such is the difference between the European hospitals, where the physician administers by the wholesale, and the American negro quarter, where the master sees that the most minute instructions of the physician is attended to, and where the wants and whims of the patient is answered by a sympathizing hand. In the latter, whatever the convalescent appetite requires, if not prohibited by the physician, is furnished, and at proper times and in proper quantities. Here the negro resumes his labour when he feels perfectly able to do so, and not like the European pauper, who, to escape the constraints of the poorhouse, and mingle with his every-day associations, goes forth, half cured and half unprovided for, to relapse into worse sickness.

Knowing, as we do, the improved moral and physical condition of the slaves of the United States and Texas over their former naked, ignorant, and cannibal condition in Africa, we feel conscious of no moral wrong in their present ownership. We believe that this relationship is the happiest both for their physical condition and *general* mental capability.

Had Mr. O'Connell, the disturber of his own country, the calumniator of ours, and the reviler of Washington, known more of this institution, both justice and common sense would have taught him that his transcendent talents might be employed in a better manner than in a lifetime of abuse of that country which has opened wide the door of competence and happiness to hundreds of thousands of his own destitute countrymen. We have the evidence of hundreds and thousands of as honest Irishmen as Mr. O'Connell, that the worst possible condition of our negroes is far better than millions of their own citizens; and while we deeply sympathize with these suffering millions, our sympathy can never excite them to an unwise opposition to their own government; that sympathy is to be found in our open houses, in our well-filled granaries, around our hospitable hearths, and deeply rooted in our political Constitution.

It cannot be denied that within the last twenty years a wonderful revolution has taken place in the United States in the improvement of the slave's condition, and that this improvement is still going on. The legislatures of the states have interposed their protection, while a true domestic economy has demonstrated the fact, that the better fed and clothed, the more profitable the negro. That which has done most for this improvement is a charitable morality, already wide, and still spreading throughout the slave portion of the Union. That just public opinion throughout the country, which stamps the bad master as the bad man, has done, and is still doing more for this improvement than all other causes. The master who would be guilty of wanton cruelty towards his slave is marked by his neighbour as a mean man; and, feeling this blighting judgment in all his intercourse, he alters this treatment as he would avoid any other act which would bring upon him public reprobation.

It was the writer's fortune to have been born a slave-owner in one of the most densely-populated slave districts of the Roanoke, and a twenty years' acquaintance in the Southern slave portion of the United States has convinced him of the truth of these remarks. He believes that he hazards nothing in the assertion that the general condition of the Southern slaves is infinitely superior to that of the free people of colour in the North. He will extend his remarks to Texas, and, from an eight years' residence in this republic, assert, from positive knowledge, that the condition of her slaves are incomparably superior to the free negroes of the North, and better than any other portion of the slaves of the South. And why? Because here is a climate better suited to their constitutions, and a soil more capable of a free and abundant produce, which makes the necessaries of living cheaper.

The truth of this remark will not be difficult of comprehension when we state the fact that a beeve weighing from seven hundred to one thousand pounds can be raised in Texas at a less expense to the owner than a chicken can in Virginia, in which its owner finds his profits in raising and selling at one dime. The last season, in a large portion of Texas, a market could not be had for pork at one cent per pound, and corn at twelve cents per bushel. In illustration of this subject, one other fact may not be out of place here—that in most any portion of Texas, the best beeves may be purchased at an amount which the hides and tallow will bring in market, leaving the large amount of flesh without cost to the consumer. It may be asked with propriety by a person unacquainted with this fact, Why does not the raiser butcher his own beeves, and thereby save the flesh? There are good reasons why he does not. It is his business to *rear* cattle, and not to *butcher* them. Large stocks are owned by persons who have but little else, and whose occupation it is to brand the calf when young, and look after the herd sufficiently, while raising, to keep them together. He consequently has neither time nor means to prepare the hides or tallow for market, and sells the beeves on foot at his cow-pen.

With these facts before us, how worthless should be that specious but mistaken fanaticism which dwells with such eloquence about slavery, which excites such false sympathies about the "traffic in human blood," and which seeks to level three millions of human beings to the wretched misery and wants of the free negroes of the North, or the freed cast of Mexico.

I am justified in my observations while in Mexico by all late writers, that the boasted freedom of that country is a slavery in its horrid realities which attaches nowhere to the descendants of Englishmen; that their freedom is only in name, for want and wretchedness, general ignorance and slavish humility, are seen there such as I have never, in a solitary instance, witnessed in the slave portion of the United States. Mr. Stephens, in his late work on Yucatan, gives the following description of this freedom in that country, which I copy, from its faithfulness to my own observation throughout Mexico. He says: "Looking into the corridor, we saw the poor Indian on his knees on the pavement, with his arms clasped around the knees of another Indian, so as to present his back fairly to the lash. At every blow he rose on one knee, and sent forth a piercing cry.

He seemed struggling to retain it, but it burst forth in spite of all his efforts. His whole bearing showed the subdued character of the present Indians, and with the last stripe the expression of his face seemed that of thankfulness for not getting more. Without uttering a word, he crept to the major domo, took his hand, kissed it, and walked away. No sense of degradation crossed his mind. Indeed, so humble is this once fierce people, that they have a proverb of their own, '*Los Indios no oyen sino po las nalas*'—the Indians only hear through their backs."

As I have said before, having been born and brought up in the slave portion of the United States, and been the owner of slaves all my life, I do aver that I never saw or heard of such a case of slavish humility, of servile abasement, which, if anything could, should have disarmed law of its justice, and unnerved the vengeance of a bloodhound. It is true that I have often known slaves improperly punished, and equally true that I have more frequently known them to escape just punishment; but I again repeat, that I never saw or heard in the United States such abasement as Mr. Stephens relates, and many instances which I witnessed myself in Mexico, where, at each stroke of the lash, the miserable Péon praises his God, "*Alabo à Dios*," on account of his master's mercy.

It was common, upon our arrival at a hacienda in Mexico, to be struck with the conspicuous position of the *stocks*, a machine for punishment. This machine is made of two pieces of timber, each about thirty feet in length, and three inches thick by twelve in breadth. These timbers are placed one upon the other edgewise, and at every few feet there is a hole large enough for one's neck, and a smaller one on each side for the wrist. For dereliction of duty, among other punishments, the petit tyrant, who presides over these estates as alcalde, condemns the poor Péon's neck and wrist to this cruel duress; and the amount of punishment may be estimated at these haciendas when we state that these machines, each capable of punishing twelve or fifteen at a time, were filled. I cannot err in saying that, if the owner of negroes in the United States were to permit such an instrument of torture upon his plantation, public reprobation, universal and overwhelming, would cause him to abandon the neighbourhood thus outraged. Neither in the United States nor in Texas will the intelligence of the age allow of vindictive punishment, even were that demoniac feeling the constitutional inheritance of so brave and proud a people.*

* Since writing the above, both truth and candour require the author to state, that in his travels in Texas he has witnessed, upon the plantation of one of the citizens of the republic, treatment of his slaves which forms the only exception, in this community, of what is above asserted. I witnessed working at the cotton scaffold three Africans wearing what the overseer familiarly called "necklaces." This "necklace" consisted of a circular piece of iron, the ends of which were fastened upon the back of the head with a stout padlock. This circular iron band rested in front upon the mouth, attached to which was another iron inserted in the open mouth. A second iron band was welded at right angles to the first, immediately in front of the mouth, and pass-

With these facts, which are familiar to the intelligence of the South, ought the anti-slavery fanaticism of the North to be viewed in any other light than unpardonable ignorance or unwarrantable impudence? This remarkable fact is observable, that those who mostly concern themselves about this institution are those who know least about it; and when they have occasionally had a response from better intelligence, it has been unfortunate for their cause that such response is traceable to the demagogue, who hopes to gather from such a harvest stores which will serve his ambition. When a gifted and leading Northern politician has dignified it as a "great moral question which must and will be heard," it was unfortunate for that individual, with his great and comprehensive intellect, that he was so little acquainted with the real institution, or it is hardly probable that he would

---

ed over the top of the head, thence down in the direction of the padlock behind. Thus "necklaced," these slaves had neither power to eat, drink, nor speak, and at stated periods the "necklace" was taken off to afford them sustenance. They were working bareheaded, under a burning August sun, in the 29th degree of north latitude. The reader can best imagine to himself the power of the sun upon these irons, and they in contact with the naked flesh. I could imagine no crime so heinous as to justify the punishment of this damnable machine. Upon inquiry, I was informed that they were made to wear these machines to prevent them from "eating dirt," a desire occasioned by a morbid appetite which I have known both in white and black. I have since learned that these irons were to prevent them from absconding.

I am sensible that the abolitionist will triumph at this circumstance; yet they will have but a lean argument in condemning the humanity of a thousand good on account of the cruelty of one bad master. It would be as reasonable were the censorious to condemn the whole Protestant Church for the crimes of one pastor, or the amours of a bishop.

have endorsed a popular fallacy—a sophism such as schoolboys may debate in their college walls, but such as practical experience does not justify.

In Mexico I saw a number of negroes who had absconded from Texas, and in no case did I see one whose condition was bettered, but, in most instances, vastly worse. I saw several anxious to return to their owners, and nearly all, by a few months' residence, were as degraded as the mass of Mexicans. They were extremely destitute; they who previously never had a care, and who knew it was their master's business to clothe, feed, and provide them with every necessary, now found liberty an unreal phantom; they found in it a licentious indulgence, which, instead of giving them food and raiment, brought in its train misery and wo.

After all, I am forced to the conclusion that slavery, as applied to this institution, is but an ugly name, and liberty, as applied to nineteen twentieths of the people of Mexico, but a handsome one, and that the true condition of these two countries would warrant a reverse of these terms; that they are in either, *eo nomine*, arbitrary. Let us look into the mines and manufactories of European countries—let us go among their destitute millions—let us look into the workshops and factories of our own free North, and compare their condition—we are forced to believe that the liberty of the former is a delusion, while the slavery of the latter is the better condition.

From these condensed reasons, it is plain to my

mind that no circumstances can ever occur which will allow the abolition of slavery throughout the United States, and permit the manumitted slaves to an equal participation either in the rights of domicil or citizenship. It is equally clear, that while it is not the will of those interested at present to allow it, yet, if it were, neither individuals nor government have the means either of purchasing or transporting this population to Africa. If, then, no such means at present exist, how much better able would government be at the end of twenty-five years, when the amount required would be doubled, and at fifty years, when it would be quadrupled? It is a reasonable calculation, that at the end of fifty years the coloured population of the United States will exceed twelve millions; and, estimating their then value by their average value for the last fifty years, with the cost of transporting them to Africa, it would exceed the national debt of Great Britain, or three times the amount of every specie dollar in circulation throughout Christendom, and would require all the navies of Great Britain, France, Russia, and the United States twelve years to transport them, allowing each vessel to make three trips per annum, and carry three hundred souls each over and above their own complement of men.

If we look to what most certainly will be the aggregate of this population within the lifetime of many of our children now born, and estimating that aggregate by their average increase for the last fifty years, we conclude that the generation now coming upon the stage will see the monstrous whole of twenty millions. To the political philanthropist, who may reasonably calculate many changes of interest and policy, which may by this time spring up between the master and these probable unprofitable millions, his mind should seek to provide for them against a destiny so impending. A sure and certain provision is in the reach of the politicians of that country. It requires boldness to avow it, but that boldness is based upon the great necessity of the case, and, as such, the justice of nations will acquiesce in the measure. To provide these existing and forthcoming millions with a country accessible, and a climate suitable to that physical constitution which the great Author of the universe has given them, our southern boundary should extend to the twentieth degree of north latitude, and nearly all will be accomplished which human wisdom can provide. Here is a country in soil, climate, and every other consideration far superior to the best portions of their native continent, within reach, and in the immediate direction of that great tide of emigration which is fast sweeping them from the ungenial and unprofitable North. By the immediate contiguity of this country to the United States, it will cost no greater outlay of means to transport them than the natural course of events will create and provide for.

If the object of the abolitionist is benevolence to the black race—if he wishes to avert this possible calamity and ruin—he should urge upon his government the acquisition of that which will most certainly effect it. Without professing to see farther in futurity than the lights which past experience will justify, it does appear to my mind that in seventy years, when the coloured population of the United States shall have increased to twenty, and the white, in their proportionate ratio, to one hundred and thirty millions, many, very many reasons teach that so many people, so differently marked by nature, cannot live in harmony within the present limits of that country. That in view of the case, whether their relative political condition shall remain as at present, or undergo the worst radical changes, the same good reasons urge this measure. How solicitous, then, should the busy politician of that country now feel, when, in acting, or in failing to act upon this subject, he knows that the weal or wo of his children, and his children's children, is so directly concerned. He should approach the subject with the anxiety of a father who wishes to leave to his offspring the inheritance of no litigious interest, and feels that in its present settlement he *wills* to that posterity a long and glorious welfare.

If the declaration of the English government is uninfluenced by national aggrandizement, but alone by the philanthropic desire of promoting the welfare and happiness of this race, she must rejoice in an event so calculated to promote this end as the settlement of this country with the blacks of the

United States. It is a law well settled, both in the physiology of animals and plants, that the farther you remove either from their natural climate, so in proportion to that distance are they subject to an increase of disease. The United States census of 1840 has given a melancholy instance of this fact in the returns from the two extremes of that Republic: in the State of Maine, being the most northern, one is either deaf, dumb, blind, or an idiot, out of every twelve, while in Florida, the most southern, one out of each eleven hundred and five are thus afflicted, the difference in favour of southern climate being ninety-two to one. Allowing that much of this disease in Maine is the result of freeing a people incapable of properly providing for themselves, still these facts must be so convincing to the philanthropist as to cause him to use all proper means to restore the coloured race to as near their native climate as practicable

APPENDIX.

No. I.

A List of Texians who Fought in the Battle of Mier on the 25th *and* 26th *December,* 1842.

No.	Names.	Residence.	Nativity.	Remarks.
1	Ackerman, Peter,	Bastrop,	New-York.	
2	Alexander, John R.,	Brazoria,	Indiana.	
3	Alexander, Matthew,	Jackson,	Tennessee.	
4	Alexander, W. A.,	Milam,	Ohio.	
5	Allen, David,	Harris,	Virginia.	
6	Anderson, George,	Victoria,	Scotland.	
7	Armstrong, Alexander,	Fort Bend,	Louisiana.	
8	Armstrong, James C.,	Washington,	Tennessee.	
9	Arthur, F.,	Fayette,	Massachusetts.	
10	Atwood, William,		England.	
11	Austin, James,	Brazoria,	Missouri.	
12	Baker, John R.,	Refugio,	Tennessee,	**Captain.**
13	Barber, James,	Bastrop,	Massachusetts.	
14	Barney, Daniel F.,	Washington,	Kentucky.	
15	Barney, T. A.	Fort Bend,	Vermont.	
16	Bassett, R. P.,	Washington,	Kentucky.	
17	Beale, Robert,	Fort Bend,	Dist. Columbia.	
18	Beard, Robert,	Fort Bend,	Missouri.	
19	Beard, William,	Fort Bend,	Missouri.	
20	Beasley, D. H. E.,	Brazoria,	North Carolina.	
21	Bell, Thomas W.,	Fayette,	North Carolina.	
22	Bennett, Samuel P.,	Austin,	Tennessee.	
23	Berry, Bate J.,	Jackson,	Indiana.	
24	Berry, Joseph,	Jackson,	Indiana.	
25	Bideler, John,	Milam,	Pennsylvania.	
26	Blackburn, John,	Fayette,	Tennessee.	
27	Blanton, John B.,	Fayette,	Georgia.	
28	Bobo, Lynn,	Victoria,	South Carolina.	
29	Boon, Benjamin,		Missouri.	
30	Boswell, Ransom,	Milam,	Georgia.	
31	Bowman, B. F.,	Bastrop,	New-York.	
32	Bray, F.,	Victoria,	Germany.	

No.	Names.	Residence.	Nativity.	Remarks.
33	Brennan, John,	Victoria,	New-York.	
34	Brennem, Richard F.,	Travis,	Kentucky,	M.D.
35	Bridger, Henry,	Gonzales,	Pennsylvania.	
36	Brown, Richard,	Liberty,	South Carolina.	
37	Brush, Gilbert R.,	Fort Bend,	New-York,	Boy.
38	Bryant, W. B. C.,	Fort Bend.		
39	Burras, A. T.,	Austin,	Kentucky.	
40	Burk, James,	Fort Bend,	Ohio.	
41	Bush, ——,	Washington,	Canada.	
42	Buster, Claudius,	Washington,	Kentucky,	Captain.
43	Calvert, John,		Tennessee.	
44	Cameron, Ewin,	Victoria,	Scotland,	Captain.
45	Canfield, Israel,	Refugio,	New-Jersey.	
46	Carter, William T.,	Victoria,	North Carolina.	
47	Cash, L. L.,	Victoria,	Pennsylvania.	
48	Censibeau, T. J.,	Washington,	Tennessee.	
49	Chalk, Winfield,	Milam,	Virginia.	
50	Clark, Willis G.,	Jackson,	Missouri.	
51	Clarke, Charles,	Brazoria,	New-York,	Lieutenant.
52	Clopton, William,	Bastrop,	Tennessee,	Lieutenant.
53	Cocke, J. D.,	Harris,	Virginia.	
54	Cody, W. H.,	Austin,	Tennessee.	
55	Colville, Thomas,	Harris,	Scotland.	
56	Copeland, Willis,	Nacogdoches,	Ohio.	
57	Cox, Thomas W.,	Fayette,	Kentucky,	Lieutenant.
58	Crawford, Robert M.,		Ireland.	
59	Crittenden, George B.,	Fort Bend,	Kentucky,	Lieutenant.
60	Davis, Campbell,	Washington,	Tennessee.	
61	Davis, Daniel,	Victoria,	Kentucky.	
62	Davis, Thomas,	Washington,	New-York.	
63	Davis, William,	Bastrop,	Maryland.	
64	Davis, W. K.,	Fort Bend,	Alabama.	
65	Dickson, ——,	Harrison,	Indiana.	
66	Dillon, John F.,	Victoria,	Tennessee.	
67	Dougherty, Patrick,		Ireland.	
68	Douglas, Freeman W.,	Brazoria,	Georgia,	Lieutenant.
69	Downes, N. G.,	Victoria,	Connecticut.	
70	Dunbar, William,	Bastrop,	Tennessee.	
71	Dunham, Robert,	Montgomery,	Tennessee.	
72	Dusenberry, John,	Harris,	New-York.	
73	Eastland, William M.,	Fayette,	Tennessee,	Captain.

APPENDIX NO. I. 439

No.	Names.	Residence.	Nativity.	Remarks.
74	Edwards, Leonidas D. F.,	Washington,	Tennessee.	
75	Este, Edward,	Harris,	New-Jersey.	
76	Fisher, William S.,	Washington,	Virginia,	Commander.
77	Fitzgerald, John,	Fort Bend,	Ireland.	
78	Frensley, William H.,	Fort Bend,	Tennessee.	
79	Gattis, D. H.,	Travis,	Alabama.	
80	Gibson, F. M.,	Fort Bend,	Georgia,	Qu'rmaster.
81	Gibson, William,	Travis,	Ohio.	
82	Glascock, James A.,	Victoria,	Kentucky.	
83	Gleason, Cyrus K.,	Victoria,	New-York.	
84	Goodman, Stephen,	Fort Bend,	Alabama.	
85	Green, Thomas J.,	Brazoria,	North Carolina,	{ Com. of flotilla and r't. wing.
86	Grosjean, P. C.,		France.	
87	Grubs, F.,	Montgomery,	Alabama.	
88	Hallowell, Daniel A.,		Tennessee.	
89	Hanna, ——,	Montgomery,	South Carolina.	
90	Hannom, William H.,	Washington,	Georgia.	
91	Harris, Robert,	Travis,	Mississippi.	
92	Harrison, F. W. T.,	Washington,	Alabama.	
93	Harvey, John,	Brazoria,	Kentucky.	
94	Hasmore, William H.,		Georgia.	
95	Hays, Lewis,		South Carolina.	
96	Heddenburg, Abr'm. D.,	Montgomery,	New-York.	
97	Henrie, Daniel Drake,	Brazoria,	Ohio,	{ Late Midship. in U. S. N.
98	Hensley, Charles,	Washington,	Tennessee.	
99	Hill, Asa,	Fayette,	North Carolina.	
100	Hill, Charles,	Bastrop,	England.	
101	Hill, Jeffrey,	Fayette,	Georgia.	
102	Hill, John,	Fayette,	Georgia,	{ The smallest boy at Mier adopted by Santa Anna.
103	Hoffer, John,		Pennsylvania.	
104	Holderman, Allen,	Bastrop,	Kentucky.	
105	Hopson, William,	Gonzales,	Kentucky.	
106	Hugh, Frank,	Milam,	Pennsylvania.	
107	Humphries, J. J.,	Milam,	Tennessee.	
108	Irvin, John,		Pennsylvania.	
109	Isam, Zed., *alias* Iceland,	Gonzales,	Germany.	
110	Jackson, A.,	Harris,	Ireland.	
111	Jackson, Edward B.,	Liberty,	Pennsylvania.	
112	Johnson, Jack,	Bexar,	Virginia.	

No.	Names.	Residence.	Nativity.	Remarks.
113	Jones, John E.,	Harris,	England.	
114	Jones, Thomas L.,	Travis,	Kentucky.	
115	Jones, Wiley,	Milam,	Alabama.	
116	Journie, H.,	Matagorda,	New-York.	
117	Kaigler, William,	Bexar,	Georgia.	
118	Kaughman, E. G.,	Bastrop,	Tennessee.	
119	Kean, Edward,	Washington,	Kentucky.	
120	Kean, Richard,	Washington,	Kentucky.	
121	Kelly, Charles S.,	Fort Bend,	Connecticut.	
122	King, R. B.,	Montgomery,	Tennessee.	
123	Kirkendall, Hanks,	Fort Bend,	Tennessee.	
124	Lacy, John,	Galveston,	Ireland.	
125	Laforge, A. B.,	Liberty,	New-York.	
126	Lee, Alfred A.,	Victoria,	North Carolina,	Lieutenant.
127	Lehan, Jerry,	Victoria,	Ireland.	
128	Lewis, A. J.,	Brazoria,	Alabama.	
129	Lewis, William B.,	Victoria,	Ohio.	
130	Livergood, G. H.,	Jackson,	Pennsylvania.	
131	Locherman, Stanley,	Colorado.		
132	Lord, George,	Victoria,	England.	
133	Lusk, P. H.,	Washington,	Tennessee.	
134	Lyon, Samuel C.,	Brazoria,	England,	Sailingmaster
135	Lyons, Patrick,	Milam,	Ireland.	
136	Mahan, Patrick,	Victoria,	Ireland.	
137	Malby, T. D.,		Connecticut.	
138	Mallen, Nathan,	Bexar,	Massachusetts.	
139	Martin, William,	Jackson,	Kentucky.	
140	Matthews, Alexander,	Gonzales.	Tennessee.	
141	Maxwell, P. M.,	Liberty,	Illinois.	
142	Middleton, Bemoni,	Liberty,	Illinois.	
143	Middleton, William B.,	Montgomery,	Illinois.	
144	Miller, William (Dutch),		Germany.	
145	Miller, William,	Brazoria,	Tennessee.	
146	Millon, W. E. (late Capt.),	Harris,	Virginia.	
147	Mills, John,	Victoria.	Tennessee.	
148	Mills, Lawson,	Victoria,	Tennessee.	
149	Mitchell, William,	Washington,	Missouri.	
150	Moore, William H.,	Milam,	Canada.	
151	Moore, William,	Fort Bend,	Missouri.	
152	Morehead, Jonathan,	Victoria,	Germany	
153	Morgan, John,	Bastrop,	England.	

APPENDIX NO. I.

No.	Names.	Residence.	Nativity.	Remarks.
154	Morrell, H. B.,	Fort Bend,	Georgia.	
155	Morris, William,	Fort Bend,	Louisiana.	
156	Mosier, Abram,	Matagorda,	Louisiana.	
157	Murry, Thomas A.,	Victoria,	Ireland,	Adjutant
158	M'Cauley, Malcolm,	Harris,	Scotland.	
159	M'Cutcheon, J. D.,	Washington,	Tennessee.	
160	M'Dade, ——.			
161	M'Donald, Daniel,	Victoria,	New-York.	
162	M'Fall, Samuel,	Milam,	Missouri.	
163	M'Ginly, John,	Montgomery,	Pennsylvania.	
164	M'Illrea, William J.,	Bastrop,	Pennsylvania.	
165	M'Kendall, ——,	Harris,	Scotland.	
166	M'Laughlin, Charles,	Harris,	England,	Draughtsman
167	M'Lelland, Samuel,	Liberty,	Ireland.	
168	M'Math, ——,	Washington,	Georgia,	M.D.
169	M'Micken, James,	Victoria,	Virginia.	
170	M'Mullen, John,	Galveston,	Maryland.	
171	Nealy, James B.,	Montgomery,	Alabama.	
172	Nealy, James H.,	Austin,	South Carolina.	
173	Nelson, Thomas,	Fayette,	Tennessee.	
174	Oats, Harvey H.,	Fayette,	Kentucky.	
175	Ogden, James,	Travis,	Virginia.	
176	Oldham, William,	Milam,	Virginia.	
177	Overton, ——,	Brazos,	Mississippi.	
178	Owen, John,	Brazoria,	Pennsylvania.	
179	Peacock, James,	Victoria,	Tennessee.	
180	Phelps, Orlando,	Brazoria,	Mississippi.	
181	Pierson, J. G. W.,	Montgomery,	North Carolina,	Captain.
182	Piland, George W.,	Fort Bend,	Tennessee.	
183	Pilley, Robert M.,	Harris,	England.	
184	Pitts, E. H.,	Fort Bend,	Georgia.	
185	Porter, Elisha,	Milam,	Tennessee.	
186	Randolph, Perry,	Montgomery,	Alabama.	
187	Reese, C. K.,	Brazoria,	Kentucky,	Captain.
188	Reese, William,	Brazoria,	Kentucky,	Boy.
189	Rice, James O.,	Travis,	South Carolina.	
190	Rice, Lorenzo,	Bexar,	Maryland.	
191	Rice, Sandford,	Harris,	New-York.	
192	Riley, Francis,	Fort Bend,	Ireland.	
193	Ripley, William,	Victoria,	Pennsylvania.	
194	Roark, A. J.,	Fort Bend,	Tennessee.	

3 L

APPENDIX NO. I.

No.	Names.	Residence.	Nativity.	Remarks.
195	Roberts, C.,	Milam,	Tennessee.	
196	Roberts, H. H.,	Harris,	North Carolina.	
197	Rockyfellow, Peter,	Jackson,	New-York.	
198	Rogers, Mark,	Bastrop,	Tennessee.	
199	Rowan, William,	Fort Bend,	Georgia.	
200	Runyan, William J.,	Sabine,	Georgia.	
201	Ryan, William,	Fort Bend,	Kentucky,	Captain.
202	Sansberry, John,	Fort Bend,	Kentucky.	
203	Sargeant, Carter,	Bastrop,	Kentucky.	
204	Sargeant, William,	Bastrop,	Kentucky.	
205	Saunders, Leonidas,	Montgomery,	Tennessee.	
206	Scott, William Y.,	Milam,	Georgia.	
207	Sellers, Harvey W.,	Fayette,	Tennessee,	Boy.
208	Shepherd, J. L.,	Bastrop,	Alabama.	
209	Shepherd, William M.,	Liberty,	Virginia,	M.D.
210	Shipman, John,	Fort Bend,	Missouri,	Lieutenant.
211	Simons, Joseph,	Jackson,	England.	
212	Sinnickson, J. J.,	Brazoria,	New-Jersey,	M.D.
213	Smith, Donald,	Bastrop,	Scotland.	
214	Smith, Ezekiel,	Gonzales,	Virginia.	
215	Smith, Joseph,	Brazoria,	Kentucky.	
216	Smith, Robert,	Fayette,	Tennessee.	
217	Smith, Thomas S.,	Washington,	Maryland.	
218	St. Clair, Caleb,	Gonzales,	New-York.	
219	Stapp, W. P.,	Jackson,	Missouri.	
220	Sullivan, Daniel C.,	Milam,	Missouri.	
221	Sweizy, John,		Pennsylvania.	
222	Tanney, John,	Bastrop,	Maryland.	
223	Tatum, Thomas,	Matagorda,	Tennessee.	
224	Thompson, J. M. N.	Milam,	Tennessee.	
225	Thompson, Thomas A.,	Milam,	Kentucky.	
226	Thompson, William,	San Patricio,	England.	
227	Thurmond, Alfred S.,	Victoria,	Tennessee,	Interpreter.
228	Torrey, James N.,	Harris,	Connecticut.	
229	Toops, John,	Washington,	Ohio.	
230	Towers, Isaac,	Victoria,	New-York,	M.D.
231	Trehern, G. Washington,	Victoria,	Mississippi.	
232	Turner, Robert W.,	Victoria,	Ohio.	
233	Turnbull, James,	Victoria,	Scotland.	
234	Urie, James,	Bastrop,	South Carolina.	
235	Usher, Patrick,	Jackson,	Ireland.	

APPENDIX NO. I. 443

No.	Names.	Residence.	Nativity.	Remarks.
236	Vandyke, Wilson M.,	Jackson,	Georgia.	
237	Van Horn, William H.,	Victoria,	New-York.	
238	Van Vechten, D. H.,	Fayette,	Kentucky.	
239	Walker, Samuel H.,	Galveston,	Maryland.	
240	Wallace, William A.,	Bexar,	Virginia.	
241	Waters, Robert G.,	Fort Bend,	South Carolina.	
242	Watkins, Joseph D.,	Washington,	Louisiana.	
243	Weeks, Henry D.,	Victoria,	New-York.	
244	Whaling, Henry,	Victoria,	Indiana.	
245	White, Calvin C.,	Refugio,	Vermont.	
246	White, Francis,	Galveston,	Maryland.	
247	White, James S.,		Pennsylvania.	
248	Wilson, James C.,	Brazoria,	England.	
249	Wilson, William F.,	Liberty,	Virginia.	
250	Wilson, Zaccheus,	Montgomery,	Tennessee.	
251	Wilson, ——, (Irish),	Montgomery,	Ireland.	
252	Williams, Levi,	Bastrop,	Missouri.	
253	Willis, O. R.,		Tennessee.	
254	Willoughby, Robert,	Victoria,	England.	
255	Wing, M. C.,	Travis,	New-York.	
256	Woodland, Henry,	Harris,	Indiana.	
257	Wright, E. D.,	Washington,	North Carolina.	
258	Wyatt, J. P.,	Fayette,	Georgia.	
259	Wynn, William,	Montgomery,	Kentucky.	
260	Young, James,	Brazoria,	New-York.	
261	Zumatt, Isaac,	Jackson,	Missouri.	

A List of Texians killed at the Battle of Mier.

1 Austin, James.
2 Bassett, ——.
3 Berry, Joseph.
4 Dickson, ——.
5 Hannom, William H.
6 Hopson, William.
7 Jackson, A.
8 Jones, John E.
9 Towers, Isaac, M.D.
10 White, Calvin C.   Total, 10

A List of Texians who died of their Wounds, received at the Battle of Mier.

1 Bobo, Lynn.
2 Kirkendall, Hanks.
3 Locherman, Stanley.
4 M'Illrea, William J.
5 M'Kendall, Alexander.
6 Urie, James.   Total, 6

APPENDIX NO. I.

A List of Texians who fell at Salado in their Attack upon the Guards, 11th February, 1843.

1 Brennem, Richard F., M.D.
2 Fitzgerald, Archibald.
3 Higgerson, John.
4 Lyons, Patrick.
5 Rice, Lorenzo.

Total, 5

N. B.—Fitzgerald and Higgerson were of the Bexar prisoners, taken by General Woll in September, 1842.

A List of Texians decimated and shot at Salado by order of President Santa Anna, on March 25th, 1843.

1 Cash, L. L.
2 Cocke, James D.
3 Dunham, Robert.
4 Eastland, William M., Captain.
5 Este, Edward.
6 Harris, Robert.
7 Jones, Thomas L.
8 Mahan, Patrick.
9 Ogden, James.
10 Roberts, Charles.
11 Rowan, William.
12 Shepherd, J. L.
13 Thompson, J. M. N.
14 Torrey, James N.
15 Turnbull, James.
16 Whaling, Henry.
17 Wing, M. C.

Total 17

April 25th, 1843.—Shot by order of President Santa Anna.

Captain Ewin Cameron. Total, 1

A List of Texians who died in the Mountains after the Break at Salado.

1 Cody, William H.
2 Lewis, A. J.
3 Mitchell, William.
4 Randolph, Perry.
5 Rice, Sandford.

Total, 5

A List of Texians left in the Mountains after the Victory of Salado, and supposed to be Dead.

1 Anderson, George.
2 Bray, F.
3 Calvert, John.*
4 Morehead, Jonathan.
5 Nealy, James B.*

Total, 5

A List of Texians who died from Suffering and Starvation in Mexico.

1 Beard, Robert.
2 Beard, William.
3 Bennett, Samuel P.
4 Blanton, John B.
5 Bryant, W. B. C.
6 Burras, A. T.
7 Colville, Thomas.
8 Crawford, Robert M.
9 Grosjean, P. C.
10 Hallowell, Daniel A.
11 Hill, Charles.
12 Holderman, Allen.

* Taken upon the Rio Grande subsequently, and carried to Mexico.

APPENDIX NO. I.   445

13 Irvin, John.
14 Kaughman, E. G.
15 Martin, William.
16 Middleton, Bemoni.
17 Miller, William.
18 Miller, William.
19 Morris, William.
20 M'Dade, ——.
21 M'Lelland, Samuel.
22 Owen, John.
23 Porter, Elisha.
24 Sargeant, Carter.
25 Saunders, Leonidas.
26 Shipman, John.
27 Simons, Joseph.
28 Smith, Robert.
29 Usher, Patrick
30 Van Horn, William H.
31 White, James S.
32 Wilson, Zaccheus.
33 Willis, O. R.
34 Wyatt, J. P.
35 One other not remembered.

Total, 35

Aggregate Number of Mier men Dead 84

Released by President Santa Anna through the Intercession of General Waddy Thompson, United States Minister.

1 Canfield, Israel.*
2 Crittenden, Geo. B., Lieutenant.
3 Lusk, P. H.†
4 Phelps, Orlando (by Santa Anna)
5 Reese, William.
6 Sinnickson, J. J., M.D.
7 Waters, Robert.

Total, 7

Released through the Intercession of H. B. M.'s Minister.

1 Clarke, Charles, Lieutenant.
2 Lehan, Jerry.
3 Murry, Thomas A., Adjutant.
4 Smith, Donald.

Total, 4

Santa Anna having adopted the Boy, John Hill, released his Father and Brother.

1 Hill, Asa.
2 Hill, Jeffrey.

Total, 2

Texians who made their Escape from Mier on the Evening of the Capitulation.

1 Chalk, Winfield.
2 St. Clair, Caleb.

Total, 2

Texians who were left Wounded at Mier, and who effected their Escape.

1 Beale, Robert.
2 Bideler, John.
3 Hays, Lewis.
4 Piland, George W.
5 Mallen, Nathan.
6 Rice, James O.
7 Ripley, William.
8 Weeks, Henry D.

Total, 8

* Released by request of John Q. Adams and Mahlon Dickerson.
† Released by request of General Jackson.

APPENDIX NO. I.

Texians who effected their Escape from the City of Mexico.

1 Copeland, Willis (retaken).
2 Crawford, Robert M.
3 Dougherty, Patrick.
4 Fitzgerald, John.
5 Gattis, D. H.
6 Morgan, John.
7 Thompson, William.
8 Walker, Samuel H.
9 Wilson, James C.

Total, 9

Those who effected their Escape from the Mountains after the Victory of Salado, and arrived safely in Texas.

1 Alexander, John R.
2 Blackburn, John.
3 Cox, Thomas W., Lieutenant.
4 Oldham, William.

Total, 4

Those who escaped from the Castle of Perote, July 2d, 1843.

1 Green, Thomas J.
2 Henrie, Daniel Drake.
3 Reese, Charles K.

Total, 3

Total number of Texians killed, starved, escaped, and released, 125
Of the Mier Command, remaining in Mexico up to last advices, 136

Total 261

The following Detail, as a Camp Guard, was left upon the East Side of the Rio Grande on the 25th December, 1842, and who retreated into Texas.

Captain Buster's Company.

1 Hackstaff, ——.
2 Hensley, William.
3 Hicks, ——.
4 Hyde, A. C., Orderly Sergeant.
5 M'Quin, Major.
6 Ransom, Thomas.
7 Smith, Gabriel.
8 Turner, ——.
9 Vanham, ——.
10 Watson, Doctor.
11 Wilkerson, Warren, First Lieutenant.   Total, 11

Captain Cameron's Company.

1 Canty, John.
2 Donnall, ——.
3 Earnest, ——.
4 Ward, William.
5 Yates, A. J.   Total, 5

Captain Eastland's Company.

1 Alley, George W.
2 Ambrose, M.
3 Bissell, Theodore.
4 Buckman, Oliver.
5 Clark, ——.
6 Holton, W. S.
7 Hudson, David.
8 Marlow, Edward.
9 Vincent, E. A.   Total, 9

Captain Ryan's Company.

1 Brown, Edward.
2 Buckhannan, J.
3 Dresser, William E.
4 Gilpin, Ralph.
5 Kirkendall, Moses.
6 Lucas, Z.
7 One other not remembered.

Total, 7

APPENDIX NO. I.

Captain Reese's Company.
1 Calder, Sidney.
2 Hancock, F.
3 Phelps, Virgil.
4 Walton, George.
5 Warren, Thomas.
6 West, Gilford.   Total, 6

Captain Pearson's Company.
1 Oldham, Thomas.
2 Owens, ———.
3 Smith, George.   Total, 3

1 Bonnel, George W., First Lieutenant of the Flotilla.*
Total, 1

Total 42

Of the Sixty-seven Bexar Prisoners captured by General Woll in September, 1842, and carried into Mexico, the following made their Escape from the Castle of Perote, July 2d, 1842.

1 Barclay, Richard.
2 Cornegay, R.
3 Dalrymple, John, who succeeded in reaching Texas.
4 Forrester, John.
5 Toowig, John.
Total, 5

Those who made their Escape from the Castle at the same time, but were recaptured.

1 Allen, Isaac.
2 Beck, T. B.
3 Davis, D. J.
4 Elley, Augustus.
5 Hancock, Thomas.
6 Ogden, D. C.
7 Stone, Samuel C.
8 Young, John.

Released by Santa Anna.
1 Robinson, James H. (Lawyer Robinson, his Commissioner). Total, 1

Released through the Intercession of General Waddy Thompson, the United States Minister.
1 Hutchinson, Judge.
2 Jones, William E.
3 Maverick, S. H.
Total, 3

Released through the Intercession of General Andrew Jackson.
1 Bradley, John.   Total, 1

Killed at Salado, February 11th, 1843.
1 Fitzgerald, Archibald.   2 Higgerson, John.   Total, 2

* It has already been explained how Major Bonnel, Doctor Watson, and Private Hackstaff came to be left at the Camp.

APPENDIX NO. I.

Those who died in Prison in Mexico.

1 Booker, Shields, M.D.
2 Crews, ———.
3 Cunningham, ———.
4 Grey, French S.
5 Jackson, ———.
6 Trapnell, John.
7 Trimble (Tecolote).
8 Woods, Norman.   Total, 8

Those who escaped from Mexico.

1 Hatch, George.
2 Morgan, ———.
3 Neal, ———.   Total, 3

General Waddy Thompson, the United States Minister, upon leaving Mexico, procured the Liberation of the following, being the Remainder of the Bexar Prisoners alive, with the exception of George Van Ness, who was a Santa Fé Prisoner.

1 Alsbarry, A. H.
2 Allen, Isaac.
3 Beck, T. B.
4 Brown, Edward.
5 Brown, James H.
6 Bugg, William.
7 Colquhoun, Lodovic.
8 Davis, D. J.
9 Elley, Augustus.
10 Faison, Nathaniel.
11 Glenn, Simeon.
12 Hancock, Thomas.
13 Herbert, Nathaniel.
14 Hurrell, M.
15 Johnson, Chauncey.
16 Lehman, John.
17 Leslie, A. J.
18 Lee, John.
19 Manton, Edward.
20 Monell, A. H.
21 Morgan, J. C.
22 M'Kay, Francis.
23 Neighbours, R. C.
24 Nobles, S. L.
25 Ogden, D. C.
26 Perry, John.
27 Peterson, C. W.
28 Raper, M. L. B.
29 Robinson, Joseph.
30 Schaffer, George.
31 Shaw, Joseph.
32 Smith, John.
33 Stone, Samuel C.
34 Trueheart, James L.
35 Voss, J. G. A.
36 Young, John.   Total, 36

1 Novell, Samuel, previously, and, 2 Van Ness, George, subsequently, released.   Total, 2

Total 61

We have no knowledge of the six remaining Bexar prisoners, but presume they have perished with their companions.

The patriotic Antonio Navarro, one of the Santa Fé prisoners, who was confined in the Accordada, the most loathsome and infamous prison in Mex-

APPENDIX NO. I.

ico, where he, for more than two years, suffered more than the horrors of death, has been lately sent to the Castle of San Juan d'Ulloa, where the humanity of the "magnanimous" nation has consigned him to the *Vomita*.*

The Places of Nativity and Residence of those engaged in the Battle of Mier, December 25th and 26th, 1842.

Residence.			Nos.	Residence.		Nos.
Austin	County,	Texas,	4	Alabama,	United States,	10
Bastrop	"	"	18	Connecticut,	"	3
Bexar	"	"	5	Georgia,	"	17
Brazoria	"	"	18	Illinois,	"	4
Brazos	"	"	1	Indiana,	"	5
Colorado	"	"	1	Kentucky,	"	28
Fayette	"	"	15	Louisiana,	"	4
Fort Bend	"	"	28	Maryland,	"	7
Galveston	"	"	4	Massachusetts,	"	3
Gonzales	"	"	6	Mississippi,	"	4
Harris	"	"	17	Missouri,	"	13
Harrison	"	"	1	New-Jersey,	"	2
Jackson	"	"	12	New-York,	"	21
Liberty	"	"	9	North Carolina,	"	10
Matagorda	"	"	3	Ohio,	"	8
Milam	"	"	17	Pennsylvania,	"	13
Montgomery	"	"	14	South Carolina,	"	8
Nacogdoches	"	"	1	Tennessee,	"	42
Refugio	"	"	2	Vermont,	"	2
Sabine	"	"	1	Virginia,	"	14
San Patricio	"	"	1	District of Columbia,	"	1
Travis	"	"	8			
Victoria	"	"	35	Number from the United States,		219
Washington	"	"	23	England, } English subjects, 34		12
Not claiming residence			17	Ireland,		13
				Scotland,		7
Total			261	Canada,		2
				France		1
				Germany		4
				Nativity not known . .		3
				Total . . .		261

* During the State Revolution in Mexico, Colonel Navarro escaped from the Castle of San Juan d'Ulloa, and has safely arrived in Texas, where he was met by the warmest congratulations of his friends and countrymen.

The following Mier Prisoners made their Escape from the Castle of Perote on the 25th of March, 1844. The first Nine upon the List reached their Homes in safety, and the remaining Seven were recaptured.

1 Arthur, Francis.	9 Laforge, A. B.
2 Frensley, William H.	10 Moore, William.
3 Gleason, Cyrus K.	11 Runyan, William T.
4 Goodman, Stephen.	12 Smith, T.
5 Johnson, John.	13 Tanney, John.
6 Jones, Wiley.	14 Toops, John.
7 Kean, Richard.	15 Wright, E. D.
8 Kean, Edward.	16 Wynn, William. Total, 16

No. II.

The following correspondence, published soon after the return of the author from Mexico, will speak for itself, and satisfy every one who will take the pains to examine it of the infamous agency President Houston had in the murder of our countrymen in Mexico:

' To the People of Texas,—However unpleasant it may be to appear before you through the columns of a newspaper, it is a matter in which I have at present no choice. The President of your Republic on the one hand, and your countrymen now in chains, and the most odious slavery in Mexico on the other, are the parties at issue. I, more fortunate than they, favoured by an all-wise Providence, and an energy befitting the fearful task, with some few of my comrades, escaped through the walls of Perote some weeks since. A solemn duty I owe myself, my unfortunate fellow-prisoners, and my country, demands of me, with the evidences in my possession, to disabuse the public mind in what has been affirmed on one hand, and unblushingly denied by President Houston and his partisans on the other, to wit: 'That he wrote, or caused to be written, to Mexico, by Captain Charles Elliott, her Britannic majesty's chargé d'affaires at Galveston, *that the Mier prisoners had entered Mexico contrary to law and authority.*'

" Whatever may have been the ostensible pretext of General Houston's communication—and he pretends to ask mercy for his countrymen—yet his high authority that the Mier men had entered Mexico contrary to law and authority furnished the tyrant of that country all the legal pretext he could have desired in slaking his bloodthirsty vengeance upon the citizens of our country. It would, indeed, be an unjust denial of that personal and political acumen which General Houston's friends claim for

APPENDIX NO. II. 451

him, to say that he could not foresee the consequences of that communication. The murder of our twenty-seven countrymen at Tampico, of Colonel Fannin and his brave four hundred, of many of the Santa Fé prisoners, and a thousand other acts of savage cruelty inflicted upon us during this war by Mexico, all too plainly told General Houston that *his* asking 'mercy for the Mier men' would not weigh a feather in the balance against Santa Anna's cold-blooded vindictiveness, after he (Houston) had in effect pronounced them *brigands and marauders* upon Mexico. One year previous to the battle of Mier the bloody tyrant had published a decree 'that in future the war with Texas should be conducted upon the principles of civilized warfare,' and the Mier men, under their articles of capitulation, were guaranteed in a full observance of this decree. It was necessary, then, before he could once more, in the face of these solemn guarantees and the civilized world, dip his hands in the blood of your countrymen, to have some *legal pretext* for so doing. General Houston furnished him that *pretext*, and the murder of the brave Cameron, Cocke, Dunham, Ogden, Eastland, Jones, and their comrades in death, is the consequence, and their blood is upon his head.

"While myself and companions were incarcerated in the vilest dungeon in Mexico, and had no power of speaking upon this subject, General Houston and his partisans boldly denied the charge, and referred exultingly to the secretary of state's letter, published in June, to the Hon. Ashbel Smith, our minister in London. One word of this letter—wherefore put it off from the battle of Mier in December up to June? All the evils which it sought to remedy was of six months' standing. From the date of our inglorious surrender at Mier on the 26th of December, up to the middle of March, we had been treated with all the consideration which our articles of capitulation guarantied; then comes this '*merciful*' death-warrant of General Houston. Santa Anna forthwith orders General Mexier, Governor of Cohuilla, to shoot the whole of our prisoners in his charge, numbering one hundred and seventy odd. This brave soldier refused positively so to do; and three days after, the order, through the influence of the foreign ministers, was countermanded. Governor Mexier was then ordered to decimate them, which he also refused to do, for which he was broke of his commission, and banished the country; when a murderous wretch was specially charged with the execution of this horrible *black bean lottery*, and thus fell those brave men, who had so often staked their lives in defence of your liberty. After this most unjust and infamous butchery, which was on the 25th of March, the balance of the Mier men were still in the most imminent peril. On the 25th of April, the brave and lamented Cameron was taken out and shot without any cause being given. Immediately, however, after the first order for shooting our men had gone forth, we lost no time in writing home for evidences of General Houston's falsehood. They were furnished by the bushel. Among these were his ridiculous and bombastic newspaper gasconade, in answer to Santa Anna's letter to General Hamilton—his numerous war proclamations—his bloody war speeches at Galveston and elsewhere—his proclamation of the 16th of September, 1842, calling upon all of the first class of militia of the counties west of the Trinity, and under which proclamation we came out, and in which he authorized the men to ' *call to their lead a man of wisdom, valour, and experience,*' and '*pursue the enemy into Mexico, and chastise him for his insolence and wrongs.*' Also the law of Texas of January, 1840, authorizing us to elect our commander, and last, though not least, the Constitution of your country, by which foreigners, at least, are taught to believe that President Houston's *dictum* is not superior to that sacred instrument. These were the evidences which General Thompson so humanely alludes to in his letter of the 10th of June, to his Excellency Mr. Doyle, and which armed him so completely against the machinations of your President and the bloodthirsty vengeance of his friend Santa Anna.

"Feeling now that the last blood had flowed which it was in the power of General Houston's vindictiveness to the Mier command to shed, and many of my prison companions looking to me to vindicate them against the foul aspersions of their unjust President, on the 29th of May I wrote to General Thompson to preserve me a copy of the letter which General Houston had caused to be written to Mexico. In doing so, I felt a duty more weighty, and far more sacred, than any obligation to the living. The honest reputation of the dead was the only legacy bequeathed by these murdered heroes to their mourning friends and destitute wives and children : that I shall be in any way instrumental in perpetuating the record that their husbands and fathers did not die robbers, as President Houston pronounced them, will be to me a lasting gratification ; while to them, in long years to come, they may look back upon the fact as their proudest recollection, that the traducer of the dead was proved their slanderer and murderer.

"Can it be possible that President Houston has a friend so blinded in his party zeal as not to know that Commodore Moore and the whole of his crew would have been shot, had they by any chance of war fallen into the hands of the Mexicans, after President Houston's proclamation of piracy against him ? yet the Mier case is one point, with this difference, that they were already in the hands of the Mexicans, and it suited General Houston's policy to have them killed off more secretly, and under some *pretence* of mercy.

"My letter to General Thompson of the 29th of May, above alluded to, produced the following correspondence between him and the Hon. Mr. Doyle (letters numbered 1, 2, 3, 4), and from General Thompson to myself (numbered 5 and 6). By this correspondence it will be seen that I am first referred to the author of the letter for a copy, and in the event of refusal, then General Thompson promises his statement of its contents. Upon my arrival in Galveston, I addressed letter No. 7 to Captain Elliott. His answer, No. 8, shows his refusal to furnish said letter, which brought forth my reply, No. 9. I should then have applied to President Houston for the copy in question, but Mr. S. H. Walker, one of my fellow-prisoners lately escaped from Mexico, having applied to General Houston for the same, received General Houston's verbal denial of the existence of such letter. This correspondence will show that Captain Elliott, Mr. Doyle, General Thompson—all, except your President, are too honourable to deny the existence of the letter, and he does it with the same unblushing hardihood which has caused him to deny a thousand things he has uttered. Vice and crime delight in darkness, and General Houston may have supposed that his blunt denial would stop all inquiry upon the subject, but in this he adds moral turpitude to heinous guilt, and therefore deserves the more the execrations of his countrymen.

"Fellow-citizens, well may you ponder upon the political condition of your country, and some seek refuge in acknowledging the supremacy of degraded Mexico, some in abolition, some in annexation, when such things are allowed. What a commentary upon our government! If the poorest man were to commit murder upon his neighbour, he would be hanged therefor; but President Houston, in the unchecked practice of every political enormity, can do so by the regiment and fleet without punishment. I am, very respectfully, your old friend,

"THOMAS J. GREEN.

"*November 10th, 1845.*"

(No. 1.)

Mexico, June 8th, 1843.

My dear Sir,—I send you herewith a letter recently received from General T. J. Green, of Texas, and shall be obliged to you for an extract of that portion of the letter of Mr. Elliott to Mr. Packenham to which General Green alludes. I deem it proper to add, that although the communications made to me of the contents of Captain Elliott's, either by Mr. Packenham or yourself, were not of a confidential character, nor did I consider that any such confidence was implied, yet I neither made any communication on the subject to General Green, nor authorized any one else to do so. I am, &c., &c., &c.,

(Signed), WADDY THOMPSON.

Hon. Percy W. Doyle.

(No. 2.)

Mexico, June 9th, 1843.

My dear General,—I beg to acknowledge the receipt of your letter of yesterday's date, enclosing one you had received from General T. J. Green, of Texas, and requesting me to give you an extract of a letter written by Captain Elliott, her majesty's chargé de affaires in Texas, to Mr. Packenham on the subject of the Texian prisoners. I regret to be obliged to refuse the request you make, for the letter is a private one, and not addressed to me; I therefore do not feel authorized to give any extract from it. With respect to the communication made to you by Mr. Packenham, I cannot, of course, know how far it was looked upon as confidential by him, but I am led to suppose that, in saying what he did, he was actuated by the same feelings as myself, when I spoke to you on the same subject, namely, that any communication I made to you was certainly for the purpose of aiding each other in any steps we might be induced to take for the benefit of those unfortunate prisoners, but certainly not to be communicated to any one else, and especially not to them. I much fear that this knowledge they have obtained, as you observe, unauthorized by you, may be the means of doing them farther injury.

I am, &c., &c., &c.,   PERCY W. DOYLE.
General Waddy Thompson.

(No. 3.)

Mexico, June 10th, 1843.

My dear Sir,—I have received your note of yesterday, and regret that you should not feel yourself at liberty to give me the extract from the letter of Mr. Elliott to Mr. Packenham for which I asked. I should not have considered it necessary to say anything more on the subject but for the remark which you make as to the communications which were made to me having been regarded as confidential: if so, and I have spoken to any one of them, I have been in fault; and as I do not so consider it, I feel it to be my duty to say, that neither by Mr. Packenham nor yourself was any intimation given to me that the communication was to be so regarded, and I cannot see anything in the nature of the communication itself which in any degree implied such confidence. I am at a loss to imagine how it could have aided us, in the protection of the prisoners of Mier, to have known that they were brigands and not prisoners of war, and therefore not entitled to our protection. If such was the case, it was proper that it should be known; if it was not, and there was some mistake about the matter, it was due to those unfortunate men, whose lives were in jeopardy, that this mistake should be corrected, and not less so to me, who had interfered in my official character, and said to the minister of foreign relations in strong, but altogether respectful language, that my government would expect that all the privileges of prisoners of war would be extended to *them*; and although I made no communication on the subject to the prisoners, I rejoice to know that the fact of my having mentioned the subject to others, by whom it was communicated to them, has been the means of furnishing me with the most conclusive evidence that the expedition was authorized by the Texas government; that the officers were appointed by that government, and express orders given to cross the Rio Grande; and that, therefore, these men were entitled to all the rights of prisoners of war. But as you seem to regard the communication made to me as of a confidential character, I shall make no statement on the subject for the present. It is in the power of President Houston or Captain Elliott to cause the letter of the latter to Mr. Packenham to be published, which I hope will be promptly done. If it should not be, or if, when published, it does not correspond with the communication made to me of its contents, I shall feel bound to state what these communications were. I am, &c., &c., &c.,

      (Signed),   WADDY THOMPSON.

Hon. Percy W. Doyle.

(No. 4.)

Mexico, June 11th, 1843.

My dear General,—I have the honour to acknowledge the receipt of your letter of yesterday's date.

My object in making the observations I did in that letter was simply that you might be made aware of the light in which I wished the communications I made to you, or any other connected with the business of our respective missions, should be considered. I am, &c., &c., &c.,

      (Signed),   PERCY W. DOYLE.

General Waddy Thompson.

(No. 5.)

Mexico, June 13th, 1843.

To General T. J. Green:

Sir,—I beg leave to present to you the enclosed copy of correspondence between Mr. Percy W. Doyle, the British chargé d'affaires, and myself, upon the subject of your letter of the 29th of May. I trust you will be satisfied that, upon the footing on which Mr. Doyle has placed the matter, it would be improper for me to say more at present.

Very respectfully, &c., &c.,

      (Signed),   WADDY THOMPSON.

The following is an extract from another letter from General Thompson to General Green, also dated 13th June, 1843:

You can very distinctly see by my notes to Mr. Doyle what my statement will be.

(No. 7.)

Galveston, Nov. 6th, 1843.

To his Excellency Charles Elliott, H. B. M.
Chargé d'Affaires for Texas.

Sir,—Feeling a deep interest in the fate of my late fellow-prisoners, and that it is a duty I owe my country that the causes which led to the foul murder of a portion of them, under the order of President Santa Anna, should be known, and believing that their massacre was the result of the correspondence of President Houston with your excellency, which was forwarded by you to Mr. Packenham, I respectfully ask a copy of General Houston's letter to you, and of yours to Mr. Packenham.

You will see from the enclosed copy of correspondence between General Thompson and Mr. Doyle, that the contingency upon which I am authorized to make General Thompson's statement public is the failure to procure those letters. I am, very respectfully, your ob't serv't,

(Signed), THOMAS J. GREEN.

(No. 8.)

Galveston, Nov. 7th, 1843.

Sir,—I have the honour to acknowledge your letter of the 6th instant, and, as a general rule, I must decline to furnish you with copies of any correspondence between other persons and myself. I have the honour to remain, sir, your obedient servant,

(Signed), CHARLES ELLIOTT.

General Thomas J. Green.

(No. 9.)

Galveston, Nov. 8th, 1843.

To his Excellency Charles Elliott, H. B. M.
Chargé d'Affaires for Texas.

Sir,—I have the honour to acknowledge your note of yesterday in answer to mine of the 6th instant, and can readily allow, as a "*general rule*," the propriety of your not furnishing copies of your correspondence; but the correspondence I requested was of such an extraordinary character, I cannot believe it should come under such "*general rule.*" Your excellency, therefore, will allow me most respectfully to state more at length the reasons of that application.

Upon the arrival of myself and companions at Tacubaya, near the city of Mexico, about the 15th of March last, we were several times informed by gentlemen who had it direct from General Thompson, the United

States minister near that court, that you had, at the request of President Houston, written to H. B. M. minister, Mr. Packenham, to this purport, "*that though the Mier prisoners had entered Mexico contrary to law and authority, yet he, Houston, begged mercy for them,*" &c.

The high authority of President Houston, that the Mier prisoners were *brigands*, endorsed by the still higher authority of her Britannic majesty's chargé d'affaires residing at their homes, gave the President of Mexico all the legal right he desired to shoot them. The whole history of our war shows that he could desire nothing more than such legal pretext to execute upon Texians the bloodiest vengeance. We had been prisoners of war from the 26th of December up to the middle of March, and under our articles of capitulation had been treated as such. Then comes, to say the least of it, your unfortunate letter, which took from us all protection of that capitulation, which legalized our murders, and proved a death-warrant to the whole of my brave companions. Most fortunately for them, three days after the bloody order had gone into the hands of a soldier too just and too brave to execute it, the remonstrance of the foreign ministers got it countermanded; but still, their influence could not prevent the execution of your countryman, the brave Cameron, and his seventeen companions. Justice to the memory of these brave spirits and their destitute wives and children calls loudly upon me to place their murder where it rightly belongs. With this view, before leaving Perote, I wrote to the American minister near Mexico to procure me a copy of your letter from Mr. Doyle, H. B. M. minister, who succeeded Mr. Packenham, which correspondence I had the honour of enclosing to your excellency yesterday.

It is not my desire to criminate your excellency with a foreknowledge of the consequences of this unfortunate letter; of your humanity I have a more exalted opinion; but when your excellency has been made the unwitting instrument of communication by which this melancholy, bloody, hellish tragedy has been perpetrated upon the best men of our country, justice, both to yourself and government, requires that the *whole* truth should be told, and the blame rest upon the head of him who projected it. Your excellency has been sufficiently unfortunate in being the innocent medium of this fell execution, and its cruel author, the least of all men, deserves screening at your hands by the suppression of the least portion of the truth; and I have yet to learn how such suppression can promote the ends of justice. I must be allowed the opinion, that whatever rule of diplomacy governs your official station, you have no right to hold anything as private to myself or companions which affect our lives or liberty

Very respectfully, your excellency's obedient servant,

THOMAS J. GREEN.

Having failed to procure a copy of the letter in question, either from Captain Elliott or President Houston, to whom I was referred by General Thompson, I applied to him for a statement of its contents, which the following correspondence will explain, and which was soon after published in Texas.

" *To the Public.*

" Duty to our brave and unfortunate countrymen in the dungeons of Mexico caused me to lay before the public, some months since, the correspondence between the United States and English ministers in that country, relative to the letter which General Houston had written to Mexico, denouncing the Mier prisoners as brigands, and which caused their decimation and subsequent suffering. No honest man, even of the most blinded partisans of President Houston, who read that correspondence, doubted for a moment the statement of the facts therein set forth, though President Houston and his forces in Texas had for months previous to that time denied most solemnly that he had ever written or caused to be written such a letter to Mexico. As soon as he found that I had returned from that country, armed with the proofs of his bloody murder of our countrymen, he, in his speech in the Presbyterian Church at Houston, in November, for the first time admitted the facts and said, ' *it was not, my friends, Captain Elliott's letter which produced the mischief ;*' but charges the murder upon General Hunt and the ' Telegraph,' for publishing a letter of the former, on the 18th of January previous.

" This subterfuge of President Houston in falsely quoting said letter, and so preposterous and unjust a supposition as that the publication of the letter of a private gentleman in a Texas newspaper could be sufficient with the Mexican government for such a shocking deed, did not satisfy the public mind. On the 12th of December, a few days thereafter, President Houston, in his annual message to Congress, changed his ground of defence, and said ' that it was a retaliation on account of those under General Somerville, who robbed Laredo ;' thus charging this bloody deed to his particular friends of Washington and Montgomery counties, who returned under Colonel Bennett from that place. This last defence of the President, more frivolous than the former, shows under what awkward extremes guilt will seek shelter.

" Perhaps it would have been unnecessary for me to have said more upon this subject, so well convinced was the public mind of President Houston's criminal and malicious agency in having my comrades shot, and others starved for the want of bread, had not some newspapers in his interest recently insulted public intelligence by speaking of ' *his kind feelings for those men.*' This most unblushing and barefaced insult, as well to the memories of those hundred and odd whose deaths he caused, as to the remaining half in chains and slavery, is my excuse, if one were necessary, for again obtruding myself upon the public.

"Though our last Congress placed to the credit of our prisoners in Mexico thirty thousand dollars, under the most positive and peremptory injunctions upon President Houston '*forthwith*' to supply them, not one dollar has been sent them. When the President is asked why he has not sent the money to these men, he adds insult to their misfortunes by saying that they are better off than they would be at their homes.

"No man of sane intellect, whatever may be his devotion, personal or political, to President Houston, after reading the annexed correspondence, can for a moment doubt that he was the malicious, vindictive, cold-blooded author of the execution.

"Very respectfully, your obedient servant,
"THOMAS J. GREEN."

New-Orleans, April 14th, 1844.

Sir,—I have had the honour to receive your letter of the 8th of November, in which you inform me that President Houston not only disavows having authorized Captain Elliott to write such a letter to the Hon. Richard Packenham, as it was reported that he had done, but that he also asserts that no communication to that effect had ever been made to me by Mr. Packenham or Mr. Doyle. If President Houston had confined himself to the disavowal of having authorized such a letter to have been written, I do not know that, upon mature reflection, I should have considered it my duty to have made any statement upon the subject; but as the matter now stands, I have no alternative left me. I therefore send you the accompanying statement, with a note from Benjamin E. Green, Esq., and another addressed by me to Mr. Doyle. I trust that nothing farther can be required of me in the matter. You, sir, very well know that my name has been involved in the affair by no officious interference in it, and it has been made public contrary to my advice and wishes. The fact of such a letter having been written came to my knowledge while endeavouring, under the express orders of my government (given in a similar case), to protect those brave and unfortunate men, the prisoners of Mier. It was a matter of such a character that it was impossible I could have been either indifferent or mistaken about it. I have furnished General Houston with a copy of this statement. I have the honour to be, very respectfully, your obedient servant,

WADDY THOMPSON.

General Thomas J. Green.

Mexico, Dec. 20th, 1843.

Shortly after I heard of the capture of the Texian prisoners at Mier, and having serious apprehensions that their rights as prisoners of war might be violated, I called upon the Hon. Richard Packenham to request that he would, if necessary, add his great and well-deserved influence with the Mexican government to mine, for the protection of those men. He expressed at once a willingness to do so, but said that, from what he had heard, he was afraid they were not strictly entitled to the rights of prisoners of war, because the expedition had not been authorized by the Texian government. I told him that I was very certain he was mistaken. In a subsequent interview with Mr. Packenham on the subject, he told me that he had received a letter from Captain Elliott, H. B. M. chargé d'affaires in Texas, saying that General Houston requested him (Mr. P.) to interpose his good offices in behalf of the Mier prisoners, although they might not, in strictness, be entitled to be regarded as prisoners of war, as the expedition had not been authorized by the Texian government.

Shortly after the arrival of Mr. Percy W. Doyle in Mexico, I had a conversation with him on the subject, in which he made the same statement as to the letter of Captain Elliott; and in a subsequent conversation upon the subject, he added, that he thought it probable, in saying that the expedition was not authorized, that President Houston alluded not to the original expedition, but to the continuance of it after the return to Texas of General Somerville. Although I am very sure that in this I cannot be mistaken, yet if I am, it is very easy to prove it by the production of the letter, or a statement of Mr. Packenham.

W. THOMPSON.

Mexico, December 21st, 1843.

General W. Thompson :

Dear Sir,—In compliance with your request, I called yesterday upon the Honourable Percy W. Doyle with the statement which is copied above, and which you propose to send to General T. J. Green, upon the subject of Captain Elliott's letter to Mr. Packenham, relative to the Texians taken prisoners at Mier. Mr. Doyle declined giving me a copy of Captain Elliott's letter, on the ground that it was a private letter, and not addressed to him; and after retiring to another room to compare your statement with that letter, he admitted that the statement was in every respect correct. Very respectfully, your obedient servant,

(Signed), BEN. E. GREEN.

The following protest from a committee of our countrymen, prisoners in the Castle of Perote, dated July, 1844, to the British minister near the government of Mexico, has immediate reference to the agency which President Houston had in the decimation of our men :

APPENDIX NO. II. 461

"His Excellency Charles Bankhead:

"Sir,—The undersigned, a committee of the prisoners now confined in the Castle of Perote, believing that we are abandoned by our own government, have only the alternative left of appealing to the minister of her Britannic majesty at the court of Mexico to interfere with a view of putting a termination to our suffering and imprisonment. The evidence upon which our opinion is based, that we are surrendered by our government, are, first, the letter to your predecessor by the Executive of Texas, denouncing the Mier expedition as a lawless band of adventurers, unsanctioned by the authorities of the country whence it came, and therefore unentitled to the consideration and protection which, by civilized usage and of right, belong to prisoners of war. Secondly, his withholding the means appropriated by Congress for our relief, when well apprized of our destitute and unfortunate situation. Thirdly, his entire neglect to make any exertion in our behalf, either by way of mitigating our hard fate or procuring our release. The only anxiety, within the knowledge of the undersigned, evinced by President Houston for the Texian prisoners, is to be found in the letter above referred to, which resulted in the melancholy, tragic scene at the Ranch Salado, where were executed in cold blood seventeen as brave men as ever enlisted in the holy cause and under the sacred banner of liberty. Whether this solicitude was for our weal or wo, the probable tendency of its operation, and its actual lamentable consequences, will show, not only to the satisfaction of those who executed, but those who prompted the horrid act. From this it will appear that this appeal properly emanates from the undersigned, and the sequel will show that it is appropriately addressed to your excellency the British minister.

"We believe, sir, that the government of Great Britain is under official obligation to demand our liberation. Under the auspices, and through the avowed agency of the chargé d'affaires of your government to Texas, a treaty for the mutual exchange of prisoners was entered into and solemnly ratified by the contracting parties. Texas had confidence in this treaty from the fact that your government became incidentally a party to it—your chargé d'affaires having originated it.

"The undersigned do not rest their grounds for the interference of your excellency in their behalf upon the foregoing showing alone. They appeal to you, and the whole corps diplomatique, as conservators of international law. Diplomatic agents, clothed with ministerial powers, are called ministers to the different courts to which they are sent, which term, conjoined to their official duties, implies the possession of judicial authority.

"If this position be true, you are bound to notice all infractions of the great law of nations, either in a state of peace or in the turmoils of war. It is your prerogative to control and regulate the operations of the latter state when not conducted according to the principles of humanity and the common mild usages of civilized nations.

" In the undersigned and their unfortunate comrades you have a case which solicits the controlling influence of foreign ministers. The humane maxims of international law, the acknowledged customs of civilized nations, have all alike been violated and disregarded in our cruel treatment and unjust detention.

" When taken at Mier, under treaty stipulations guarantying to us safety and consideration, we were marched on foot, through sunshine and through storm, and a portion of the way handcuffed in couples, under the tauntings and lash of merciless Mexican soldiery. In the villages and towns through which we passed, instead of being treated with the kind courtesy usually extended by generous captors to vanquished enemies, we were received amid the hisses and maledictions of the infuriated rabble, with placards staring us in the face, commemorating the defeat of the Texian adventurers and robbers, as they termed us.

" The bloody tragedies enacted on the road the undersigned refrain from recapitulating; their minds shrink with horror from the recital. Language is inadequate to express the deep agony of the heart in the bare review of such inhuman acts. Such has been our treatment on the way to Mexico, and the same harshness still continues.

" Only a few days since, one of our men, a Lieutenant Clopton, returned from the hospital in which he had been confined for five or six weeks from the wounds and bruises inflicted upon him by a large bludgeon in the hands of Captain Arroya, commandant of the castle. A few weeks ago, a pale and sickly boy was so severely beaten by the same weapon, in the hands of the same officer, as to be compelled to carry his arm in a sling for some time. In a word, we are miserably fed, badly clothed, and worked like beasts of burden. Our hard fate is rendered yet more intolerable by the fact that neither of the contending parties appear to make any active demonstrations to bring the war to a close, but rather prefer becoming the clients of Great Britain, the United States, and France. The time necessary to render their mediation effective must necessarily be long; and during this state of nominal peace we have suffered, and still continue to suffer, all the hardships of an actual state of warfare.

" Very respectfully, FENTON M. GIBSON, CLAUDIUS BUSTER, WILLIAM S. FISHER, WILLIAM RYAN, SAMUEL C. LYON, } *Committee.*"

No. III.

The following correspondence and orders are copied from "SILGO DIEZ NUEVE," "The Nineteenth Century," the official organ of the Mexican government, of July 12th, 1843, all of which proves conclusively that the propositions brought to Texas by Robinson from Santa Anna were accepted by Houston, as far as it was possible for him to do so ; that his (Houston's) commissioners were sent into Mexico to treat alone upon the *basis of those propositions,* and that the armistice which they did sign as the representatives of the "*department of Texas*" farther shows that they did treat upon *that basis,* and *that only* ; and that these evidences were in the state department of Texas at the time that President Houston sent his disgraceful message to Congress on January 1st, 1844.

Antonio Lopez de Santa Anna to Jose Maria de Tornel, Minister of War and Marine.

Manga de Clavo, Feb. 6th, 1843.

Excellent Sir,—The Texian prisoner, Mr. William Robinson, has addressed me the letter herewith transmitted, which you will please submit to his excellency the substitute President. In it he manifests a disposition to contribute, through his influence in that department, that an arrangement may take place, explaining also the terms on which it may be obtained, and reasons why he may be of service in the prosecution of so interesting an object. Robinson, perhaps, will operate solely with a desire to obtain his liberty ; but if it should not be so, and he should act in good faith, nothing can be lost on hearing him, and some favourable result may be obtained, if, through the knowledge which he has of the present difficult and very compromised situation of the colonies, he should co-operate, bring them to reflect on their own true interests, and to appreciate the characteristic generosity of the Mexican nation.

If his excellency, the substitute President, should think proper, I can hear Robinson, and determine from conversations with him, it being understood that I will not make concessions which can affect the interests and sacred rights of the nation.

As, in political affairs, opportunities occur which pass by rapidly, I believe that the action in this matter should be rapid. Hoping that you will communicate with me without delay, and accept the protestations of my considerations, I subscribe myself, &c., &c.,

ANTONIO LOPEZ DE SANTA ANNA.

APPENDIX NO. III.

Castle of Perote, January 9th, 1843.
General Antonio Lopez de Santa Anna:

Most excellent Sir,—In directing myself to your excellency in the best manner that is possible to me, I take the liberty of communicating to your excellency matters highly important for Mexico and Texas. I have resided many years in Texas as a colonist, and never have been wanting in obedience to the laws of the government of Mexico, whose goodness enabled me to enjoy fortune and prosperity; but inevitable circumstances have suspended the progressive prosperity of the Texian people. In the month of March last, General Arista directed a proclamation (and I retain perfectly in my memory the terms in which it was couched) to the people of Texas, offering protection to the persons, and respect for the property of all those citizens who would not take up arms against Mexico. General Woll, upon his entry into Bexar in September last, gave a general order, that only those should be made prisoners who were found in arms against Mexico. I, although I believed it was a party for the purpose of pillage, did not make use of my arms, and laid them down as soon as I knew they were troops of your excellency—an error which has made me appear a rebel. I now desire, as I have already desired for many years, to show my decided adhesion to the government of Mexico, for which intention I can give unquestionable proof. I am a lawyer, and, as belongs to my profession, I know something of the political and civil organization of the governments of the earth, and especially of those of the United States and Texas; and I find myself capable of giving to your excellency information that few can give. Upon my leaving Saltillo, and during my journey to this place, I conceived a plan, in conformity with ideas which had agitated my mind for some time; but, most excellent sir, fruitless would it be for me to disclose in a letter all the details of a plan, giving clear explanations, and answering the objections which might present themselves, being better able to do it personally. Nevertheless, to take advantage of the opportunity which presents itself, I write to your excellency, and permit me to say that seven and a half years of war have made the people of Texas eager for peace: they would quickly make any prudent sacrifice to reach an object so desirable, and the more so, if it were on such a basis as the reunion of Mexico and Texas. Among my companions in prison there are gentlemen who are of the same opinion as myself, who, if they had charge of a mission of this sort, would employ a powerful influence in Texas to obtain the grand object of her return to duty. The proclamation of General Arista of March last did not produce the desired effect, although it caused many to remain neutral. If the citizens who rejoiced at its contents had openly done so, they would have lost their property, and would themselves have perished. But if there had been submitted to the deliberation of the Texian people a similar proposition, and with the same force to that which has been submitted to the people of Yucatan, much would have been done, because the people in general would have been carried to an open discussion of the matter without the fear of receiving any injury. By employing these means, the most advantageous ends may be expected. The citizens would have the liberty to reflect and reason with deliberation and calmness upon the matter, and this is what does not enter into the plan of General Arista. If there is not an armistice entered into, peace cannot be established. Great, very great would be the benefits which could be acquired by these means. Among the great advantages which would result to Mexico, the following can be enumerated :

1st. During the negotiations, a great part of the Texians would receive such an impression as would be in a manner favourable to the reunion. Many would remain neutral, thereby causing the reunion of Mexico and Texas to be comparatively an object of easy execution.

2d. The liberty of the prisoners of Santa Fé, under word of honour, without the circumstance of hoping that the Texians would make prisoners to exchange for them, was an act of generosity which made, upon the sober and tranquil characters of the citizens of Texas, an impression strong enough to predispose them for the reunion.

3d. During the proposed discussion, the advantages they would receive in the sale of their cotton in the markets of Mexico would be manifested openly to the people of Texas—a money capital of near half a million of dollars annually, which will make them a specie fund which will take the place of paper money : without this, it is almost impossible to sustain their credit.

4th. It will fix the attention on the evil state of public affairs ; and then will be considered the impossibility of Texas existing as an independent state without ruining the people with taxes which they cannot bear.

5th. The evil management of affairs will also be manifest, and the people, already discontented with the administration of General Houston, will become alarmed, and will operate in a public movement such as, in my opinion, it would be difficult to resist.

6th. The discussion would give time to the old colonists to compare their former peace and prosperity with the actual destination over their misery and broken state, and would augment the desires which they have for a reunion. These are advantages which would be approved of by the people of Texas ; and in view of their taking effect, I would indicate to your excellency how appropriate it would be at the present time to name commissioners, and unite one or two of the gentlemen who are with me, who, I before said, are of my opinion ; and permit me to recommend that the steps which are to be taken in the matter should be taken immediately, for the purpose of counteracting whatever measures the Congress of Texas might take, which ought to meet the first Monday in this month; for, according to news received here by means of periodicals, part of the members of the Congress of Texas ought to meet at Austin, and part at Washington, by which means they are divided, and this will be a good opportunity to operate. Furthermore, although the Constitution provides that the Congress cannot change the form of government, they can present to the people alterations. The presentation to the Texian people of the question of reunion in the form prescribed by the Constitution is highly important as a political movement, although "Mexico does not or will not recognise the government of Texas." This being the manner prescribed, the great difficulty will be found conquered in the beginning of the affair. Pursuing such a course, the negotiations will be established, and then the people could operate without embarrassment and with efficiency.

I take advantage of the present occasion to tender to your excellency my high considerations and respect.

(Signed), J. W. ROBINSON.

General Tornel's reply to General Santa Anna's note of the 6th inst
Mexico, Feb. 11th, 1843.

Excellent Sir,—I gave to his excellency the substitute President immediate notice of your respected letter of the 6th instant, in which you were pleased to make known the affair of the Texian prisoner, Wm. Robinson, whose original letter accompanied it, and being informed of all, he advises me to request you to act with all the necessary powers to hear him and grant that which is proper; or to hear only, and transmit the result to the supreme government, in case you consider it necessary. Satisfied that your excellency will proceed in arrangements with the Texian prisoners with your customary caution and prudence, always preserving the rights and interests of the nation of which you are so glorious a defender, the government abstains from giving directions of any kind, resting, as it should, in the just opinion that your excellency should direct this matter according to your own judgment.

In the hope that you will bring it to a full termination, useful and honourable to the Republic, please accept my expressions of high consideration, &c., &c., JOSE MARIA DE TORNEL.

Antonio Lopez de Santa Anna to Jose Maria de Tornel.
Manga de Clavo, Feb. 18th, 1843.
Excellent Sir,—In accordance with the authority communicated to me

by order of his excellency the substitute President, to call the Texian prisoner, Wm. Robinson, and hear him concerning the terms in which it was considered that the reincorporation of that department with the Republic might be obtained, and the propositions which he makes to secure so desired an object, I directed him to come from the fortress of Perote to this hacienda ; and after long conferences, in which he perfectly convinced me that he was not wanting in influence or means to produce the conviction in Texas of the importance to the colonists of again embracing the protection of our laws, I have accepted and signed the propositions, a copy of which I herewith enclose to your excellency, and have set Mr. Robinson immediately at liberty, that he may, without loss of time, proceed to the fulfilment of his offices. The care and prudence which I have taken to avoid a single expression which can in any manner compromise the rights of the nation, so dear to all Mexicans, so sacred to me in my natural sentiments, because it has made me its keeper, will not escape the penetration of your excellency. And I simply announce that certain concessions can be granted that the right of sovereignty shall remain undisturbed, of which the present situation of Texas forms a necessity and guarantee that the colonists should not fail to demand as the foundation of their future tranquillity and welfare. As the whole subject is submitted to negotiations, in which the government should act with due caution, nothing should be hazarded to plant the seeds of reconciliation among the people of a department whose dispositions have been entirely alienated. In any event, entire justice shall be dispensed to the dictates of humanity and prudence, provided it be in accordance with reason, even though accompanied by the horrors of war.

Please present my expressions of esteem to his excellency the substitute President, and accept the assurance of my particular regards.

I have the honour to be, &c., &c., &c.,

ANTONIA LOPEZ DE SANTA ANNA.

The next in order is the following copy of the articles signed by Santa Anna, and despatched through Judge Robinson to this government, and which, it appears from the subsequent action of this government, was accepted by President Houston.

Manga de Clavo, Feb. 18th, 1843.

The undersigned, authorized by the supreme government of the Republic to confer with James W. Robinson, the Texian prisoner in the fortress of Perote, and take into consideration his communication, under injunction of secrecy, on matter of great importance both to Mexico and Texas, in which various propositions are made to bring to a conclusion the prolonged war between these parties, having heard all that was to be offered upon the subject, and considered deliberately each proposition, has agreed with said Robinson on certain bases directed to this object, and for the prosecution of which has appointed said Robinson, by virtue of the facilities with which he is invested, to proceed in accordance therewith, and to use those efforts which in his judgment should be most convenient and conducive to the end proposed. In virtue whereof, and in accordance with said bases, Mr. Robinson,

1st. Will explain to the inhabitants of Texas that the supreme government desires the termination of the war with that territory, not because it feels itself without means or resources to continue it until it obtains a complete triumph, but through motives of humanity and the interests of the colonists.

2d. That thus far the government offers to throw a veil over the past, granting amnesty to all whom it may affect.

3d. That as the bare interests of the inhabitants are founded on peace, tranquillity, and good order, and the security of person and property—benefits which they cannot enjoy in the continually agitated condition which is the natural consequences of war—the supreme government offers to guaranty these benefits in their full enjoyment.

4th. That the inhabitants of Texas shall lay down their arms, and recognise as an essential and unalterable condition the right of property of Mexico in this its territory, the sovereignty of the nation, its laws, rules, and general orders.

5th. That whereas this is the fundamental basis of all others, no other can be effectual unless this be admitted by Texas in its most unlimited extent, and without the slightest modification.

6th. That this part being admitted in the manner aforesaid, Texas may appoint its own functionaries and authorities, military and political, in accordance with the general Constitution of the Republic.

7th. That Mexican troops shall not be sent to Texas, the said department taking care to provide for its own security on the frontiers, covering them with its own forces, composed of citizens resident within it.

8th. That in regard to the legislative power, the respective *departmental Junta* shall have power, in virtue of its attribute, to propose to the general Congress for approval or decree such laws as may be considered proper for the good government of Texas.

9th. And, finally, that Texas shall conform in all other matters to such regulations as may be established for the other departments of the Republic.

These bases being understood, and Mr. Robinson having engaged to fulfil his commission in accordance with all, and with the utmost efficacy and zeal, it is understood that the supreme government will receive with satisfaction the notice of a favourable result of his laudable efforts, or any commission which may be directed to the capital, where I shall go within a few days to resume the reins of government. I authorize for this purpose, and grant to the said Robinson his liberty, and permission to leave the Republic at his pleasure, congratulating myself on the opportunity which permits me to be the means of establishing this agreement, from the precise fulfilment of which, if its results prove favourable, we may hope the complete pacification of Texas, and its reincorporation in the Mexican Republic, of which it is an integral part.

In confirmation of which, I grant this document to said Robinson at my hacienda of Manga de Clavo, on the 18th of February, 1843.

ANTONIO LOPEZ DE SANTA ANNA.

Next follows a letter of some length, from Jose Maria de Tornel to Santa Anna, of which we copy only the first paragraph, that being all that is of any interest to our readers:

Mexico, February 23d, 1843.

Most excellent Sir,—On receipt of your respected communication of the 18th instant, I submitted it to his excellency, the substitute President, and not only is he informed of, but also well satisfied with the prudence and extraordinary integrity with which your excellency has availed yourself of the disposition manifested by the Texian prisoner, Mr. Robinson, to contribute, by his personal influence, to a settlement of the affairs of Texas; and his excellency believes that the propositions drawn up and subscribed by your excellency will protect the national rights and the general principles of our political organization, *without the hazard of any concession which the colonists may demand as a guaranty of their future fate.*

Office of Foreign Relations and Government,
Mexico, July 7th, 1843.

Most excellent Sir,—Mr. Percy W. Doyle, her Britannic majesty's chargé d'affaires, has addressed to me a communication, a copy of which I transmit to your excellency, in which he explains what has been done in pursuance of the propositions of which Mr. Robinson was the bearer, for the purpose of bringing to a conclusion the evils of the war between Mexico and Texas. Copy No. 2 is the copy of the proclamation of Houston on the armistice which Mr. Doyle has transmitted to me, and No. 3 is to advise your excellency of my reply to that gentleman, in accordance with the supreme order of his excellency the substitute President, and also in accordance with the communications which I have received on the subject from the office. God and liberty! BOCANEGRA.

(No. 1.)
Percy W. Doyle to the Minister of Foreign Relations and Government.
Mexico, July 6th, 1843.

Having known for some time that, by means of Robinson, one of the Texian prisoners set at liberty, proposals have been addressed to the government of Texas, which I have received, and which might result in the establishment of peace, I advised his excellency the President of this circumstance, and he replied to me that he was disposed to receive Texian commissioners who might be sent to treat on the proposed conditions, acceding, farther, to the propositions which I made him, that a declaration of armistice should be made, in order to carry on the negotiations. In consequence, I informed the chargé d'affaires of her majesty in Texas of what had occurred without loss of time, and in consequence of the communication between that gentleman and the government of Texas, President Houston has published a decree, of which I have the honour to enclose a copy, in which he directs that hostilities shall cease forthwith on the frontier of Texas. I have the honour to advise your excellency that it may be brought to the notice of his excellency, that he may communicate to me the measures which the said decree, a copy of which is enclosed, may suggest, in order that I may inform the chargé d'affaires of her majesty in Texas for the information of her government.

I have the honour to be, with the highest consideration, your most obedient humble servant, PERCY W. DOYLE.

Next follows (No. 2) Houston's proclamation, the publication of which we consider quite unnecessary here.

No. 3 is a letter of J. M. de Bocanegra to Percy W. Doyle:

National Palace, Mexico, July 7th, 1843.

Dear Sir,—*By your letter, under date of yesterday, I am informed of what has taken place in consequence of the proposals of which the lawyer Robinson,* one of the Texian prisoners, was the bearer, *to terminate* the war which Mexico has sustained with the just purpose of preserving her territory entire. I have also received a copy of the provision (proclamation) dictated on the armistice, which result has been obtained by the measures taken by you through the gentleman charged with the affairs of her Britannic majesty near said Mr. Houston. I have brought this to the notice of his excellency the provisional President, and he has advised me forthwith to render you his thanks, as I have the honour to do, for the part you have taken in a matter of so great importance, and of which Mexico has not lost sight. The good offices and actions which you have been pleased to interpose in the matter merit a special mention and corresponding gratitude ; therefore, his excellency the President, instigated by the best motives, has directed that the necessary orders shall issue from the office of war for the suspension of hostilities between Mexico and Texas, as is expressed in the annexed copies which I have the honour to transmit you, and the fulfilment of which will be exact and rigorous. With this beginning, his excellency the President will see with satisfaction that you should make known to Mr. Houston, through said agent of her Britannic majesty in Texas, that commissioners may come with competent instructions, *based upon the propositions which Robinson took*, with the understanding that their journey to Mexico may be made by sea or land, and that they will be received and treated like those from Yucatan, as his excellency is animated with the best and purest intentions towards both departments.

In manifesting to you the manner in which your notice has been received, and the measures which, in consequence, have been taken so conformable to his designs, I have the honour to repeat my considerations as your most affectionate and obedient servant. S. M. B.

J. M. DE BOCANEGRA.

The following is a copy of the instructions despatched to General Woll by Tornel, minister of war and marine, on the reception of General Houston's proclamation of armistice ; or, in other words, it is the proclamation of armistice on the part of Mexico :

Mexico, July 7th, 1843.
To General Adrian Woll, Commander-in-chief
    of the Army of the North.

Excellent Sir,—By the accompanying documents you will be fully informed that Mr. Samuel Houston has proclaimed an armistice in the department of Texas, in consequence of the admission of the propositions which the lawyer, Mr. Robinson, made, that they might be made the basis for a discussion, the result of which should be an agreement whereby the rights of the Republic and its interests should be combined with those of Texas. And as the operations of government should always be accompanied by a consequent and unchangeable good faith, it has resolved, in the name of the nation, upon the propositions of armistice, and that it be confirmed by both parties *according to the laws of war*.

In consequence, his excellency the provisional President directs me to advise you that hostilities with Texas are suspended for a time at all parts on the line of your command, retiring your advanced posts, spies, parties of observation, and all forces destined to molest the enemy, suspending during the armistice your march to the centre of Texas with a strong division of cavalry, yourself being personally in command, according to your orders of the 2d and 28th of June, and those of the 5th instant, forwarded by your aid-de-camp Jose Washington Eayrs. Notwithstanding, you will not fail to employ the $180,000, which I have remitted to you in two parts, in the regulation, enlistment, and equipment of the said division of forces under your command, nor the other means placed at your disposition; because, while the negotiation may not reach a definite conclusion, we should prepare in peace for war, as the sacred interests of the Republic demand.

That the armistice may be proclaimed according to the terms prescribed by the usages and practice of war, you will officially advise Mr. Samuel Houston to nominate commissioners, who, in conjunction with those appointed by you, will be subject to the following regulations:

1st. The armistice shall be submitted to the supreme government, but hostilities shall be immediately suspended.

2d. It shall be stipulated in the armistice that the so called government of Texas shall send commissioners to the capital of the Republic, who shall make to the supreme government those propositions which they shall consider correct, on the *basis of the propositions which the lawyer Robinson conveyed*, and which will be matter of discussion.

3d. The armistice shall continue during the time necessary for the purpose; but a prudent time shall be agreed upon for the renewal of hostilities, when either of the parties shall so determine, giving previous notice, as is customary in like cases.

4th. The commissioners shall enjoy the same securities granted to those sent from the department of Yucatan, and, on their arrival, stay, and return, shall be protected by the Mexican laws and authorities.

His excellency the provisional President has full confidence in your circumspection in the exercise of the powers conferred upon you—a general so deserving of gratitude for leading the arms of the Republic to the acquisition of new glories on the field of Texas.

I present to your excellency my sentiments of the highest consideration and esteem, &c. JOSE MARIA DE TORNEL.

Following the above is the armistice agreed upon by the Texian commissioners, acknowledging Texas as a "*department of Mexico*," which it is unnecessary to insert here.

The following is the manifesto from General Adrian Woll, of the Mexican army, to President Houston, informing him of the recommencement of hostilities against the usurpers of Texas for a non-compliance with the armistice entered into by their commissioners:

First Brigade of the North, Headquarters.

The delay fixed by the supreme government in the armistice concluded the 15th of February of the present year with the commissioners having expired, his excellency the President has called to mind that, from the 11th of the present month, hostilities are reopened against the inhabitants of this department, and I communicate to you the declaration of his excellency. I also make known to you that my government has seen, with well-founded indignation, the perfidies of the inhabitants of the said territory towards a republic whose generous conduct to them they misunderstood in relation to a question in which they were thought to be acting in good faith. They have abused the confidence of the Republic by violating the conditions of the armistice respecting the commissioners, who, according to the fourth article of said armistice, should have repaired to the city of Mexico, in order to regulate our differences so far as their propositions might be admissible. His excellency the President, convinced that the honour and dignity of the nation require the chastisement of a conduct so little creditable, has ordered me to apprize you of his resolution, so that it may be well understood that it is not through timidity or want of power, but because his excellency has always listened to the voice of humanity, that hostilities were not commenced at the period fixed by the armistice.

Notwithstanding my regret in thinking that blood is once more to flow, yet in transmitting to you the declaration of the President, I enjoy the satisfaction to find that justice is on the side of our cause, which reposes on sacred and imprescriptible rights. In this we place our confidence, as well as in the valour of our troops. When the struggle shall once more begin, the civilized world will judge between us, and the fortune of war cannot but be favourable to those who fight for their country against usurpers.

I have the honour to renew to you assurances of my high consideration.

Headquarters, Micr, 10th June, 1841.

ADRIAN WOLL.

To Gen. Sam. Houston.

No. IV.

DR. SINNICKSON'S STATEMENT ABOUT THE "WHITE FLAG" AT THE BATTLE OF MIER.

When I was taken prisoner (at the Battle of Mier), I was immediately conveyed to General Ampudia, the commander-in-chief of the Mexican army then there, who, after interrogating me, through the medium of an interpreter, respecting the numbers of the Texian force, and the name of their commanding officer, ordered that I should bear a flag to Colonel Fisher, demanding an immediate surrender. Perceiving that I gave no reply, and evinced no disposition to obey such an order, he said that it was useless for me to refuse, as I should be compelled to do it. He seized me by the shoulder, while Colonel Carasco laid hold upon the other, and forced me to the corner of a street leading in the direction of our troops, dictating at the time the following message to me, to be delivered to the Texian commander, viz.: "Say to Colonel Fisher that he must surrender with his whole force in five minutes, or I will cause them all to be put to the sword, and give no quarter—to accomplish this, I have 1700 regular troops, and look every moment for a re-enforcement of 800—and that, if he will cause his troops to lay down their arms, and surrender in that time, their lives shall be spared, and they shall be treated with all the humanity and deference due them as prisoners of war; and, furthermore, I will exercise my influence with the supreme government to prevent their being marched to the city of Mexico, but to have them retained east of the mountains until they are released or exchanged."

Accompanied by a Mexican soldier, as I entered our lines I discovered Colonel Fisher, who, when he perceived me, advanced a short distance to a low stone wall. When we met, I informed him that I had been compelled to bear a flag with a verbal message to him, and while relating the purport of it, the incessant discharge of musketry prevented him from hearing: motioning for me to remain silent, he gave orders for the firing to cease. So soon as it had discontinued, he turned to me and inquired, "What does this flag mean?" I then repeated what has been stated above. After concluding, I watched closely and eagerly for a reply. Without saying a word, he cast his eyes upon the ground as if undetermined, and endeavouring to decide upon what course he should pursue. Meditating in this position for a brief period, he at length came to some conclusion, when he leaped the wall and advanced to the position occupied by Cameron and Ryan's companies particularly, without taking any farther notice of me, either by word or sign. I instantly followed to

APPENDIX NO. IV. 475

await his instructions. He called together a council of his officers, at which time the Mexican officers took the opportunity to venture within our lines. What occurred from this time you had an opportunity of becoming as well acquainted with as myself.

The preceding, sir, is a brief statement of facts, as they transpired between the colonel and myself. I do not wish to increase the length of this paper so as to become wearisome to the reader, yet I cannot conclude without mentioning some circumstances relative to this matter that, I trust, will enable the reader to arrive at a just and impartial opinion. I presume it is well known that during an action, when an order is given by an officer to his inferiors in rank, and the obedience of which is necessary in securing the safety and success of a body of men, that a disobedience most frequently is considered as a direct violation of the regulations of the military code, and renders the offender liable to the severest punishment that can be inflicted upon him, instantaneously, and that without the convening of a military court. Had I voluntarily disobeyed any order that Colonel Fisher states he gave me, why did he not enforce upon me the penalty as the results of its violation? He held a pistol in his hand at the time, and would have been held justifiable in making immediate use of it upon me.

Again: Does it not appear improbable that he should have commanded me to return with the flag without having any knowledge of the object for which it was sent, as he could know nothing of its errand excepting from conjecture? He had as much right to suppose, as otherwise, that the enemy wished to enter into some terms with him for their own safety, as well as that of their wounded, and the town with its inhabitants; for he is well aware that a commander will always, whenever within his power, after he is defeated, make the best stipulations he can with his victor.

You will recollect I had an interview with the colonel in the morning of Friday, the 30th December, a short time previous to our men being marched off to Matamoras. In the conversation I then held with him, he never intimated, in the slightest degree, that he had given me such an order, but, on the contrary, when the subject of my bearing the flag was introduced, he assured me that himself nor any other person had or could attach any censure to me for the course I was compelled to pursue. Moreover, I do most positively assert, that during my imprisonment I had frequent conversations with the men, as well as the officers, in relation to our capitulation, and not one of them ever mentioned to me of having heard of such an order being given, or ever passed a word of condemnation upon me for my conduct during any period of that engagement.

Having already extended this communication to a much greater length than I intended, I shall add nothing more than a sincere desire that your publication may have an extensive circulation, and that it may be written both justly and impartially.

   Most respectfully yours,   JOHN J. SINNICKSON.
 To General Thomas J. Green.

No. V.

The following is a List of the Mier Prisoners who were released on the 16th of September, 1844, by the Mexican Government, and who arrived in New-Orleans per Schooner Creole, Captain Dessechi, which sailed on the 22d of September: passage, thirteen days from Vera Cruz. Several Mier Prisoners remained in Mexico, and others took a different route home.

Ackerman, P. A.
Alexander, M.
Allen, David.
Armstrong, A.
Arthur, Francis.
Baker, J. R., Captain.
Barney, Daniel F.
Bassett, R. P.
Beasley, D. H. E.
Bell, T. W.
Berry, Bate J.
Bowman, B. F.
Boon, B. Z.
Brennan, John.
Bridger, H.
Brown, Richard.
Brush, G. R.
Bush, G. W.
Buster, C., Captain.
Calvert, John.
Censibeau, T. J.
Clark, Willis G.
Clopton, W., Lieutenant.
Copeland, W.
Davis, Thomas.
Davis, William.
Davis, W. K.
Dillon, J. F.

Douglas, Freeman W., Lieutenant.
Downes, N. G.
Dunbar, William.
Edwards, Leonidas D. F.
Fisher, William S., Colonel.
Frensley, William H.
Gibson, F. M., Quartermaster.
Gibson, William.
Glascock, James A.
Goodman, S.
Grubs, F.
Hanna, A. B.
Harvey, John.
Harrison, F. W. T.
Heddenburg, Abraham D.
Hensley, C.
Hoffer, John.
Humphries, J. J.
Jackson, Edward B.
Journie, H.
Kaigler, William.
Kelly, Charles S.
King, R. B.
Lacy, John.
Lewis, A. J.
Lee, A. A., Lieutenant.
Livergood, J. H.
Lord, George.

Lovergy, J.
Lyon, S. C., Sailingmaster.
Matthews, Alexander.
Maxwell, P. M.
Middleton, William B.
Miller, Henry.
Millon, W. E.
Mills, John.
Mills, Lawson.
Morrell, H. B.
M'Cutcheon, J. D.
M'Fall, Samuel.
M'Ginly, John.
M'Mullen, John.
Nealy, James B.
Nelson, Thomas.
Oats, H. H.
Overton, D.
Peacock, James.
Phillips, James.
Pierson, J. G. W., Captain.
Pilley, Robert M.
Pitts, E. H.
Riley, F.
Roberts, H. H.

Rogers, Mark.
Roark, A. J.
Runyan, William J.
Sargeant, W.
Sansberry, John.
Sellers, Harvey W.
Smith, J.
Sullivan, Daniel C.
Tanney, John
Thompson, Thomas A.
Thurmond, Alfred S.
Toops, John.
Trehern, George Washington.
Turner, R. W.
Vandyke, Wilson M.
Van Vechten, D. H.
Watkins, Joseph D.
White, F.
Whitehurst, F.
Williams, Levi.
Willoughby, R.
Woodland, H.
Young, James.
Zumatt, Isaac.

The following Five were Released a few Weeks previous to the above.

Armstrong, James C.,
Ryan, William, Captain,
Tatum, Thomas,
Wallace, William A.,
Wilson, William F.,
} Liberated by Petition from many Members of the United States Congress.

No. VI.

THOUGH the Eighth Congress of the Republic of Texas, in December, 1843, voted an appropriation of fifteen thousand dollars to our countrymen in the Mexican prisons; and again, in February, 1844, fifteen thousand dollars in addition to the first appropriation (see Journals of the House of Representatives, Eighth Congress, page 450), yet, EIGHT MONTHS thereafter, when public opinion in Texas forced him (President Houston) to pay some little regard to these most peremptory laws of the land, he condescended to place to their use two thousand dollars, two hundred of which was, by special provision of the law, paid over to our unfortunate countryman, Antonio Navarro. This was done by sending a special agent with the paltry sum, whose pay and expenses must have come to fifty per cent. of the amount which our one hundred and twenty surviving countrymen received, when a bank deposite in New-Orleans, against which they could have drawn, would have been worth from six to eight per cent. premium. It will be recollected, that when *this* insulting show of regard for our prisoners was made by President Houston, both himself and newspapers in Texas were boasting of "the par circulation," "surplus in the treasury," " great receipts in the custom-house," &c., &c.

What we have said, and the abundant proof heretofore furnished, cannot fail to satisfy every impartial reader that President Houston's first object was to have the whole of the Mier men shot in Mexico, when he wrote to that government, through the British minister, that "they had entered that country without authority," and consequently were "robbers and marauders;" and failing in this, to have any but the brave Captain Cameron and each tenth man shot, his second plan was to starve the remainder to death in Mexican dungeons. This he wellnigh effected by a usurpation of the laws of the land which voted them bread, and which the remnant of their muster-roll will show.

He who deals in falsehood is ever in danger of self-conviction, and such has been President Houston's misfortune. From the Battle of Mier up to the fall of 1843, both the President and his partisans in Texas were busy in denying that he ever wrote such a letter to the British minister as was charged and proven upon him, and that the Mier commander had had his orders to invade Mexico. But on the 27th of January, 1844, when that excitement had measurably subsided, and to subserve his vindictiveness towards a gallant soldier, Colonel William G. Cooke, he forgets his former denials, and in his veto message of this date (see Journals of House of Representatives, Eighth Congress, page 375) he writes as follows:

Executive Department, Washington, Jan. 27th, 1844.
To the Honourable the House of Representatives:

The Executive regrets to find himself under the necessity of withholding his assent from the bill for the relief of William G. Cooke, late acting quartermaster general. The reasons which impel him to do so are, as he conceives, of the most forcible character.

In the first place, the government never promised those who should participate in the late campaign to the Rio Grande anything more than authority to march, such ammunition and arms as could be furnished, and the spoils acquired from the enemy, according to the laws of civilized warfare. This fact is shown by the accompanying note from the secretary of war and marine, which is intended to form a part of this message, and the published declarations of the Executive himself. In an address to the people of Texas, dated July, 1842, and published in the newspapers of the day, the Executive remarked, in reference to the contemplated expedition, that "the government will promise nothing but authority to march, and such supplies of ammunition as may be needful for the campaign. *They must look to the Valley of the Rio Grande for remuneration.* The government will claim no portion of the spoils: they will be divided among the victors. The flag of Texas will accompany the expedition."

From this it will be perceived that the government was guarded against incurring any pecuniary responsibilities on account of the campaign. For this reason, they were authorized to cross the Rio Grande, "and make such reprisals upon Mexico as civilized and honourable warfare would justify in the relations then existing with the common enemy." The Executive knew full well at that period, as he does now, that the means of the country could not sustain the expense of the expedition, and hence he based his call to the citizen soldiers of the Republic upon what he believed to be their patriotic desire and readiness to engage in the undertaking; and because he knew the inability of the country to pay them for their services, he plainly told them they must look "for remuneration to the Valley of the Rio Grande."

. . . . It is just that all should be regarded on the same footing, and the claims of no one preferred to those of all the rest. The widows and orphans of the brave and unfortunate decimated have not petitioned Congress for pay or relief, &c. SAM. HOUSTON.

Thus, in one short year, in subserving this vindictive hatred of one individual, he furnishes the world from under his own hand the evidences of his guilt; and, notwithstanding the many falsehoods which he asserted, and some of his partisans reiterated about his desire to serve our suffering fellow-citizens in the Mexican prisons, we absolutely see them released, without any influence or agency of his, at a distance of more than a thousand miles from their homes, with ONE DOLLAR each, which the charity of the "*magnanimous nation*" gave them to bear their expenses. We see them turned loose upon the levée of New-Orleans in the greatest possible destitution, covered with filth and rags, and sustained by the charity of the good people of that city; and thus we see them begging their way back to Texas, with one proud feeling still uppermost in their bosoms—to die for the honour and liberty of that country whose executive chief had slandered them all—had murdered some—had starved by piecemeal many, and basely insulted the remainder when in chains ! What a moral reflection this for Mexico, and how hopeless, should it prove, is her vain hope of reconquering such a people !

In the face of the foregoing facts, President Houston has had the shameless hardihood, in his last annual message to the Ninth Congress, dated December 4th, 1844, to say, that "the laws of the last Congress touching our prisoners in Mexico were carried out as fully and as speedily as circumstances would permit."

No. VII.

November 29th, 1844.

General Thomas J. Green:

Dear Sir,—I have perused, with infinite pleasure, your manuscript detailing the Battle of Mier, the captivity, imprisonment, and sufferings of yourself and fellow-prisoners in the loathsome Castle of Perote, together with your adventurous and successful escape from that almost impregnable fortress.

The spirit-stirring incidents, from the commencement to the end of your journal, cannot fail to excite a lively interest in the breast of every reader.

With myself, and your numerous friends in this country, your details have peculiar interest, from our knowledge of the fidelity with which they are given. Independent of my knowledge of the frankness of your character, an intimate acquaintance with many of your fellow-prisoners, with whom I have had frequent conversations, enables me to judge the correctness of your narrative. Permit me, therefore, to solicit the publication of your journal as soon as practicable, inasmuch as it is immediately connected with our Revolution, and forms one of the important events attending its progress.

Most respectfully, your friend and obedient servant,

B. T. ARCHER.

Oakland, January 4th, 1845.

General Thomas J. Green:

Dear Sir,—Our mutual friend, Dr. Archer, informs me that you have prepared a minute account of the Battle of Mier, and of the incidents, anterior and subsequent, connected with that brilliant though calamitous event.

There are but few instances in which the great superiority of Texian arms over those of our boastful enemies have been more fully illustrated than in that conflict, which has elicited so little of the public sympathy, and attracted so small a share of admiration. It is no new idea that success is necessary to applause. The fame of the brief and almost unresisted onslaught of San Jacinto, of eighteen minutes' continuance, has resounded throughout the world, and in the imaginations of the uninformed, has wreathed the brow of the nominal commander, who was literally *compelled* into the chase, with the garland of heroism, while the protracted and bloody battle of Mier has scarcely been perpetuated by newspaper advertisement. There is, however, consolation in the thought that, although one's contemporaries may fail to do justice to his public acts, and may confer unmerited plaudits upon the recreant and unworthy, a better-informed and more dispassionate posterity will render honour to whom honour is due.

Among the seventeen decimated victims of your late companions in suffering was a brother of Mrs. B.'s, and it is natural that we should feel a more than common interest in the events you have related. In all my reflections upon that most atrocious act of an atrocious tyrant, to save whose life, during the great excitement at Velasco in 1836, my own was imminently jeoparded, I have not been able to divest my mind of a suspicion that General Houston is and will be held, by a heart-searching God, morally guilty of that most abominable massacre. His gratuitous, uncalled for, and extraordinary communication to Santa Anna, through the agency of the British minister, officially denounced you and your companions in arms as without the pale of nationality, and, consequently, as outlawed brigands, and liable to be dealt with as such. There certainly was no political necessity for that pragmatic, and, if not designed for some wicked purpose connected with the destiny of you unfortunate prisoners, most silly and useless communication. It is well known that by far the major part of Colonel Fisher's command were the political opponents of the wily demagogue, and that some of them were the objects of his special personal enmity; and those who know General Houston as well as you and I do, know that he never forgave an enemy or sustained a professed friendship beyond his own interest or convenience. His utter destitution of moral principle, and, signally, his habitual and entire disregard of *the truth*, render it no breach of charity to suspect him, on slighter evidence than is furnished in this instance, of an extreme of baseness.

I speak advisedly, and, I trust, without an undue feeling of personal hostility. Political feelings I have long since discarded as far as is consistent with the duties we all owe to the society we live in.

I beg you will not long withhold the product of your interesting labours from the public. Give us "the truth, the whole truth, and nothing but the truth," and let venal critics and rewarded editors, sometime bedecked with the *ermine*, gnaw upon it until their venom fails or their rewards cease. Very respectfully, your friend and obedient servant,

DAVID G. BURNET.

Austin, January 10th, 1845.

Dear General,— .... Since the release of our countrymen, prisoners in Mexico, I hope there will be nothing to divert your mind from the completion of the work in which I found you engaged last spring—I mean the journal of your Mier expedition, and the events subsequent to it. I have been looking for some time for its announcement as being ready for the press. That it will lose any portion of its interest by time I have no fear, but still, to cause it to be generally read and *more* anxiously sought after, the incidents which it relates must not become stale on the public mind. .... Your friend and servant, JAMES WEBB.

No. VIII.

The following letter from her Britannic majesty's chargé d'affaires, Captain Charles Elliott, to Hon. Anson Jones, secretary of state of the Republic of Texas, will speak for itself. That both the President and secretary of state made these assurances to Captain Elliott they did not deny; but the secretary in answer says, " *Whatever has been done, therefore, in relation to this subject, has been in obedience to the requirements of their acts*" (the Congress).

Galveston, March 22d, 1844.

To the Honourable Anson Jones, &c., &c.
    Washington, on the Brazos.

The undersigned, her Britannic majesty's chargé de affaires to the Republic of Texas, has lately had the honour to acquaint Mr. Jones that her majesty's government was engaged in continued efforts to induce the government of Mexico to acknowledge the independence of Texas; and he has now the gratification to add that renewed communications have taken place between the governments of her majesty and that of the King of the French, and that his majesty has expressed his concurrence in the purposes of the queen, and signified his pleasure to command the French minister at Mexico to join his continued friendly assistance to that of her majesty's representative.

But, adverting to the proposals of the government of the United States respecting annexation, to the recent mission of distinguished citizens of Texas to Washington on the Potomac, and to the impression so general

APPENDIX NO. VIII. 483

in Texas that negotiations having that object in view are either in progress or in contemplation, the undersigned finds it his duty to express the hope that the government of Texas will furnish him with explanations on the subject for transmission to her majesty's government. He is sure that they will be made in that spirit of frank and friendly unreserve which has always characterized the intercourse of the two governments.

It must be unnecessary to say that the undersigned is perfectly aware of the President's personal opinions on this subject, and he has not failed, agreeably to the President's wish, to communicate to her majesty's government his excellency's determination to sustain the independence of the Republic, and his excellency's confident hope that the people would uphold him in that course. Indeed, referring to the conferences which the undersigned had the honour to have with the President and Mr. Jones at Galveston during last autumn, he can suppose that the mission to Washington of the gentlemen in question has been directed by a wise desire to avoid any cause of offence or irritation to the government of the United States, and to explain with frankness that the government of Texas could not entertain the subject at all, even if all other obstacles were removed, after the former rejection of such an arrangement of the United States, and wholly without reason, to know that the Senate of the United States would ratify now or in future.

The Congress of Texas, however, has met and separated since the date of the communications to her majesty's government to which the undersigned has referred, and the President will feel with force that it is just and necessary, in the present appearance of circumstances, that there should be no room for the least uncertainty on the part of the governments engaged in the behalf of Texas at Mexico; for it is not to be supposed that they could continue to press the government of Mexico to settle upon one basis while there was any reason to surmise that negotiations were either in actual existence or in contemplation proposing a combination of a totally different nature. It is manifest, on the other hand, that a distinct disavowal on the part of the government of Texas of any intention to consent to such a scheme, either now or perspectively, could not fail to strengthen the hands of the ministers of their majesties, the Queen and the King of the French, at Mexico.

Confiding in the steadfastness of the people of Texas to the pledges in the fundamental acts of their national existence, several of the great powers have acknowledged the independence of this Republic, and entered into treaties with it. While that confidence subsists, it may be depended upon that the government of her majesty will never relax in its friendly efforts to induce the government of Mexico to adjust on the policy so forcibly pressed on the attention of her majesty's government by the government of Texas, not adopted without mature deliberation by her majesty's government, and in their judgment equally necessary for the security of Mexico, and the strength and prosperity of Texas.

The undersigned takes this occasion to renew to Mr. Jones the expression of the sentiments of regard and distinguished consideration with which he has the honour to remain his faithful and most obedient servant,

(Signed), CHARLES ELLIOTT.

No. IX.

The following extracts from my journal in 1836, a part of which had been copied into " General Foote's History of Texas," will explain Santa Anna's unforgiving malignity towards myself :

"*June* 1, 1836.—Arrived at Velasco on board the steamer Ocean, in company with the schooner Pennsylvania and 230 of my brigade, having ordered the remainder, under Major T. W. Ward, to Labacca Bay. Upon my arrival, I found a large number of the citizens of the country in great excitement about Santa Anna's being sent home to Mexico, he being at that time on board the '*Invincible*,' in the offing, ready to sail. President Burnet had sent him on board said vessel to carry out a treaty in good faith, which General Samuel Houston had promised upon the battle-field of San Jacinto. Still the people of the country believed him (Santa Anna) faithless, and clamoured violently against his sailing. Denunciations and violent threats were issued both against the President and all who should aid or abet his sailing. Public meetings were held, and violent speeches made against the measure. In this state of things, President Burnet addressed me a note, requesting an interview, and asking my opinion in this emergency. I told him that, as to any violence being offered to him or his cabinet, I pledged my honour to shield him and them with my life ; but that I was of opinion that, in accordance with the overwhelming public will of the citizens of the country, he should remand the prisoner ashore, and await that public will to determine his fate. The President promptly replied that he would do so.

" Accordingly, the next day, he issued an order to Captain Jeremiah Brown, of the Invincible, to bring the prisoner on shore. Santa Anna returned for answer that he would never leave that vessel alive. A second order was issued, and a similar reply provoked. The President then nominated a committee, composed of Colonel B. F. Smith, Baily Hardeman, and Generals Hunt and Henderson, to visit the Invincible, and bring him ashore. The first-named gentleman refusing to act, the remainder of the committee called upon me, as the head military officer at the post, to accompany them, and bring the prisoner off, according to the President's wish.

"*Three o'clock, P.M.*—We arrived on board the Invincible, where we found the prisoner in a state of extreme agitation, lying in his berth upon his back, alternately raving like a madman and crying like a child; now denying that he had any agency in the massacre at Goliad; anon, threatening to take away his own life sooner than go ashore, to be delivered up to what he called the *new* army from the United States, which he believed to be bent on his destruction. The prisoner continued to act this strange part for about two hours; stating, meanwhile, that he had taken largely of opium, and would soon die. I assured him that, if he could rely upon the word of an American officer, he might consider me as pledged that there was not a soldier under my command who would even do him insult while under my protection. This declaration had no visible effect in dissipating the uneasiness of the prisoner; and his aid-de-camp, Colonel Almonte, finally declared to us that all assurances to him, in his existing condition, would be useless, as his mind was entirely under the control of an overwhelming dread of popular phrensy; that he, Colonel Almonte, knew the American character well enough to have full confidence in the assurances which I had given. All this time the prisoner continued lying upon his back in his berth, and his respiration seemed to me exceedingly difficult. After waiting some minutes longer, I called the surgeon of the Invincible, and requested him to feel the prisoner's pulse, and report his true situation. He complied with my request, and reported his pulse to be perfectly healthy in its vibrations, when I again intimated to the prisoner the necessity of going ashore. He begged twenty minutes' longer respite; upon which, I announced to the captain that it would be necessary to send forward his master-of-arms, and have him ironed without delay. When the irons were brought within his view, the prisoner immediately jumped up, adjusted his collar, put on his hat, and stated his readiness to accompany us. Upon getting on deck, he saw a sentinel, evinced much agitation, and presented his bosom, evidently believing that he was about to be put to death. I took his arm, desired him to be composed, and conducted him to the captain's gig-boat, into which we descended, in company with Mr. Hardeman, Colonel Almonte, and Captain Brown, and rowed for the shore; the other boat bringing the balance of the committee, and Santa Anna's private secretary. On reaching the mouth of the Brasos River, Santa Anna took fresh alarm at a body of Texian soldiers and citizens whom he saw collected upon the beach on the Velasco side, and threatened to drown himself if the boat was not pulled over to the western bank. I explained to him that the crowd had been drawn together by curiosity alone, and intended no violence; and farther suggested that, if he was ambitious of fully acting the character of *Napoleon the Second* (so he styled himself up to his defeat), he could do so by taking the Texian flag, which he would find in the stern of the boat, and calmly wave it in view of the assembly, in token of his respect for the cause which they were pledged to maintain. His countenance brightened at the suggestion, and he accordingly took the flag. So soon as the boat arrived within about ten paces of the shore, I announced to him that then was the time to wave the flag, rising myself at the same time, and giving the word to the crowd, '*Three times three!*' when the whole company cheered, while the prisoner attempted tremulously to wave it, in which he had to be assisted by Captain Brown, so physically unnerved was he for the task. We continued our course up the river, passing the schooner Pennsylvania and steamer Ocean, from both of which vessels we were cheered. Landing at Quintana, upon the western bank, we met President Burnet, and surrendered the prisoner to him. The President turned to me and said, 'General Green, I deliver the prisoner over to your charge, and shall hold you responsible for his safe keeping.' From being the most frightened human being I ever saw, the prisoner at once regained confidence and appeared cheerful. The truth of my promises had been demonstrated by taking him safely through a crowd of citizens and soldiers, whom he thought bent upon his blood.

"It was now near night, and having ordered my cabin on board the steamer to be put in readiness for the reception of the prisoner, we continued to walk until our supper was announced. During this walk, I was struck with the address both of the prisoner and his interpreter, Colonel Almonte, in endeavouring to impress upon me the certainty of his carrying out the treaty, and the sooner he should reach Mexico, the more power he would have in so doing. I took the ground that the people of Texas were not convinced of that fact; and as for myself, that it was childish to tell me that there was anything either *legally* or *morally binding* upon the prisoner to carry out a promise made by him while in duress.

"At half past six our supper was served. It was as good as money could have purchased at the time, and a good one for hungry men. It is true that it was not served in as bright metal, and under as many covers as my guest was used to in the palace of the Montezumas, but, considering his late devastations in Texas, we were lucky in having so good a one. It consisted of an abundance of good beefsteaks and gravy, served in a bright tin pan, with good bread, and, what was remarkable for this stage of our Revolution, a knife and fork each. The tin pan was set upon a narrow bench, and my august guest and myself straddled said bench—inward face!—with our knees touching, we *cutting*, *sopping*, and *eating* a bountiful meal out of said tin pan!

APPENDIX NO. IX.

"Colonel Almonte and the private secretary of the prisoner stood by in attendance upon him, while my orderly served each of us a pint of coffee in tin cups: the said cups, though sufficiently bright inside, were quite sooty upon the outside. Holding up my cup, I pleasantly remarked to Santa Anna, that, when I visited Mexico, I should expect him to give me coffee in brighter metal. Placing his hand upon his heart, in the most Christian earnestness he replied, 'Ah! yes, my dear general, I do long for this unfortunate war to be over, and then I want to see you in Mexico, where I can reciprocate your kindness.'*

"In a few days I was ordered, with what forces I had at Velasco, up the Brasos to repel an Indian incursion, and turned the prisoner over to the President.

"On the day after I marched from Velasco, Santa Anna made a protest to President Burnet against his detention as prisoner, &c., in which much of his unjust spite seemed levelled at me. He says, 'I repeat that I protest against the President and cabinet's condescension in issuing their orders for that measure' (bringing him ashore), 'thereby making a show of me before those men, as in former times was done with the chiefs of conquered nations, considering them as trophies of their victories: with this difference, that in my case a solemn treaty already existed.' It is hardly necessary for me to say that President Burnet's answer to said protest was triumphant."

* While a prisoner in Mexico, I related this anecdote to a Mexican officer, and jocularly requested him to say to the dictator, his master, "that I had visited Mexico, though not in the manner we spoke of at Velasco in 1836." The only answer I ever received was twenty pounds of iron, and an order to perform menial labour. Having no power to resist the irons, I promptly replied that I would die under any tortures he might choose to inflict upon me sooner than submit to the latter degradation. The order was several times repeated, accompanied with severe threats, and my countrymen will bear me witness that it was as often resisted with the most open contempt.

THE END.

The Far Western Frontier

An Arno Press Collection

[Angel, Myron, editor]. **History of Nevada.** 1881.

Barnes, Demas. **From the Atlantic to the Pacific, Overland.** 1866.

Beadle, J[ohn] H[anson]. **The Undeveloped West; Or, Five Years in the Territories.** [1873].

Bidwell, John. **Echoes of the Past:** An Account of the First Emigrant Train to California. [1914].

Bowles, Samuel. **Our New West.** 1869.

Browne, J[ohn] Ross. **Adventures in the Apache Country.** 1871.

Browne, J[ohn] Ross. **Report of the Debates in the Convention of California, on the Formation of the State Constitution.** 1850.

Byers, W[illiam] N. and J[ohn] H. Kellom. **Hand Book to the Gold Fields of Nebraska and Kansas.** 1859.

Carvalho, S[olomon] N. **Incidents of Travel and Adventure in the Far West; with Col. Fremont's Last Expedition Across the Rocky Mountains.** 1857.

Clayton, William. **William Clayton's Journal.** 1921.

Cooke, P[hilip] St. G[eorge]. **Scenes and Adventures in the Army.** 1857.

Cornwallis, Kinahan. **The New El Dorado; Or, British Columbia.** 1858.

Davis, W[illiam] W. H. **El Gringo; Or, New Mexico and Her People.** 1857.

De Quille, Dan. (William Wright). **A History of the Comstock Silver Lode & Mines.** 1889.

Delano, A[lonzo]. **Life on the Plains and Among the Diggings;** Being Scenes and Adventures of an Overland Journey to California. 1854.

Ferguson, Charles D. **The Experiences of a Forty-niner in California.** (Originally published as *The Experiences of a Forty-niner During Thirty-four Years' Residence in California and Australia*). 1888.

Forbes, Alexander. **California:** A History of Upper and Lower California. 1839.

Fossett, Frank. **Colorado:** Its Gold and Silver Mines, Farms and Stock Ranges, and Health and Pleasure Resorts. 1879.

The Gold Mines of California: Two Guidebooks. 1973.

Gray, W[illiam] H[enry]. **A History of Oregon, 1792–1849.** 1870.

Green, Thomas J. **Journal of the Texian Expedition Against Mier.** 1845.

Henry, W[illiam] S[eaton]. **Campaign Sketches of the War with Mexico.** 1847.

[Hildreth, James]. **Dragoon Campaigns to the Rocky Mountains.** 1836.

Hines, Gustavus. **Oregon:** Its History, Condition and Prospects. 1851.

Holley, Mary Austin. **Texas:** Observations, Historical, Geographical and Descriptive. 1833.

Hollister, Ovando J[ames]. **The Mines of Colorado.** 1867.

Hughes, John T. **Doniphan's Expedition.** 1847.

Johnston, W[illiam] G. **Experiences of a Forty-niner.** 1892.

Jones, Anson. **Memoranda and Official Correspondence Relating to the Republic of Texas, Its History and Annexation.** 1859.

Kelly, William. **An Excursion to California Over the Prairie, Rocky Mountains, and Great Sierra Nevada.** 1851. 2 Volumes in 1.

Lee, D[aniel] and J[oseph] H. Frost. **Ten Years in Oregon.** 1844.

Macfie, Matthew. **Vancouver Island and British Columbia.** 1865.

Marsh, James B. **Four Years in the Rockies; Or, the Adventures of Isaac P. Rose.** 1884.

Mowry, Sylvester. **Arizona and Sonora:** The Geography, History, and Resources of the Silver Region of North America. 1864.

Mullan, John. **Miners and Travelers' Guide to Oregon, Washington, Idaho, Montana, Wyoming, and Colorado.** 1865.

Newell, C[hester]. **History of the Revolution in Texas.** 1838.

Parker, A[mos] A[ndrew]. **Trip to the West and Texas.** 1835.

Pattie, James O[hio]. **The Personal Narrative of James O. Pattie, of Kentucky.** 1831.

Rae, W[illiam] F[raser]. **Westward by Rail:** The New Route to the East. 1871.

Ryan, William Redmond. **Personal Adventures in Upper and Lower California, in 1848–9.** 1850/1851. 2 Volumes in 1.

Shaw, William. **Golden Dreams and Waking Realities:** Being the Adventures of a Gold-Seeker in California and the Pacific Islands. 1851.

Stuart, Granville. **Montana As It Is:** Being a General Description of its Resources. 1865.

Texas in 1840, Or the Emigrant's Guide to the New Republic. 1840.

Thornton, J. Quinn. **Oregon and California in 1848.** 1849. 2 Volumes in 1.

Upham, Samuel C. **Notes of a Voyage to California via Cape Horn, Together with Scenes in El Dorado, in the Years 1849–'50.** 1878.

Woods, Daniel B. **Sixteen Months at the Gold Diggings.** 1851.

Young, F[rank] G., editor. **The Correspondence and Journals of Captain Nathaniel J. Wyeth, 1831–6.** 1899.

Library
Sampson Technical Institute